The Making of the Israeli Far-Right

The Making of the Israeli Far-Right

Abba Ahimeir and Zionist Ideology

Peter Bergamin

I.B. TAURIS

LONDON • NEW YORK • OXFORD • NEW DELHI • SYDNEY

I.B. TAURIS
Bloomsbury Publishing Plc
50 Bedford Square, London, WC1B 3DP, UK
1385 Broadway, New York, NY 10018, USA
29 Earlsfort Terrace, Dublin 2, Ireland

BLOOMSBURY, I.B. TAURIS and the I.B. Tauris logo are trademarks of
Bloomsbury Publishing Plc

First published in Great Britain 2020
Paperback edition published 2021

Cover design: Adriana Brioso
Cover image: Abba Ahimeir standing next to wall on which is written
'Don't participate in the census' ('al tepakdu'), Jerusalem, 1931.
Courtesy of the Jabotinsky Institute in Israel.

A catalogue record for this book is available from the British Library.

A catalogue record for this book is available from the Library of Congress

ISBN HB: 978-1-7883-1-4534
PB: 978-0-7556-4500-8
eISBN: 978-1-8386-0-4790
ePDF: 978-1-8386-0-4783

Series: Library of Middle East History

Typeset by Deanta Global Publishing Services, Chennai, India

For my teachers

Contents

Acknowledgements

A large portion of the research that I carried out for this study took place in archives, and I am indebted to staff members at the various institutes that I visited. I wish to thank, in particular: Mag. Barbara Bieringer at the University of Vienna, Yishai Ben-Arieh at the Lavon Institute in Tel Aviv, Amira Stern and her staff, especially Olga Gechman and Ira Berdan, at the Jabotinsky Institute, Tel Aviv, and Dr Cesar Merchan-Hamman and his staff, especially Mila Zeidler and Michael Fischer, at the Leopold Muller Memorial Library, University of Oxford.

In addition, various friends and colleagues have been very generous with their time, and have provided valuable input into this study. In particular, I would like to thank:

During undergraduate study at SOAS, University of London: Prof Emeritus Colin Shindler, Prof Emeritus Tudor Parfitt, Dr Tamar Drukker and Dr Nir Cohen; at the Hebrew University of Jerusalem: Prof Emeritus Gideon Shimoni, Prof Israel Yuval, and Yonatan Kaplan.

During postgraduate study at the University of Oxford: Prof Martin Goodman, Dr Sara Hirschhorn, Prof Alison Salvesen, Prof Glenda Abramson, Prof David Leopold, Prof Ros Ballaster, Prof Paul Lodge, Dr Helen Lacey, Lucinda Rumsey, Baroness Helena Kennedy, Dr Dana Mills, Dr Alex Beard, Gil Zahavi, Lova Chechik, Will Ferris, Jack Edmunds, Christopher Parton and Rebecca Abrams.

In Jerusalem: Rabbi Ada Zavidov, Rabbi Hillel Millgram, Cantor Evan Cohen, Avital Ben-Horin (ז"ל), Hildi Mohr, Bianca Zaoui and Tamar Perles.

In Tel Aviv: Ruth Rosowsky, Yossi Kister and Uri Appenzeller.
In Washington, DC: Prof Arie Dubnov.
In Durham, NC: Prof Malachi Hacohen.
In Heidelberg: Dr Johannes Becke.
In Toronto: Nimrod Lin.

The Ahimeir family have been gracious and exceedingly generous with their time and assistance to this study. Yaacov Ahimeir and Ze'eva Ahimeir-Zavidov were very kind in discussing particular aspects of their father's life. As mentioned above, Ahimeir's granddaughter, my dear friend Ada Zavidov, has gone above and beyond the call of duty in the service of this project. And this study would have been inconceivable without the support and considerable assistance of Yossi Ahimeir. His encyclopaedic knowledge and invaluable insights regarding both his father's life and work and the world of Revisionist Zionism helped to expedite every aspect of my research.

Once again, at the University of Oxford, I have had the benefit and honour of being guided by a Triple Entente of outstanding historians. Prof Abigail Green lent considerable expertise and assistance towards my discussions of Fascism and Revolution. Prof David Rechter has been a bastion of support, both as my administrative supervisor and as an academic. Finally, Prof Derek Penslar has been the most perfectly rigorous supervisor that I could ever have hoped to have. His eagle eye, brilliant insights and ability to connect the dots in the most sophisticated of ways have set a very high bar indeed. I will miss our work together as much as I shall endeavour to replicate Derek's high standard in the future.

Part of Chapter 3 is based on my chapter 'Revolutionary Fascist or Fascist Revolutionary: Abba Ahimeir and the Success of Revolutionary Zionism', in Jacob Frank and Sebastian Kunze (eds), *Jewish Radicalisms: Historical Perspectives on a Phenomenon of Global Modernity. European Jewish Studies* vol 39. It is used here by the kind permission of the publishing house Walter DeGruyter.

Finally, I wish to thank Sophie Rudland, my editor at I.B. Tauris for her unwavering interest and support, since we first met to discuss this project, in 2016.

Introduction

*I do not want to know how God created the world. I'm not interested in
this or that phenomenon, in the spectrum of this or that element. I want to
know His thoughts, the rest are details.*

–Albert Einstein[1]

In the long and varied cast list of characters who compete for privilege of place
in the recounting of Zionist history, few cut such a maligned, misunderstood
and, indeed, tragic figure as does Abba Ahimeir (1897–1962). A highly educated
cultural historian, Ahimeir gained notoriety mainly as a journalist, political
activist and – alongside the poet Uri Zvi Greenberg (1896–1981) and writer
Yehoshua Yevin (1891–1970) – leader of the 'Maximalist' faction of Zeʾev
Jabotinsky's (1880–1940) Revisionist Zionist Party in British Mandate Palestine
during the late 1920s and early 1930s. Of the three Maximalist leaders, Ahimeir
was arguably the most ideologically influential, viscerally outspoken and
politically engaged. While purportedly captivated by Jabotinsky's persona,
Ahimeir nonetheless posed, at times, a very real threat to his mentor's leadership.
This was especially true within the Yishuv (the Jewish settlements in pre-state
Israel/Palestine) from 1930 onwards, when Jabotinsky's return had been barred
by the British authorities. While too often marginalised in the past, Ahimeir's
historical importance and ideological influence are gradually being given the
recognition that they deserve. Indeed, the distinguished historian of the Israeli
Right, Colin Shindler, contends that the title of 'Father of the Revolt' should be
shared equally between Jabotinsky and Ahimeir.[2]

*   *   *

This book traces Ahimeir's ideological genesis. While his influence upon the
Zionist Right is undeniable, the lack of analysis surrounding his ideological
contribution has caused the scope and importance of this influence to be
undervalued. Thus, this study seeks to comprehensively understand Ahimeir's

ideological stance and its development, and to position him more accurately within the contexts of the Zionist Right, the historical timeframe in which he was active and the Zionist movement in general. It contends not only that Ahimeir's unique ideological position formed the backbone of Revisionist Maximalism in Mandate Palestine, but that, as a *Madrikh* (leader) for the Revisionist Youth Group Betar and teacher at the Betar Leadership Training School, his ideological influence upon the Revisionist youth movement was far greater than is often recognised.

This study will demonstrate that Ahimeir's initial fascination with – and tentative embrace of – Italian Fascism began three to six years earlier than is generally believed, and that his apparent fundamental ideological shift from Left to Right was not at all the radical move that it is considered to be. Ahimeir's true relationship to both of these political positions will be re-evaluated. A key element in reassessing Ahimeir's ideological development is an understanding of his embrace of Spenglerian theory, which, far from being a mere research interest, exerted a fundamental influence upon him throughout his life. Thus, I contend that Ahimeir's output and actions should be (re-)examined with this consideration in mind.

Furthermore, this study will show that both Ahimeir's loyalty to and gradual disillusionment with various Labour Zionist organisations, including his own party, HaPoel HaTzair (The Young Worker), were based as much on pragmatic necessity as they were on ideology. Indeed, it will conclude that Ahimeir's ideological path was set already in 1924, by the time he emigrated to British Mandate Palestine, and before he joined HaPoel HaTzair. This study contends that the political ideologies of the Revisionist Party and its heirs owe a greater debt to Ahimeir than is generally accepted. Furthermore, Ahimeir's particular case study allows scope for a more general engagement with several intellectual-historical concepts, such as Messianism, Revolution and Fascism. A major underlying thesis of this study concerns the challenges of writing 'difficult history', and the obligation to approach such a challenge in as neutral a manner as possible. For example, the fact that, in 1924, Italian Fascism could represent a viable and attractive political option for both its country's Jewish citizens, and indeed for Ahimeir, as will be demonstrated, should be understood in its historical context, and not be analysed with a disproportionate degree of historical hindsight. Equally, there is no escaping the fact that Ahimeir was a controversial figure who espoused, at times, some highly controversial ideas. Recognition of such facts should not preclude a historically accurate presentation of his life and ideological development.

For a short period of time – from 1928 to 1934 – Ahimeir was a leading figure in the Yishuv, and his influence, and indeed personality and popularity, often outweighed that of Revisionist Party leader Ze'ev Jabotinsky. The fact that figures like Menachem Begin (1913-92) later minimised Ahimeir's influence upon them had more to do with political savvy, self-promotion and certainly self-preservation than with historical accuracy. This study will paint a historically more accurate picture.

*   *   *

A Zionist from his earliest days, Ahimeir was born Abba Shaul ben Isaac Gaissinovitch, or Haissinovich, on 2 November 1897 in Dolghi, White Russia. Although the family was neither particularly religious nor Zionist, Gaissinovitch was, by the age of six, already studying under the tutelage of the young Yiddish and Hebrew poet David Shimoni (1891–1956). In 1907, two years after the family moved to Bobruisk, the young Gaissinovitch enrolled at the Russian Private Gymnasium, and supplemented his curriculum with Hebrew and Talmud study. It was during this period that he became acquainted with the future Labour Zionist leader Berl Katznelson (1887–1944), who also lived in Bobruisk. Katznelson emigrated to Ottoman-Palestine shortly thereafter, in 1909.

Catalysed by an avid interest in Hebrew literature, Jewish culture and history, and a burgeoning identification with Socialism and Zionism, the fourteen-year-old Abba Gaissinovitch asked his parents for permission to study at the newly opened Herzliya Gymnasium in Tel Aviv. The Gymnasium was the first Hebrew High School to open in Tel Aviv, and was an iconic institution. Many of the figures who would go on to play important roles in pre- and early-state Israel were alumni of the Gymnasium, including the future prime minister of Israel, Moshe Sharett (1894–1965) and poet Avraham Shlonsky (1900–73). Rather surprisingly perhaps, Gaissinovitch's request was granted, and in October 1912, the fourteen-year-old made the journey to Ottoman-ruled Palestine. He was chaperoned by his older sister Bluma, who shared her brother's youthful zeal for both Zionism and Socialism. Upon arrival, he quickly renewed his acquaintance with Katznelson, who introduced the pair into Socialist circles. Notably, Gaissinovitch purchased his first 'Zionist shekel' there in 1913, at the ripe old age of fifteen.

The young student returned home to Bobruisk in July 1914 with the intention of spending merely the summer vacation with his family, but the outbreak of the First World War in September forced Gaissinovitch to remain in Russia for its duration. From 1916 he was active with the Bobruisk Zionist Youth Group, and in May 1917 attended the Russian Zionist Conference in Petrograd. In July and August of that year, Gaissinovitch went to Batumi in the northern Caucasus, in present-day Georgia, to participate in training under the auspices of Joseph Trumpeldor's (1880–1920) HeHalutz (The Pioneer) organisation, an initiative designed to prepare young agricultural 'pioneers' for emigration to Ottoman-Palestine. While there, however, he contracted malaria and was forced to return to Bobruisk.

The October Revolution erupted on 7 November 1917, and further complicated Gaissinovitch's extended sojourn in his native Russia. At the end of 1918, and in a Russia now in the midst of revolutionary turmoil, Gaissinovitch matriculated at the University of Kiev, in the faculties of History and Literature. Tragically, on 19 April 1919, his beloved younger brother Meir – a committed Bolshevik, and officer in the Red Army – was killed in battle with Polish forces. The trauma of his brother's death had a profound, and lasting, impact on Gaissinovitch. Indeed, he found it impossible to remain in Russia, and began studies at the University of Liège in Belgium in 1920, before moving on to the University of Vienna the following year. Chapter 1 will begin at this point in Ahimeir's life.

*   *   *

Several terms are used regularly throughout this work, and although each one will be given more extensive discussion in the chapters to follow, it is perhaps useful at this stage to provide a basic outline of how each is understood for the purposes of this study.

Revisionism, or Revisionist Zionism, was an ideological strain of Zionism that was established in 1925 by Ze'ev Jabotinsky. It existed, at first (until 1935), under the umbrella of the World Zionist Organisation. Jabotinsky's breakaway action was catalysed by his rejection of the 1922 Churchill White Paper, which – through its recognition of the newly created Hashemite Kingdom of Transjordan in a portion of the historical biblical Land of Israel – limited the western border of any future Jewish state to the west bank of the river Jordan. Revisionist Zionism advocated not only a return to 'pure' Political Zionism as originally envisaged by Theodor Herzl, which sought the establishment of a Jewish national home through political means (or, more specifically, that international approval gained through diplomatic initiative should precede practical settlement of the land), but also the establishment of a Jewish state on both sides of the river Jordan.[3]

Maximalism or Maximalist Zionism or, indeed, Maximalist Revisionism was a radical ideological stream within Revisionist Zionism. It was established in the Yishuv, in the wake of the 1929 Arab riots, and its leaders were Abba Ahimeir, Uri Zvi Greenberg and Yehoshua Yevin. The Maximalists, while accepting the territorial demands of the Revisionists, differed ideologically from Jabotinsky and the general Revisionists in several key areas. First, unlike Jabotinsky, who consistently advocated a path of diplomacy with the British, the Maximalists fought, both ideologically and actively, against the British government in Palestine, which they saw as antisemitic, and anti-Zionist.[4] Second, the Maximalists rejected Jabotinsky's policy of *Havlagah* (defensive restraint) towards both the Arabs and British, and advocated, instead, a much more proactive, militaristic approach. Third, Maximalist rhetoric was imbued with Secular-Messianic overtones. Finally, the Maximalists wanted the Revisionists to adopt a modus operandi that was predicated on Italian Fascism, with Jabotinsky as leader.[5]

The concept of 'ideology', so very central to this study, is very much a product of Enlightenment thinking. The word appeared first in French, at the end of the eighteenth century, as a quite literal linguistic amalgamation of 'science' and 'ideas'.[6] Over time, the word's use and reception developed both a positive and pejorative understanding: thus, 'ideology' could denote either a noble 'philosophy of the mind' or ignoble 'false consciousness and unreality', depending on the situation.[7] Nonetheless – and putting all etymological interest aside – for the purposes of this study, Shimoni's definition of ideology – 'a coherent, action-oriented set of ideas that provides those who subscribe to it with a comprehensive cognitive map of their position and purposes' – is most accurate, and useful.[8]

Equally a product of the Enlightenment, but somewhat less straightforward in cognizance, is the notion of 'aesthetic'. The word was derived, and Hellenised, by Alexander Baumgarten (1714–62) as a synthesis of 'senses' and 'perception'.[9] *Merriam-Webster* gives a modern definition of 'aesthetic' as, 'a branch of philosophy dealing with the nature of beauty, art, and taste and with the creation and appreciation of beauty', which may also represent a 'particular theory or conception of beauty or art, a particular taste for or approach to what is pleasing to the senses'.[10]

At the risk of oversimplification, it could be said that an ideology is what one believes, while the means which one chooses to express that belief may be seen as an aesthetic expression of that ideology. One might further conclude, then, that an ideology may also possess an aesthetic.[11] The recognition of such a cognitive differentiation between the two concepts will be useful throughout this study. There are occasions when various ideologies might appear to overlap – for example, when discussing the Maximalists and the general Revisionists – yet the aesthetics employed to aid the expression of these ideologies might differ considerably, and vice versa. For example, his concentration on militaristic precision and comportment and the choice of brown for the group's uniform have led some to conclude that Jabotinsky foresaw an embrace of Fascist ideology for the youth of Betar.[12] However, as noted earlier, the fact that he may have borrowed, if only unwittingly, from Fascist aesthetic should in no way lead to the conclusion that Jabotinsky advocated Fascist ideology. For Ahimeir and the Maximalists, the case was altogether different, as will be seen.

* * *

Although not primarily a narrative history, this study does proceed chronologically. Its five chapters cover the years 1921–34: from the year Ahimeir began his doctoral studies in Vienna, until the years of the Arlosoroff murder and the subsequent trials that cost Ahimeir his political reputation. Once again, the focus of this study is on Ahimeir's ideological development. Be that as it may, for the reader who is hitherto unfamiliar with the figure of Abba Ahimeir, I believe that the present narrative also stands on its own as a comprehensive historical account of Ahimeir's life and work over the years covered. In addition, it should be remembered that Ahimeir was a prolific writer. A truly thorough study and analysis of the many and varied articles, letters, unpublished essays and diary entries, all written by Ahimeir between 1921 and 1934, would take years, and would most likely produce a book running to thousands of pages in length. Thus, although comprehensive, this study is not exhaustive. Therefore, as a methodological tool and in the name of variety, I chose, in each chapter, to privilege one particular type of archival source over another – academic, journalistic, testimonial and so on – and which varies from chapter to chapter, as follows:

The first chapter concentrates on Ahimeir's academic magnum opus: his unpublished doctoral dissertation on Oswald Spengler's *Der Untergang des Abendlandes* (The Decline of the West), which he wrote at the University of Vienna, between 1921 and 1924. It also examines his first publications in the American Hebrew journal *HaToren*, which notably contained his first article on Mussolini and Italian Fascism. As noted earlier, this period in Ahimeir's ideological development is often all but ignored by Zionist historians. Nonetheless, it will be demonstrated that it was precisely during this period that Ahimeir set the ideological course upon which he would continue.

The second chapter examines Ahimeir's first years in British Mandate Palestine, and membership in the moderate, Labour-oriented party, HaPoel HaTzair, through a focus on his journalistic output in both the party's eponymous newspaper and the right-oriented newspaper, *HaAretz*. In his articles from the years 1924–8, we can trace Ahimeir's gradual disillusionment with HaPoel HaTzair and the political organisation of the Yishuv, as well as see the first signs of his ability and willingness to court controversy in print.

Chapter 3 details Ahimeir's departure from HaPoel HaTzair for Jabotinsky's Revisionist Zionist Party at the beginning of 1928. It then provides a discussion and analysis of the series of articles he wrote under the rubric 'From the Notebook of a Fascist', in his new position at the newspaper *Doar HaYom*. Finally, it uses the more conceptual, phenomenological discussion of the intellectual concepts of Fascism and Revolution, detailed earlier, to better understand and position Ahimeir's embrace of each.

Chapter 4 privileges unpublished contemporary training manuals from the Revisionist Youth Group Betar and the Betar Leadership Training School, alongside unpublished reminiscences by the school's founder Yirmiahu Halpern, in order to paint a comprehensive overview of both groups' ideological positions and practical organisation and Ahimeir's contribution to both, from 1929 to 1930. Furthermore, I undertake a close reading of the first section of his final book, *Yudaikah* – one of only two books that Ahimeir published during his own lifetime – in an attempt to better understand his very particular ideological conception of Jewish history and civilisation. This is one section where I depart from my otherwise almost exclusive use of contemporary documents or personal memoirs of the period. *Yudaikah* is one of the few works where we get a glimpse of Ahimeir the cultural historian, and therefore merits such a methodological departure.

Finally, this study concludes with a focus on Ahimeir as a political activist, beginning with his formation in 1930 of the semi-underground, anti-British, resistance group Brit HaBiryonim and then proceeding to his arrest in conjunction with Arlosoroff's murder in June 1934, and the subsequent trials that Ahimeir stood. Fittingly, for a discussion of a group that was itself semi-clandestine, my methodological focus in this chapter has been on documents that are themselves 'semi-clandestine' in nature: court transcripts and evidence seized for both the Arlosoroff and Brit HaBiryonim trials, almost all of which have not been viewed since the time of their production. Such an approach gives the unique impression of observing, first-hand, the conversations, thoughts and, indeed, frustrations of a group that was 'speaking' freely, without fear of being heard. Ahimeir's reminiscences, written years later, round out the documentary evidence used in this chapter, and paint a more comprehensive picture of the workings of the organisation that was the ideological exemplar for the more extreme paramilitary groups, Irgun and Lehi.

At the end of each chapter, I draw conclusions that are more specifically related to each of the subjects discussed. Nonetheless, standing back somewhat, a broader consideration of this study's more specific findings has allowed me to make some further observations which suggest possible explanations for the gradual radicalisation of Herzlian Political Zionism. Finally, the study very briefly considers Ahimeir's politico-ideological legacy, before making some final overall conclusions regarding both a more accurate dating of his ideological genesis, and some methodological shortcomings that exist in the extant body of scholarship, which have – I contend – until now prevented a truly comprehensive understanding of Ahimeir's ideological development.

1

Academic

It is perhaps not unfitting to begin this first chapter in the study of Ahimeir's ideological genesis on the ideas that he himself explored and developed in his one academic work: his doctoral thesis *Bermerkungen zu Spenglers Auffassung Russlands* (Remarks on Spengler's Conception of Russia), which he wrote from 1921 to 1924, as a student at the University of Vienna.[1] In order to establish the ideological basis over which would, eventually, unfold an array of concepts that could be as extreme as they could be contradictory, it is methodologically imperative to undertake a close reading of the thesis. Indeed, such action reveals a surprising degree of ideological maturity in this often-overlooked work.

The renowned cultural historian George L. Mosse remarked that Spengler's *The Decline of the West* had more impact through its title than its content, and it has allegedly influenced figures as diverse as the Nazi Propaganda Minister Joseph Goebbels, conductor Wilhelm Furtwängler, historian Arnold J. Toynbee and literary theorist Northrop Frye.[2] The work could as easily resonate with German racial theorists and antisemites as it could with future Jewish ultra-nationalist intellectuals. Indeed, it is clear that Gaissinovitch not only became a Spenglerian at this early stage but also remained so, to varying degrees throughout his life. And although his dissertation may deal with material that appears to have no connection at all with the future Ahimeir's ideology, Zionism, or even Judaism, it should be remembered that the primary intention at this early stage is to focus on Gaissinovitch the Spenglerian, and not the 'Zionist Gaissinovitch as Spenglerian', or even the 'Jewish Gaissinovitch as Spenglerian'. His thesis, while certainly written by a 'Jewish Zionist', was not at all written from that point of view. Conversely, although he described his time in Vienna as the 'period where my interest in Zionism was at its nadir', this does not mean that we are not confronted with the 'Zionist' or 'Jewish' Gaissinovitch.[3] Indeed, a close examination of his thesis will show that these themes never lurked too far beneath the surface.

Throughout this chapter, I will use the term 'small peoples'. This particular usage refers to a formulation coined – after the Czech writer Milan Kundera – by the Israeli historian Uriel Abulof, and which he defines as 'a smaller ethnic community that exists in constant confrontation with the arrogant ignorance of the mighty, characterized by uncertainty and individual doubt about the very existence of the collective self'.[4] The theme of 'small peoples' recurs throughout Gaissinovitch's work and its importance will be discussed later in the chapter. Of course, this is not to say that – were it even possible – Gaissinovitch was conscious of the term, but rather that Abulof's formulation gives us a useful analytical tool when analysing certain, sometimes unconscious, thematic trends in Gaissinovitch's thesis.

Vienna

In 1920, Gaissinovitch left the University of Kiev and Communist Russia. Memories of the Great War and a revolution that had claimed the life of his brother Meir had left him embittered and disillusioned. Indeed, the trauma of his brother's death prompted, that same year, a name change in his memory: from Gaissinovitch to 'Ahi-Meir', or 'Ahimeir' – literally 'my brother Meir' – as he would eventually come to be known.[5] For the time being, on paper at least, he remained Abba Gaissinovitch. After a short stint at the University of Liège, he transferred, with best friend Josef Katznelson, to the University of Vienna, where he was matriculated in the winter semester of 1921–2 as a doctoral candidate in the Faculty of Philosophy, reading Modern and Medieval History, and Art History.[6]

In the autumn of 1921, Austria was entering the third year of the First Republic as a nation beset by economic, political and ideological upheaval. The rate of inflation had been growing dramatically since the previous June, when Chancellor Johann Schober (1874–1932) assumed office to head a coalition between the Christian Socialist and German People's Party that was representative of the two prevailing politico-ideological trends of the period. By contrast, the city of Vienna had in 1919 elected its first Social Democrat mayor, Jakob Reuman (1823–1925), setting in motion a trend that – with the notable exception 1934-1945 – continues to this day. The notorious 'Knight from Rosenau', the politician Georg von Schönerer (1842–1921), had died on 14 August, and although he had not posed a political threat since the demise of his pan-German Party in 1907, his radical German-nationalist, antisemitic, anti-liberal (and indeed anti-Catholic, -capitalist and -Hapsburg) ideology influenced the increasingly radical *Burschenschaften* (student fraternities), and others who took up the *Kampf für das deutsche Volk*, not least the young Adolf Hitler.[7]

Perhaps one of the best examples of the various irreconcilabilities that competed for – and together, contributed to – Viennese politico-cultural hegemony in Europe can be seen in the figure of the composer Richard Strauss, who was director of the Vienna State Opera during the period of Ahimeir's study. Strauss, as a composer, was the standard bearer of fin-de-siècle decadence. His operas *Salome* and *Elektra* pushed the boundaries of tonality, musicianship and – owing to their difficult subject matter – audience reception. As a conductor, however, Strauss was cool, calculating and completely without sentiment. Himself a foreigner – he was Bavarian – Strauss nonetheless epitomised the Viennese *über*-civilised, bourgeois intellectual. His operatic collaborations with the Viennese dramatist Hugo von Hofmannsthal – who, as the son of an upper-class Catholic mother, and titled Jewish bank-manager father, likewise epitomised Vienna of a certain class and age – are still considered to represent the most valiant attempts at reconciling music and text that exist in the genre. Furthermore, Strauss's son Franz would, in 1923, marry a Jew and go on to father two sons who were 'racially' Jewish – a fact that might best explain Strauss's eventual acceptance of the role of presidency of the German *Reichsmusikkammer*, in 1933. Those in search of ideological consistency would be well-advised to avoid Vienna during the interwar period.

Indeed – all Viennese bourgeois liberal cosmopolitanism aside – in reaction to a staggering increase in both antisemitism and broader nationalistic trends, Vienna's Jewish community slowly also began to organise itself along nationalist lines. The University of Vienna itself was a bastion of Zionist activity throughout this period, mainly in reaction to the increase of pan-German nationalistic fervour from within the student body. The university's Jewish students aligned with the burgeoning Jewish nationalist movement in two ways. Internally, they officially joined the Zionist Organisation and paid its membership fee, the 'Zionist Shekel'. Externally, from 1910 onwards, nationalistic Jewish students – and by 1910, one-third of the university's Jews had so defined themselves – began to list *Jüdisch* (Yiddish) as mother tongue in their student records, when registering for each new academic year.[8] Eventually, however, since Yiddish was considered a German dialect, it was, over time, supplanted by the linguistically and ideologically more satisfactory 'Hebrew'. Nevertheless, since neither language was officially recognised by the Danube Monarchy, this was a gesture charged as much with political subversion as it was with nationalist fervour. Gaissinovitch, who as a student at the Herzliya Gymnasium in Tel Aviv had, already in 1913, purchased his first Zionist Shekel, thus also made his Zionist leanings public in Vienna. His student record for his first year lists his mother tongue as 'Russian', but the following year he changed it to 'Hebrew'.[9]

Gaissinovitch's sojourn in Vienna witnessed a power struggle between two 'Roberts' – Weltsch (1891–1982) and Stricker (1879–1944) – over control of the primary institutions within the Austrian Zionist movement. The neo-Romantic, intellectual Weltsch had come from Prague in 1918 to work in the Zionist administrative office and was thus well-positioned to further pursue his own political ambitions. By 1925 he had become involved with the newly founded Brit Shalom movement in Palestine, which sought the establishment of a bi-national state characterised by equal rights for both Jews and Arabs. His opponent Stricker was active in Austrian politics and the Viennese Zionist movement, and founded the Jewish daily newspaper *Wiener Morgenzeitung* in 1919. He was a pro-Habsburg liberal democrat who, over time, moved further to the Right. He joined Ze'ev Jabotinsky's Revisionist Party in 1931 and served, eventually, as one of its vice presidents.[10] It is thus no surprise that, on one hand, Weltsch and Stricker did not see eye to eye, and on the other, that the two future Revisionist leading figures, Stricker and Gaissinovitch, became acquainted with each other during this time.[11]

It was in this colourful, highly charged milieu that Gaissinovitch would spend the next six semesters. In Vienna, he pursued a comprehensive curriculum that included courses as varied as History of Latin, Political Social Movements in Russia, History of the Balkans, History of the Middle Ages, Psychology, German History, German Painting, Shakespeare, The Philosophy of Hegel, Byzantine History and Schopenhauer.[12] Notably, he studied *Staatskirche* (state church) under Hans Uebersberger (1877–1962), Introduction and Study of History, Theoretical Principles of the Science of History and Politics with Wilhelm Bauer (1877–1953) and The Age of the Reformation under Heinrich Srbik (1878–1951).

A cursory look into the backgrounds of these three professors yields some rather interesting information. Uebersberger was a lecturer in Eastern European history and would serve as rector of the university from 1930 to 1931. Bauer, who appears to have been Gaissinovitch's supervisor, lectured in general modern history, and had just published his influential *Einführung in das Studium der Geschichte* (Introduction to the Study of History), in 1921. The two would later examine Gaissinovitch's dissertation and recommend that he be awarded his doctorate. Srbik was a professor of General History who, in 1920, had written a book on Wallenstein's murder and was working on a two-volume biography of Prince Metternich that would eventually be published in 1925. Notably – and ominously – from 1938 to 1945 he served as president of the Austrian Academy of Sciences.

Close friends as well as colleagues, Bauer and Srbik were both suspended, along with their colleague Otto Brunner, in 1945 and forced into early retirement.[13] Their strong pan-German agenda was seen to have influenced and compromised their teaching throughout the years of Austria's annexation, and cast doubt on their future 'ability to unconditionally support the new, independent Austrian Republic': a legalistic euphemism used to describe those who had collaborated with the National Socialists.[14] Indeed, all three academics were members of various pan-German, nationalist *Burschenschaften* in Austria.[15] Unfortunately, Gaissinovitch left no account of the relationship between himself and these three professors, and the only extant comments that exist vice versa are by Bauer and Uebersberger, and pertain only to his dissertation (see the following discussion). Thus, we are left to speculate on the nature of the attitudes between Gaissinovitch – who certainly made no effort to hide his Jewish heritage and Zionist leanings during his time in Vienna – and the pan-German, and most likely antisemitic, academic trio.

Gaissinovitch submitted his doctoral thesis entitled *Bermerkungen zu Spenglers Auffassung Russlands* (Remarks on Spengler's Conception of Russia) to the Faculty of Philosophy at the University of Vienna, on 31 March 1924, and on 8 June of that year was awarded his Ph.D. Comprising a mere eighty-seven pages, including a bibliography that lists only eighteen, mainly secondary sources, one is struck at first glance by the difference in methodological approach when compared with a contemporary doctoral thesis. Indeed, within those eighty-seven pages there exists neither a single footnote nor citation.

Although such practice seems strange to a contemporary academic eye, it was nonetheless accepted. The University of Vienna's 1872 Reform Laws, in consideration of doctoral dissertations submitted to the Faculty of Philosophy, were vague, and stated only that candidates exercised free choice over the form of their dissertations so long as they could demonstrate sufficient knowledge of their topics.[16] Thus it was possible to submit a freely formed treatise on a particular subject, and indeed, it appears that this is what Gaissinovitch did. Perhaps less a scholarly study of Spengler's work than a 'philosophical rebuttal', the dissertation reads more like a series of remarks delivered from one cultural historian, if not 'philosopher', to another. An introduction is followed by six chapters: 'Arabian Culture', '*Mujik* and *Fellah*', 'Tolstoy and Dostoyevsky', 'One

Sixth of the Mainland', 'The Revolution and Its Consequences' and 'To Whom the Last Word in Europe?'.

Untergang

The first volume of Oswald Spengler's magnum opus *The Decline of the West* (*Der Untergang des Abendlandes*) appeared in 1918, and bore the title *Form and Actuality* (*Gestalt und Wirklichkeit*). A second volume, *Perspectives of World History* (*Welthistorische Perspektiven*), followed in 1922, one year after Gaissinovitch had begun his doctoral research. Spengler believed that the real utility in his approach was in its attempt at

> predetermining history, of following the still untravelled stages in the destiny of a Culture, and specifically of the only Culture of our time and on our planet which is actually in the phase of fulfilment – the West-European-American.[17]

Such a revolutionary, meta-historical methodology required a new cognitive and analytical strategy. Spengler eschewed the traditional grouping of one 'long' world history into temporal periods – ancient, medieval and modern – in favour of a less Eurocentric approach that grouped world history by epochal 'Cultures', which could then be studied comparatively.[18] Furthermore, a Spenglerian 'Culture' is like all other 'biological' phenomena: a living organism that possesses a life cycle of its own, and which, in this case, lasts approximately 1,500 years. It comprises four predetermined, temporally fixed stages that correspond to the life-cycle of human beings – childhood, youth, maturity and old age – or the four seasons: spring, summer, autumn and winter.

The pre-cultural, 'childhood' phase of a Spenglerian Culture lasts approximately 500 years and is characterised by much change, albeit unconscious, as the 'germinating' Culture leads an almost directionless, somnambulistic existence. Eventually, however, like a butterfly from a cocoon, a new Culture emerges out of what Spengler calls a 'proto-spirituality of ever-childish humanity', into its two major periods of development: youth, which lasts approximately 500 years, and maturity, which lasts approximately 300 years.[19] The period of 'youth' is marked by religious zeal, and its ruthless defence: Spengler characterises actions in this phase as 'warm-blooded' and impulsive, and settlement is in the countryside, as feudal organisation begins to predominate. The 'mature' phase represents the pinnacle of creativity, expression and fulfilment of each Culture, as country marketplaces grow into towns that – in turn – enable scientific, artistic, political and philosophical evolution.

The final stage – 'old age' – sees 'culture' transformed into 'civilisation'. This period is ruled by cool intellect and calculated reason that act completely independently of passion and instinct. Towns become cities, and finally 'megalopolitan' centres, where rationalisation prevails and cultural decay is widespread. Religion becomes dogma, science and philosophy become rational analysis, prophetic vision becomes journalistic superficiality, art becomes technique and history is no longer 'made', but is 'studied'. Worst of all, money – the prime indicator of a 'rootless' Culture – assumes a central, irresistible role. All traces of rural life are abandoned in favour of the stone 'cosmopolis', at which point the Culture's blood 'congeals', a sure sign of its demise. Indeed, 'warm' blood, and money – 'congealed-blood' – were, for Spengler, polar opposites. Blood as a life-force plays a central role in Spenglerian ideology, hence his glorification of the 'warm-blooded primitive' versus his debasement of 'cold-blooded civilisation' and his overall mistrust of reason.

The 'civilised' population, 'culturally-rootless' once again, begins anew to wander aimlessly, similar to its predecessors in the 'childhood' stage, but now evolved into 'intellectual drifters' that Spengler calls *fellaheen*. And although indicative of a Culture that was now firmly in decline, this final phase does not manifest itself without various forms of resistance. Spengler believed that the increase in supernatural belief and flirtation with 'pseudo-religion' that were indicative of this phase marked the advent of a Culture's second, albeit corrupted, 'childhood'. At the same time, those few who had remained in the countryside – the 'simple' folk – now come to the fore, in what Spengler calls a 'Second Religiosity'. In spite of its promise, however, this Second Religiosity lacks vitality; it brings forth no new religion and is therefore quickly converted into the already extant religion of the *fellaheen*. All distinctions between the religions of city and province become blurred in a religion that no longer experiences any form of historical progression. Eventually, a 'new' Culture – one nonetheless predicated on the former, 'ossified', Culture – would emerge, led by a new elite of warm-blooded barbarians, and begin the process anew. Indeed, Spengler specifically appropriates the Arabic term for peasant farmers, since he believed that the 'real' *fellaheen* that existed at the time of writing were both remnants of a now-dead Arabian Culture, and the prototypes of what would eventually become the new barbarian elite – the 'proto-spirituality of ever-childish humanity' – of a reborn Arabian Culture.

Although the parallels with the Nietzschean *Übermensch* are rather obvious, the Hegelian overtones should also not go unnoticed. Spengler's theory of Cultural evolution is not completely dissimilar to Hegel's concept of dialectical 'becoming': a Spenglerian Culture comprises not only Hegelian thesis (culture) and antithesis (civilisation) but also – in the idea of cultural rebirth led by the 'New Barbarian' – a synthesis of the two, which then serves as the point of reference for a new dialectical process. The real point of departure from Hegel is that, for Spengler, Cultures are independent 'biological' organisms, and thus lack any sort of universal truth, although they may, in fact, share similar spiritual ideals. As such, he rejects Hegel's idea of one overriding history of humankind that develops teleologically for the notion of several smaller self-sufficient, biologically predetermined historical Cultures that all develop in a similar manner. As he noted:

> Here I would protest against two assumptions that have so far vitiated all historical thought: the assertion of an ultimate aim of mankind as a whole and the denial of there being ultimate aims at all. The life *has* an aim. It is the fulfilment of that which was ordained at its conception. ... 'Historical' man ... is the man of a Culture that is in full march towards self-fulfilment. Before this, after this, outside this, man is *historyless*.[20]

He also rejected Darwin, in favour of Goethe, who he believed, in his essay *Geistesepochen* (Spiritual Epochs), had 'characterized the four parts of a Culture – its preliminary, early, late, and civilized stages – with such a depth of insight that even today there is nothing to add'.[21] Spengler thus uses Goethe's theory as the template for his own theory of Cultural biological predetermination. He believed that the idea of Darwinian evolution was refuted in nature, especially in palaeontology, but also – remarkably – in the study of human evolution:

> As for mankind, discoveries of the Diluvial age indicate more and more pointedly that the man-forms existing then correspond to those living now; there is not the slightest trace of evolution towards a race of greater utilitarian 'fitness'. And the continued failure to find man in the Tertiary discoveries indicates more and more clearly that the human life-form, like every other, originates in a sudden mutation (*Wandlung*) of which the 'whence', 'how', and 'why' remain an impenetrable secret.[22]

Indeed, because Cultures appeared – like any other life form – as a 'sudden mutation', and consequently had similar life-cycles with parallel stages of development, Spengler believed that corresponding periods of different Cultures could be studied comparatively. He terms this 'Morphology'.[23] Accordingly, parallel events that occurred during corresponding spiritual epochs in any particular Culture are considered, in Spenglerian methodology, 'morphologically contemporaneous'. Thus, in Spenglerian analysis, Plato and Goethe were – morphologically speaking – 'contemporaries', in spite of the fact that they lived 1,500 years apart, since each assumed a similar role at a corresponding period in the development of his particular – Classical and Western, respectively – Culture.[24] Moreover, Spengler borrowed the mineralogical term 'pseudomorphosis' to describe a situation where an older Culture cuts short a younger Culture's evolutional self-expression, and thus prevents it from 'becoming': from evolving into its own Spenglerian-predetermined mature Culture. Cultures may superficially borrow from each other, but can never substantially assume each other's characteristics.

Spengler identified six Cultures which he believed had completed their respective life-cycles: Egyptian, Babylonian, Classical, Chinese, Indian and Arabian. He identified a further two, incomplete, Cultures: Mayan, which had begun its cycle but met with a sudden end, and Western, which was still extant, but in the process of decline, having already entered its phase of 'old age' or 'winter'. He further distinguished between 'Apollonian' (ancient Roman and Greek), 'Magian' (Jewish from 500 BCE, Persian, Arabian, early Christian) and 'Faustian' (Western) Cultures.

Gaissinovitch's homeland, Russia, was – for Spengler – in a state of pseudomorphosis, a process that had begun in 1703 when Peter the Great founded St Petersburg. Until this period, Russia had been 'morphologically contemporaneous' with Europe during its 'pre-cultural' and 'spring' epochs. From 1703, 'Old Russian' Culture was abandoned in favour of an emulation of Western Culture. Spengler pits Tolstoy against Dostoyevsky: the 'Western', 'revolutionary' father of Bolshevism *cum* social reformer, versus the 'Asiatic', saintly figure who represented primeval Russia, and – consequently – the Russia to come. Thus for Spengler, the 1917 revolution was less the revolt of a disenfranchised, urbanised proletariat, as it was the innate yearning of a town-less, primitive *mujik* (Russian peasant) for his own life-form, religion and history.[25] A Spenglerian reading sees the Bolsheviks as the epitome of a megalopolitan 'civilised' – in other words, at the end of its life cycle – Western European society. Nonetheless, because of Russia's unique pseudo-morphological state with the Spenglerian 'Western' Culture, the Bolsheviks could only ever attempt to emulate Western European society. Consequently, for Spengler, Marxist rhetoric, a product of 'civilised' Western Europe, was nothing more than pure, rationalist fetishism. The reason that the revolution had been successful in Russia and not, for example, in Germany or Austria was due to ideology, but rather to the strong *mujik* element that characterised it (and was lacking in the others) and because the strong, almost exclusively Marxist, fanatical element represented the 'flirtation with pseudo-religion', and 'Second Religiousness' that characterised the end of the life cycle of a Spenglerian Culture.

Mosse isolated three important concepts that could be deduced from Spengler's work. First was the concept of biological determinism, the idea of historical cycles joining up together. In Spenglerian theory, however, 'biology' was not associated with material, but rather metaphysical, force. The particular Culture then witnessed the killing of this force through modernity, thereby creating the necessity for a cultural rebirth, as exemplified in the concept of the 'New Barbarian'. Second was the idea that hope for the future lay with this 'New Barbarian'. Third was Spengler's distinction between 'culture' and 'civilization', the deep and metaphysical versus the confined and superficial.[26]

Although Gaissinovitch's thesis concentrates on what he sees as Spengler's misconception of Russia in *The Decline of the West*, he perhaps not surprisingly devotes a considerable amount of time to what he sees as his mentor's misconception of Jews and Judaism. Spengler placed the Jews – along with the Persians, Syrians and Arabs – under the greater umbrella of 'Magian' culture, which had been awakened from its 'childhood' at the same time as the ascendency of Christianity. The preceding six hundred years, from approximately 500 BCE to 100 CE, had represented nothing more than a 'pre-cultural' preparation for this more mature stage. Until that point – that is, during the period of the Israelite tribes, the Exodus from Egypt and even the First Temple Period – Spengler considered the Jews part of ancient Babylonian Culture, and Israel only one of the many tribes that made up its character. Magian Culture was dominated by a unique affinity with the 'Light and Good' that emanated from above, and therefore belonged spiritually to the divine community of the *Jedermann*. There was no Magian nation, language or homeland, because religious mission precluded territorial expansion. And, since submission to the commands of 'Light and Good' took precedence over all else, there existed among the Magian peoples no separation between ecclesiastical and civil law.[27]

With the Jewish Dispersion came, from approximately 1000 CE, a juxtaposition of Magian upon Faustian Culture.[28] Since each Culture was at a different developmental stage of its particular life cycle, the Jews, 'civilised and cosmopolitan', were – since Magian culture had already reached its zenith with Islam – almost Spenglerian *fellaheen*, while the people in the Western Culture among whom they dwelt were only now just making their transition from the primitive 'pre-cultural' stage to the early development of the 'youth' epoch.[29]

Consequently, Spengler posits, 'mutual hate and contempt [was] due not to race-distinction, but to *difference of phase*'.[30] The 'megalopolitan' ghetto was displaced into the Gothic country town. Thus, the apparent Jewish aptitude for monetary affairs as well as the phenomenon of the *Judengasse* – where domestic life, moneylending and petty trade were all carried out at close quarters – was a millennium ahead of the Western cultures in which it operated. Judaism, as a religion, had run its course, and was by this point timeless and devoid of any historical development. Only with the Enlightenment, and subsequent intellectualisation – and thus 'civilisation' – of Faustian Culture could the Jews find a sort of affinity with the surrounding, more dominant Culture. Indeed, because of their advanced *fellaheen* state, the Jews were in a position to 'poison' and take advantage of the economic, scientific and cultural advancements made by the newly civilised Western society. Nonetheless, Spengler thought that Western European Jewry was losing its inner cohesion, due to its 'rootless' disregard for the metaphysical in favour of the economic, the gradual disappearance of the Magian business sense and – notably – its lack of homeland.[31] Spengler concluded that the 'Jewish Consensus' had 'saved its life by shutting itself off in the ghetto'; now that those walls had come down, it was 'fragmented and faced with dissolution'.[32] Ironically, this was a conclusion often reached within the Western European Jewish community itself, although it cited different causes.

Gaissinovitch and Spengler

> Spengler gives [us] the most exhaustive and profound expression of longing felt by the Europeans of the 20th century after the vanished beauty of the old Europe.[33]

So begins Gaissinovitch's dissertation on Spengler: with a qualitative assessment of the overall mood pervading *The Decline of the West,* and his acknowledgement of the 'expression of longing' which, Gaissinovitch believes, in his rather hagiographic introduction, was precisely what rendered the book worth reading. His recognition that Spengler's longing for the golden age of European culture was a common phenomenon during the empty, directionless, transitional period that occurs between two historical epochs, is an analysis that is not only Spenglerian but possibly even somewhat autobiographical. Gaissinovitch had been forced, by the outbreak of the First World War, to turn a visit with his parents in Bobruisk, Russia, into an indefinite stay. He only finally returned to

Palestine one month after being awarded his doctorate in the summer of 1924, ten years after assuming that he was merely leaving for a summer holiday. Thus Gaissinovitch himself also stood in a transitional period between two defining epochs, and doubtless some of the longing he felt was that of the young Zionist towards Zion, to which he so desperately wished to return.

Gaissinovitch found *The Decline of the West* to be absolutely, and uniquely, au courant: a product of the end of the war, viewed through the prism of a defeated Germany and accordingly saturated with all the necessary pessimism that such an unprecedented situation might effect. Indeed, the German intelligentsia – of which Spengler considered himself a member – had, at the beginning of the war, looked forward to the 'messianic' fulfilment of a role it had aspired to since the Middle Ages, one that facilitated greater German cultural and ideological influence in Europe. However, history had quashed this hope. Thus, *The Decline of the West* was written not only from the point of view of a section of the intelligentsia of a Germany that had lost the war but also from the point of view of a section of the intelligentsia of a Germany that had *expected to win the war, but had lost.* Hence the nostalgia for the past that pervaded Spengler's book, 'like the lamentations of a mature man for the vanished happiness of youth'.[34] Due to Germany's defeat in the war, Gaissinovitch posits in his introduction that 'Europe's future belongs to Russia', a fact that was recognised by 'every German'. In consideration of both Gaissinovitch's virulent anti-Bolshevism, and the de facto status quo of a post–Treaty of Versailles Europe, this seems a bizarre claim. Why not one of the other Allied nations? Or indeed Poland, which, under the conditions of the Versailles Treaty, was now given international sanction for political self-determination? Gaissinovitch's claim rings hollow, and was most likely contrived in order to justify his concentration on Russia in his thesis. Indeed, he contradicts his own contention by the end of his dissertation, as will be seen.

Gaissinovitch concludes his Introduction with no thesis, no discussion of Spenglerian theory, no outline and only the single, fleeting, mention of Russia, noted earlier. The lack of a clear thesis would seem to support the argument that Gaissinovitch is writing more from the perspective of a 'fellow-philosopher', than a scholar. As such, we see Gaissinovitch assume a role that the later Abba Ahimeir would adopt for the rest of his life: that of the sagacious critic. In spite of his rapturous acceptance of Spengler's work, Gaissinovitch still knows better. And here perhaps, as later in life, he sabotages his scholarly authority through an all-too premature assumption of such a role.

Curiously, Gaissinovitch begins his study of Spengler's conception of Russia with a chapter on his conception of Arabian Culture.[35] It is telling that we first hear not from Gaissinovitch the cultural historian and philosopher, but rather, from Gaissinovitch the Zionist. He immediately rejects Spengler's position, adapted from the historians Ernest Renan (1823–92) and Theodor Mommsen (1817–1903), that the Jews were a nation without a land, and that Jerusalem – while perhaps a mecca for them – was neither their spiritual centre nor homeland.[36] Had Jerusalem merely been a 'mecca', he argues, the Jews would not have been able to wage such an intensive fight against an enormous Roman empire that had been at its zenith. For Gaissinovitch, the Jews represent their own Spenglerian Culture, although perhaps that of a 'small people'. Jerusalem was not a mecca, it was the capital of a small-peoples' sovereign nation, one that was forced into existential confrontation with a larger, stronger oppressor. Indeed – in a notable analysis for the future Ahimeir – he uses Spenglerian theory to show that both Jewish Palestine and Russia had demonstrated similar demographic settlement at their respective morphologically contemporaneous revolutionary periods: the Jewish Revolt in 70 CE and the Russian Revolution in 1917.

The Israeli historian Yaacov Shavit has previously recognised Gaissinovitch's belief that a nation's birthplace formed its 'character and consciousness', as well as his 'view that the formative years of the Jewish people were the period of their wanderings in the desert'.[37] The Spenglerian dimension inherent in Shavit's observation should, perhaps, be highlighted.[38] He discusses how Ahimeir applied Spengler's historiosophical and morphological methodologies to Jewish history, and saw the phenomenon of *halakhic* (pertaining to Jewish law) Judaism as the development of system of mere legal codes that had become necessary because of the stagnation of what had once been a 'living', spontaneous Judaism. Two thousand years of Diasporic exile had only sought to push Judaism further behind this contrived legalistic structure of fulfilment of commandments, an analysis which is certainly supported by a close reading of the dissertation on Spengler. Shavit correctly concludes that Ahimeir 'found in Spengler a basis for his individual interpretation of the history of the Jewish people'. In Shavit's analysis, this is the reason that Gaissinovitch considered an imperative of Zionism to be the redemption of the 'Jewish people from the decadence of civilization and to redeem it to sovereign, national patterns of existence in its national territory'.[39] The preceding discussion confirms this. Indeed, Shavit's conclusion, that Ahimeir saw a return to the Land of Israel as 'a return to the source of vitality – a necessary condition for transforming Judaism into a "Culture"'– lacks perhaps only the further indication of just how completely Spenglerian a conclusion this is.[40]

Gaissinovitch continues with his discussion of Jewish history – again, telling for a thesis on Russia, which at this stage in his study he has all but ignored – by comparing the present-day Jewish Diaspora with Jewish colonisation in the Hellenistic world. Although Jews had settled throughout all of the Mediterranean, he notes that Palestine had nonetheless continued to remain the single Jewish centre until a full 150 years after the destruction of Jerusalem. The Jewish community in Mesopotamia, which had existed since the Babylonian exile, had developed only much later, when the Talmudic academies were founded after the destruction of the Second Temple. And in Alexandria, although Jewish culture certainly did become Hellenised to some degree, it had essentially remained Jewish. Furthermore, Gaissinovitch disagrees with Spengler's analysis that pitted the Jewish prophets as 'morphological contemporaries' with Zarathustra. For him, a true analysis of the situation would see Zarathustra as morphologically contemporaneous, rather, with Moses, Paul, Mohammed and Confucius. Spengler considered prophethood to be a characteristically Magian phenomenon. Gaissinovitch rejects his mentor's contention, and thus realigns the Jewish prophets to be 'morphologically contemporaneous' with the Church Fathers: Augustine, Tertullian, John of Chrysostom, et al. The fact that Gaissinovitch calls them the 'Christian prophets' highlights their functional similarity as Spenglerian morphological contemporaries, and as such, his analysis does appear to be an improvement on Spengler.[41] Indeed, just as the Jewish prophets had struggled against pagan worship and the foreign cultural influence of Egypt, so the 'Christian prophets' likewise struggled against paganism and the foreign cultural influence of Greece. In further support of his break with Spengler on this point, Gaissinovitch notes that prophets establish no new religion themselves, but rather they augment, deepen and purify one's faith in the struggle against foreign influence. Indeed, they buttress a 'small people's' faith in itself.

The destruction of the first Jewish temple and subsequent Babylonian exile were events of great importance to the Jews, and here, finally, he slowly brings Russia into the discussion. Gaissinovitch sees the Chaldeans – the Semitic tribe (900–665 BCE) that was eventually assimilated into Babylon – and the Tatars – the various nomadic Turco-Mongolian tribes that existed from approximately 1243, and that were eventually assimilated as part of Tsarist Russia in 1598 – as 'morphological contemporaries' in their respective Jewish and Russian historical developments. Both tribes were influenced by the culture of their respective occupying forces, albeit with differing results. For Gaissinovitch, the Jewish situation had resulted in preservation of culture but loss of homeland, while in Russia the opposite had occurred. In his notably Spenglerian analysis, every Culture experienced a similar 'Yoke of the Tatars' – a struggle of a 'small people' against a greater oppressor – at some point in the course of its historical development.

Leaving Russia aside, once again, Gaissinovitch further criticises Spengler for basing his views of Jewish and Persian culture on the theories of the German historian Eduard Meyer (1855–1930), who suggested the strong influence of Zoroastrianism on Judaism during the Babylonian exile.[42] Meyer had further posited that 'Judaism' had begun only after the Jews returned from Babylonian Exile, in the days of Ezra and Nehemiah. Before that, only the 'Israelitic' faith had existed. Gaissinovitch refutes Meyer's claim by noting that the Jews had, in fact, brought forth no new religion at the end of the Babylonian exile. Indeed, Gaissinovitch saw Ezra's religious innovations, which fought assimilation and forbade intermarriage, as not particularly significant in the history of the Jewish People. As such, he considers Ezra (480–440 BCE) – the scribe who had led thousands of Judeans back to Jerusalem from exile in Babylon, in 458 BCE – to be 'morphologically contemporaneous' with Luther: both were great reformers, but neither was unique in his particular role when compared with his morphological contemporaries in other Cultures, for example, Buddha or Mohammed. And Spengler further erred, according to Gaissinovitch, by seeing in Buddha a symptom of India's decline and not recognising him for the reformer that he was. Furthermore, notably, and in marked contrast to Spengler, Gaissinovitch believes that Islam imparted no new religious ideas to the Persians and Syrians. He sees it as merely theologically more radical and more aggressive in its proselytism. Indeed, he notes that reformation was a marked characteristic of every religion's historical development, whether Apollonian, Faustian or Magian.

And not surprisingly, since he believed that the Jews represented their own Spenglerian Culture, Gaissinovitch goes to great lengths to disprove Spengler's contention that *all* Magian peoples were nations without a land. It was a subject close to his heart, and he contends that the existence of the Jewish Diaspora in no way supported Spengler's allegation. Although he does agree with Spengler's assertion that Diaspora Jewry existed completely independently of the metropolis in Palestine, Gaissinovitch sees it, in this respect, as no different from any other general colonisation project. In spite of this observation, he notes that while it was common for a particular colony to have little political dependence on its metropolis, Gaissinovitch does admit that cultural congruence was, in fact, common. He cites the example of the United States, which despite immigration from all over Central Europe had remained 'culturally' – but not 'politically' – an English colony. Thus, for Gaissinovitch, only a cultural bond could evolve between a colony and its metropolis, never a political one. This is how he explains the possibility of Jewish national rebirth: Jewish political independence was merely latent – a result of exile – and doomed to remain so unless the situation of exile could be negated. Finally, it is significant that Gaissinovitch does not fundamentally disagree with Spengler's assessment of the Jews as a 'people without a land', but, instead, sees this landlessness as neither an exclusively Magian nor a permanent and unchangeable trait.[43]

Gaissinovitch now turns properly to Russia, and specifically to Spengler's misconception that its cultural position in relation to the West was morphologically contemporaneous with Arabia's position in relation to the Ancient world. Disagreeing with Spengler, Gaissinovitch finds that Russia represents a single people – a 'small people' – the Arabians, an amalgamation of many peoples. Gaissinovitch explains the appearance of Mohammed in Arabia and Luther in Europe as major incidents of international importance that demonstrated the morphological contemporaneousness of the two reformers. Islam reformed Southwest Asia and North Africa in the same way that the Reformation 'purified' Western Christianity from the 'heathenness' of Catholicism. Notably – in consideration of the future Ahimeir's embracement of Revisionist Zionist ideology – Gaissinovitch believed that Mohammed preached an 'extreme *monistic* form of the religion of the Persians, Syrians, and Egyptians'.[44] And here, Gaissinovitch does draw a parallel with Russia: but it is with the Russia of Bolshevism, which was virulently monistic in its ideological message, and not – as Spengler opines – with the Russia of romantic-nationalist 'Dostoyevskyism'.

Gaissinovitch notes that Russia was first 'discovered' by the West when the English discovered Muscovy in the sixteenth century. At this first juncture between a Western Culture that was still in its period of Spenglerian 'youth' and a much younger Russian Culture, the English had encountered a people as different in outward appearance as they were in religious affiliation, and who were more Oriental than Occidental.[45] Predictably, the Europeans saw in Muscovy a barbaric land, a 'small people' that was ripe for colonial exploitation. However, they faced fierce opposition from a population infused with national pride. But although the Russians successfully thwarted any English colonial enterprise, they could ultimately not deny the superiority of certain elements in Western Culture. Thus, by the end of the seventeenth century and the rule of Peter the Great, Western cultural influence had triumphed, and dominated in the former 'Eastern, Magian land', as this 'small people' – now locked in Spenglerian pseudomorphosis with Western Culture – sought to emulate and transform itself into a 'large people'. For Gaissinovitch, this period represented the first of two decisive victories of Westernisation. Russia was 'rediscovered' by the West during the French Revolution and Napoleonic invasion, which led to a period of great French political and cultural influence in Russian life. Indeed, Gaissinovitch makes it clear that a 'small people' could not reject the political dominance of a 'large people', and accept only its cultural influence, without the latter becoming the dominant culture. The third and final time that the West 'discovered' Russia, according to Gaissinovitch – although he might have more accurately said vice versa – coincided with the Great War and Russian Revolution, and which saw Russian culture 'rediscover' itself, but through Western ideals. Indeed, for Gaissinovitch, Bolshevism marked the second decisive victory of Westernisation in Russia, but one that, paradoxically, sought to reclaim the cultural-national character of the Russian Spenglerian Culture. Ideologically, however, this was an impossible expectation since, as will be discussed next and if we accept Gaissinovitch's analysis, Bolshevism was an ideological product of Western, and not Russian, Culture. This observation seems to indicate that Gaissinovitch considered Russia – for better or for worse – to be in transition from a 'small people' to a larger 'civilisation' that could now stand on its own, and pose its own threat to a former potential oppressor.

Turning to Russian urban organisation, Gaissinovitch highlights what he believes is a fundamental flaw in Spengler's view that the Russian city was like a foreign body in Russian national life, there 'only for the satisfaction and utility of the Court, the administration, [and] the traders', but not the general population.[46] He argues that Moscow and St Petersburg were both established in the natural development of a Russian national economy, culture and politic, and their foreigners had assimilated more quickly into Russian life than had, for example, the Czechs in Vienna. Indeed, St Petersburg, in spite of its mixed ethnic history, was, in Gaissinovitch's opinion, more characteristically Russian than Spengler's characteristically 'Arabian' cities: Alexandria and Constantinople. St Petersburg was a political and spiritual centre, home to the most Western and epicurean form of Russian culture. Moreover, it is notable that it was the figure of Peter the Great, with his conservative nationalist agenda, that embodied for Gaissinovitch the quintessential Russian historical figure.

In addition to Yaacov Shavit, discussed earlier, the historian Eran Kaplan has also highlighted Gaissinovitch-Ahimeir's general acceptance of Spenglerian theory. Nonetheless, he concludes that Gaissinovitch ultimately rejected Spengler's conception of Russia. He contends that Gaissinovitch saw Russia as a unique case because it had developed in a 'hermetically sealed cultural environment'.[47] However, it is clear from a closer reading of Gaissinovitch's dissertation – which certainly agrees fundamentally with Spengler's assertion that Russia had started out as its own Culture, but had now become locked in Spenglerian pseudomorphosis with the West – that this is not necessarily the case. Certainly the last paragraph of Gaissinovitch's chapter 'Arabian Culture' suggests such a conclusion. However, in later chapters, Gaissinovitch goes on to highlight Russian resistance to Western *dominance* but not, in fact, to Western *cultural influence*, which had – by the time of Peter the Great – triumphed, and continued to prevail through the Napoleonic invasion through to its present-day influence in the Russian Revolution. Furthermore, Gaissinovitch rejects Spengler's conception of the Russian *mujik* as an 'eastern' *fellah* by arguing that the former longed for the city, that is to say – if one applies the filter of Spenglerian analysis – demonstrated decidedly Western traits. Thus, to a certain degree, Gaissinovitch does accept the fact that Russia was a 'son of the west', but rather rejects Spengler's opinion that it was a '*backward* son of the west'.[48]

Moving on to the Russian cultural sphere, Gaissinovitch devotes considerable discussion to the relationship between the writers Leo Tolstoy (1828–1910) and Fyodor Dostoyevsky (1821–81), and a Spenglerian reading and comparison of each.[49] Once again, his discussion is often more interesting for the light it sheds on Gaissinovitch's own political and ideological positions than it is for a comprehensive cultural-ideological insight into either man. In *The Decline of the West*, Spengler had claimed there was only one Christianity, and its sole modern exponent was Dostoyevsky. For Spengler, Dostoyevsky was the archetypical Russian: the purest expression of the Russian spirit, its 'Mohammed' or 'Goethe'. By contrast, however, Gaissinovitch notes that, in fact, Christianity contained both reforming and traditional ideological trajectories, and, indeed, from its very beginning. Paul, whom Gaissinovitch calls the 'apostle of the Gentiles' and 'Revisionist of Christianity', had actually opposed Jesus's own brother James, who had himself advocated the perpetuation of Jewish tradition in Christianity.[50] Clearly, Dostoyevsky could not possibly represent both ideological streams. Indeed, Gaissinovitch notes that Dostoyevsky and his disciples were eager supporters of the Russian Orthodox Church, and Dostoyevsky had pejoratively declared Socialism the 'New Catholicism'. And in opposition to Spengler, who called Dostoyevsky a 'peasant', Gaissinovitch considers Dostoyevsky a 'civilised' urbanite, both in reality and as a writer.[51] Interestingly, Gaissinovitch notes that Dostoyevsky discussed the 'Socialist' tendencies of Pope Leo X in a journalistic series entitled 'Diary of a Writer', much in the same way that the future Abba Ahimeir would, only four years later and also in journalistic form, extol the virtues of a similarly nascent political movement in his 'From the Notebook of a Fascist' articles.[52] This observation, of course, raises the question of whether the former bore some influence on the latter and whether the titular parallels are more than coincidence.

Moving on now to Dostoyevsky's antithetical colleague, Gaissinovitch believed, unlike Spengler, that Tolstoy – a 'thinking sectarian' – had negated the Church, historical Christianity and almost all Christian literature. However, Gaissinovitch disagrees with Spengler's assertion that Tolstoy was no Christian. He argues that Tolstoy's Christianity was simply more pragmatic: he demanded improvement in the existential situation of the common man, and his works address the themes of Socialist thought, anarchy and negation of urban culture. In spite of this fact, and in opposition to Spengler, Gaissinovitch does not consider Tolstoy a Marxist. The fact that, in the 1880s, during the suppression of the Nihilist uprising – in which the anarchistic revolutionary group was quashed in the wake of the assassination of Tsar Nicholas II by members of the related Narodnaya Volya – many members of the Russian intelligentsia, doubting the worth of the revolution, settled in the countryside and became farmers was, for Gaissinovitch, a consequence of Tolstoy's ideological influence. Indeed, Gaissinovitch believed that Tolstoy was as much an opponent of the revolution as he was of despotic rule and the Church, and called him a 'cultured' ruralist who hated the city and who was drawn to 'Buddhistic passivity' and 'Oriental tranquillity'. This view stood in direct contrast to Spengler's, in which Tolstoy was the aristocrat who, weary of urban life, had escaped to the countryside. Gaissinovitch described Tolstoy as a 'patriarch' whose way of life and creative output had merely fallen from favour.

Thus, Gaissinovitch essentially reverses Spengler's conception of the two men: he pits Tolstoy, the cultured ruralist, against Dostoyevsky, the civilised urbanite. He nonetheless places them on equal footing, similar to other great figures who epitomised the dichotomy between 'culture' and 'civilisation', or perhaps again, Hegelian thesis and antithesis: Goethe and Schiller, Leonardo and Michelangelo, or Kant and Hegel. Thus for Gaissinovitch, both figures can be seen to be if not exactly dialectically complimentary, then certainly able to coexist. This is a fundamental departure from Spengler, who saw – at least within a single people – 'culture' and 'civilisation' as consecutively occurring phenomena.

And again, Gaissinovitch introduces the Jewish element into the discussion by comparing the 'civilised' Talmudists of the Priestly code – who in Ezra's redaction led to the present-day rabbis – with the 'cultured' Prophets who developed, in Gaissinovitch's reading, from Isaiah, through Jesus, to Bialik. This reading is interesting not only because it recalls the Spenglerian, and indeed greater Romantic, dichotomy between 'culture' and 'civilisation' but also because it is – if we remove Jesus from the equation – the classic Zionist reading. And once again it implies that, in light of the discussion earlier, Gaissinovitch sees both phenomena as able to coexist. Thus, 'culture' competes with, and exists alongside, 'civilisation', Goethe alongside Schiller, *Tanakh* alongside Talmud and not least, Zion(ism) alongside *Galut* (Exile). Nonetheless, although able to coexist, there is a qualitative hierarchy. In consideration of Gaissinovitch's already very pronounced Zionist leanings, this formulation is certainly not accidental.

Indeed, Shavit reaches a similar conclusion through different means, although his argument lacks the universal and metaphysical dimensions contained in the discussion earlier. Nonetheless, he does highlight Gaissinovitch-Ahimeir's contention that both 'cultural' and 'civilizational' forces worked concurrently within the Jewish Culture, an observation which, although congruent with the discussion earlier, nonetheless reveals a marked divergence from Spengler's conception of Judaism. And Shavit goes on to delineate Ahimeir's particular understanding of these two concepts: '"Culture" is the authentic, original expression of an organic, national unit, while "civilization" is a geographical, cosmopolitan concept … Judaism is constantly confronted with the "principle of culture" versus the "principle of civilization"'; it contains a permanent dichotomous tension.[53]

Turning back to nineteenth-century Russia, Gaissinovitch names Tolstoy as the creator of modern anarchism. His rejection of any type of domination was characteristically Russian, and therefore also indicative of Tolstoy's true Russianness. It demonstrated that he was a child of his time and of his people as they stood on the threshold of a great revolution. This had, for Gaissinovitch, morphologically contemporaneous historical precedents. He identified an 'anarchistic spirit' in ancient Judea just before the destruction of Jerusalem, and which he saw embodied by the extremist sects of the Essenes and Sicarii.[54] He also cites the extreme Puritans just before Oliver Cromwell's (1599–1658) revolution and English Civil Wars (1642–51), the Moravian Anabaptist brotherhoods before the Thirty Years' War (1618–48) and the Anabaptists in Germany before the Reformation (1517). All were anarchistic in their 'political' affiliations, which were dictated, rather, by extreme religious devotion; all had preceded some form of revolutionary change, be it religious or political. And here again, we catch glimpses of the future Abba Ahimeir, a figure who would come to see anarchy as the harbinger of revolution in the struggle of a 'small people' against its perceived oppressor, a 'culture' against a 'civilisation'. As will be seen in Chapter 5, Ahimeir would go on to form the semi-underground resistance group Brit HaBiryonim in 1930. Itself characterised by an 'anarchistic spirit', the group attempted to effect a Zionist revolution against the British rule in Mandatory Palestine; in other words, a revolution of a 'small peoples' against its perceived oppressor, once again: culture against civilisation.

In an attempt to better explain the ideological nature of Tolstoy's anarchism, Gaissinovitch notes that it was not at all influenced by ideas that had been imported from the 'civilised' West; rather it was a product of the organic development of a 'cultured' Russia. In marked contrast to Spengler once again, he considers Tolstoy, from every perspective – artistic, religious, political and socio-critical – to be quintessentially Russian. Furthermore, and notably, Gaissinovitch believed that Tolstoy's religious ideas had neither an impact on the Russian intelligentsia – since its members were infused with secular Western revolutionary ideals – nor on the sectarian movement, the rationalist movement of the peasants; if anything, the converse was true. Tolstoy had converted to Christianity later in life, after observing the apparent ease of acceptance of death demonstrated by the Russian peasant class. But he rejected the Eastern Orthodox Church, which was, as an institution alongside the state, one of the foci of his anarchism. Nonetheless, Gaissinovitch notes that Russian Orthodoxy had never enjoyed the organisational strength or the ideological and societal influence that had Catholicism.

Thus in Gaissinovitch's analysis, Spengler was incorrect to concentrate on the influence of the religious ideas of Tolstoy and Dostoyevsky on the Russian intelligentsia. The opponents of Bolshevism had come armed, predominantly, with Western, secular 'worldly' concepts: Liberalism, nationalism and moderate Socialism.[55] They were catalysed by historical and economic motives, but rarely religious ones. He did not agree with Spengler's prediction for a resurgence of religion in Russia, and could not foresee Marxism being supplanted in favour of a renewed interest in Christianity, especially since religious feeling had never been very developed in Russia. For Gaissinovitch the Russian Revolution was absolutely a victory of Western ideals. But its critics among the Russian intelligentsia were, notably, also influenced by the Western Cultural sphere.

In an attempt to explain the reasons for such ideological disparity between the masses and the intelligentsia, Gaissinovitch notes that in Spengler's own Germany, Goethe – whom Spengler named, alongside Nietzsche, as one 'to whom I owe practically everything'[56] – had really only remained topical in elite circles, while the racial theories of Gobineau and Chamberlain, and the class theories of Marx, had become popular with the masses. And here, he finds the connection to Russia. The 'literary' Dostoyevsky belonged to the elite, whereas the 'religious' Dostoyevsky – which Gaissinovitch saw as the expression of the Magian spirit – had enjoyed minimal influence. Furthermore, Gaissinovitch reminds his reader that cultural treasures were effective only if they were successfully disseminated 'downwards' to the masses: Nietzsche's ideas – although well-known in intellectual spheres – had not managed to take root in more popular circles. If this was true in the case of the educated, 'rationalistic' Germans, then, for Gaissinovitch, it was so to an even greater degree in Russia, with its disproportionately high number of illiterates.

Gaissinovitch goes on to note that the struggle between the Bolsheviks and their opponents had been predicated on Western European socio-economic and nationalistic ideologies. And the Russian Orthodox Church and the peasant sectarians – that is, the dominant Russian society of Dostoyevsky's writings – had remained passive throughout the horrible tragedy of the Russian Revolution. Indeed, Dostoyevsky, as a loyal student of Fichte and Hegel, had, himself, preached nationalism. Thus his real influence was literary rather than societal. In spite of this observation, Gaissinovitch notes that the Russian anarchistic spirit had all but disappeared after the events of the previous ten years, as the Russians had, ironically perhaps, learned to take a more positive attitude towards state power.

For Gaissinovitch, the Russian Revolution represented a further victory: that of Western ideology over Slavophilism. The latter phenomenon was a conscious ideological movement, organised by some members of the Russian intelligentsia who sought to restore Slavic and Russian over Western European cultural dominance in the land. Ultimately, however, they failed. Indeed, both the Bolsheviks and Social Revolutionaries had been influenced by Western ideology, although the latter had started out less so. Gaissinovitch believed that Spengler – who knew Russia only through books – had really misunderstood the decisive influence of the West upon the Russian Revolution. He had perhaps, so Gaissinovitch believed, developed a particularistic conception about the revolution through reading works such as the political poet Alexander Blok's (1880–1921) *Die Zwölf* (The Twelve) and *Die Skythen* (The Scythians). According to Gaissinovitch, both poems – apocalyptic in tone towards Europe – were embraced by the 'so-called leftist Social Revolutionaries' and had, in reality, but minimal influence upon the events of the revolution. Instead, Gaissinovitch remarks that the 'whole of Bolshevism suckled on the breast of the West'.[57] Furthermore, he notes, perhaps with some degree of cynicism, not only that Lenin had learned Marxist theory from Marx but that he also copied his teacher in the essentially Western nature of his private life. Gaissinovitch believed that

Marx's Western European Jewish roots had endowed him with the influences of German, French and English culture in equal measure, and it was precisely this Western European cosmopolitan archetype that became the symbol of the Russian Revolution.

In Spenglerian terms then, the less-Magian Bolsheviks were victorious over their more-Magian Social Revolutionary opponents, in spite of the fact that the latter were originally considered by the Russian peasants to be the true heroes of the revolution. It should be remembered, once again, that Gaissinovitch himself had consistently eschewed Bolshevism for Zionism, yet his brother Meir had not, and with tragic consequences. Thus, both the Spenglerian and Zionist Gaissinovitch come together here in his rejection of Marx – the 'civilised' cosmopolitan archetype of a Western Europe in decline, who was refuted both for his Western-ness and his Socialist agenda. And once again, in pitting Zionism against Marxism, nationalist individualism against political universalism, Gaissinovitch places his hope for the future in the cause of the 'small people'.

To add further dimension to his contention that the Russian Revolution was a victory of Western ideals, Gaissinovitch notes that the Soviet Commissars were, in fact, the direct heirs to the Tsars and Emperors: indeed, the Bolsheviks had overcome the rest of the Socialists much in the way that the Grand Dukes of Moscow overcame their feudal blood relatives. Thus the Russian Revolution was a victory of city over village, state over anarchy, centralism over federalism, Western-ness over Eastern-ness, civilisation over culture. The observation is also noteworthy because it seems to indicate that Gaissinovitch envisioned two, or possibly three (see the following discussion) Spenglerian Russian Cultures – Imperial and Soviet, old and new, more Eastern and more Western – that could be compared against each other using Spengler's technique of pseudomorphosis. Nonetheless, in spite of this apparent Western victory, Gaissinovitch believes that the Russian Revolution would be no more successful in unifying Europe – presumably through the advocacy of Socialist ideals – than had been the attempts of Charlemagne, Innocent III, Napoleon, or the Hohenzollerns, who, it would appear, Gaissinovitch sees as morphological contemporaries.

In effect, he views Russia's political development as analogous to that of other Western European countries where centralism had previously dominated, most notably France and England. Indeed, these two very 'Western' cultures – along with Spengler's 'Magian' Russia – had all watched as centralised rule conquered feudalism, the Church and free cities. Thus, for Gaissinovitch, a true Spenglerian analysis of Russia's political development saw the Prince of Moscow – Ivan I Kalita

(1288–1340) – and his family (until the fall of the Rurik Dynasty, in 1598) as 'morphological contemporaries' of the Plantagenets (1154–1399), Valois (1284–1589), Tudors (1485–1603), Bourbons (1272–1830) and Romanovs (1613–1917). The very fact that he could list both Ivan I and the Romanovs as 'morphological contemporaries' indicates that Gaissinovitch conceived of two Russias: pre- and post-Petrovic. Or indeed, in consideration of Gaissinovitch's comparison of pre- and post-revolutionary Russia, discussed earlier, even three: pre-Petrovic, post-Petrovic Imperial and post-revolutionary Soviet Russia. Rather notably, he ranks Lenin, the revolutionary, as a 'morphological contemporary' of Cromwell, Robespierre and Calvin; indeed, he saw the Bolsheviks as less an organised party than a holy order, or rather, a 'modern Jesuit order in the fullest sense'.[58] Thus for Gaissinovitch, the Russian Revolution was not the result of Dostoyevskian Russian nationalist spirit, but rather a reaction to the political structure that embodied by Russian centralism. Notably, Gaissinovitch sees all revolution as a direct consequence of centralism, as was evidenced in the histories of Rome, England, France and Russia. And, he further observes that if one considered the cases of Greece, Italy and Germany, then the converse was also true. Indeed, within ten years, the future Abba Ahimeir would apply this observation to his own political situation, and develop the concept of 'Revolutionary Zionism' in the face of a centralist British administration.

From all of these examples and comparisons, Gaissinovitch ultimately concludes that Russia is – in every respect – a Western state. This conclusion stands in contrast to Spengler, who believed that in the future, the Magian spirit of Dostoyevsky would form not only Russian but also Western culture. In order to address Spengler's position, Gaissinovitch compares pre- and post-revolutionary Russia, England, Germany and France. He notes that the chiliastic spirit that gripped pre-revolutionary Russia and that saw it transform political-economic science into the religion of revolution, had been replaced with a questioning of – failed – ideals, and a strengthening of the positivist spirit. In the case of England, the puritan element became intensified after the English Civil War, and was, ultimately, transformed into capitalist ideology. Post-revolutionary Germany became the hotbed for Socialist ideology, whether Marxist, evolutionary or academic. And post-revolutionary France was characterised by a 'sober', positivistic society that would be mirrored and magnified in the Russia of the future, much in the same way that social ideals in the French Revolution were mirrored and magnified in the Russian Revolution. Thus all three nations had, post-revolution, moved yet further towards Western ideals, and therefore also Spenglerian 'civilisation'.

Kaplan correctly highlights Ahimeir's claim that revolutions do not necessarily follow the most sophisticated ideologies, but instead those that are best able to unite a people.[59] Be that as it may, although he did see anarchy as a fundamentally Russian creation, Gaissinovitch nonetheless viewed Russian anarchism as not influential in the face of the much greater ideological influence that came from the West. Indeed, that had been Russia's downfall: Gaissinovitch's ultimate conclusion is that Russia is – or more precisely, *had become* – a Western state. Thus, although Gaissinovitch may disagree with Spengler's conception of Russia, he does not, essentially, disagree with his conclusion. For Gaissinovitch, the devil is in the details.

He concludes, in a perhaps not un-Spenglerian manner, that if one wanted to see the Russia of the future, one should look to the France and England of the present; in other words, to the West, and not to Spengler, who mistakenly foresaw the triumph of the Dostoyevskian Slavophil-nationalist spirit in Russia's future. This is not to say that Gaissinovitch sees the positivism that characterised post-revolutionary England, France and now Russia as an optimistic development. But he nonetheless finds a great similarity between their political and cultural development and finds it is no accident that Spengler – a German – cannot completely comprehend the Russian Revolution, since Germany's political and cultural evolution was much more similar to that of Central Europe.

In a short denouement, Gaissinovitch rather interestingly predicts what he believes will play out on the European landscape.[60] For him, Russian culture could occupy the same place in European history as Arabian Culture had in the ancient world. Since Russia was not young, as Spengler erroneously believed, it would not – could not, if Spengler's theory was correct – have the 'last word' in Europe. According to Gaissinovitch, this would go to other nations younger than Russia: the many 'small peoples' scattered along the shores of the Baltic Sea – which he refers to as the 'future Mediterranean of Europe' – the Danube and the Balkan Peninsula. Much in the way that Russia before Pushkin, through lack of its own culture – and here we see Gaissinovitch draw yet another temporal demarcation for the analysis of Russian history – fell prey to French influences, these newer nations were now busy trying to arrest those of Germany and Russia upon their own cultures.

In Spenglerian terms, urban life in these nations was still in its embryonic stage; Gaissinovitch notes that their peasants were *mujiks* and not *fellaheen*. Of all of these, Albania was the youngest nation, and continued to exist in a primitive condition of tribal organisation. Gaissinovitch sees these small nations as similar to the lands of Western Asia and North Africa before Islamification of the region had turned the area into one single body. But unlike Western Asia and North Africa, all attempts at turning the lands of the Balkans, and those along the Danube, into a single pan-European entity had so far been unsuccessful. Thus, Gaissinovitch concludes, the future – he calls it the 'last word' – in Europe belongs to these people, and not, as Spengler mistakenly opines, to Russia.

Academic reception

Spengler's work enjoyed both popularity and considerable influence for a very short period that lasted from his book's publication until the end of the Second World War, and it is obvious from Gaissinovitch's rapturous enthusiasm in his thesis introduction that he considered *The Decline of the West* to be a cultural-historical breakthrough. Not only was he familiar enough with it to produce a doctoral thesis on it but he also felt that he had absorbed the book's message enough to suggest improvements on Spengler's theory. Thus, in consideration of Gaissinovitch's remarks, we should conclude that his study reflected both a thorough understanding of *The Decline of the West*, and an accurate attempt to criticise certain aspects of the latter's theory in relation to Russia.

Hans Uebersberger found Gaissinovitch's assessment that Spengler's lack of familiarity with Russia in history, culture and literature negatively affected his view towards the nation when formulating his theory, 'rather apt',[61] and found that his study 'reflected not only great erudition but also a strong, independent sense of judgement'. Wilhelm Bauer was more reserved, remarking that Gaissinovitch was not able to fulfil his task, merely by means of philological methodology. He pointed to the danger of criticising Spengler's 'unproven and un-provable' assumptions with opinions that are equally so, and noted that Gaissinovitch did not always successfully avoid falling into this trap.[62] Nonetheless, he continued, Gaissinovitch did succeed in understanding Spengler from a historian's point of view and successfully grasped and resolved the problems that presented themselves.[63] Yaacov Shavit's assessment, that Ahimeir was 'lacking in methodology', was not that of a lone voice.[64] And Bauer's comment regarding Spengler's 'unproven and un-provable' theory is striking. If Bauer was indeed Gaissinovitch's thesis supervisor, his comment seems to imply a cynical and cautious approach to Spengler, and suggests that the idea to write on *The Decline of the West* was wholly Gaissinovitch's. In any case, Gaissinovitch was awarded the doctorate.

Gaissinovitch's own conclusions are also noteworthy. He considered Russia, ultimately, to be a Western state, and it is clear that he placed great value on the milieu of Russian high culture that had informed his own childhood and education. Spengler, on the other hand, saw Russia as a relatively young, undeveloped Culture locked in a 'pseudomorphical' state with Faustian Culture. In principle Gaissinovitch agrees, but considers Russia to be much older than Spengler does. As such, it had become an integral part of Western Culture, not only influenced by but also influential upon it. And herein lies the problem for Gaissinovitch. Russia's adoption of Western European, 'Faustian', Culture had caused it to lose its own. In its quest for cultural evolution it had become part of a greater 'civilisation'. Although Gaissinovitch is never explicit, it appears from his final conclusions that he considered Russia, if not directly linked to the present decline of Western Europe, then nonetheless on its coattails. His chapter 'To Whom the Last Word in Europe' seems to imply this. Thus, Gaissinovitch in no way rejected Spengler's conception of Russia as a Culture in decline.[65] In point of fact he is saying quite the opposite, and his message here is clear: that true national culture should never be compromised, no matter what the reason, as this would mark the beginning of the Culture's decline. This conviction would become a central principle of the future Ahimeir's maximalist ideology and is the root of his uncompromising territorial and ultra-nationalist stance. It also explains his rejection of Marx's Socialism and universalism, both examples of cultural 'compromise' in the name of civilised 'evolution'.[66]

The lack of a clear thesis is one of the most frustrating aspects of Gaissinovitch's study. Without one we are obliged to speculate, and doubtless much of this could have been alleviated had he laid his cards on the table in his introduction. Nonetheless, the fact that Gaissinovitch so carefully picks apart Spengler's theory with regard not only to Russia but also to Jewish history helps lead to the most far-reaching conclusions of this study. In spite of all that he rejects in Spengler, we must conclude that there is much, much more – by implication – that he accepts. Gaissinovitch writes not from the point of view of a critic of Spenglerian theory, but from that of a Spenglerian who takes issue with certain details of that theory. Furthermore, a close reading of the work shows the first mention of themes that will occupy the future Revisionist ideologue, from Monism, to the Sicarii, anarchy and revolution. That he remained to some degree a Spenglerian cannot be doubted. Shavit quotes an article, 'Poland in Palestine', published in *HaMashkif* on 24 January 1941, where Ahimeir writes:

By absorbing the cosmopolitan ideas of Russian and German egotism, we [Zionists] absorbed a deadly poison. It is indeed a great error that our generation absorbed so little of nineteenth-century Polish culture. This was not the culture of all mankind, or of the individual, but rather the culture of the nation. Goethe,

Dostoyevsky and Tolstoy poisoned us, the sons of a people fighting for its national survival, while the superb writers and poets of Polish literature could have invigorated us.[67]

In 1941, then, Ahimeir was still influenced both by Spenglerian methodology and by themes that he had set out in his thesis on Spengler. Once again he pits a 'culture' – Poland – against a 'civilisation' – Russia and Germany – the plight of a 'small people' in the face of a larger, cultural threat. Furthermore, he bemoans the fact that one 'small people' – again, Poland – was not given the opportunity to influence another – the Zionists – and that they instead allowed themselves to be influenced by more 'civilised', less 'cultural' Western 'egotism'. Kaplan also cites examples of Spengler's continued influence on Ahimeir, and notes that Ahimeir believed that the Hebrew nation could only revitalise itself by 'returning to the pre-exilic Israelite ethos of the warrior judges who had roamed the ancient land'.[68] Compare this with Spengler's conception of a culture in its post-civilised stage, where intellectual drifters called *fellaheen* wander aimlessly before regenerating themselves – from their own stock – into a 'new' culture.[69] When Ahimeir wrote thirty-five years later that the *'Tanakh* is dripping with blood. Especially the historical sections ... In terms of bloodshed, the "Book of Books" – "bleeding with blood" – is second to none, with the exceptions of Homer and Shakespeare',[70] it is still possible to see his recognition of the Spenglerian concept of necessary bloodshed at the hand of the hot-tempered *Urmensch* as an integral part in the early development of a Culture.

In spite of this observation, it is the theme of 'small peoples', who were locked in various struggles against their larger, more dominant oppressors, which really dominates his thesis. Be it Cromwellian England over Victorian England, *mujik* over *fellah*, prophet over pagan, *Tanakh*ist over Talmudist, Albania over Western Europe, Jew over Gentile or Zion over *Galut*, Gaissinovitch sides consistently with the underdogs, the 'small peoples'. For him, 'small peoples' represent 'culture' and 'larger peoples', 'civilisation'. The former is a sign of cultural ascendance, the latter of cultural decline.

Thus between Gaissinovitch's acceptance of Spengler's conception of a Russia that had begun as its own culture but was now existing in a 'pseudomorphical' state with 'civilised', 'Faustian' Culture and his own observation that Russia's adoption of Western European, 'Faustian' Culture had caused it to lose its own, there is a warning: Russia stands out as an exemplar, a case study of what can happen if a 'small people' allows itself to become overshadowed by a 'larger people', a 'culture' by a 'civilisation'. Hence, the deeper subject of Gaissinovitch's study – if perhaps only unconsciously so – is the Jews who, as a 'small people', faced continued existential threat, be it real or, in this case, cultural, through pseudomorphosis. Such a 'pseudomorphical' state must, therefore, be prevented. Consequently, anarchistic engagement becomes acceptable in the struggle of a 'little people' against its oppressor. Gaissinovitch, it should be remembered, considered anarchy to be not only a Russian phenomenon but also a common harbinger of revolution. Indeed, the fact that Russian anarchism was not influential had, in fact, contributed to its 'cultural' defeat, at the hands of 'civilised', Western ideals.

Revolution, then, was the deciding factor between the preservation of 'culture' and the bastardisation of 'civilisation'. It was thus not only acceptable but obligatory. This principle is a central tenet in the ideology of the future Ahimeir, who, as will be discussed, coined the term 'Revolutionary Zionism'. Gaissinovitch uses Spenglerian analysis to explain the plight that 'small peoples' face in the attempt to preserve their 'cultural' independence from the influence of a more dominant 'civilisation'. I would even suggest that the Russian-Jewish-Zionist Gaissinovitch sees himself in that very role, vis à vis the German-Gentile-Pan-European Spengler. A Spenglerian reading would present all of this as a predetermined part of a Culture's life cycle. But Gaissinovitch, in an attempt to out-Spengler Spengler – whose message was, ultimately, optimistic – believes that we may learn from Russia's example and prevent such a phenomenon from occurring with other 'small peoples', be they Albanian, Lithuanian or most important: Jewish. However, whereas Spengler foresaw the blood necessary for cultural rebirth in the form of the 'New Barbarian', Gaissinovitch saw it in the form of revolution.

First publications

Concurrent with Gaissinovitch's doctoral study were his first publications, in the American Hebrew monthly *HaToren* (The Mast). Notably, these were now signed 'Abba Ahimeir', which appears to have acted as Gaissinovitch's nom de plume until his return to Palestine in 1925, when he discontinued the use of 'Gaissinovitch' for good. Between August 1922 and December 1925, he contributed a total of six articles to the publication.

HaToren had begun in June 1913 as an initiative of the newly formed Ahiever society, and had both variable publication frequency and editorial control before it ceased publication, in December 1925, after approximately 320 issues.[71] Formed in 1909, the Ahiever society was a by-product of the American Jewish immigration explosion that occurred between 1880 and 1924. By the time that the first issue of *HaToren* saw the light of day, America had already accepted over 2 million Jewish immigrants. The Ahiever society reflected the changing character of the younger immigrants, who were influenced by the *Haskalah* – the 'Jewish Enlightenment' – in a different way than previous generations had been. This younger generation now viewed Hebrew as the cultural-linguistic basis of Jewish national rebirth. As the Hebrew literature scholar Alan Mintz noted, 'Hebrew, in its catholic embrace, was the ground itself of the new national reality, the essence of the revolution.'[72] The Ahiever Hebraists pitted themselves firmly against the Yiddishists, as a 'cultural elite' that considered the Hebrew revival as the cornerstone of a greater movement for Jewish nationalism, and saw the logical furtherance of *maskilic* religious Hebrew literature in the more au courant form of belles-lettres.[73] As a high-quality, Hebrew-language periodical that featured articles and essays dedicated to the development of Hebrew literature proper, *HaToren* began to address this shift in ideology.

Mintz suggests three reasons why the publication of a new periodical was seen to be the best way forward for the Ahiever Hebraists. First, it mirrored similar successful endeavours of the Berlin – in *Hameasaf* (The Collector) – and Odessa – in *Hashiloakh* (The Dispatch) – Haskalahs, as well as partisan journals from *Eretz Israel*, for example, *HaPoel HaTzair*. If America were to establish itself as a centre for Hebrew-language and Jewish national revival, then it had a tried and true exemplar in the form of the periodical. Second, as an organ that presented topical discussion and relevant commentary, the journal represented the most prudent and opportune means for disseminating this new cultural-literary form. Finally, it addressed the lack of geographical congruity that was peculiar to the American Hebraist movement by giving voice to those who were situated outside of the major American Jewish centres.[74]

Until December 1915, *HaToren* was published, with occasional interruptions, as a monthly journal. It sought to present 'all that is healthy and fresh in American Judaism', and strove to speak 'to the Hebrew community on the difficulties of our life, its arrangements and its correction'.[75] In March 1915, the journal became a weekly publication, under the new editorship of the Hebrew writer and son-in-law of Shalom Aleichem, Isaac Dov (Y.D.) Berkowitz. Shmarya Levin joined him as co-editor in 1916. Under their leadership the journal successfully combined the Hebrew national-literary spirit of Odessa with topical, Political-Zionist thought. They hoped to address the 'thousands of Hebrew readers in America who, though they yearn for the Hebrew language and see it as the way to individual and national repair and restoration, are slipping away and growing further distant from Hebrew each year'.[76] In the editors' eyes, this distance was the result of

> impatience and annoyance with the failure of Hebrew to establish itself in America and provide them with the very minimum: a reliable Hebrew organ of expression [that would] concentrate within it the scattered Hebraist readers on these shores and ... be for them as a sanctuary in miniature and gradually create something unprecedented for which we all pray: a Hebrew environment.[77]

Indeed, the creation of such an environment took on an even greater urgency in view of the cessation of Hebrew cultural activity in both Eretz Israel and Russia, after the outbreak of the First World War.

The Hebrew journalist Reuven Brainin replaced Berkowitz and Levin in August 1918, and in June 1921 – owing to a decline in readership – the journal reverted back to a monthly format. Between 1919 and 1922, publication of *HaToren* was taken over by the American Zionist Federation, which – due to the journal's unprofitability – proved ultimately to be too great a financial risk. The newly formed independent Safruth Publishing Company finally assumed the journal's publication, until its demise in December of 1925. At its zenith, circulation for *HaToren* reached the 13,000 mark.

It was during this final period of the journal's publication that Ahimeir contributed a total of six articles: 'The First (I): German Jewry' (August 1922), 'The First (II): Moses Hess and German Jewry' (January 1923), 'Whose Bialik?' (May 1923), 'Some Thoughts on Fascism' (August 1923), 'Sparks of Russian Literature' (December 1923) and 'Sparks from Russian Literature' (November–December 1925). Hence, he was represented in the journal's final issue. Although his dissertation on Spengler seldom dealt directly with European Jewish and Zionist themes, Ahimeir's articles for *HaToren* saw him do just that, sometimes applying Spenglerian comparative techniques, sometimes reworking certain themes in order to more directly confront them from a Jewish and/or Zionist perspective.

Of these, the most interesting and relevant by far is Ahimeir's fourth article, 'Some Thoughts on Fascism', published in August 1923.[78] Far from representing the first attempts of a young scholar to get published, this essay looks ahead to the future politico-ideological Ahimeir, not only in terms of content but also in his literary style. Most importantly, it reveals an Ahimeir who was already, in 1923, interested in and seemingly enamoured with the new Italian political movement:

> Today I saw – finally – a picture of Fascists on the cover of an illustrated weekly. … In the picture … we see the Fascists dressed in black shirts, right arm outstretched, no hats covering their black hair. Some young girls fell in love with these youths, with their swift gait and glistening eyes. Is it possible not to become enamoured? … Youths in black shirts, [their] eyes glistening with an abundance of faith in these defining moments, their right arms raised at their sides. How could the lasses not fall in love? … And the children of Italy have invented for themselves a new game: they play 'Fascists'. The little brother emulates the actions of his older brother. The majority of the young one are without black shirt. But even they are able to raise their right arms.[79]

Ahimeir begins as he intends to carry on, his remarks not those of a simple observer, but rather one who has experienced an epiphany. He compares the status quo in Italy with that of Russia: in Italy the communists had been beaten – their world turned upside down – while the Russians continued to live under what Ahimeir calls the 'tribe of the oppressor', as he refers to the Bolsheviks.

He makes his first attempt at articulating themes that would, by 1926, become central to Ahimeirian ideology: the cult of violence, readiness for self-sacrifice, the importance of action over word and the centrality of an engaged youth:

> And why do we become embittered by Fascism … by its deeds of violence? All of these youngsters … are ready to kill and be killed for the 'sake of the homeland' … so that the name of the Fascist leader will be recorded in history. … The movement increases their life spirit. Is the youth guilty [of the fact] that he has so much verve, but nowhere to squander it? … Our epoch is one of men of action. … [They] rely on their weapons, they are the rulers, they set the tone, in many lands.[80]

Ahimeir draws parallels between Fascist Italy and other movements of national rebirth – those of Turkey and Ataturk, Greece and Sinn Fein in Ireland – which he notes were all 'military' in nature.[81] They had all 'turned to the sword' and to the masses, and used the youth of their respective nations as their base. By contrast, the countries that were victorious in the Great War – France, England, Russia and America – had all consequently sought leadership in journalists and lawyers, 'men of the book', as Ahimeir calls them – Clemenceau, Lloyd George, Trotsky and Harding – and whom he saw as the 'Bonapartists of our time'.

For him it was no coincidence that Italy turned to Fascism and Russia to Bolshevism. The former, lacking the traits of a 'small people', looked backwards to a rich historical past; the latter, through the Slavophilism of Herzen – which, as a contrived movement led by intellectuals, Ahimeir had contrasted, in his dissertation, with a more culturally pure Tolstoyan Russian spirit – focused on the Socialist International, discarded national memory and looked only to the future. Ahimeir finds some similarity between the Fascists and the Junkers, the ultra-conservative, landowning Prussian elite who staunchly supported the German monarchy and military: although the former was more of a mass movement, both shared similar aspirations. And noting that the Junkers had played a pivotal role in the outbreak of the European war, Ahimeir then asks – rather ominously – 'What will come on the heels of Fascism?'[82]

More salient still is Ahimeir's analysis of how all of this bears upon the situation of Russian Jewry. Bolshevism, in looking only to the future, had pulled up Russian history 'by its roots'; the Bolsheviks not only had negated the heroic element in the key players of Russian history, but furthermore, had had the insolence to tarnish them as 'oppressors of the people'. Ahimeir notes that, in a similar vein, the Russian non-Zionist Jewish Socialist groups – the *Bund*, the *Yevsektsiya* and the *Kultur Lige*[83] – had likewise all denied a brilliant Jewish past.[84] 'By contrast', Ahimeir continues, 'Zionism – our national movement – is based on the history and all of the past culture of our people'.[85] Indeed, for Ahimeir the historian, it was neither possible nor desirable to ignore a people's proud national-cultural history. It was an exercise doomed to failure. Thus, if we accept his earlier claim that Fascism looked backwards to Italy's proud, rich historical past, we see Ahimeir not only provide further justification for the rejection of Socialism but also – notably – make a first, albeit tentative, ideological link between the aspirations of Fascism and Zionism.

Ahimeir now introduces another theme that would occupy him in the future: that of the crisis of parliamentarianism. Italian parliamentarianism – which he called a mere 'imitation' of that of other countries – had gone bankrupt. It had not evolved organically, as in England; been 'sanctified' through revolution, as in France; nor reflected regional religious separatism, as in Germany. It had embodied all the negative aspects of parliamentarianism and none of the positive. In fact, he observes, those that were currently speaking about a general crisis in parliamentarianism were forgetting all too easily that this apparent crisis had occurred in the same countries in which parliamentarianism had never flourished in the first place.[86]

Addressing the ideological nature of Fascism and Bolshevism, Ahimeir notes that although the two movements differed in aspiration, they were essentially the same in spirit; there was an ideological distance, but not a psychological one.

Both sought to dictate the societal status quo, both excelled in impatience for other opinions, both inhibited mutual understanding within society. More to the point, Ahimeir believed that the masses of these two movements belonged to a single psychological type: 'In the eyes of the historian of the future to come', he remarks astutely, 'there will be no great difference between these two movements. ... The Fascist, like the Bolshevik, each of them is certain, that the leaders of their movements are the greatest historical heroes that have arisen for humankind'.[87]

Indeed, the concept of the 'active', 'historical hero' or 'hero-as-maker-of history' is one that would become a central tenet of Ahimeir's ideology.[88] As will be seen, his essay from 1926, 'The Scroll of the Sicarii', is based on the idea that the true heroes in history are men and women of action, and furthermore, that their historical importance should be elevated and not negated. Interestingly, the term 'hero of history', often associated with Ahimeir, also appears in Spengler, who wrote:

> We can distinguish the adventurer or successful man who is destitute of inward greatness (like Danton or Robespierre) from the Hero of history by the fact that his personal destiny displays only the traits of the common destiny. Certain names may ring, but "the Jacobins" collectively and not individuals amongst them were the type that dominated the time.[89]

Thus Spengler placed importance on heroism in the service of the collective and the greater good over 'heroic' action that merely served individual purpose. In the original German, he uses the term *Heroen der Geschichte* and not the more Germanic *Helden der Geschichte*, thereby lending a certain Classical understanding – that of one prepared to sacrifice oneself in service of the greater good – to the term, as Spengler understands it. Undeniably, this is also how Ahimeir understands and utilises the term.[90] Consequently, one might speculate that this was a concept that Ahimeir took from Spengler.

Ahimeir goes on to note that both Fascism and Bolshevism place emphasis on deed over word, and the Fascists or Bolsheviks from the masses must not think for themselves but rather fulfil the command of their leaders, whom he calls the 'high priests', Mussolini and Lenin. Both movements sought to 'dumb down' public thought; both were based on the cult of authority. And furthermore, according to Ahimeir, 'Mussolini understood what Lenin did not: that his teaching was nationalist; Lenin's, internationalist'. The former had stimulated national egotism, the latter, class egotism.

Ahimeir concludes this seminal article by speculating on the future of Fascism. He notes that when the Bolsheviks came to power, they were not expected to last for more than five years. Yet they had remained in power, and there were few who would now predict an end to their rule. He remarks that while only two years previously it was thought that Russian life would adapt to Bolshevism, Bolshevism had now, in fact, adapted to Russian life. And Fascism, in Ahimeir's opinion, would face the same fate. The question for him was whether a strong democratic movement that could, or would, combat the chauvinism of Fascism might be founded in Italy in the future. Although the Italian Socialist movement was strong – 'too strong' in Ahimeir's opinion – it had nonetheless not managed to achieve the same standing as that of German Socialism. And Italian Liberalism – 'a hotbed of political competitors' – was not united, and in any case had lost many of its supporters to the Fascists. Its role as the 'vigorous fighter of Communism' had not yet roused strong opposition to Fascism and this is why Ahimeir believed that it was not yet 'showing its claws'. Nonetheless – and notably – Ahimeir does recognise Fascism's potential for terrorist engagement. And in spite of all his apparent rapture for the new movement, he is still at this time unable – or unwilling – to predict whether it will enjoy any sort of political longevity.

In this essay we see Ahimeir come into his own; ideologically, politically and – not least – in terms of his literary style, which combines a rich historical knowledge, sharp intellectual analysis and visceral matter-of-factness. We are no longer confronted with the writings of a young essayist and scholar, but rather with those of a politically engaged young ideologue. Almost all of the themes that would occupy Ahimeir over the next ten years culminating with the period of Brit HaBiryonim are present here, and apparently for the first time: the power of youth; the preference for men of action over word; the concept of 'heroes of history' and 'heroes as makers of history'; the importance of drawing on a rich historical past; the acceptance of violence – indeed, the readiness to 'kill or be killed' – if required in the service of the national cause; disdain for Bolshevism, Socialism and Liberalism; the crisis of parliamentarianism; and not least, the beginnings of the idea that Fascism may represent a viable modus operandi for Zionism. As stated earlier, Ahimeir – whether consciously or unconsciously – relegates Zionism here to the same ideological camp as Fascism. The fact that this already occupies a place in his own thought and ideological development – in 1923, while still a doctoral student in Vienna – is noteworthy indeed. It contradicts the common perception that Ahimeir confronted Fascist ideology only sometime between 1926 and 1928.[91] Indeed, Ahimeir later admitted as much, himself: on a postcard written in 1933 and bearing Mussolini's picture, he confessed that 'for ten years I am searching for a Jewish Mussolini'.[92]

Perhaps, then, it was not Ahimeir's interest in Zionism itself that had 'reached its nadir' during his period of study in Vienna, but rather his interest in an increasingly ideologically diluted Zionism, and frustration at its lack of forward direction. As we shall see, an embrace of 1920s Italian Fascist ideology would eventually, for Ahimeir, serve as the way out of this conundrum.

Pioneer, Journalist

Young worker

This chapter concentrates on the years 1924–7: Ahimeir's return to Palestine, his stint as a young Zionist 'pioneer' and his slow disillusionment with the Yishuv Left. It focuses on his considerable journalistic output from the period in order to trace the very subtle ideological development that was beginning to ferment in him.

In the summer of 1924, shortly after receiving his doctorate in Vienna, Ahimeir made his 'second *aliyah*' to what was now British Mandate Palestine. This time it would be permanent. He quickly set about establishing himself and joined the moderately Socialist party HaPoel HaTzair ('The Young Worker'). Formed in Ottoman-Palestine in 1905, HaPoel HaTzair was a product of the much greater Second and Third Aliyot, and its members formed a portion of the ideologically charged kernel of both immigration waves.[1] They were young Zionists who had come from Eastern Europe – in the wake of the Kishinev pogroms in 1903, and violence that had followed the revolutions in 1905 and 1917 – full of political ideology, principles and organisation. What this small core of ideologues lacked in number – the vast majority of immigrants to Palestine during the period were motivated far more by the need to escape existential threat, than by any form of Zionist ideology – it made up for in influence. In spite of its often-varied and disparate ideological positions and party affiliations – HeHalutz ('The Pioneer'), Poale Zion ('Zionist Workers'), Tzeirei Zion ('Zionist Youth'), 'HaShomer HaTzair ('The Young Guard') and Ahdut HaAvodah ('The Labour Union') were, in addition to HaPoel HaTzair, all represented – the lasting impact that this small, but highly motivated, core made on the political, social and structural organisation of the Yishuv can be seen to this day.

Although HaPoel HaTzair was Socialist, the party was not Marxist. Perhaps best embodied in the figure of its ideological mentor A. D. Gordon (1856–1922), the 'worker-intellectuals'[2] of HaPoel HaTzair – who were concerned with 'labour' but not 'the worker' – were determined to establish themselves in Palestine through the '[Jewish] conquest of labour' and the land and to stimulate a Hebrew linguistic and cultural revival that would turn the land into a flourishing Hebrew cultural centre.[3] At its annual conference of 1919-20, the party spelled out four primary objectives:

1. The upbuilding of Eretz Israel on the foundations of self-labor and national ownership of land;
2. The establishment of Jewish society in Eretz Israel on foundations of social justice (*tzedek*) and equality in the economic, cultural and political senses;
3. The Hebrew language as the absolute function of our lives and our national culture, both in Eretz Israel and in the Diaspora;
4. The preparation of the nation in the Diaspora and its Hebrew-language education towards labor and ascent to Eretz Israel.[4]

Much has been written about the fact that Ahimeir would eventually make a great political leap from Left to Right in a matter of only two years. However, I believe this claim requires re-examination and redefinition, or at least a more thorough contextualisation.[5] Ahimeir had always rejected Marxism and Communism; the death of his brother Meir had only sought to reinforce this refutation. And eventually, as his friend and supporter, the historian Josef Nedava, noted, '[Ahimeir's] hatred of Communism also brought him [around] to the revocation of Socialism; indeed [for him], the two of them shared a single source.'[6] In point of fact, the true Socialist in the family was his sister Bluma, and she remained so throughout her entire life. It was she who had accompanied Ahimeir to the Yishuv in 1912, when he was fourteen years old. It is thus highly likely that Ahimeir's apparent early embrace of Socialist ideals sprang from the influence of his older sister, on one hand, and his Zionism, which, in Bobruisk at that time, could find expression only in combination with some degree of Socialist ideology, on the other.

Indeed, for a secular, anti-communist, *oleh* (immigrant) arriving in British Mandate Palestine in 1924, there were only two choices for political affiliation: the more truculently Socialist Ahdut HaAvodah, which was a member of the Socialist International, and HaPoel HaTzair, which was not. The latter was certainly the more moderate option, and a party that defined itself as outlined earlier would be an obvious choice for someone who had participated in Trumpeldor's HeHalutz organisation. Indeed, it is rather notable that Ahimeir did not join Ahdut HaAvodah, as his old friend from Bobruisk, Berl Katznelson, with whom he had remained in close contact throughout his years in Vienna, had become – alongside Yitzhak Tabenkin (1888–1971) and David Ben-Gurion (1886–1973) – one of the leading figures in the party.[7] One might have expected Ahimeir to affiliate himself with a party in whose ranks – owing to strong personal connections – he could, feasibly, move up with ease. However, this was not the case. Furthermore, as Shindler has noted, there was a marked contrast between members of HaPoel HaTzair who had emigrated to the Yishuv already before the October Revolution and those members who had experienced it first-hand, and arrived in Palestine ex post facto. This latter group, many of whom had sat in Soviet prisons, had experienced a very different reality to the Soviet 'dream' that was still espoused by HaPoel HaTzair in the Yishuv. The dissident group which they formed within the party – Kvutzot HaAmlanim – would eventually go on to find much ideological congruence with the Revisionist Party. It is very likely that Ahimeir, although he joined the party only upon his arrival in the Yishuv, identified more with this latter group.[8]

Moreover, in 1920, HaPoel HaTzair and Ahdut HaAvodah had formed HaHistadrut HaKlalit shel HaOvdim B'Eretz Yisrael (The General Federation of Labourers in the Land of Israel'), known simply as the Histadrut. A sort of 'super union' that boasted an employment agency, Bank HaPoalim (The Workers' Bank), immigration office and health care agency (*Kupat Holim Klalit*), the Histadrut quickly gained a monopoly over the workforce in the Yishuv. In the year before Ahimeir immigrated, almost 50 per cent of the Jewish workforce were Histadrut members; by 1927 that percentage had increased to seventy.[9] While it professed loyalty to Socialist ideology when it was founded, the Histadrut – under the leadership of David Ben-Gurion, who had been elected secretary in 1921 – had arguably shed, or at least tempered, many of its Socialist ideals by the time Ahimeir returned to Palestine. Although three of the four parties who had members serving on the Histadrut council (Ahdut HaAvodah, HaShomer HaTzair and the Left Poale Tzion) purportedly aligned themselves with the international plight of the worker, the Histadrut was – in reality – a restricted club. In practice it was not at all internationally Socialist but rather nationally so, and excluded not only non-Jewish labour but also those Jewish workers unaffiliated with one of the four parties that were represented in its council. Simply put: if one wanted to work, one joined the Histadrut, and one of its representative parties.

Through the Histadrut, Ahimeir secured a job as a librarian for its Cultural Committee, in Zikhron Yaakov, and as a teacher in the *Kibbutzim* (agricultural collectives) of Nahalal and Geva. These were perhaps not the most prestigious positions for a young graduate; however, considering the work conditions in

Palestine at the time, Ahimeir did not fare too badly. Certainly he was successful in securing a position that was, to some degree, academic. Indeed, the majority of work available during this period was concentrated in the areas of either ideologically motivated agrarian labour – industry, which had begun in 1920 and whose endeavours included Shemen Oil and Solel Boneh Paving and Building – or 'traditional' Jewish occupations such as artisanship and small-scale commerce, which, although forming the basis for urban economy in the Yishuv, was – owing to its size and entrepreneurial nature – usually the undertaking of the business owner and his family alone.

Was, then, Ahimeir's membership in HaPoel HaTzair a marriage of convenience? Possibly, possibly not. His articles from 1924–6, written for the party's journal, give away very little of his true ideological stance. In reality, the articles very often give a much better impression of what he stood against. I would argue that Ahimeir's political affiliation at this time was ambivalent at best: he was certainly Zionist before Socialist, nationalist before internationalist, an intellectual before a pioneer; a Trumpeldor-ist perhaps, but that is a moot point. The figure of Trumpeldor was appropriated – or misappropriated, as the case may be – as an ideological mentor by both the Left and the burgeoning Right. The 1920s saw a period of ideological transition in the Zionist Organisation and the Yishuv, due mainly to the issuing of the 1922 Churchill White Paper.[10] As will be detailed in the following section, Ze'ev Jabotinsky – in reaction to the Zionist Organisation's position on the White Paper – would go on to form the Revisionist Zionist Party, but only one year after Ahimeir's arrival. The case of Trumpeldor – whom the Left could glorify as a Zionist Pioneer, the Right as a Zionist Nationalist – epitomises the basic ideological chasm that was developing, within both the Yishuv and the greater Zionist Organisation.[11] Thus, Ahimeir – who was himself in a state of personal transition – presumably chose the party that stood closest to his own ideals; or if not, at least the party that did not espouse what he rejected. His eventual and much touted 'defection' from HaPoel HaTzair to the Revisionists in 1928 was, at the time of his arrival in 1924, quite simply not an option.

Journalist

Within a year of his arrival, Ahimeir began to publish articles in the party's journal, *HaPoel HaTzair*. For the first year (from April 1925 until May 1926) these took the form of essays on cultural and political figures: the Russian writer Mikhail Gershenzon (1868–1925), the writer and revolutionary Boris Savinkov (1879–1925), the Socialist theorists Henri de Saint-Simon (1760–1825) and Ferdinand Lassalle (1825–64), and – rather surprisingly – the sexual theorists, Otto Weininger (1880–1903) and Sigmund Freud (1856–1939). With the exception of Saint-Simon and Lassalle, there is little to justify Ahimeir's choice of topics for a journal dedicated to the 'young worker'. It is highly likely that Ahimeir merely took advantage of the fact that he now had a forum for showcasing his vast cultural-historical knowledge.

Indeed, the articles are less interesting for Ahimeir's treatment of his respective subjects as they are for showing us – in light of his various observations – how his own ideological development was progressing. Themes that would play a central role in Ahimeir's future ideology are confronted in his articles written for *HaPoel HaTzair*. And although, at this early stage, they are still viewed through the lens of whatever particular subject he happens to be discussing, it is nonetheless notable that the manner of Ahimeir discussion very often reflects his own identification with – or rejection of – a particular theme. Thus, his apparently innocuous observation that 'nationalism, for Gershenzon, is the primary spiritual expression of a people … in the first instance its cultural treasures and not those of its policies' is perhaps not a completely empty one.[12] Even less so his remark that 'assimilation is [for Gershenzon] the most natural public manifestation of Jewry', a concept which, he concludes, is the root of Gershenzon's opposition to Zionism. More perplexing still, for Ahimeir, is the fact that '[Gershenzon] arrived at the paradox that Zionism is more foreign to the Jewish people than assimilation'.[13] By way of explanation, Ahimeir notes that Gershenzon was one of many who had 'returned to their roots' – in his case, Judaism – in the light of the Russian Revolution, but who – Ahimeir believed – as a student of German philosophy, was too abstract a thinker to get close to Zionism. 'Perhaps death got in the way of his going down this path?' he muses.

Ahimeir's choice, however, of Savinkov – a Socialist revolutionary terrorist, whom he calls the 'Don Quixote of the Russian Revolution' – as the subject for an article in the journal of a party that was decidedly non-revolutionary – indeed pacifist – is noteworthy indeed.[14] Savinkov was a Russian revolutionary figure, politician and writer, who actively resisted both imperial and Bolshevik rule. He played a decisive role in the assassinations of Minister of the Interior, Vyacheslav von Plehve (1904) and Grand Duke, Sergei Aleksandrovitch (1906), which his book *The Pale Horse* documents in fictional form. A member of the Social Revolutionary Party, Savinkov became Kerensky's Deputy Minister of War in the Russian Provisional Government in July 1917. In 1918, he established

'The Union for the Defence of the Fatherland and Freedom', an underground paramilitary group. It is likely that Ahimeir had the group in mind when he founded Brit HaBiryonim in 1930, although he did not name them as being influential (see Chapter 5).

As a 'child of the West ... not a product of revolutionary teaching like Lenin ... but a fighter in the revolutionary war', Ahimeir sees Savinkov's utility in the fact that he was a man of action. Once again, we see Ahimeir's partiality for action over word, in a developing ideology that begins to see the true historical hero as one who actively sets about to become a conscious 'Maker of History', in contrast – if only implicitly – to what Spengler might have called a mere 'Writer of History'. Notable for Ahimeir – and for a study of his ideological development – is his discussion of *The Pale Horse*, written in 1909, as Savinkov was beginning to gain notoriety as a leader of the revolution:

> [It is] the story [Roman] of a terrorist, whose soul questions and cannot find an answer [to the question of] whether it is allowed or forbidden to kill: if allowed, who sanctions [it], and why am I allowed [to kill] while another is forbidden? The problem of acceptable means constantly occupied Savinkov the author.[15]

This very dialectic would form the central theme of Ahimeir's 1926 essay 'The Scroll of the Sicarii', and the parallel between Ahimeir and Savinkov is too great to assume that the 'problem of acceptable means' was not something that also occupied Ahimeir, at this time. The question is whether Ahimeir's own engagement with the concept of 'acceptable means for killing' was ignited by his article on Savinkov, or Ahimeir's article betrayed an already present, personal debate with the topic. Either way, it is doubtful if, at this early stage, Ahimeir's occupation with the theme went any further than that of mere philosophical consideration. However, the fact that the idea of 'killing by acceptable means' appears in *The Pale Horse* suggests that the concept – presented by Ahimeir in his essay as simply another option towards the realisation of a revolutionary objective – was perhaps less 'revolutionary', than 'commonplace'. Were there precedents – now made known to him through Savinkov's work – that enabled Ahimeir to even consider the option of 'killing through acceptable means?' If so, such an observation might demonstrate that Ahimeir – far from creating his own 'revolutionary' ideology with regard to killing – was simply building upon a precedent already set by others, and indeed – as in Savinkov's case – those from a completely different politico-ideological background. While not excusing such behaviour, recognition of this perhaps uncomfortable fact demonstrates that Ahimeir was not alone in his occupation with such themes. Nonetheless, it is noteworthy that such a theme was considered at all, in the journal of an ostensibly pacifist party..

Even when addressing subject matter that is more in line with the party's ideological bent, Ahimeir surprises in his ability – indeed, compulsion – for examining such subject matter from an unconventional angle. Thus, an essay penned for the 100th anniversary of Saint-Simon's death, on 19 May 1925, considers the ideological development of the concept of 'Socialist' Saint-Simonianism vis à vis the de facto 'historic', ideological thought of the 'aristocrat' Saint-Simon, himself.[16] Ahimeir's observation that 'modern socialism sprouted and grew from liberalism, both in worldview and economic theory' leads him to conclude that it was 'nothing more and nothing less than modern bourgeois teaching'. For Ahimeir, then, Saint-Simon had been no true Socialist at all, but rather a 'classic' Liberal theoretician.

In spite of this apparent fact, Ahimeir contends that his students had unduly concentrated on, and developed, the Socialist core of Saint-Simon's thought. Furthermore, perhaps predictively, they had introduced a certain 'religious' element to it, as well. The result was what Ahimeir terms 'western religious liberalism', which, through its apparent scientific spiritual content, had helped to fill what he saw as the 'spiritual' void that had been created by movements such as Freemasonry. Nonetheless, Saint-Simonianism's 'human commandments', as Ahimeir calls them – and it is not clear whether he refers here to Saint-Simon's *On the Reorganisation of European Society* (1814) or perhaps to *The New Christianity* (1825) – were, for him, fully in line with the 'empty ritual and cheap ceremony' of Freemasonry.[17] As such, Saint-Simonianism was absolutely a product of its time. It represented a form of civil religion that had begun, inter alia, in the Masonic Lodge, a fact that also rendered it short-lived, to eventually become supplanted by the more 'utopian socialism' of Proudhon. However:

> After the passing of many decades, as students gave up preaching the mechanical religion of Saint-Simonianism, and became [instead] the capitalist business managers of France, who went on to become rich in the days of Louis Philippe and Napoleon III, [Saint-Simonianism was revived]. His books 'went forth' from within the *genizah* of the national library, [and] Saint-Simon become a theoretician of Socialism, and his students, founders of the first modern socialist movement.[18]

Therefore, Ahimeir sees hypocrisy in the Marxist placement of Saint-Simon among the utopian Socialists; for him, Saint-Simon's ideology was neither Socialist nor utopian. Indeed, as the ideological founder of Positivism – the 'teaching of scientific temperance', in Ahimeir's delineation – Saint-Simon could not, by definition, be utopian. Of course, Ahimeir's main intention in his article is to take a jibe at the development of a certain utopian Socialism – Saint-Simonianism – which, he believed had little in common with the ideological outlook of its eponym. His observations regarding the secular, 'civil religiosity' that was bound up in utopian Socialism – including Marxist-Socialism – are noteworthy in consideration of Ahimeir's later embrace of both Secular Messianism and, of course, Fascism: two quintessential examples of civil religion.

A more surprising contribution is Ahimeir's article on the sexual theories of Weininger and Freud.[19] Although both men were Viennese Jews, they differed in ideology, approach and conclusions, and Ahimeir pits one against the other. In spite of the article's subject matter – and its apparent unrelatedness to this study – Ahimeir's discussion, nonetheless, does yield some notable conclusions, which allow us to paint a more detailed picture of his own, developing, ideological stance.

Ahimeir describes Weininger as a metaphysical Dualist – 'a synthesis between Schopenhauer and Nietzsche' – who isolated and treated male and female elements, in all living matter, as separate – but competing – phenomena. For Weininger, the male element was strong, sure, productive, morally upright and rational, while the female element was weak, anxious, morally questionable and irrational. Composed of a varying degree of each, all human beings oscillated between the maleness and the femaleness of their particular constitution.[20] More importantly, Weininger had applied these characteristics of maleness and femaleness to ethnic groups, and the pseudoscientific overtones – different, but not completely dissimilar to Spengler – should be noted. Indeed, in spite, or perhaps because, of his own Jewish pedigree, Weininger classified the Indo-Germanic Aryan as the most masculine ethic group, and the Jews the most feminine. For Ahimeir – and later, for Nazi propagandists – such a dualistic approach likened Weininger's sexual theories to Arthur de Gobineau's (1816–82) racial theories and indeed, interestingly, to Marx's theory of class war. Nonetheless, Ahimeir himself could, at times, similarly see the world in terms of binary opposites, as will be discussed in more detail in Chapter 4.

Not surprisingly, Ahimeir places Freud on the opposite end of the scientific methodological spectrum to Weininger. He describes Freud as an empiricist who followed the path forged by Darwin, one who 'lacked completely the dualism that was characteristic of Marx, Gobineau, and Weininger', and who believed that its own "sex-life' occupied the living being more than anything [else] '. In Ahimeir's analysis, Freud belongs to the scientific tradition that sees life itself as a single phenomenon, 'not merely the most important, but indeed, the only', and there are perhaps Spenglerian overtones in his observation. Moreover, Ahimeir believes that the goal of psychoanalysis – to reveal the concealed unconsciousness – carried with it the danger of doing more harm than good, and one wonders how Freud might have analysed his comment. Also noteworthy is Ahimeir's observation that 'for Freud, in general, the problem of "good" and "bad" – the central point in Weininger – does not exist'. This a not uninteresting statement in consideration of Ahimeir's ruminations on Savinkov. Indeed, what might have represented an ideological hurdle in the article on Savinkov, could now perhaps – by embracing Freud – be rendered ideologically obsolete.

Ahimeir thus – albeit almost certainly unconsciously – makes some important ideological links in these three articles. On one side, he groups together the dualist approaches of Marx, Gobineau, Weininger and possibly Savinkov, and pits them against the holistic-, perhaps pseudo-, empiricism of Saint-Simon, Freud and possibly Gershenzon, a perhaps not wholly un-dualistic approach itself. Ahimeir recognises the danger for society inherent in the acceptance of not only dualist, 'either-or' theories – he notes that Gobineau's racial theory had led to German antisemitism and that Marxist theory in reductio ad absurdum had produced Russian Bolshevism – but also, but to a lesser extent, one-sided theories such as Freud's that were unprovable. Perhaps Ahimeir had Wilhelm Bauer's comments on his own dissertation in his head – on the danger of criticising Spengler's 'unproven and un-provable' assumptions with opinions that are equally so – when he reached his own conclusion on Freud. Be that as it may, Ahimeir believes that although Freudian psychoanalysis remained – for the time being – only important in the realm of scholarship, it carried the potential for becoming a 'life teaching'. Nevertheless, and with no apparent sense of irony, he concludes that 'those wishing to see the world and life from [only] one angle, will see only the partial picture and not the full picture'. To a certain degree then, Freud is also rejected, if only because of his one-sided, all-consuming focus on sex. For Ahimeir, a more satisfactory ideological approach would lie somewhere between Weininger's dualism that concentrated on sex as a biological gender, and Freud's holism that concentrated on sex as a primal act.

At this stage it is worth taking account of Ahimeir's 'public' ideological development, as expressed in print, at the end of his first year in Mandate Palestine. Themes already considered become more concrete in his developing ideological thought. Ahimeir recognises that nationalism must be achieved, in the first instance, through the recognition of political statehood, and not merely through cultural rebirth. And he further develops his conviction of the importance of action over word, and pits the 'action' of Savinkov's 'Revolutionary War' against the 'word' of Lenin's 'Revolutionary Teaching', as an example. In his comparison of the 'utopian' dualist, Weininger, and the holistic empiricist, Freud, Ahimeir is able – by rejecting the absolutist extremism in both – to define more clearly his own ideological standpoint. As a Positivist he deals with the reality of the situation he finds himself in. Hence Ahimeir also allows himself – through his self-identification with Savinkov's situation in *The Pale Horse* – to begin to consider the permissibility of killing. Not satisfied with being a theorist who seeks to look at the world from only one angle, Ahimeir, in his developing *Weltanschauung*, seems to be searching, increasingly, for a satisfactory ideological and methodological combination of scientific dualism and utopian holism, an important ideological transition on his way to the embrace of Monism, and eventually Fascism. This developing ideological position would influence Ahimeir's attitude towards the unfolding of events during the General Strike in England, and the way that worker's movements in Britain, Russia and the Yishuv had handled them.

The turning point

The English General Strike occurred between 3 and 13 May 1926, and was a response from the Trades and Union Commission (TUC) to the lockout of 800,000 coal miners who were faced with the prospect of a longer working day and the more than 30 per cent reduction in wages that they had endured over the last seven years. Prime Minister Stanley Baldwin had appointed Sir Herbert Samuel – who, the year before, had returned to England after five years as High Commissioner to Palestine – to head a committee that would make recommendations for the improvement of the mining industry. The report, published on 10 March 1926, advised not only a lengthening of the miners' workday but also a further reduction in wages.[21] The Miner's Delegate Conference – acting independently of the Industrial Committee of the General Council – passed a resolution rejecting both of these recommendations, which resulted in a stalemate with the mine owners. In mid-April, the mine owners gave the required fourteen days' notice of their intention to terminate their existing contracts with their employees, and replace them with contracts that were in line with the recommendations of the Samuel Commission Report. Failure to accept the new contracts would result in a lockout and, in fact, this is what transpired on 1 May 1926.

The TUC – backed into a corner – were forced to call a general strike in support of the miners, which took effect at 11:59 pm on Monday 3 May. It was a confrontation that they were ill-prepared for. The government denounced the strike as 'unconstitutional and illegal', and indeed, it maintained the upper hand throughout the period of the strike.[22] Worse still, there was little inconvenience to the British public outside of the urban centres. Thus, the General Council called off their strike on 12 May, a move which added further insult to the injury of the striking miners, who continued their resistance. But although many of them continued to strike until as late as November, the majority were forced, by existential need, back to work. And it was not only the miners who suffered a heavy blow. As the strike's biographer, Daniel F. Calhoun observed: 'The English political left was disabled for a generation, and much that was imaginative, thoughtful, humane and good in British life and thought did not again get a serious hearing until after the Second World War.'[23]Indeed, in the wake of the botched industrial action, more than half a million workers quit the TUC, and – perhaps more ominously – by September 1926, the membership of the Communist Party of Great Britain had doubled.[24]

Furthermore, the TUC had been playing a game of cat and mouse with the Soviets for over a year before the strike began. While on the one hand happy for the attention they received from Russia, the TUC was also, on the other, keen to avoid being seen by the British public as a revolutionary agitator in the universal class struggle. Hence, when the Russians gave the TUC notice of their intent to raise over 2 million roubles to aid the striking British workers, and to transfer 250,000 roubles of that sum with immediate effect, the TUC found themselves backed into a corner. The acceptance of aid from Soviet Russia carried with it the suggestion that the two groups might be collaborating in the name of the proletarian 'revolution'. Furthermore, since the initiative was organised by the All-Union Central Council of Trade Unions – an organ of the Soviet government – the TUC wanted to avoid any perception of aiding entryism by the Soviets into British politics. Thus – according to the newspaper *The British Worker* – the TUC 'informed the Russian Trade Unions, in a courteous communication, that they are unable to accept the offer, and the cheque has been returned'.[25]

In point of fact, the money was not returned, but rather rerouted to the Miner's Federation of Great Britain, to help towards the costs of the strike. In total, the Russian miners eventually contributed £1,233,788 – an astonishing sum – to their British counterparts, 'over two-thirds of all funds collected and more than 90 per cent of the receipts from outside Britain'.[26] In the name of comradely solidarity, the Histadrut also sent a token donation of one hundred Palestinian Pounds to the striking miners, on behalf of the various workers parties in the Yishuv. This was the backdrop to Ahimeir's article, in Issue 29, 1926 of the journal *HaPoel HaTzair*, 'Reflections of a Proletarian on the English Strike'.[27]

Ahimeir's headline is, in itself, somewhat provocative: as a librarian for the Histadrut and a teacher in Zikhron Yaakov, he must have hardly considered himself a true member of the proletariat. Nonetheless, he wastes no time in pointing out some of the apparently questionable reporting of the strike by the *Yishuv Labour* newspaper:

> 'Davar' – a worker's newspaper in Eretz Israel – had in the first days of the strike, in a huge headline, declared victory for the workers. The expert in English affairs on the editorial staff of *Davar* was certain of th[is] victory from his headquarters in Tel Aviv. To Cook, leader of the workers [in England], the victory was not [at all] clear, from his headquarters in London.[28]

While he recognises the utility of industrial action as a 'useful weapon at the hands of the worker's movement', Ahimeir is also quick to point out the danger of it becoming, if overused, an act of betrayal for that same worker's movement. Indeed, he notes that in Italy and England – countries where industrial action had become an all-too-common occurrence – the strike had served only to feed the fire of the Fascists, who in effect had been the ones responsible for the introduction of strikebreaking.[29] Familiarity had thus bred contempt.

And with regard to the hundred pounds sent on behalf of the Zionist Yishuv, Ahimeir notes sarcastically:

> Good that the Jewish workers – [themselves] 'striking' from [having] zero work – sent [money] to the striking English workers who want to improve their working conditions. Good that we sent our hundred. 'Send your bread forth upon the waters'.[30] Perhaps this hundred will be beneficial for us and the Daily Herold will cease [with] its attitude towards our movement.[31]

But it is for the Soviet donation and the Miner's Federation of Great Britain's handling of the affair that Ahimeir saves his strongest criticism. While first remarking on the vast difference in donation amount between the Yishuv's 100 pounds and the Russians' '260,000 Pounds [sic]' – 'this elephant will cover our mosquito' – Ahimeir notes, with disdain, that Alistair Cook, the secretary of the

MFGB, eventually accepted the Russian monies, but only after the strike had officially ended. Indeed, he spells out the injustice:

> Now, after the strike has ended, Cook has agreed to accept this sum. One has to wonder. Even if the affairs of Russia aren't fully understandable to him, it is known that the situation of the Russian worker is worse and bitterer than that of the English worker. ... In an official manner the Russian miners sent the sum of £260,000 to the English miners. As far as I am aware, there are not half a million miners in the whole of the Soviet Union. But supposing there are half a million, it would mean that each Russian miner issued more than half an English pound to the English strike. It would actually be interesting to know how much a Russian miner earns each month. [One who is] employed and not jobless [that is].[32]

And if there was doubt remaining in his reader's mind that Cook and the MFGB had handled the whole affair in the most odious of manners, Ahimeir further clarifies:

> The USSR's motives in sending this sum are known: propaganda. How many hungry [mouths] would it be possible to feed in Russia, with the sum taken by the *Komintern* to feed the fire of the Universal Revolution? With this money it would be possible to save all the children without shelter in the whole of the USSR, but these things are [well-] known. In Russia there are hidden intentions and programs. But how did Cook and his colleagues agree to accept this huge sum – the fruit of sweat and blood of the wretched masses of Eastern Europe? Was the situation of the Russian workers really not known to the managers of the Trade Unions, the real situation?[33]

Even more acerbically, Ahimeir exposes what – for him – is the greatest absurdity of all:

> The Soviet government worries about the English miners, collects huge sums from its citizens with help of the police, and at the same time it turns to the bourgeoisie of New York, etc. to come to [the] help [of] the Jews of the *shtetls* of White Russia and Ukraine that were destroyed, not without its [the Soviet government's] own culpability.[34]

Ahimeir had thus reached a politico-ideological standpoint from which he would never retreat. His recognition of the hypocrisy surrounding the TUC's rejection, and the MFGB's subsequent acceptance, of the Soviet government's not unconditional support set him on a path that would increasingly isolate him, ideologically and practically, from both HaPoel HaTzair and the labour movement in the Yishuv. It is interesting to note that Ahimeir's well-considered insight and cynically forthright assessment of the situation has, in fact, stood the test of time. As Calhoun concluded:

> [The Soviet donations] averaged out to almost 3 shillings from every Soviet trade unionist, over twice as much per person as organized British workers were willing to pay. Considering Russians earned only a fraction of what their English counterparts received, it was an extraordinary total. Bernard Pares calculated that Russian miners at the time were taking home only about 22s.6. a week, less than their locked-out English counterparts were drawing in strike pay. It was 'disgraceful', he observed, that the Soviets should be dunned for any contribution at all.[35]

Ahimeir's strongly worded exposé of what might generously be described as the poor judgement inherent within the international workers' movement – in the journal of one of its own parties – could not go unnoticed. Indeed, it brought about harsh criticism in what was to become a public mudslinging between Ahimeir and two prominent members of the labour movement – Moshe Shertok and David Zakai – in its newspaper *Davar.*

The papers in the Yishuv had followed the strike with avid interest. *Davar* was an initiative of the Histadrut, its first issue had appeared just less than one year earlier, on 1 June 1925, and bore the title *Davar - Iton Poalei Eretz Yisrael*: 'Davar – Newspaper of [the] Eretz Israel Workers'. Its first editor was Ahimeir's old friend from Bobruisk, Berl Katznelson. On 3 May 1926, *Davar* carried the headline 'The Miners' Strike in England', alongside an account detailing 'The Final Night Before the Declaration of the Strike'.[36] The same day, the English daily *The Palestine Bulletin* reported the British government's ultimatum to the trade unions.[37] The following day, the front page of each paper declared – in Hebrew and English, respectively – 'General Strike in England'. Both papers also documented the return of the Soviet money by the TUC. *Davar* noted on 10 May 1926 that 'the TUC ... had discussed the question [of accepting the Soviets' cheque] at length and decided to send a polite reply expressing their gratitude but also their inability to accept the sum of money'. The sum stated by *Davar* was to be 'several thousand pounds'. *The Palestine Bulletin* was more specific in its edition the following day, reporting that 'The Congress of Trade Unions has returned the cheque for 1,500,000 roubles, raised by the Russian workers, to the Soviet Trade Unions, with a polite note declining the contribution to its funds'. The discrepancy in amounts – Ahimeir's claim of £260,000, Calhoun's probably more accurate 250,000 roubles, *The Palestine Bulletin's* 1,500,000 roubles – is of no great issue for this discussion, and is most likely a case of having got lost in translation, as it were. The real discrepancy was in how each paper reported the end of the General Strike, on 13 May 1926. *The Palestine Bulletin* announced simply the 'End of the General Strike', with the sub-headline, 'Sir Herbert Samuel's Triumph'. *Davar*, however, declared – erroneously – 'The Strike in England has Ended in Victory for the Workers'. The inherent irony in the latter headline was too much for Ahimeir, and his disdain for the MFGB, TUC and the Soviets was matched only by his *Schadenfreude* at *Davar*'s rather premature ejaculation.

Not surprisingly, his article set off a flurry of objection, which, in print, took the form of letters to the editor of *Davar*. The paper published the first rebuttal from fellow journalist and Labour Party member David Zakai on 7 June 1926. Zakai takes Ahimeir to task, not merely for his mockery of the contribution from the Histadrut – 'he is not the first to laugh … his predecessors have already laughed in *HaAretz* and in conversations of those who sit in coffeehouses of Tel Aviv' – but in the bitterly ironic tone that Ahimeir took. Zakai thought that Ahimeir had thus latently slandered all public workers in the Yishuv as 'merchants and usurers', a common derogatory expression used against Jews by Gentiles since the Middle Ages. And the fact that Ahimeir had called himself a 'proletarian' in the article's headline, and signed it from 'Kibbutz Geva' had, for Zakai, in no way mitigated the effect of Ahimeir's slanderous tone.

Four days later, Moshe Shertok – who would go on to become Moshe Sharett, the future minister of foreign affairs and the second prime minister of the State of Israel, but who was, at this time, still a member of Ahdut HaAvodah and regular contributor to *Davar* – expressed his thoughts on Ahimeir's article. First of all, he corrects Ahimeir's facts: *Davar* had not declared a workers' victory during the first days of the strike, but rather at the end. In support of this he, rather pedantically, lists each headline that *Davar* had published, from the 3 to 13 May. 'Why, then, did Ahimeir write things that weren't true?' he asks. And although it was true that *Davar* had subsequently retracted its declaration of a workers' victory, Shertok argues that, on 13 May, it was generally assumed that the end of the general strike would also spell the end of the miners' lockout. He maintains that Ahimeir would have drawn the same conclusion himself, had he written his article on 13 May, and not after the fourteenth, when the truth was clear for all to see. Moreover, Shertok believed that *Davar*'s subsequent admission of the strike's failure had only further underscored the paper's journalistic integrity. Indeed, Shertok concludes that 'Ahimeir's *Schadenfreude* at catching *Davar* "in the act" had not changed that fact'.

On 24 June 1926, *Davar* published Ahimeir's rebuttal to both letters, as well as a new reply from Shertok.[38] Ahimeir defends his use of the term 'proletarian', which he used as it was understood in 'classic socialist literature', in other words, as an economic concept. Indeed, he clarifies that, as a man who is 'without property except for his clothes and his basket of books, a man who works until the afternoon in the common room of the kibbutz and after that teaches at the same kibbutz on behalf of the Cultural Association – I think that a man such as this may think of himself as a proletarian'.[39] More importantly, Shertok had – in reality – not answered Ahimeir, but rather the editorial staff of *HaPoel HaTzair*, who apparently had edited Ahimeir's handwritten article, which – according to him – had originally stated:

> The reports of the victory in our paper reminds me of the reports of the Russian, Austrian, and Turkish adversary from the battlefield. The reported victory, [and the report of] the many thousands of POW's, [caused] patriotic parades, and after that [the reporters] were forced to report the bitter truth.[40]

Addressing Zakai – 'I may be a Pharisee and you a Sadducee, or vice versa. But let's not be hypocrites' – Ahimeir defends the 'crimes and sins' that he had voiced publicly as representative of what the whole of the Worker's Executive – 'both the Sadducees and the Pharisees' – were thinking when they received word of the transfer of the 100 pounds by the Histadrut. 'By the way', he adds sarcastically, '[it's] a wonder that [the Worker's Executive] did not find it necessary to print the sums that the workers of other countries had sent. *Davka HaAretz* printed the sums and it is interesting to compare them in order to marvel at the "[honey-] pot" of international solidarity'. And he adds, 'is it not in the [very] spirit of "Send your bread forth" [etc.], that we wine and dine the editors of the New York papers?'

Ahimeir believes that Shertok's justification of *Davar's* editorial position was due to the fragmentary nature in which the reports were received. He suggests, sarcastically, that instead of such a rationalisation, '[Shertok] would do better to compare the "non-partisan" *Davar* with other "partisan" papers from the beginning of the strike, such as *Vorwärts* and the *Arbeiter Zeitung*'. Ahimeir's implication, of course, is that the whole of the labour press was unanimous in its collusion in reporting that the strike had resulted in victory for the workers. Nonetheless – and most startling – Ahimeir admits that he, himself, had not seen the foreign papers, but was sure that they 'shout' as loudly as *Davar* had. While ignoring Shertok's point that *Davar* had only declared the workers' victory at the end of the strike, and not at the beginning – as Ahimeir had erroneously reported – Ahimeir nonetheless admits he had hurt his colleagues – albeit 'lovingly' – and he apologises if he has hurt anyone personally.

Shertok's reply follows immediately. He accepts Ahimeir's corrections, but pushes the point about Ahimeir's false accusation, that *Davar* had declared the workers' victory from the first days of the strike. He had not only *not* admitted his mistake but also continued 'to ignore things written in black and white'. Furthermore, Ahimeir's accusations were untrue. First, according to Shertok, the reports had not been received in a fragmentary nature, but rather in great detail, so much so that *Davar* had not been able to give anything more than the main points. Neither had they been full of contradictions. Second, the reports were not contrasting, since the majority of them had been taken from Reuters News Agency who 'even in Ahimeir's opinion [must be] clear of the guilt of excessive devotion to the interests of the strikers'. He continues:

> But I explained that the short reports that we received after the cancellation of the strike misled us, as they had many others, in different locations. One assumed that Samuel's conditions were the government's conditions, and hence one would think of the end of the strike as [representing] a victory.

Furthermore, Shertok rejects Ahimeir's comparison of *Davar* with the *Arbeiter Zeitung*: the latter publication had, in fact, been 'imbued with the spirit of war and security much more than *Davar*'. And what had Ahimeir meant by 'non-partisan?' For Shertok, 'Nothing was non-partisan in the "generational war" between the exploiters and the exploited; *Davar* had not enlisted such non-partisanship'. Regarding Ahimeir's comment, 'Send your bread forth [etc.]', Shertok charges 'Comrade' Ahimeir with accusing anyone in the party who doesn't think in the same way as he (Ahimeir), to be a hypocrite, and concludes by addressing him directly:

> If you meant to express the notion of our brotherly solidarity in the universal war of the worker, you [will] also take our position and that of our [class war] here in the land, or is it that he [*sic*] comes to object to the intention of the senders [of the £100], and to make this sending of help to the strikers devoid of all class- and human-content and to show it merely as manipulation. If he really thinks the latter, [then] certainly he is not speaking for each and every one of us. For me, the argument is finished.[41]

Essentially, Ahimeir was told, in a public forum, to toe the party line. This very public airing of laundry between the three members of the same party sowed the seeds for an ever-increasing ideological schism that was opening up between Ahimeir and HaPoel HaTzair, and can be accurately pinpointed as the beginning of Ahimeir's slow departure from the party. It is perhaps interesting to note that Zakai refers – sarcastically – to 'our friend Ahimeir'. Shertok is much more formal, and in line with party ideology: it is 'Comrade Ahimeir' ('*HaHaver* Ahimeir') whom he addresses, and indeed, redresses. Ahimeir, for his part, refers to Shertok simply by name, while Zakai is 'my friend'. One might wonder if the address 'Comrade' ever formed part of Ahimeir's vocabulary.

Changes

The year that had passed between the time of Ahimeir's *aliyah* and his article on the General Strike in England witnessed a major political reorganisation in both world- and Yishuv-Zionism. In 1923, at loggerheads with his colleague and the Zionist Organization's chairman, Chaim Weizmann, Ze'ev Jabotinsky tendered his resignation from the Executive Council of the group. Two years later, in April 1925, he founded the Brit HaTzionim HaRevizionistim (*HaTzohar* for short), or the Revisionist Zionist movement.

The beginning of the Zionist Right as a separate political entity can be traced back three years prior to Jabotinsky's rejection of the Churchill White Paper of 1922. In it, Winston Churchill, then colonial secretary, underscored Britain's commitment to the establishment of a Jewish National Home in Palestine – as had been outlined in the Balfour Declaration of 2 November 1917 – but at the same time delineated the Hashemite Emirate of Transjordan, which was to have the Jordan River as its eastern border. The White Paper was a double-edged sword for the Zionist Organisation, and spelled its first major disappointment since the hopeful precedent set by the Balfour Declaration, in 1917. It also underscored the conflicting, irreconcilable, promises that Britain had made to both the Zionists and Arabs during the war. Indeed, the 1922 White Paper cautioned that

> unauthorized statements have been made to the effect that the purpose in view is to create a wholly Jewish Palestine. Phrases have been used such as that Palestine is to become 'as Jewish as England is English'. HMG regard any such expectation as impracticable and have no such aim in view. Nor have they at any time contemplated, as appears to be feared by the Arab Delegation, the disappearance or the subordination of the Arabic population, language or culture in Palestine. They would draw attention to the fact that the terms of

the Declaration referred to do not contemplate that Palestine as a whole should be converted into a Jewish National Home, but that such a Home should be founded in Palestine.[42]

Although critical of the paper, the Zionist Organization (ZO) nonetheless begrudgingly accepted it. It had hoped to create a Jewish majority state in all of the biblical Land of Israel, but stopped short of stating this, emphatically. The Churchill 1922 White Paper quashed this hope, and the passive position of the ZO effected Jabotinsky's resignation from its Executive Council. It led to the formation of a group within its ranks that called for a review – a revision – of the Labour- and ZO-endorsed 'practical', settlement-based Zionist ideology that had been its strategic modus operandi up to that point. Jabotinsky and his circle advocated a return to Zionism in its essential, Herzlian, 'political' form; furthermore, they demanded territorial maximalism, and active lobbying of British policy and practice. Nevertheless, Jabotinsky – like Weizmann, a staunch Anglophile – still believed in Britain's intention and ability to fulfil its mandatory obligations, and he consistently advocated a path of diplomacy with the Mandatory power, for his new party. Be that as it may, the Revisionist Party, founded in 1925, represented the first organised party to stand on the right of the Zionist political spectrum, and Ahimeir cannot have helped but notice the new movement.

From the period following the British miners' strike, Ahimeir's articles become more focused on themes that were certainly occupying his own thoughts: nationalism and nationalist expression, the shortcomings of democracy and its problems with the British Empire, and, once again, the wretchedness of the British miners' strike. The first of these articles is a cultural-historical essay on Ahad Ha'am (Asher Ginsberg, 1856-1927), the writer and Zionist philosopher who was the father of Cultural Zionism, which opposed Herzlian Political Zionism.[43] A strong critic of Herzl, Ahad Ha'am believed it was more important to (re-) establish a Jewish cultural centre than a sovereign territorial polity in the Land of Israel. Ahimeir notes that Ahad Ha'am concerned himself less with the idea of Israel as a land than he did with 'Israeli-ness' as a culture. Consequently, his nationalism was 'abstract': not the means to an end, but the end-goal, itself. In this sense, according to Ahimeir, it differed from that of 'Lilienblum, Herzl or ours, the nationalism of the Worker's Movement in the Yishuv', who espoused 'nationalism of means but not end-goal'. Of course, for Ahimeir – who, it should be noted, continued to see himself as a steadfast member of the 'Worker's Movement of the Yishuv' – nationalism represented both means and end; thus it is interesting to see him make such a distinction here. Ahimeir traces the idea of 'abstract' nationalism back through the German Romantic poets and artists, and the idealist philosophers Hegel, Fichte, Schlegel and others. He finds it noteworthy that it was *davka* on the threshold of the Napoleonic Wars of 1813–15, that what he calls German 'Impractical Nationalism' had begun to flourish. Ahimeir believed that it was precisely this type of abstract and philosophical nationalism – one that was based on the notion of the primordial nation or *Volk* – that 'roused the hearts [of the nation] towards concrete deeds'.[44] Thus, Ahimeir not only identifies the necessity for an abstract, romantic, *völkisch*-nationalist element in nationalist organisation but also recognises its ability to catalyse political-nationalist organisation.[45]

In this manner, we continue to see the increasingly organic nature of Ahimeir's own nationalist ideology developing, one that comprised the philanthropic nationalism of the writer Moshe Leib Lilienblum (1843–1910), the politico-diplomatic nationalism of Herzl, the nationalism of HaPoel HaTzair Hebrew labourer's conquest of the land and, finally, standing behind all of this – and based on philosophical ideals that could and would catalyse direct action – the 'abstract nationalism' of Ahad Ha'am. Furthermore, Ahimeir takes from the German Romantics the idea that each nationalism has its own particular mission, one that has – as its fundamental goal – humanitarian salvation through national hegemony. Indeed, he continues, 'this is the national mission-concept of Israel, the messianic idea; so the idea of primordial antiquity of Israel's culture, so to speak, begins with the first prophets, [those] of the generation of First Isaiah'. Ahimeir thus establishes both the birthplace and the historical period of Jewish national cultural-historical legitimacy, and links Jewish nationalism and Messianism, a phenomenon that will be discussed in more detail in Chapter 5. And he notes that 'Until recently, neither Judaism in general, nor the individual Jew has asked, "In the name of what is this suffering [and] pain of exile, and where are we going?"' Zionism thus provided a concrete political goal for the Jewish nation, after almost 2,000 years of aimless wandering. In spite of his observation, Ahimeir believed that the Jews had managed – over the past 1,800 years, and in spite of external crises – to maintain a 'harmonic spirit' from within. He describes Ahad Ha'am's idealistic world view as that of a 'pure Positivist' who had been influenced by all Jewish rationality and culture from the Middle Ages to the present day. This description, perhaps, also applies to Ahimeir, himself, but for the fact that his influences hark back as far as the *Tanakh*ic period, and indeed before.

And an article written for *Davar* in the autumn of 1926 on the fate of the Young Turks movement is particularly interesting for both the historical and ideological observations which he makes.[46] First and foremost, the article's subject matter reveals an Ahimeir who was, to some degree, au courant with revolutionary movements outside of Europe. Ahimeir had lived in both Ottoman- and British Mandatory- Palestine; thus his discussion of a revolutionary, nationalist, political reform movement that had likewise occurred in the Ottoman Empire is significant. Once again, in a nod to Spengler, Ahimeir notes the parallels between historically similar events. He sees the Young Turks – moderate reformers – as similar to the moderates during the period of the Jewish-Roman wars, the Dantonists and Girondists during the French Revolution, and the Mensheviks during the Russian Revolution. Indeed, all had suffered a similar fate: the moderate movements were all destroyed by their more extreme counterparts: the 'Sicarii-terrorists', Jacobins and Bolsheviks. However, he notes that while the other cases had represented a victory of politics over military, the victory of the Kemalists over the Young Turks represented a victory of military over politics. Most tragic of all, for Ahimeir, was the fact that the Young Turks had 'fallen' at the hands of their ideological allies.

Not only does Ahimeir, at this stage, equate the Sicarii with the Bolsheviks, but he also makes clear his belief in the inevitability of the victory of extreme movements over moderate movements. Furthermore, Ahimeir had that same year, as will be discussed in Chapter Five, penned, but not published, his essay 'The Scroll of the Sicarii'. The essay – which the sentencing judge at the Brit HaBiryonim trial in 1934 would rule had demonstrated a glorification of political murder – would be used as evidence to convict Ahimeir of being in possession of seditious literature. Thus, this first, matter-of-fact mention of the Sicarii in print is noteworthy, if only in retrospect of events as they would unfold eight years later.[47]

Ahimeir then turns to the theme of democracy, and more specifically, to the question of its feasibility, in the future.[48] Drawing a distinction between democracy as ideology and democracy as a practice, he notes that since the end of the Great War, most countries had now come under some form of 'practical' democratic rule. The most obvious exceptions – Lenin's Russia and Mussolini's Italy – represented, for Ahimeir, a 'Revolutionary Dictatorship' and a Bonapartist regime, respectively.[49] Thus not only does he see Bolshevism as the true form of dictatorial rule, but – equally as important – he also sees Italian Fascism as both a more conservative form of Socialism, and a more populist form of imperial rule; indeed, a 'Third Way', in every respect. Notably, in Ahimeir's eyes, Bolshevism was the more radical movement: an important observation for understanding his eventual embrace of Fascist ideology.

Nonetheless, the fact that democratic rule was becoming increasingly widespread was contrasted, for Ahimeir, by the fact that democratic ideology was – in both its 'systemic development' and its current form – unsatisfactory. In democratic nations:

> The[ir] political situation, the interrelations between nations, plus the[ir] cultural situation does not assume the opinions of the liberals and radicals, and in addition to this, the economic situation does not assume the opinions of the Socialist movement.[50]

For Ahimeir, this discrepancy – between democratic ideology and democratic rule – was an ever-widening schism. The current situations in Poland and Mexico served as examples of what could happen when democratic ideology rejected the democratic rule that it had formerly supported in the form of parliamentarianism: both nations had turned to Dictatorship. Ahimeir continues:

> It is possible to follow without difficulty the development of affairs that is brought [on] by this 'Neo-Democracy'. In the past, democracy was the monopoly of the Liberals; they have [since] dropped it, and now its disciples are the moderate Socialists. As a result of the World War and the Russian Revolution, the Socialist camp suffered a rupture: on one side stood the Social Democrats, on the other side, the Communists. Also, however, for Socialism, which had chosen the path of democracy, [there was a] lack of patience that Liberalism excelled at. Recent years [have seen] the introduction of changes and the abolition of democratic rule. ... Moderate Socialism is now the subject of a 'Neo-Democracy' that is permeated by mistrust in democratic rule.[51]

'Neo-Democracy' indicated, for Ahimeir, an ever-increasing trend towards Conservatism which was no longer the domain of only the upper classes. In this manner, 'true' democratic rule had been conquered by conservative elements; thus the interests of the unions – the prime examples of Ahimeir's conservative 'Neo-Democracy' – were beginning to replace those of parliament. Only Ramsay MacDonald in England and the Social Democrats in Germany had, in Ahimeir's eyes, remained loyal to true democratic rule.

The best examples of this discrepancy between democratic ideology and democratic rule could, for him, be seen in Poland, where only the Yiddish papers – apparently in an act of self-deception – had made the distinction in calling the powers of the Polish government 'fascist' and those of Pilsudski 'democratic'. 'In truth', Ahimeir clarifies, 'Pilsudski is the Polish fascist'. He had used the military, under his own command, as a means of legitimate government, and had done so in line with all the legality of democratic rule, even though this 'democratic rule' now took on a much more conservative form. And here Ahimeir makes his point: 'One cannot cast a doubt on Pilsudski's democratic ideology, but, in practice, what is [really] the difference between him and Mussolini?' Also in Turkey, he notes, Kemal had conducted military 'trials' for his opponents – 'in the name of democratic ideology' – but throughout these, nonetheless, the 'guillotine had continued to work without respite'.

Most importantly, for Ahimeir, 'even' Mussolini – who followed in the ideological footsteps of Mazzini, Garibaldi and Cavour – espoused democratic ideals, although they took on his own particular form. In other words, Ahimeir considered Mussolini – in his mantle as the resurrector of Bonapartism – a democrat in spirit, although one who took the form of a democratic dictator like Cesar and, again, like Cesar, '[would fall] at the hands of the Roman conservatives'.[52]

Ahimeir's conclusions are noteworthy: democratic rule – the product of Liberalism – was now being conquered throughout the world by Conservatism:

> Those who possess democratic ideology, who aspire to changes [improvements] in society, are not able to come to terms with this situation and turn more and more to dictatorship in one form or another. The realisation that Parliamentarianism interferes with the 'spiritual' opinions and the aspirations of modernity also pushes for the creation of a new ideology of democracy like that which we see in the actions of Pilsudski, Clemm, Mussolini, Kemal Pasha and in the rule of Otto Bauer – who advocates a 'tin dictatorship'– and with the radical trends in the Worker's [*sic*] Party in England.[53]

And Ahimeir gives us yet further clues regarding his ever-developing attitude towards Western political change when he names the phenomenon of political Conservatism – a newer player on the field of democracy – as the one true force that was currently fighting the spread of extreme nationalism.[54] The Great War had put an end to the 'denial' that was bound up in the Universalist ideals of Liberalism and Socialism, as 'Nationalism ceased to be the inheritance of Conservatism alone'. Indeed, Ahimeir believes that nationalist interests could be seen even in extreme versions of Marxist-Socialism – in present-day Russia – which had adapted, in no small way, to the concept of nationalism. In Italy, ironically perhaps, the conservative Catholic elements were now experiencing more difficulty fighting Fascism than they were Socialism. And in a statement that perhaps best highlights Ahimeir's current ideological quandary, he declares that

> there is currently no serious person who really believes that Socialism is peace. ... If Socialism was promised [its] ideal realisation [but] at the price of a 'good war', it is doubtful if it would stand the test.[55]

And indeed, he comes to the central conclusion of his article, one that might also now just as easily be used for Ahimeir himself: 'Between the ideal and the form of realisation that it takes, [there] lies always an abyss'.[56]

Ahimeir makes one further important observation, when he concludes that the despair which followed the failure of the 1848 revolutions had produced two results for those who had put their faith in the ideal of democracy as a 'religion of progress': the moderates had adopted an air of scepticism, on one hand, while the extremists had adopted a belief in dictatorship, on the other. Furthermore, and notably, he believes that Socialism was experiencing a similar fate in the twentieth century. Indeed, as he observes, 'The Russian experiment blinds the eyes [of society]'.[57] Nonetheless, Ahimeir finds in these uncomfortable truths no room for despair: 'One needs only to replace the belief in the ideal goal [itself] with the belief in the means, on the path to the ideal'. Thus, ideals are fine, as long as they are not clung to with false piety; indeed, as always, 'action' should be privileged over 'word'. In support of this claim, Ahimeir notes that, currently, in Russia – 'now that the damage of 1917 is gone' – already no one really cares if they are ruled by a Bolshevik dictatorship, a parliament of moderate Socialists and radical Liberals, or even the (re-)legitimisation of (the Tzar) Romanov.

For him, the weakness of Socialism does not lie in the fact that it fails to get rid of society's self-destructive tendencies, but rather that it is not able to stimulate any sort of national-cultural reawakening. Any attempt at the realisation of an ideal brings with it the danger of disappointment and despair. 'However', Ahimeir notes, rather importantly, 'on the path to idealism, people are elevated by deeds of heroism', upon which he does not elaborate, although the implication is of some form of self-sacrifice. Nonetheless, he points out that the 'golden ages' of a culture always occur during periods of peace. Furthermore, and in rare agreement with Marx, he notes that one could speak about mass production only with disdain. Where Ahimeir differs from Marx is in his belief that the individual would remain the creator also in the future; a public ideal was rarely realised through any sort of mass-cultural creation. Thus Ahimeir warns that the Yishuv faced a similar danger to that of America: that the life of its residents would become a life of 'structural'– and not 'creative'– work. This was to be avoided, in spite of its apparent attraction; a perhaps confusing remark for someone who was looking increasingly towards Fascism – a movement that was decidedly not individualistic – as a viable ideological-practical framework.

Ahimeir's gradual shift – from pioneer idealist to disillusioned cynic – can be seen in the remaining articles that he penned for *HaPoel HaTzair*. Throughout 1926 and the first half of 1927, he was a regular contributor. After that, he contributed only two articles, at the end of 1927. The last two articles that appear in 1926 focus on Britain and Fascism, topics that would soon become inextricably intertwined in Ahimeir's ideological world.[58] First, however, he revisits the failed Miners' Strike, the phenomenon that had recently effected his own disillusionment with the worker's movement, which Ahimeir blames on the 'particularly stubborn', conservative nature of English nationalism, one which rejected any sort of foreign ideological influence.[59] Hence the failure of the Soviets – 'custodians of radical Socialism' – to make a propagandistic inroad, during the strike. Ahimeir notes that the 1926 strike, like those in 1912 and 1921 before it, was centred on purely economic considerations – the length of the workday and wage increase – and not ideological ones, as had been the case in similar instances on the continent. The strike had thus, in his assessment, 'exposed the nakedness' of international solidarity, in a similar way that the events of August 1914 had done, as they pushed Europe into war. Indeed, English public opinion, with regard to the cause of the striking miners, was, for the most part, indifferent. But even worse for Ahimeir was the fact that the English trade unions, like their American counterparts, were not at all influenced by the demonstrations of professional unity shown by 'other' workers' parties in the same way that their colleagues on the continent had been influenced by, for example, Socialist, Catholic and Fascist political unity during their corresponding periods of industrial action. This fact, for Ahimeir, made it difficult to predict whether the unsuccessful strike would result in the introduction of a more moderate or more radical stream of politics into British political life.

Notably, Ahimeir once again confronts the subject of Italian Fascism.[60] As a review of Robert Michels' *Sozialismus und Fascismus als politische Strömungen in Italien: historische Studien* (Socialism and Fascism as Political Currents in Italy: Historical Studies), the article can, at times, pose problems in determining which material should be attributed to Michels, and which to Ahimeir. Thus, one should proceed with caution when using the article as an absolute indicator of Ahimeir's own developing politico-ideological shift. While it certainly demonstrates his ongoing fascination with Mussolini's movement, Ahimeir's 1923 article in *HaToren* is far more unadulterated and unequivocal. Nonetheless, there are still several observations that we may take from the 1926 article.

As Ahimeir's first – and to this point, only – book review, we should conclude that he considered Michels's book to be a significant work, whether because of the importance and depth of its analysis and conclusions, or merely because it was one of the first books to be published that dealt with the subject matter as such. Second, while extolling Michels's extreme objectivity throughout, Ahimeir also bemoans the book's lack of ideological analysis. Michels, as a professor of economics, discussed only the economic causes of Fascism, and not the 'historical-romantic' basis that enabled the formation of an 'extreme political movement' in Italy. The importance for this study is the fact that Ahimeir's criticism of Michels makes absolutely clear to us that Ahimeir places a very high value on the question of ideology. Indeed, ideology, historical context and national culture – in his opinion – had played as decisive a role as had economic considerations in effecting Italy's recent political embrace of Fascism. This revelation should come as no great surprise, considering that Ahimeir was a cultural historian. We will see a similar dichotomous parallel – cultural-history versus economics – in Chapter 5, when comparing the *völkisch* element in both Ahimeir's and Arlosoroff's concepts of Jewish nationalism.

Moreover – and we may assume that this is where the attraction lay, for Ahimeir – Michels sees Bolshevism and Fascism as two complementary – yet, also competing – ideologies: Bolshevism played 'Remus' to Fascism's 'Romulus'.[61] Both traced their roots to the war: the Catholic *Menschenmaterial* (human materiel or manpower) from Italy's towns and villages that had fought in the war had become the supporters of Fascism; its Socialist opponents had – likewise, in its wake – become more extreme. Furthermore, for Michels, the occupation of the factories in August 1920 had been a key factor in the decisive push towards the dual phenomena of both Bolshevism and Fascism in Italy. And, most importantly – like the mythological brothers – Romulus would go on to kill Remus. Indeed, Michels had isolated three reasons why Socialism had lost out at the hands of Fascism. First, the fatalism that was inherent in Marxist-Socialism was disadvantageous vis à vis the more constructive activism of Fascism. Second, the *Menschenmaterial* of Socialism was altogether older than that of Fascism, which was centred on a youth that had – due to the war – been instilled with a military spirit. Third, Socialism's 'humanistic' element had caused the more 'activist' Syndicalist elements to embrace Fascism. Thus, the desire for 'positive' action over 'negative' words had been responsible for the defection of a large number of Italian Socialists to the Fascist camp, a fact that was certainly not lost on Ahimeir. He further notes Michels's claim that the Italian Marxists had produced the theory that the Italian people were generally more proletarian than the 'bourgeois' English, German, French and American nations, a fact that had led to the exploitation of the Italians by these other nations, and was a further example, for Ahimeir, of a smaller nation fighting to preserve its national-cultural identity in face of more dominant nations.

Finally, Ahimeir highlights Michels's conclusion that there was, in fact, no Italian imperial economy because the Italian colonial settlements were not economically self-sufficient. Thus, Italian Imperialism was more of a political phenomenon, and this fact is what had produced the curious alliance with the Socialists and Syndicalists during the war in Tripoli. In this respect – and rather notably – Ahimeir draws an analogy here with the British 'Imperial' efforts in the Yishuv.

As previously stated, Ahimeir continued to be a regular contributor to *HaPoel HaTzair* throughout the first half of 1927. His articles are, for the most part, innocuous cultural-historical essays that demonstrate a rich historical knowledge and ability for sophisticated analysis, but generally give little indication of Ahimeir's own changing ideological development. Perhaps he felt the need to more effectively 'toe the party line', in the wake of the controversy caused by his article on the British Miners' Strike. Or perhaps his own politico-ideological position was still too ambiguous to allow him to write with absolute conviction. More than likely, Ahimeir had simply lost interest in producing thought-provoking essays for an audience that he believed was unwilling to think outside of its own ideological constraints.

Be that as it may, there are noteworthy observations that, in their analysis, do give us some indication of his own developing thought. For example, Ahimeir notes that it was not only England – as stated in his article on the Miners' Strike – but also the whole of the 'Anglo-Saxon' world that was currently showing a very united conservative front.[62] For Ahimeir, the reasons for this were clear: England and its dominions, including all of North America, were satiated as a consequence of what he calls – in a nod to Spengler – 'civilizational flourishing', in other words, imperial territorial, economic and cultural expansion. This trend towards Conservatism was balanced out by other progressive ideological strains, historically in the form of Liberalism, but now also in the form of Labour. Yet Ahimeir wonders whether the Labour Party would ultimately adopt an ideological platform that was more traditionally liberal, or more traditionally Socialist. Indeed, he reminds his reader, according to Marxist theory, England – due to its robust economic situation – would have needed to be one of the first countries to accept and adopt Socialist ideology and practice. Of course, this had not been the case. In point of fact, Ahimeir believes that the Labour Party espoused, essentially, nothing more than 'pure Liberal ideas' at the expense of true Socialist aspirations.

Notably, he also details the previous, unsuccessful, attempt at forming a 'Third Party' in England, the phenomenon of Chartism, which – in a further nod to Spengler – Ahimeir believes had earlier occupied the same ideological position as the current Labour movement:

> Both turned to the masses and tried to draw them along with them. The Chartists had a liberal content, but the means they used were almost revolutionary. … Labour was the opposite: its means were liberal, more moderate than the means of the Chartists, but its program was less liberal than that of the Chartists. In the 1840s the third party disappeared at the hands of the second, Liberalism. [This is] Exactly what has just occurred to the 'Third Party' in North America. Similar to that, the fate of Labour will be different to that of Chartism. Now the third party in England goes on to devour the second, one of the historical parties of the English public movement. But that is for the future.[63]

Thus Ahimeir saw the British Labour Party's true strength in the fact that it had shed much of its Socialist content, and had 'turned to the masses'. He implies that the current success of the party was due to its ability to espouse liberal values in everything but name. Although not at all Fascist, the Labour Party did provide a third option, and the similarity with Italy in this respect could not have been lost on Ahimeir. As will be discussed next, the very appeal of Mussolini's Fascists was their ability to provide a 'Third Way', one that combined Socialist intent with more conservative, yet – in their opinion – liberal values. Undoubtedly, this attractive ideological mix was what drew Ahimeir to the movement.

Dictatorship

But it is the question of dictatorship that occupies Ahimeir; not so much its ideological validity, but rather its successful practical implantation. Indeed, he comes to his final positive conclusions on dictatorship and Fascism in a rather roundabout manner, one that seeks, perhaps, to empirically prove their viability by citing current – successful – exemplars. Hence, Ahimeir's discussion of Portugal, a country which, after a long history of monarchy, now found itself ruled by what he sees as a 'Praetorian military dictatorship'.[64] And not for the first time he uses the example of one country as an analogy for the current status quo in much of the rest of Europe. Thus his statement that the now obsolete battle between Monarchism and Republicanism had been replaced by a more current one, between Dictatorship and parliamentarianism. Recent events in Spain, Greece and China had all pointed to an emergent struggle between military dictatorship and parliamentary rule that was slowly becoming the status quo. Although still hesitant to state his own position on the matter – at least in print, where he remarks that 'much will depend on the "correctness" of the Spanish dictatorship'[65] – Ahimeir nonetheless leaves no doubt in his reader's mind that, at present, there are no other viable options for European political organisation. As noted earlier, Ahimeir had previously made his disdain for parliamentarianism quite clear. Thus, while he still does not deliver a straightforward advocacy for dictatorship, he certainly indicates, if only passively, that it is currently the most feasible option in Europe. And he is even less clear as to whether he believes such a development would represent a welcome change, or an unhappy necessity. Either way, Ahimeir's conclusion – and again, at least in print, it remains an implied conclusion – reflects more a cool-headed intellectual analysis than it does any sort of emotional enthusiasm. Nonetheless, the writing was on the wall for the future of European political organisation in general, and for Ahimeir – wittingly or unwittingly – in particular. Ahimeir has reached the mid-point – chronologically and ideologically – in his shift from pioneer idealist to cynical pragmatist that had been catalysed by the events surrounding the English Miners' Strike. The next year would see this shift become more pronounced in his own politico-ideological thought.

From early 1927, Ahimeir had also now become a regular contributor to the Hebrew daily newspaper *HaAretz*. Unlike his articles penned for *HaPoel HaTzair*, which covered a vast range of topics and disciplines, those written for *HaAretz* are almost exclusively political or politico-historical in nature, and it may be the case that he fulfilled the role of political correspondent. For the most part, the articles throughout 1927 concentrate on the situation in a post-war Europe that was now characterised by a Bolshevik Russia, a Fascist Italy, the consequences of the Versailles Treaty and a crisis in Socialism that was a result of all of these factors. However, in addition – and notably – Ahimeir also begins increasingly to write about political life in the Yishuv, and – specifically – the degree to which he believes both the British and Jewish leaderships were mishandling the situation there.

His first article in *HaAretz*, entitled 'Trotzkyism', had appeared already in 1925.[66] Now, the tenth anniversary of the February and October Revolutions provided Ahimeir with the opportunity to reflect further upon the effectiveness of a decade of Bolshevik rule. The first of these articles, which dealt with the February 1917 revolution, appeared in *HaPoel HaTzair*, the remaining articles appeared in *HaAretz*, in November 1927.[67] Ahimeir – who, it should be remembered, had not only experienced the events first-hand but also lost his brother Meir as a consequence of the revolution – not surprisingly, takes a rather cynical attitude in his analyses.

For Ahimeir, the period from February to April 1917 in revolutionary Russia had been the 'honeymoon phase'. The February revolution had successfully toppled the ancien regime and rule had transferred to the people, led by the Russian intelligentsia with Kerensky at its head. Nonetheless, the period was marked by partisan self-interest and unrealistic expectation from all directions, from the extreme Socialists to the Imperialists: 'They were all dreamers', Ahimeir notes, cynically.[68] The problem, as Ahimeir sees it, is that 'Kerensky-ism' was 'a doctrine and not a deed'. Its adherents – who naively believed in a bright future for Russia, and indeed all of humanity – had made 'aesthetic' and not practical decisions. Indeed, nobody was prepared to die for the ideals of Kerensky-ism, Ahimeir remarks, notably.[69] And this privilege of 'word' over 'action' had, in fact, been the fatal flaw for Kerensky's government:

> The Russian intelligentsia, like every intelligentsia on the threshold of a great revolution (with us it was the Essenes, the first Christians) sought to introduce moral foundation into politics and didn't know that – as today – one should expect failure from such politics.[70]

Lenin's greatness, for Ahimeir, was in his ability to separate politics from ethics. Of course, for the anti-Bolshevik Ahimeir, this ability could represent only an 'objective greatness'. Indeed, Ahimeir believed that the consequences of the October Revolution had merely served, once again, to create a rift between a Russian public that had no say in governmental affairs, and an elite group of rulers that did not take public opinion into account. This short-lived honeymoon period for Russia had ended on 5 April, when Lenin arrived in St Petersburg.[71] And, Ahimeir remarks cynically, with the October Revolution, 'Russia returned to its historical destiny – oppression of all public freedom'.[72]

But, he notes, the Bolshevik government's need to stay in power had, paradoxically – but necessarily – led to a compromise in the ideals of Bolshevism. For Ahimeir, one was not possible without the other:

> Lenin led the Bolsheviks to think that they were ruling Russia – Here is the secret of their success. Ten years of rule show how the goal – the ideal – became the means, and how the means – rule – became the goal.[73]

Delving further into the reasons behind the resilience of Lenin's dictatorship, Ahimeir notes that the peace that had followed in the wake of the Treaty of Brest-Litovsk had not brought about economic improvement in Russia, but rather, had spawned only civil war and increased antisemitism due to the nationalist fervour that it had stoked.[74] And it was precisely after this civil war that Lenin's 'dictatorship was strengthened'.[75] In fact, until Lenin had compromised on his economic principles, there had been only economic decline. As Ahimeir summarises, rather succinctly: Lenin had begun with the realisation of Marx's *The Capital* and *The Communist Manifesto*, and finished with the realisation of Hobbes's *Leviathan*, by means of Machiavelli's *The Prince*.[76] Accordingly, Ahimeir admired Lenin, if only objectively so, due to his ability to remain pragmatic, and place 'deed' over 'doctrine', through 'dictatorship', if necessary. And, as Shindler has noted, Ahimeir prized Lenin's singleness of purpose and ability to coalesce, and spoke of his desire for 'our own 1917' in Zionism, which – like the Bolshevik Revolution, as Ahimeir saw it – would be inspired more by nationalist than by Socialist interests.[77]

Turning, once again, to the political organisation of post-war Europe, Ahimeir notes that Italy's political situation since 1918 was similar to Germany's before 1918: there had been attempted revolution, but in the end, Imperialism had won out. Italy was thus now ideologically situated between revolutionary Leftist Russia and a Germany that had – at least until 1918 – stood somewhat further, to the 'Napoleonic', Imperialist, Right.[78] Then, using the Versailles Treaty as a foundation, Ahimeir divides Europe into two groups: the 'Pro-Versailles Parliamentarians' – comprising England, France and to a lesser degree, Poland – and the 'Anti-Versailles Anti-Parliamentarians' comprising Germany, Austria, Hungary, Romania, Bulgaria and the European nations surrounding the Caspian Sea, and Italy. Ahimeir considers the 'Anti-Versailles' faction 'politically hungry'; indeed, this fact was evidenced in the 'proactive political deeds' that characterised Russian Bolshevism, Austromarxism and – above all – Italian Fascism. Notably, Ahimeir sees the phenomenon of Italian Fascism as indicative of a nation that felt itself unrewarded by the fruits of its victory in the Great War. Furthermore, in spite of Germany's defeat and the conditions incumbent upon it as laid out in the Versailles Treaty, Ahimeir found that the nations most disadvantaged by the treaty were, in fact, Austria and Hungary.

Moreover, Russia's political ambitions in Western Europe had been overcome by England; the events that transpired during the General Strike had been decisive in Soviet Russia's politico-ideological defeat. Thus, Ahimeir sees the current 'resurrection' of Eastern Europe – led by Russia – as very much an anti-British movement.[79] Again, he believes that the conservative nature of the English was the key factor in England's actions: the perceived 'radical' nature of the Miners' Strike had put an end to the idea of the strike as a useful tool for influencing British politics. Ahimeir believes that in Britain, for Socialists and Conservatives alike, the 'strike' had become not only anachronistic, but, in fact, an obstacle for the British worker. British Conservatism was its most popular – and effective – mode of cultural and political self-preservation, and Ahimeir notes a prevailing influence of Fascism in the current form of English Conservatism. This is notable, since it demonstrates, perhaps, an inability for Ahimeir to successfully place Fascism on the political spectrum. For him, in Italy and Russia, Fascism represented extreme political trends: Imperialism and nationalist-Socialism in the former, and Bolshevik and internationalist-Socialism, in the latter. And in England – true to its national character, he notes – Ahimeir sees the Fascist element playing itself out on the societal, but not political, field.

An editorial written for the Jewish new year, Rosh HaShanah 1927, gave Ahimeir the opportunity to take stock of the political development in the world during the past year.[80] And again, as with many of his articles, his reflections also give us a good indication of his own politico-ideological state of affairs. Not surprisingly, many themes from previous articles are once again presented, in an attempt to analyse the political atmosphere of the past year.

Above all, Ahimeir notes the general lack of ideological drive that had characterised European politics in 1927. He notes that every current European politico-ideological dichotomy – whether between absolutism and constitutionalism, monarchism and parliamentarianism, or most important, dictatorship and parliamentarianism – represented the respective trend towards either 'rule from above' or 'rule by the people'. He sees the last of these diametrically opposed concepts – dictatorship and parliamentarianism – as the 'true' enemies of the age, and cites the case of Russia – where parliamentarianism had merely served as a transitional phase between monarchism and dictatorship – in support of his contention. Only the countries that were 'truly' parliamentarian – England and France – had seen parliamentarian ideology strengthen; those that practised what Ahimeir calls an 'imitative' form of parliamentarianism – Spain, Italy, Poland, Hungary, Lithuania, Bulgaria – had, in fact, seen parliamentarianism replaced by dictatorship.

Furthermore, Ahimeir believed that dictatorship occupied a seminal position in the unfolding of recent critical developments within the international Socialist movement, and could be linked directly to the rift between moderate and extreme Socialists: the former had gone in the direction of parliamentarianism, the latter in the direction of dictatorship. Again, he cites England and Russia – and indeed, Germany and Russia – as examples of where this ideological conflict was currently being played out. However, he notes that German parliamentarianism was currently in danger of being defeated by what he calls 'Dictatorial Monarchism'. It is unclear here whether Ahimeir is referring to Hitler – whose ban on public speaking had been lifted that year, and who had led the first of the Nazi Party rallies to take place in Nuremburg, in August – or Hindenburg, who only eight days earlier, on 18 September 1927, had rejected any and all German culpability for the Great War.

Turning now to the Middle- and Far East, but notably, not to British Mandatory Palestine, Ahimeir notes an increasing trend – as evidenced in recent developments in Turkey, Iran, Afghanistan and China – towards the view that Soviet Russia was the 'enemy'. He predicts that – without a doubt – the nations of the 'East' would begin to turn to Britain for aid in the coming years, although Ahimeir is clear that such a development would not necessarily be a positive one. Indeed, Ahimeir remarks on how the 'divide and conquer' method of British Imperialism had only served to further enslave any nation that found itself under British colonial rule, and he cites Egypt as a rather notable example of this phenomenon. Nonetheless – and here he certainly refers to British rule in Palestine, and the Jewish population which it oversaw – Ahimeir believes that a 'people of progress' could potentially threaten this very particular type of British Imperial Rule. In support of his claim, Ahimeir notes that British imperial success in China was due to the 'peaceful nature' of the land, and was completely unlike that of India, where Britain had needed many years to impose its rule. The implication is that in Palestine, Britain had, with the Jews, a similarly peaceful people with which to implement its mandatory obligations. Of course, Ahimeir would prove himself wrong in this respect, in only a few short years, as will be discussed in Chapter 5.

Ahimeir concludes by looking to America, a nation at the 'summit of its economic development', one where both Parliamentarian France and Fascist Italy could vie for its attention and affection. Nonetheless, America was viewed as a dangerous enemy by some, notably Latin American nations such as Mexico and Argentina and, of course, Soviet Russia. While not directly bemoaning America's economic success, Ahimeir does – perhaps not unsurprisingly – lament its increasing cultural dominance. Post-Versailles Germany – a nation that had, until recently, represented the pinnacle of Western cultural achievement – had now taken a backseat to America, with its 'radio, motion picture, and aircraft'. Indeed, as he concludes, cynically: 'America has conquered the world not only with the dollar'.

In spite of the fact that 1927 represented, for Ahimeir, a 'Grey Year' – one that had been characterised by both 'fissures in the West' and 'rebirth of the East' in the years following the Locarno Treaties – he does see some signs of 'awakening' in the West that 'lent great hope for the future'.. And Ahimeir's seemingly innocuous final remark, that this era of 'sunset' – Spenglerian 'decline', perhaps? – had 'revealed its youth' – the Spenglerian Primeval Man? – that was now preparing to 'take to the cultural and public stages in the world', represented a concept upon which he would increasingly focus, throughout the coming year. In point of fact, the three months separating the beginning of the Jewish and secular new year would act as a final fermentation period for Ahimeir, before he sought to more actively address some of the inequalities that, for him, existed in the sociopolitical realm of the Yishuv. His articles in *HaAretz* for the remainder of 1927 reflect this shift in his thinking.

A rather elucidatory article about Catalonia shows us some of the subtleties that had developed in Ahimeir's broader ideological thought.[81] A microcosm of his doctoral dissertation, the article nonetheless goes further in its politico-ideological analysis and conclusions. By first separating Spanish Liberalism from that of the rest of Europe, Ahimeir seeks to show how the spread of what he calls 'acute' Liberalism – in other words, anarchy – was particular to Spain, and therefore differed from the spread of 'moderate' Liberalism – in other words, Socialism – that had occurred throughout the rest of Western Europe. To a large degree, Ahimeir believes that this was a not illogical phenomenon, due to a Spanish proclivity for radicalism in general, and also to the particularistic concept of *Pronunciamiento*.[82] It is worth noting that, similar to his observations in his dissertation, Ahimeir does not use the term 'anarchy' to denote an outright rejection of political organisation, but rather a rejection of centralised political organisation, as was embodied in the concept of the state in general, and – in the case of Catalonia – Madrid, in particular. This is implied not only through context but also by Ahimeir's use of the term 'Federalist Anarchism', and his linking of this type of anarchism directly to Bakunin and his conception of 'Collectivist Anarchism', and Proudhon's 'Anarcho-Syndicalism'. Federalist Anarchism was thus – for Ahimeir – a non-Marxist and less radical form of anarchy, which he believes Spain, and especially Catalonia, had best embodied. And once again, as he concluded in his dissertation vis à vis Russia, Ahimeir concludes that Catalonia's embrace of this more 'generic' – he uses the word 'assimilationist' – movement had led to the downfall of the Catalonian nationalist movement.

Furthermore, Spain – through its recent embrace of Primo di Riviera's (1870–1930) dictatorship – had hammered the final nail into the coffin of Spanish Anarchic-Federalism, and ushered in an era of National Syndicalism. Nonetheless, Ahimeir notes that Riviera's Spain lacked the Imperialist ambitions of Mussolini's Italy, and was thus perhaps more similar to French Bonapartism than Italian Fascism. Moreover, Ahimeir sees the concept of *Pronunciamiento* –

a 'rule of generals' – as more in line with the current military dictatorships in Latin America, and not Europe. Catalonia erred by ignoring its nationalist element in favour of broader, international, political aims, and had thus forfeited its chance for national sovereignty. The Catalan nation had been let down by its liberals and – notably – its intellectuals, a lesson not lost on Ahimeir. He was now more determined than ever to ensure that the Zionist movement in the Yishuv would not suffer such a fate, by casting off its nationalist ambitions in favour of internationalist, 'assimilationist' ideologies.

Undoubtedly, the concept of *Pronunciamiento* must have held some attraction for Ahimeir. Indeed, a cornerstone of Zionist ideology was Leon Pinsker's essay *Autoemancipation*, published in September 1882. In it, Pinsker argued that the concept of civil emancipation for Europe's Jews had now become obsolete, due mainly to fact that they lacked their own territorial polity. He thus believed that the time had come for the Jewish nation to emancipate itself, by founding a land of its own. Eventually, and undeniably, the solution offered by Zionism would come to be the most salient of all the various modi operandi for effecting Pinsker's concept of Jewish national autoemancipation. Zionism itself was – by its very definition – a declaration of intent to effect, if not a coup d'état, then certainly a revolution for European Jewry, its own *Pronunciamiento*. Ahimeir must certainly have recognised the ideological similarity between the two concepts.

Although Ahimeir sees, in the example of Catalonia, what could transpire when nationalist desire was ignored, he nonetheless considers the Spanish incarnation of military dictatorship as too extreme and self-serving. He is clear that the most intellectually and pragmatically satisfactory approach for Zionist ambitions is the style of dictatorship embodied in the Fascism of Mussolini. The movement was led by the Italian intellectual bourgeoisie as much as by its military generals; it did not ignore nationalistic ambition, but neither did it ignore Italy's rich cultural foundations; it eschewed ineffectual Italian Liberal parliamentarianism, while at the same time took into consideration the importance of some form of Syndicalist political organisation. And finally – in what must surely have carried some weight for Ahimeir – Mussolini's Fascism enjoyed strong Jewish representation and influence at every level.[83] Indeed, it is to the more general theme of the Jewish contribution to European politico-ideological development that Ahimeir now turns.[84]

For him, Austromarxism and Bolshevik Russia represented the only current instances where extreme Socialism had conquered moderate Socialism. In every other European country that was ruled by a Socialist government, moderate Socialism – characterised by a commitment to parliamentarianism and democracy and opposition to revolutionary action – had won out. He notes that the Austrian Social Democratic movement was the only movement in the world that embodied 'true' Marxism, but was, in fact, more a movement of intellectuals – 'armchair Socialists'– than workers.[85] Such a phenomenon could, in Ahimeir's estimation, occur only in a metropolis such as Vienna – the city of his student days – and for the following reason: Vienna's recent 'Jewish assimilation explosion' had led to the dual phenomena of increased Catholic antisemitism and the Austromarxism of the Social Democratic Party.

But Austromarxism was itself now split between the more moderate 'Goyim, with Karl Renner at their head' and the 'true', extreme Austromarxism, led by the Jews Otto Bauer and Max Adler. For Ahimeir, the strong Jewish presence in, and influence upon, movements of 'extreme' Socialism – whether Austromarxist or Bolshevik – was due to the fact that both Austria and Russia had allowed the assimilation of Jewish masses into their greater, Gentile societies. The Jews, now assimilated and with no real religion of their own, expressed their 'religious fervour', instead, on the political field; hence, Ahimeir believes, their tendency towards extreme forms of political engagement. Such action, in turn, fuelled antisemitism. It was an unavoidable vicious circle. Thus, Ahimeir not only implies that all Jewish political engagement was tinged with some degree of a 'Secular-Messianic' element but also now – notably – states categorically what he had only alluded to in his doctoral dissertation: if Jewish 'Culture' allowed itself to become overshadowed, influenced and bastardised by a 'larger Culture', the resultant assimilation would spell its cultural and existential downfall,

> because in every movement where the hand of Israel is in the middle, and the voice of Jacob is heard loudly, it is certain that our brethren, the *Bnei Israel*, [will] experience [there] extreme division … the course of Soviet bureaucracy is *Judenrein*, and not by accident.[86]

In point of fact – perhaps predictably so – Ahimeir believes that the only form of 'moderate' Socialism that enjoyed a strong Jewish influence was in the Yishuv. He believes the reason for this phenomenon was because the Jewish intelligentsia in Palestine was experiencing its first taste of a homeland, if not yet one that was its own:

> Only the national feeling, that saved the majority of European countries from turning into movements of religious fanatics, performed the same miracle in relation to the Jewish society in Eretz Israel.[87]

Thus Ahimeir could not be clearer in his contention that nationalism was a substitute for religion in reductio ad absurdum. Nonetheless, as Ahimeir himself noted, Jewish assimilation without a national home had, historically, led only to more extreme political engagement. It was slowly becoming clear to him that the situation of the Jews in the Yishuv vis à vis British rule in Mandate Palestine was – in its present state – really nothing more than Jewish assimilation within a greater Gentile society. The fact that this was occurring in the Jews' historical homeland only added insult to injury. Indeed, Ahimeir predicts that as long as they remained stateless, the Jews in Palestine would – as had occurred with the Jews of Austria and Russia – also need to turn towards more extreme political engagement. Thus, he finally directs his attention towards the need for Jewish autoemancipation; in this case, however, Jewish autoemancipation from British Mandatory rule in Palestine.

The title of Ahimeir's article – he uses Hillel's quote, 'If I Am Not For Myself, Who Will Be For Me?' – is telling.[88] British rule in Palestine was, for him, like 'India in miniature'. Both lands were divided into two parts. The cities and ports – on the more lucrative urban exterior – were managed by the British administration; the primitive interior of each land – with no connection to the wider world – continued to be administered by noble elites. For Ahimeir, the corresponding areas in Eretz Israel were represented by Mandate Palestine, and Transjordan: a 'Jewish' section, rich in 'quality but not quantity'; and an Arab interior, rich in 'quantity but not quality'. The fact that, in the ten years since the Balfour Declaration had been issued, the minimum expectations of the Zionists had not been realised was due to both the conservative style of British rule and the immature nature of the Jewish administration. Ahimeir – notably, still a member of HaPoel HaTzair – believes that only Jabotinsky and the Revisionist movement offered, at present, a viable way out of the current complacent situation, because they demanded 'changes in the political character of British colonisation'. Ahimeir pits Jabotinsky's 'political maximalism' against Samuel's and Weizmann's 'political minimalism': complacent 'vegetarianism' – a term borrowed from Jabotinsky to denote the weakness of the Yishuv Socialists – which Ahimeir sees as no different to the politics of the *Galut*. Furthermore, in spite of the high quality of the Jewish *Menschenmaterial* that was brought to the region – and noting cynically that, in contrast, 'there is no great difference between the Arab settlements in Cairo and Jerusalem' – the Yishuv was, paradoxically, not any closer to its realisation of a national homeland than it had been before Britain had assumed the Mandate.

For the first time, Ahimeir speaks out, in print, directly against the Histadrut, and notes – in the spirit of 'whoever is not for us, is against us' – that the organisation was happy to comply with the British for building the 'winding road from Jaffa to Petah Tikvah [but] not [for] real help in building the land'.

Thus, like the Sinn Fein in Ireland, Ahimeir believes it is now also time for the Zionist movement to adopt the motto, 'If I am not for myself, who will be?' and go the route of other national liberation groups. Indeed, he declares the 'Age of Pioneering' to be over, 'perhaps never to return'. And in its place, Ahimeir calls on the Zionist movement to adopt the ideology of revolution.

Ahimeir's concept of revolution is – as spelled out here – rather idiosyncratic, and was doubtless predicated on the state of affairs that existed at that time between the Zionist movement and the British Mandatory government. It has two parts: first, a requisite 'imperialist moment', one that would, 'unlike in the socialist understanding [of the term]', carry some form of utopian promise – 'a revolution of *Weltanschauung*' – but one that would, ultimately, not be given fulfilment. The ideological dichotomy thus caused – between utopian promise, and Imperialist self-interest – would lead, in turn, to a period of disillusionment that would finally – and necessarily – effect a 'literal' revolution, in the traditional political insurrectionary sense. Ahimeir's theory does not come out of nowhere: it describes exactly the situation that Zionists found themselves with regard to the British at the time that Ahimeir wrote his article. His call for revolution was therefore catalysed by precisely such a period of grave disillusionment with an Imperialist – specifically, a 'British-imperialist' – moment.

Ahimeir warns the Zionist movement that it must escape from the 'vegetarian-utopian mire' in which it was now immersed, otherwise it would be taken over by those with new blood, and who would be willing to perform the deeds necessary to realise what Ahimeir calls 'Egoism of the State'.[89] The Spenglerian overtones are clear, as Ahimeir recognises the requisite shift that was now necessary – indeed, predestined – for the evolution of Zionist ideology and practice. As an ardent Spenglerian, Ahimeir must certainly have seen this shift in evolutionary-deterministic terms:

> From now on we must desist from basing the movement of Zionist Youth on 'Pioneering' in the accepted sense of the word … we need to go to the youth in *Galut* and … we need to give them a systematic Zionist education; Zionism without any conditions, Zionism of not only one generation.[90]

The aforementioned quote appeared in an article that was a reply to criticism that Ahimeir had received in *Davar* for his increasingly extreme rhetoric.[91] It was clear to him that the time had come for a return to Herzlian Political Zionism, now to be spearheaded by a new movement of Zionist youth – the Spenglerian New Barbarian, perhaps? But although the allusion to Jabotinsky's Revisionist Zionist Party is unmistakeable, Ahimeir remained – for the time being – a member of

HaPoel HaTzair. Nonetheless, he could not sustain – neither personally nor professionally – his continued existence in such a state of ideological Purgatory much longer. Indeed, an article written five days later on the subject of South Tyrol saw Ahimeir speak out so strongly in favour of Italian Fascism – '[It is] no wonder [Mussolini] aspires to transfer these Tyrolean Germans in northern Italy to Calabria in the south [*sic*], and to bring from Calabria Italians to settle in Tyrol', he notes – that it was followed by a disclaimer from the editorial board of *HaAretz*.[92]

Thus the period spanning from May 1926 to the end of 1927 brought about realisations and developments in Ahimeir's own politico-ideological thought that allowed him to reach a point of no return – and thereby put him in a sort of metaphorical state of *Agnut* – vis à vis HaPoel HaTzair, and, indeed, the Labour Left in the Jewish Yishuv.[93] He was not alone. Two of Ahimeir's colleagues from the party – poet and journalist Uri Zvi Greenberg and writer and journalist Yehoshua Yevin – had also been experiencing a similar process of disillusionment. The beginning of 1928 would see all three men leave HaPoel HaTzair, and join Ze'ev Jabotinsky's Revisionist Zionist movement.

Fascist, Revisionist, Revolutionary

It had been clear ever since his article on the British coal miners' strike, in May 1926, that Ahimeir's marriage with HaPoel HaTzair was an unhappy one. Nonetheless, he went through the motions, if rather unconvincingly so, and remained in the party for another eighteen months. When Ahimeir finally did part company with his comrades in HaPoel HaTzair, he did so along with the poet Uri Zvi Greenberg and writer and journalist Yehoshua Yevin. The year 1928 would see the trio join Jabotinsky's Revisionist Zionist Party and gradually, from August 1929, affiliate a considerable portion of its members in the Yishuv with what became known as the 'Maximalist' arm of the party, which they led.

Ahimeir had been engaging with the concept of revolution since his dissertation on Spengler, and with Fascism since his article in *HaToren*, as discussed in Chapter 1. During the course of 1928, he would now publicly advocate the embrace of Fascism as a strategy in bringing about a revolution in Zionism. This chapter will examine Ahimeir's first appearance as a representative of the Revisionist Party, at the Conference of the Bloc for Revisionist Labour, in February 1928, and the series of articles that he penned for *Doar HaYom* (The Daily Post), which bore the title 'From the Notebook of a Fascist'. Finally, based on these discussions, I will try to more accurately position the nature of Ahimeir's understanding, advocacy and practice of the ideas of Fascism and revolution than has perhaps been the case previously.

The Unholy Trinity

In spite of the overarching association of Ahimeir with Greenberg and Yevin, it is not immediately clear when the members of the now-infamous trio actually became acquainted with one another. What is clear, however, is that they joined Ze'ev Jabotinsky's Revisionist Zionist Party in one fell swoop, at the Conference of the Bloc for Revisionist Labour, which took place at *moshav* (settlement village) Nahalat Yehuda on 10 and 11 February 1928.[1]

If one takes a step backwards when examining the lives of Yehoshua Heshel Yevin, Uri Zvi Greenberg and Abba Ahimeir, one is struck by an overriding similarity of experience in several areas of their various upbringings. All three hailed from Central-Eastern Europe – Ahimeir and Yevin from within the Pale of Settlement, Greenberg from just outside – received schooling in Hebrew, and gained proficiency in the language at a young age. In addition, they were all forced to experience first-hand the various atrocities that occurred in Central and Eastern Europe between 1914 and 1918, through involvement – active or passive, as the case may be – in either the First World War, the October Revolution, the ensuing pogroms that it spawned or indeed all of these. A final unifying factor was the trio's initial engagement with, and membership in, HaPoel HaTzair.[2]

Yehoshua Heshel Yevin was born in Vinnitsa, Ukraine in 1891. He lost both parents when he was four and a half, and went to live with his maternal grandmother in Mezritch. He eventually attended the Hebrew Gymnasium in Vilna where he received a traditional Jewish education, and was active in the *Yavneh* Hebrew School group, before going on to the University of Moscow to study medicine. Upon graduating he was drafted into the Russian Army; he served as a surgeon throughout the First World War, the trauma and horror of which were later reflected in his literary works. After the war he practised as a physician in Vilna and wrote fiction in his spare time. By 1922, Yevin had dedicated himself completely to writing, and moved to Berlin that same year. He became active in the Marxist-Zionist workers' movement, Poale Zion, published in their journal and earned a living as translator and writer. In 1924 – the same year as Ahimeir – he moved with his family to British Mandate Palestine where he – again, like Ahimeir – wrote for various Labour publications, and taught in the Jezreel Valley, for the cultural committee of the Histadrut.

Uri Zvi Greenberg hailed from Galicia, in the Austro-Hungarian Empire, where he was born in 1896, in the town of Bialikamin. The family, prominent *Hassidim* (a sect of Jewish ultra-orthodoxy), moved to Lviv when he was still young, and it was there that he was educated. His first poems in Hebrew and Yiddish were published while he was still in his late teens. In 1915, Greenberg was conscripted into the Austrian army, and served on the Serbian front before he deserted in 1917, unable to bear the horrors of war any longer. By the time that Poland declared independence from Austro-Hungary, on 11 November 1918, he had returned to Lviv. Greenberg thus experienced first-hand the ensuing pogrom that broke out ten days later, and he was forced to participate in a mock execution with his parents and six sisters. Both traumas were to have a lasting effect upon him, and profoundly influenced both his artistic output and ideological thought. After brief sojourns in Warsaw and Berlin, Greenberg moved to British Mandate Palestine at the end of 1923, where Berl Katznelson hired him as a regular contributor to *Davar*.

The Conference of the Bloc for Revisionist Labour was the turning point for the non-Socialist nationalist worker. The decision to form an organisation that challenged the hegemony and partisanship of the Histadrut set an important precedent in the Yishuv. Furthermore, the conference marked the first occasion where the three future Maximalist Revisionist leaders appeared together.[3] Indeed, the very presence of the trio apparently served to boost the morale of the Revisionist-nationalist Labour movement, and Ahimeir, Greenberg and Yevin were thus instrumental in assisting the creation of an alternative 'nationalist' workers' Bloc within the Histadrut.[4] The conference discussions revolved around the 'abnormal character of the Left [-ist] Histadrut'. It was called upon to act in a 'professional' – in other words, non-partisan – manner and to 'disassociate itself from all of the currently accepted institutions from the Zionist movement'.[5] The crux of the discussion hinged on the question of whether or not it was possible to change the character of the Histadrut or whether it would be better to establish a separate professional body, altogether. The more moderate members of the conference remained faithful to the Internationalist ideal that 'workers were workers', and that the Bloc should operate under the umbrella of the existing Histadrut; others – notably, Ahimeir, Greenberg and Yevin – called for the foundation of a separate Histadrut for non-Socialist nationalist workers.

The conference concluded with a compromise: the foundation of the Revisionist Labour Bloc would occur within the framework of the Histadrut, but the group would enjoy a certain measure of independence in the treatment of work issues. The intention was to free the non-Socialist nationalist worker from his dependence on the bureaucrats who currently 'allocated the working day, and guard[ed] the loaf of bread of the worker'.[6] The Bloc decided to work towards the goal of separating the 'professional organisation' – the Histadrut – from the labour exchanges, and from other areas of activity that did not – indeed, should not – require Histadrut membership.[7]

Ahimeir had previously – in articles in *HaPoel HaTzair* and *HaAretz* – declared the end of the 'Pioneering Era', and in the days preceding the conference, he now expounded upon this claim.[8] In his view, philanthropy had bred corruption; indeed, he believed that the one grave error of Baron Edmond de Rothschild –

who set up the Palestine Jewish Colonisation Association in 1924, and provided the financial backing for many vineries and farming communities in Palestine – had been in investing capital in building up the land as an agricultural endeavour, and not 'The Land' as a nationalist endeavour. If the Histadrut wanted to save itself, it needed – in Ahimeir's opinion – to abandon its path of philanthropic appeal: 'The Return to Zion will not be redeemed in *Tzedakah* (charity)', he declared.[9] Instead of Zionist ideological *halutzim* (pioneers), he believed that Eretz Israel now needed 'Pioneers of Private Capital'. Indeed, the clerk who sat in his office and pushed paper all day was not at all interested in the success of public enterprise in the same way that the merchant was interested in the success of his own private enterprise. And he adds, notably:

> Private capital doesn't fear the organised worker ..., private capital fears the purported *intelligent*. ... Just as the government doesn't need to act as counsel for [the] capital, neither does the *intelligent* need to act as counsel for the worker.[10]

Ahimeir characterised a healthy workers' movement as one that was trade-unionised, but devoid of intelligentsia – as in the Anglo-Saxon world – and thus unlike the unhealthy 'revolutionary' workers' movement in Eastern Europe, one that abounded with bourgeois *intelligenti*. He saw the future for the Zionist movement in Eretz Israel as one that successfully combined a robust workers' movement with healthy private capitalist enterprise. If the ideological similarity to Mussolini's Fascist movement was not obvious through implication, Ahimeir now makes this connection crystal clear. He notes that Fascism had 'placed its arm' on the politics and culture of Italy but hadn't touched the economy; thus for Ahimeir, it was no wonder that Italy now found itself in a situation of economic boom. Ahimeir's revolution was not to be an economic one, but a 'revolution of the spirit', a '"Third Way" that stood, ideologically, between Marxism and capitalism'.[11]

Not only does he reject the economic policies of the Yishuv leadership in favour of what he sees as the more practical Revisionist approach to private capital, but Ahimeir now also makes clear his disdain for the 'enemies' within both the Jewish Diasporic and Yishuv Zionist communities; from the Orthodoxy, to the Liberal Assimilationists, Revolutionary Socialists and Territorialists.[12] The latter group – who were willing to settle in any land where Jewish national sovereignty could be realised – lacked the utopian Messianic element of the Eretz Israel-oriented Zionists. Indeed, Ahimeir intensifies the almost religious fervour of his message, stating manifesto-like:

> Zionism – this is our national component[13]. Zionism – this is the national promise of our people. At the moment when the Jewish nation stood in danger,

at the moment where our national ideals appeared as written by the Prophets, at this self-same time came the beginning of Zionism. ... Zionism is organic. ... Territorialism lacks a past, therefore has no future ... Zionism guards our nation from rabbinic embalmment.[14]

Furthermore, Ahimeir notes that Zionism – and from his context we must assume that he now means Revisionist Zionism, although it is not mentioned by name – would guard the Jewish nation from Marxism, and from becoming the commissary of a destructive mixture of Socialism and Zionism. The concepts of Zionist secular Messianism and civil religion will be discussed in greater detail later. For now, it suffices to point out this very early nod in the direction of secular Messianism, a device that would eventually become a central defining characteristic of the Maximalist arm of the Revisionist Zionist Party.

Ahimeir's final article in *HaAretz* appeared in September, and was – not uninterestingly – a commentary on Hermann Graf Kayserling's book *Spengler der Tatsachenmensch* (*Spengler, the Man of Facts*).[15] He would not contribute to the paper again until he penned a series of four articles in 1955 that focused on his own 'Second *Aliyah*' to Palestine, in 1924.

In August 1928, Ahimeir began writing for what would shortly become the Revisionist mouthpiece, the daily newspaper *Doar HaYom*, which at that time was still a commercial daily under the editorship of Itamar Ben Avi (1882–1943). The son of the linguist and modern Hebrew revivalist Eliezer Ben Yehudah (1858–1922), Ben Avi was the first child in the Yishuv – if not anywhere – to grow up speaking Modern Hebrew as his mother tongue. He began to publish the newspaper in August 1919, almost exactly nine years to the day before Ahimeir's first article appeared on 10 August 1928. It was geared towards the growing generation of children whose parents had been part of the first *Aliyah* but who were born and raised in Palestine, as well as religious Sephardim who had been living there for generations. The paper sought to distance itself from what it saw as the conservative, Euro- and especially Russian-centric stance of the editorial board of *HaAretz*, and although politically unaffiliated until Ze'ev Jabotinsky took over its editorship in December 1928, the paper nonetheless took a right-wing stance, and featured sensationalist headlines and photographs to accompany lead articles. It was sharply critical of the Left-wing institutions in the Yishuv, and the hegemony that they enjoyed.[16] When Jabotinsky became editor, the paper took on a more obviously Revisionist-political stance, and its circulation peaked.[17] Jabotinsky appointed Shlomo Gepstein (1882–1961) as editor, although Gepstein's editorship was eventually taken over in a coup staged by Ahimeir, Yevin and Wolfgang von Weisl, in 1929.

In true form, Ahimeir's first article, *Opozitziah shel Kollelim*, written still as a guest contributor, came with a rather confrontational footnote to the editor, which the paper preserved in publication:

> *Nota bene* if a place is given to such affairs in your newspaper. I do not agree with the general direction of your newspaper. As far as I was aware, our press should indeed be a fighter, but one for blurring the classes. ... And I am a mere political Zionist, and I have nothing literary to express in this regard; [not] my opinion, freely. Therefore, I ask of you: treat me as a guest who passes by ... at our existing newspapers, and do not give me a home, rather a guesthouse.[18]

His request notwithstanding, Ahimeir would indeed take up permanent residence at *Doar HaYom* within six weeks, as one of its most prominent journalists.

One month later, on 7 and 8 September 1928, a second conference of the Bloc for Revisionist Labour took place, in Tel Aviv. This time seventeen delegates from ten branches met and focused on organisational problems, such as the need to expand the Bloc outside of Palestine, and within the framework of *HeHalutz* and Revisionist movements. This is notable not only because it demonstrates some link – if not ideological, then certainly practical – between the pioneer training programme and the ever-growing Revisionist Party but also because it shows that the Bloc aimed to be as equally partisan as the Labour Left in securing the loyalties of future *olim* (immigrants), so that they would file into the Revisionist ranks, immediately upon arrival in the Yishuv. Indeed, there had been a steady increase in the numbers of Betar training graduates outside of Palestine, since it was founded in Riga in 1923, and the Bloc thought it necessary to prepare for, and maximise upon, this increase.[19]

Participants in the conference also noted that the situation in the Histadrut had become more severe since its complete takeover by Ahdut HaAvodah. The already tenuously professional organisation was now the mouthpiece for a single party, as was the newspaper *Davar*. In addition, they noted that the 'nationalist worker' – in other words, the Revisionist worker – continued to be discriminated against in the Histadrut labour exchanges and that ongoing strike action by members of the Left further worsened this situation and caused huge damage to the economy as a result. The motto of the platform of the second conference was 'Compulsory National Arbitration!'[20]

In spite of its frustration with the Histadrut, the question of the Bloc for Revisionist Labour's relationship to the larger union was not discussed. The question was raised as to whether it should leave the Histadrut completely, since such action would overcome the existing complications. In the end, however, it was decided, once again, that the Bloc should remain within the Histadrut, at least for the time being. There was a further, substantial discussion revolving around settlement issues, where dissatisfaction with the ideology of 'work for work's sake' and prioritisation of the group over the individual was fermenting. These non-Socialist nationalist workers appear to have had their fill of Socialist ideology in practice, and there was a general feeling of wanting to escape the *kvutzot* (communal farms). Indeed, one member even suggested the establishment of a settlement framework that focused more on the individual.[21]

Notebook of a Fascist

Later that month, on 21 September – still two months before Jabotinsky's appointment – *Doar HaYom* made clear to its readers – once again, in almost manifesto-like form – that the paper's editorial direction and staff were changing. With the suitably sensationalist headline, '"*Doar HaYom*" On Its Way Forward – The Experiment and Its Success – Participation of New Regular Contributors and Upcoming Publication of Three Enchanting Tales', the paper explained its new role and direction it would take, in what it saw as the 'Journalistic Revolution' currently occurring in the Yishuv.[22] The paper's circulation had increased significantly, due – in the opinion of the editor – to the fact that the paper's readership had discerned the improvements that it introduced in recent weeks, specifically the 'procurement of excellent and desired writers, living, energetic to work'. Not that the daily was to become a 'decent newspaper' – 'God forbid!' Rather, it intended to cover all issues that presently faced the Yishuv, 'from among the Hebrews and from among our neighbours, the Arabs'. It is interesting to note that the paper neither hints at what particular issues might be current with the neighbouring Arab population, nor does it mention the British government that oversaw both communities.

The paper listed Abba Ahimeir as a new regular contributor, now no longer a 'guest who passes by'. Chosen because of 'his former membership in the leftist camp ... [He] knew well [how] to expose our readers to the hidden arteries [that ran] between the nationalists and the socialists'. Thus we should note that, however unsatisfactory the terms 'left' and 'right' might be for any discussion of Yishuv political organisation – and indeed Ahimeir's own nationalism and Fascism, as will be discussed later – they were nonetheless used to differentiate Yishuv Socialism from Yishuv nationalism. And it should be further noted that although the article documents Ahimeir's departure from the 'leftist camp', the term 'right' does not appear; neither in relation to Ahimeir's present political affiliation, nor to the Yishuv 'nationalists' in general.[23] That these observations should neither serve in any way to mitigate the consciously bellicose, revolutionary sentiment that the paper's editorial board now expressed by taking this decidedly nationalist route is perhaps best summed up in this sentence from the same lead article: '[Already] On the first day an explosive article has been printed in relation to the revolution [occurring] in our Hebrew papers, by one of the most well-known teachers in our land'.[24]

The 'well-known teacher' was none other than Abba Ahimeir, and the 'explosive article' appeared under the rubric 'For the Ears of the Nation [People]', and was entitled, 'In the Matter of Jabotinsky's Visa'.[25] More important still was the fact that this was the first in a series of nine articles published over the following two months that bore the subheading 'From the Notebook of a Fascist'. These appeared variously under the regular *Doar HaYom* columns 'For the Ears of the Nation' and 'To the Questions of the Moment'. In spite of the series title, in general, and the article 'On the Arrival of our Duce', in particular, there is not much that renders the articles themselves particularly 'Fascist'.[26] More accurately, taken as a whole, they depict a sort of revolutionary manifesto, and lash out in every direction at the key personalities and issues that Ahimeir considers to be representative of the 'vegetarianism' that was currently running rampant in the Yishuv Zionist organisation and leadership.[27] In this respect, the articles are comprehensive. Although not yet the real-life agent provocateur that he would become, Ahimeir certainly saw the journalistic utility in the provocation that the series title effected.[28] It is clear from the articles' content and context that Ahimeir now openly embraced some degree of Fascist ideology and practice, although the latter would manifest itself only gradually, over the next three years. They cover issues as varied as Jabotinsky's return to live in Palestine and the issues surrounding it, incidents at the Western Wall on Yom Kippur and the subsequent reactions they caused, the ineffectiveness of the current Tel Aviv Municipality, the Yishuv leadership's opposition to Betar, events on the eve of Simhat Torah and so on. And again and again Ahimeir bemoans the 'vegetarianism' – the complacency and weakness – that had manifested itself in all areas of the Yishuv and its leadership.

In the first paragraph of the first article, we see already the marked change – the no holds barred, almost purely visceral approach – in what would be Ahimeir's new literary tenor:

> One would think that the government of Eretz Israel is not so completely imbecilic as to try to prevent Jabotinsky from entering the country. One would

think that the government of this land is not completely imbecilic – even though there are several Jews among its top officials, those who see everything through rose-coloured glasses[29] ... those who 'cover their lewdness' with the fig leaf of Ahad HaAm-ism.[30]

Ahimeir makes frequent use of colloquialisms – in addition to 'vegetarianism', mentioned before, he uses the more informal *Mopsim* and *Patzim* to denote the pro-Communist Hebrew Worker's Party and *HaPoel HaTzair*, respectively; *Haverim* in its Yiddish spelling (כאוורים) as a more derogatory reference to all Communist-leaning Zionists; *Gentlemeniut* (Gentlemanliness) as a pejorative description of the British pretence of polite efficiency in government of the Mandate, and those Yishuv personalities and organs that paid lip service to it; and 'nationalist youth' – in Ahimeir's usage this incorporated more than just Betar, although certainly that group, as well – as the Political Zionist corollary to Socialist and Labour youth groups. To some degree, such language undoubtedly also reflected the editorial stance and tabloid style of the paper, which now gave Ahimeir's biting sarcasm and pointed cynicism full rein.

Jabotinsky had accepted a job as vice president of the Judea Insurance Company and was set to return to Mandate Palestine in October; however, there was opposition to his visa application due to his previous political agitation during the 1921 Jaffa Riots.[31] At the time, he was convicted of possession of firearms, and although the fifteen-year prison sentence that accompanied the conviction was subsequently overturned by Herbert Samuel, Jabotinsky left Palestine for the United States in November 1921, and resettled in Europe in 1922. The Mandatory government sought for the Judea Insurance Company to guarantee that Jabotinsky 'would not engage in political activity in Palestine', something they refused to do.[32] Nonetheless, on 21 September 1928, the day of the first of the 'Notebook of a Fascist' articles, Jabotinsky's entry to Palestine was granted.[33] And in spite of the concern surrounding his visa, Jabotinsky stated that his agreement with the Judea Insurance Company assured him 'absolute freedom for his journalistic, literary and public activities'.[34]

Speaking as their spokesman, Ahimeir makes clear the 'us versus them' polarisation that existed between the 'pure', Herzlian, Political Zionism of Jabotinsky's Revisionists and both the British and the Yishuv status quo. Addressing the former, he admonishes the British for even attempting to delay Jabotinsky's visa; indeed, the process was: 'In and of itself, enough for us ... Please remember this ... Not always will they pass judgement on us ... the day will come when also we will pass judgement ...'[35] He further criticises the Yishuv leadership, which governed 'in the style of the British', and was thus no better, only perhaps more caricaturistic. He pits the *Gentlemeniut* of 'M.G.' (Moshe Gluckson, 1878–1939) of *HaAretz* ('the respectable newspaper') against 'M.B.' (Moshe Beilinson, 1889–1936) of *Davar* ('the newspaper of *Kolel Ungarin*'), who 'doesn't speak as Muscovite *Haver*, not even as a Viennese *Haver*, but in the manner of a Brusselian [*Haver*]'. Both were products of Eastern Europe and embodied the same 'vegetarian *Gentlemeniut*' of the Bolsheviks. The impression Ahimeir gives of the Yishuv infrastructure is that of a group of self-important 'big fish', from Eastern Europe, who tried to hide their provincialism and lend credibility to themselves by coating their Bolshevik rhetoric in the more appealing tones of Western European Socialists.

Taking advantage of the discussion surrounding Jabotinsky's visa, Ahimeir directly addresses the overall subject of deportation from Mandate Palestine:

> To those of us with the viewpoint of a 'State no matter what' … we need to declare again and again: We are not for free entrance to the land and we are not against expulsion from the land … we are not for free entrance of Jews to the land, but only for free entrance of Zionists. Only Zionists are necessary to us here. … [And] [w]e are not against the expulsion of *Mopsim* from the land.[36]

This is the first instance where Ahimeir calls for direct action against what he considers to be negative elements within Yishuv Zionism itself, and his language is suitably militaristic:

> We must demand with full force that each and every *Mops*, that doesn't [already] need to be removed by legal procedure, is removed from the land … the war on each and every [one or another] *Mops* does not suffice: we must fight *Mopsim and Mopsiut.*[37]

As if to reiterate his allegiance to the Monism of Jabotinsky's Revisionists, Ahimeir states clearly that Brusselian 'human rights and socialism' may well come about in 'another hundred years', once statehood had been achieved. Until then, however, 'We don't have such a luxury. In the moment that the city finds itself under siege, there is room only for the laws of "Siege Mentality."'[38]

In an article which appeared two weeks later, on 8 October 1928, Ahimeir uses a story about the Jews of Caesarea from Josephus's *Jewish Wars* as an analogy for the present attempt of the Zionist Organisation to purchase the Western Wall. In Josephus's tale, the Jews of Caesarea attempted to negotiate the purchase of their synagogue from its Caesarean-Greek owner, and even offered a much-inflated price. Not only were their attempts rejected, but the Greek owner constructed new buildings in the courtyard of the synagogue, leaving only a narrow path that could be passed through only with great difficulty.[39] Indeed, 1,000 years later, the situation was, in effect, the same. Only now, Ahimeir, ever the Spenglerian, sees the Arabs – the '*Bnei* Ishmael' – in place of the Greeks, and the British – the *Bnei Edom* – in place of the Roman government.[40] The 'narrow path' was not an empty comparison: the area around the Western Wall had become so built up over time that only a narrow path remained for anyone who wanted to pray there. As discussed in the previous chapter, Ahimeir had made it clear in earlier articles that he considered Palestine's Arab population to be less evolved than its Jewish population, and perhaps even suggest that they were 'wild savages' that needed taming.[41] Of course, this was not a view that was unique to Ahimeir. It represented the general consensus not only among members of the Yishuv but also the British administration in Palestine, and indeed most colonialist enterprises. However, in the article, Ahimeir now goes one step further, and declares also the Arab, alongside the British, as the enemy of the Zionists.

The catalyst for both renewed Jewish efforts for purchasing the Western Wall, and Ahimeir's article, was an incident that occurred on the morning of Yom Kippur – the Jewish Day of Atonement – 25 September 1928. A *mehitza* – a wooden screen traditionally used to divide male and female worshippers in synagogue – had been erected in front of the Western Wall in the afternoon before the beginning of the holiday. This prompted the *Mutawalli* of the Abu Madian Waqf, which held authority over the area of the Western Wall, to apply to the British deputy district commissioner for its removal.[42] The deputy district commissioner arrived on the evening of Yom Kippur and gave notice to those praying that the *mehitza* would have to be removed by the following morning. He was told that, since the holiday had already begun, it would be impossible to remove the screen until after the end of Yom Kippur. At 9:00 am the next morning, the British police inspector on duty – D. V. Duff – arrived with British and Arab constables (there were no Jewish police present owing to the holiday) and once again demanded the screen's removal. When they received no reply from those praying (since they were in the middle of the *Amidah*, the silent prayer that forbids talking until its completion), the officers set about to remove the *mehitza* by force. The scuffle that ensued resulted in the injury of several worshippers, including an American woman, and was considered a desecration of the holy day.

The Yishuv was united in its protest at what it saw as an unnecessary provocation and deep insult. *Davar* noted that a *mehitza* had been set up at the Western Wall on Jewish holidays for 'six or seven years before' the British began their rule.[43] Of course, in the days following the incident, both the Arab and Jewish populations – in what was now an ongoing battle for supremacy of narrative – would argue to the British that the actions of the other had upset the status quo. *Doar HaYom* ran the headline, in huge font, 'The Scandal of the Western Wall: An Empty Yom Kippur in Jerusalem at the Hands of the Police', and detailed – among other things – the 'pandemonium' that occurred, the protest to the British by Judah Magnes and Yitzhak Ben Zvi, and the 'indifference of the Governor in his replies to our [*Doar HaYom's*] investigations'.[44] Indeed, the Yishuv papers spoke – for once – almost as one voice. Moshe Beilinson of *Davar* noted the lively interference of the 'nationalist and activist institutions', who were quick to protest, commenting – perhaps rather surprisingly – 'And good they did'.[45] Notably, while the incident was front-page news for both *Davar* and *Doar HaYom* for days, the English *Palestine Bulletin*, for the most part, confined stories of the affair to its third page, under the regular rubric, 'Palestine from Day to Day'.

On 26 September, a formal complaint was lodged with the officer administering the government by representatives of the Zionist executive, the Jewish National Council, and Chief Rabbis Kook and Meir, and the Yishuv held public protest meetings – which also resulted in the cessation of all Jewish labour – from 5 pm the following day. That day, *Doar HaYom* declared the 'War of the Hebrew Nation in Eretz Israel for its [Western] Wall: [A war] not of sword nor fire, but by the strength of the will of two hundred thousand citizens in our national home, and twenty million Jews worldwide'.[46] In the days following, a further protest from the Grand Mufti of Jerusalem succeeded in obtaining the removal of the ark containing Torah scrolls situated at the Western Wall, an act that caused further outrage in the Yishuv. The General Jewish Labour Federation, in fury, insisted that the Western Wall be 'handed over to the Jewish People'.[47]

Ahimeir's article, one week later, criticises not only the British and Arabs but, pointedly, also the efforts that were currently being made by Jewish groups to purchase the Wall. Turning first to the British, he accuses them of seeing the Jews as barbarians, just as the Roman rulers in the past had done. But, he reminds them that even then, the '*Bnei Israel* were not conquered, honoured gentlemen!'[48] He points out that, in fact, the Jews were closer in culture to 'Britannia or Rome' and should not be treated as 'wild savages living on the river banks', like the 'Hindus'. In spite of his choice of metaphor, Ahimeir's implication of the Arabs here is clear. Furthermore, he reminds the British that 'His Majesty's Government' was in Palestine not only because of the 'strength of the sword' but also by approval of the 'united world, with the Zionist Organisation at its head'. This latter comment is a distortion – whether deliberate or not – of the truth: while the Mandate for

Palestine had been issued to Britain by the newly formed League of Nations in 1923, the League hardly had the Zionist Organisation 'at its head'. Ahimeir also seems to believe that the Zionist Organisation did exercise disproportionate influence over the British Mandatory government, which unfortunately resulted in the fact that government all too often 'serv[ed] the opinion of the Jewish *Kahal* (public)'. Indeed, the negative influence of the latter group could be seen in the recent affairs surrounding not only the Western Wall but also – pointedly – Jabotinsky's visa.[49] For Ahimeir, the idea of monetary purchase of the Wall stank of the Jews of the *galut*, where 'everything can be bought with gold'. He warns that 'lobbying and *Gentlemeniut* are not only not helpful, but harmful', and that the Wall should be acquired, rather, by political strength. And if this is not possible, 'if the Jews of the Galut continue to be more concerned with business, and don't see this insult to the Jewish [nation] [also] as their insult', Ahimeir thinks it then better that the Western Wall remain in its current situation, so that there will be an occasion, on every Yom Kippur, for the Goyim to abuse the Jews.

If the first two 'Notebook of a Fascist' articles had a polarising millenarian urgency about them, the third, 'In Relation to the Coming of our *Duce*', introduced a Messianic dimension to Ahimeir's narrative.[50] Indeed, Jabotinsky, who arrived in Tel Aviv on the morning of 5 October, is treated by Ahimeir as a prophet, 'who lives and walks among us … See how the king is greeted: "Blessed is he who shared his honour [with] flesh and blood."'[51] And Ahimeir calls for the need for the Jews of the Yishuv to adopt blind faith in Jabotinsky, in spite of the fact that 'we, the Jews, full of the negativity of the Galut will laugh at this blind faith'. He declares that now was the time for the Jewish nation to stop idolising the 'Psalmists of Israel', and begin idolising the idea of statehood. Just as Herzl had created Political Zionism, Jabotinsky was now fulfilling it. For the moment, Ahimeir notes, Jabotinsky's followers were in the minority, and it was up to him to organise the 'handful of people who are ready to step to his command, to create the "National Guard"'. The Betar youth in Mandate Palestine would fulfil this role, and 'guard their Duce with all vigilance', 'for' – he warns, and clearly Ahimeir refers as much to the Yishuv leadership as to the British and Arabs – 'enemies of the state are in our midst'.

In his choice of language and analogy, Ahimeir links Jabotinsky to the biblical prophets, the proud Jewish nationalists that were so unlike the 'men of the book' that were worshipped during the period of exile. Ahimeir makes the Messianic overtones in his article clear, not only by linking Jabotinsky to the proud Jewish national sovereign past but also in the awe that he holds for Jabotinsky himself as a redemptive figure. This was not the first time that a Zionist leader had been written about in such rapturous tones: Herzl had often prompted such a reaction. Moreover, the very idea of Zionism itself – as a nationalist movement that foresaw the return of the Jewish nation to its ancestral homeland – can be viewed in Messianic terms. Nonetheless, it was with Ahimeir, Greenberg and Yevin where secular or quasi-Messianism and the use of Messianic metaphor would become an ideological and motivating tool. This will be discussed in more detail subsequently.[52] For the moment it suffices to note that I use the terms 'secular Messianism' and 'quasi-Messianism' interchangeably, and understand their meaning as per Gideon Shimoni's definition of 'quasi-Messianism', as 'Messianic rhetoric not predicated on traditionalist or orthodox understanding of the messianic belief' [that does not, however] deny its mythic potency also for nonorthodox or secular Jews'.[53]

Ahimeir is able to link the phenomenon of quasi-Messianic fervour to his developing idea of the need for a revolutionary war. The result thus produced from the synthesis of these two concepts – the permissibility, if not the necessity, for self-sacrifice, if carried out in the service of the Jewish Nation – was further underscored for him by events that occurred on the evening of Simhat Torah.

On the evening of 5 October 1928, the same day that Jabotinsky arrived in Tel Aviv, members of the militant pro-Hebrew language group *Gedud Meginei HaSafa* (Battalion for the Defence of the Language) attacked members of the pro-Bolshevik, Communist, Left Poale Zion Club on Allenby Street in Tel Aviv. In the ensuing fracas, several people were injured.[54] Ahimeir declared his support for the *Gedud* in a telegram that *Doar HaYom*, on 12 October, reprinted as its main headline:

> It is good to Die For the Sake of Our Country!
> A handful of the nationalist youth that inflicted punishment on the messengers of Moscow,
> I extend to you my blessings! I am with you!
> War for us with [all] the forces of destruction until their fall! They declared the war!
> Do not fear! Well done!
> [We] will [stand] up to the vegetarians!
> Blessings of Tel–Hai!
> Yours, etc.
> Abba Ahimeir[55]

The opening line referred to Joseph Trumpeldor's purported final words after he was mortally wounded by an Arab militiaman during the battle of Tel-Hai, in March 1920. As previously noted, both the Zionist Left and Right claimed Trumpeldor as a hero; however, only the 'nationalist youth' and more specifically the Revisionist youth group Betar appropriated for themselves the greeting 'Tel–Hai!'

In the days following the attack, Ahimeir reports that the *Haverim* of the Poale Zion sent a blood-stained shirt and several rocks to the Jewish Scientific Institute (YIVO) in Vilna in order to commemorate the 'war for Yiddish in *Eretz Israel*'. According to Ahimeir, the rocks were the ones that had been used to stone the 'nationalist youth'. Apparently the members of the Left Poale Zion Club had tried to defend themselves by throwing stones and rocks at their attackers, who were members of the 'nationalist youth'. For Ahimeir this is the issue here, and not the blood-stained shirt, which presumably had belonged to one of the injured Poale Zionists. The very fact that the articles – representing for him the battle for Hebrew over Yiddish, Zion over Galut – were sent to YIVO in Vilna, the epitome of the Jewish Galut, must have been an anathema to Ahimeir. But the two places were similar in one frustrating aspect: Ahimeir bemoans the fact that in the Yishuv – like in the Galut – there were still so few who prepared to die a hero's death, instead of going like lambs to the slaughter.[56]

Ahimeir exposes the hypocrisy of the journalists 'M.G'. (Gluckson of *HaAretz*) and 'M.B'. (Beilinson of *Davar*), who were quick to condemn the event, but who – apparently in line with the long-standing tradition of the Socialist hard Left – had looked away when Communists previously attacked 'Trumpeldorists' (Betar members) in Warsaw, or when what he calls the 'Lost Youth' beat *Trumpeldorim* in Jerusalem. 'Lost Youth' (הנוער האובד) was a pointed pun on 'Labour Youth' (הנוער העובד, more literally 'The Youth That Works'), and Ahimeir makes clear his intention when he writes, 'I know the difference between *aleph* and *ayin*' (the two letters that needed to be exchanged to effect the pun). Indeed – speaking in the name of the nationalist youth – Ahimeir now declares, 'we will fight against Red Judaism until its downfall'. The nationalist youth – 'ready for battle' – have no plans to fight a war 'of recreation':

> No, Rabbotai, this war is a war. … And our Messiah will not come in the form of a poor [man] and riding on a donkey. The Messiah will come, as [do] all Messiahs, riding on top of a tank and bearing his tiding[s] to the people.[57]

If any doubts remained that this was no mere war of words, but one of deeds, propelled by a Messianic urgency that mandated self-sacrifice in the revolutionary cause, these were now dispelled. The revolution that Ahimeir saw as necessary – already while still a member of HaPoel HaTzair – was beginning to take shape. In his articles for the party's journal he had made clear his belief in the overarching importance of the youth of the nation as the vanguard for revolutionary change. He now names them; no longer merely the 'nationalist youth', or 'Trumpeldorists', but rather 'Betar', the Revisionist Party youth group.

Jabotinsky formed Betar on a visit to Riga in November 1923, the same month that he published his essay 'On the Iron Wall'. The essay bore the perceptive realisation that the Arabs would never recognise Jewish sovereignty in any part of Palestine and would, therefore, never be willing to negotiate towards it. He called for the need for a Jewish military – an 'Iron Wall' – an independent strength that would protect Jewish interests in the land, and force the Arabs into accepting a Jewish state in Palestine. In the article, Jabotinsky talks of the difference between 'our militarists' and 'our vegetarians', presaging Ahimeir's use of the latter term, which, we may be certain, was used in emulation of the Revisionist leader.[58] Betar was an acronym for 'Brit Yosef Trumpeldor' (The Covenant of Yosef Trumpeldor), although the group went one step further and substituted the Hebrew letter *tav* (ת) for the letter *tet* (ט), which gave it a mythical connection to the fortress of Betar (i.e. 'בית"ר' and not 'ביט"ר').[59] The fortress was the site of the last stand between Jews and Romans in the unsuccessful Bar Kochba revolt, and was destroyed by the Emperor Hadrian's forces in 135 CE. The group thus looked both backwards to a proud cultural, martial, past and forwards to a proud national, martial future.[60] Interestingly, the 'Notebook of a Fascist' articles show that Ahimeir spelled the group's name with a *tet* (ט) at this time, although this was corrected in posthumous publication of articles from this period.[61]

Ahimeir notes the increased opposition to both the 'nationalist youth' and Betar, which he ascribes to the lack of not only common ideology but also common language. Not only did *HaPoel HaTzair* and other groups on the Left continue to use Yiddish alongside Hebrew, but those 'haters of Zion and boycotters of Hebrew' who complained about the 'new Judaism of Brit Trumpeldor' – and here he names a certain Mr Eschel – were the same people who advocated the translation of the 'International' and Bolshevik anthems into Hebrew, anthems that the Labour Youth had used to try and drown out Betar's singing of *HaTikvah* when Jabotinsky arrived in Palestine. Although Ahimeir makes no connection in print, it seems likely that this was the catalyst for the *Gedud Meginei HaSafa* attacks later the same evening. He does, however, connect the 'Judaism of Betar' with the heroes Samson, Job and King David: the 'Judaism of Israel the Fighter … and not with the Psalmist of Israel'.[62]

Ahimeir further differentiates between his – and by implication, the Revisionist and Betar – *Weltanschauung*, and the 'Vegetarian *Weltanschauung*' that was currently prevalent in the Yishuv, and which was best expressed in the views of *HaAretz* editor Moshe Gluckson, in particular.[63] The 'vegetarians' – as Socialists – were unable to differentiate between the individual and the collective, and subsequently, unable to recognise that the latter possessed ethics and laws that differed from the former. Rather pointedly, in support of this, Ahimeir cites the permissibility – by implication, both moral and legal – to kill in the service of the collective, whereas such would be prohibited when motivated by mere personal need and interest. Ahimeir does not drop this apparent bombshell without precedent. We should remember his article on Savinkov, written in *HaPoel HaTzair*, which demonstrates that Ahimeir had been pondering the idea of the permissibility to kill at least since June 1925. And, as will be discussed, he had already, in 1926, penned – although not published – *Megillat HaSikrikin* (Scroll of the Sicarii), whose central argument revolved around this very dilemma. Indeed, the 'secret of Israel's eternity' was that it had continued to live among healthy young European nations that enjoyed a strong, masculine, political life; nations that had 'spilled blood', unlike the 'emasculated' Yishuv, which had lost 'almost what was left of its masculinity'. As Ahimeir argues, 'Every revolution requires sacrifices, [both] human and 'glass'. Blood is the oil on the wheels of revolution'.[64]

Ahimeir blames the 'vegetarianism' of people like *Davar*'s Beilinson for making it impossible for them to see that, even in a relatively peaceful revolution – like the Czech 'revolution' of 1918 that led to international recognition of the Czechoslovak National Council, and which, according to Beilinson, had been 'bloodless' – blood had most certainly been spilled, by both the leaders of the revolution and the Czech youth, even if only as an indirect result of the revolution.[65] Again: there could be no revolution without bloodshed.

Furthermore, Gluckson, Beilinson and their ilk – vanguards of the Galut, and the Russian, indeed Soviet, intelligentsia – demanded more rights for the individual, whereas, by contrast, Ahimeir demands further curtailment of the rights of the individual. The Fascist ideological overtones are obvious here, and it is clear from this context that Ahimeir's concept of 'Monism' certainly goes beyond Jabotinsky's. Ahimeir sees the most extreme form of expression of Monism in Fascism, a view that – while perhaps extreme – is certainly not illogical.[66] Moreover, he recognises that Socialism had not proved to be as successful as its proponents made it out to be: the British, American and Italian trade unions had 'nothing to do with socialism'; the professional guilds in Germany had a large Catholic membership, and those in Italy were Fascist. What did that say about the ideology of the international worker? Indeed,

Ahimeir notes that the Socialist intelligentsia was now only finding success by compromising its ideological core.[67] The Italian revolutionary Syndicalist leader Agostino Lanzillo had outlined the reasons for this ideological compromise in his 1919 book *The Dissatisfaction of Socialism*:

> The passivity that has destroyed the edifice of the socialist struggle has been due to:
>
> 1. The existence and development of socialist parties.
> 2. Social legislation.
> 3. The absence, in the proletariat, of an idealistic and voluntaristic conception of its own power.[68]

For Ahimeir, the reason was simpler still: the 'worker lives his daily life [while] the intelligentsia hallucinates about the days of the Messiah of Marx's teaching'.[69]

He thought that the best example of this in the Yishuv was in the Tel Aviv Municipality, where an 'active' minority of intellectuals had taken over the 'passive' majority.[70] Just as bad were the bourgeois property owners who believed they should control Tel Aviv because they had invested money in the city. 'Neither one nor the other [should run Tel Aviv Municipality]', says Ahimeir; 'better if the property-less [person] think[s] less of the fate of the entire city, but [rather] on the fact that he is property-less … and better that the property owner thinks about how to increase [his] assets'.

One month later, on 18 December 1928, the municipal election took place in Tel Aviv, and saw the workers' committee of the Left Histadrut move closer towards becoming a political organisation. The Histadrut appeared as its own list, in collusion with its two main parties. Of the eleven candidates for city council, seven were from Ahdut HaAvodah, four from HaPoel HaTzair. The Revisionists stood at the head of the movement that aimed to 'liberate the Yishuv from socialist hegemony and build up *Eretz Israel* on the foundations of birth right, instead', in a battle that was as much one of epoch – the *olim* of the second and third Aliyot versus those of the fourth *Aliyah* – as of ideology.[71] The latter group, which included the Bloc for Revisionist Labour, published a pamphlet that called out the hypocritical nature of the Histadrut and Labour Left:

> These men, in the name of their party-war, failed, and systematically continue to fail the vital interests of the Hebrew worker. After all, they [were the ones] that turned the Union of Workers [i.e. the Histadrut] into a castle [ivory tower] of clericalism and bureaucracy. [A]fter all, the responsibility for the criminal acts that were carried out [by way of] financial 'aid' and advances to *Solel Boneh* rests on them, after all, *they* [work] against the interests of the Hebrew worker, against

his will, without allowing the possibility to organise neutral labour exchanges. And the people that introduced ethical and public demoralisation into the ranks of the Histadrut have the *chutzpah* to call the Revisionists 'Haters of [the] Worker' [Enemies of the Worker].[72]

Finally, the Bloc appealed to the public to assist in their call for the establishment of neutral labour exchanges, which would be non-partisan and would perform its services free of charge, for any work requirement. Nonetheless, it appears that by this time Ahimeir was also dissatisfied with the Revisionist Labour Bloc: with regard to the Tel Aviv municipal election, he advocates neither the 'Gush' nor the 'Faction' (comprising the Histadrut, Ahdut HaAvodah, HaPoel HaTzair, see the following section), remarking that 'both together, stink'.[73]

Fascist Revisionist, Revisionist Fascist, or neither?

Colin Shindler maintains that, although Ahimeir joined the Revisionist Party, 'he was clearly no Revisionist'.[74] Not only did Jabotinsky – rather notoriously – consider him 'talented but too much a fascist', but Ahimeir and the Maximalists were opposed by the majority of the delegates at the Fifth World Revisionist Conference in Vienna, in 1932. Indeed, in his speech at the conference Ahimeir had sought to make an ideological distinction between Jabotinsky's Revisionism and the neo-Revisionism of the Maximalists.[75] Nonetheless, in spite of their ideological differences, Ahimeir was actively involved in the party – not least in training *madrikhim* (leaders, guides or counsellors) at the Betar training school – and the attention and praise he received from Jabotinsky at other times indicate that Jabotinsky, ever the politician, sought to balance the various ideological streams that existed in the party. Jabotinsky likened it to an orchestra which was made up of various timbres, and we might say that Ahimeir's, Greenberg's and Yevin's Maximalists embodied simply the most highly pitched group, to continue with Jabotinsky's metaphor.[76] In a similar vein – and equally as important – I contend that we should also question the validity of Ahimeir's Fascism. What was its true nature? Does it compare to current scholarly definitions of Fascism? And does this in fact matter, since, in any case, Ahimeir called himself a Fascist? Furthermore – and perhaps most important – did Ahimeir conceive of the implantation of Fascist ideology in the Yishuv, or did he use the term flippantly, in the service of mere journalistic bravado?

Perhaps the greatest obstacle to understanding and assessing the degree and validity of Ahimeir's own Fascism is the lack of scholarly consensus on a definition of the politico-ideological concept itself. Even if we narrow our parameters to Mussolini's Fascism of the mid-1920s to early 1930s, on which Ahimeir's understanding of the term is certainly predicated, we are still confronted with vast ideological disparity. The political scientist and historian of Fascism, Robert Paxton, has identified nine 'mobilising passions', which he believes 'underlie fascist actions':

1. A sense of overwhelming crisis, beyond the reach of any traditional solutions;
2. The primacy of the group, towards which one has duties superior to every right;
3. The belief that one's group is a victim; a sentiment that justifies any action;
4. Dread of the group's decline under the corrosive effect of individualistic liberalism, class conflict, and alien influences;
5. The need for closer integration of a purer community ... by exclusionary violence, if necessary;
6. The need for authority by natural chiefs (always male), culminating in a national chieftain who alone is capable of incarnating the group's historical destiny;
7. The superiority of the leader's instincts over abstract and universal reason;
8. The beauty of violence and the efficacy of will, when they are devoted to the group's success;
9. The right of the chosen people to dominate others without restraint from any kind of human or divine law.[77]

But certainly most of Paxton's 'mobilising passions' – perhaps all of them, if we understand 'group' as a social class and not national(ist) ethnicity, and 'liberalism' more in an economic-capitalistic sense – can be convincingly applied to many streams of Marxist ideology, especially Leninist-Marxism. Indeed, for the Marxist philosopher Walter Benjamin, the main difference between the two movements, if only by implication, was that 'Fascism seeks to give [the newly created proletarian masses] an expression while preserving property'.[78] But, we should remember that less radical Socialism and most streams of Liberalism also sought to redistribute wealth and change existing property structures, and that non-Fascist Conservatism also now gave the voice of the new proletarian masses 'an expression' – if only in the form of a vote, in the wake of universal suffrage – without giving any further consideration to the reform of existing property relations.[79] Thus, terms such as 'Left' and 'Right', in their traditional, post–French Revolutionary understanding, are less clear-cut than we perhaps understand them to be, and as such are certainly problematic. I believe that it is more useful, from an analytical perspective, to understand such trends functionally, and suggest therefore that we speak rather of 'totalitarian', 'radical' or 'extreme' versus 'democratic' or 'moderate' politico-ideological streams. And even here, the use of a structural approach when comparing various European political ideologies in the interwar period can be frustrating and misleading.

Of somewhat more utility – especially since this study attempts to understand both the historical development and ideological reasoning behind Ahimeir's embrace of Fascism – is the attempt to consider the phenomenon of Fascism from a philosophical position. The work of the Frankfurt School, especially that of its most prominent members, Theodor Adorno, Max Horkheimer and Walter Benjamin, is noteworthy in this respect, less for its neo-Marxist reading – although this is not uninteresting, in consideration of Ze'ev Sternhell's conclusions (see the following discussion) – but rather because its major contributions to the body of scholarship in this respect were made during, and immediately following, the period of what was arguably – in the form of Nazism – fascism's most extreme and calamitous incarnation, by intellectuals directly affected by its ideology, and who wrote from exile.[80]

Philosophers of the Frankfurt School saw the emergence of Fascism as a product of the crisis that – in the wake of the Enlightenment – threatened the concept of rational thought. Already from the time of the Greek philosophers, 'the subjective faculty of thinking was the critical agent that dissolved superstition [and] denounc[ed] mythology as false objectivity'. But, the recognition that this 'false objectivity' itself was, in fact, a subjective creation, thereby mandated a development of an 'objectivity of its own', in other words, an objectivity that existed in and of itself.[81] The current 'crisis of reason' – the anti-Enlightenment trend that had begun in the wake of the failed 1848 revolutions and become so pronounced by the interwar years – was thus due to the fundamental fact that 'at a certain point thinking either became incapable of conceiving such objectivity at all or began to negate it as a delusion'.[82] Indeed, as Horkheimer concluded, rather cynically: 'In modern times, reason has displayed a tendency to dissolve its own objective content'.[83]

Furthermore – and notably, for our understanding of the ideological trajectory that eventually led to twentieth-century ultra-nationalist political organisation – the eventual supplantation of religion by rationalist metaphysics, in the wake of the Enlightenment, created the phenomenon of 'civil religion', through which, in the 'American and French revolutions, the concept of the nation became a guiding principle'.[84] The rise of civil religion, embodied in the idea of the civic nation – which it served – created, at the same time, a fundamental dichotomy with the idea of individual self-interest that had been engendered by the industrial age and the rise of capitalism. Nonetheless, each of these phenomena, both products of the 'step from chaos to civilization, in which natural relationships no longer exert their power directly, but rather through the consciousness of men',[85] had led in its own way, through either mass production or nationalist expression, to the same result: a present-day fetishisation of 'sameness' [*Gleichheit*].[86] The 'national community' now became the new 'idol' in the practice of civil religion, but one which could:

> Eventually be maintained only by terror. This explains the tendency of liberalism to tilt over into fascism and of the intellectual and political representatives of liberalism to make their peace with its opposites. … Fascism [is] a satanic synthesis of reason and nature – the very opposite of that reconciliation of the two poles that philosophy has always dreamed of.[87]

Thus, Enlightenment itself became a radical form of 'mythical fear'.[88] The organisation of mass groups – here Adorno and Horkheimer refer specifically to the Hitler Youth, but we may substitute any mass movement from the period, be it the *fasci* in Italy or the Bolsheviks in Soviet Russia – was 'not a return to ancient Barbarism, but rather the triumph of repressive sameness'.[89] As a result, both the philosopher and politician renounced reason out of the necessity to surrender to this new reality, an action that was, itself, 'a much worse form of regression', and one that could only culminate 'in a confusing of philosophical truth with ruthless self-preservation and war'.[90] Indeed, as Adorno and Horkheimer summarised, rather cynically: 'The blindfold over the eyes of Justitia means not only that there should be no intervention in Law, but that it [that is to say, law itself] is not derived from freedom'.[91]

Perhaps, however, the most useful tactic when tracing the evolution of Fascism – certainly for understanding both Mussolini's and Ahimeir's, ideological development – is to try to analyse and understand the various intellectual- and cultural-historical trajectories that informed its development. The Israeli historian Jacob Talmon was one of the first to trace the origins of what he terms variously 'totalitarian democracy' and 'anarcho-monarchism' back to the 'eighteenth-century idea of the natural order (or general will) as an attainable, indeed inevitable and all-solving end' that results in a teleological reading of historical events.[92] As such, he sees the Jacobin proto-fascist 'Reign of Terror' and Babeuvist proto-Communist societal restructuring – both products of French Revolutionary ideology, and two sides of the same coin – as the 'two earliest versions of modern political Messianism'.[93] Both phenomena mandated the suppression of freedom and the 'legalized violence of Revolution' until their various revolutionary-teleological-political-Messianic objectives had been realised.[94] Indeed, as Talmon concludes, 'The right to Revolution and the Revolutionary (provisional) dictatorship of the proletariat (or the people) are two facets of the same thing'.[95]

More recently, Talmon's student, the historian and political scientist Ze'ev Sternhell, building on his teacher's theories, has explained the emergence of Fascism as a result of a crisis in Marxism, and the product of a very specific revision thereof. In Sternhell's reading, the fact that, by the first years of the twentieth century, Marx's predictions for a proletarian revolution that would destroy capitalism, and the power structures that it necessitated, had failed to transpire, led to an ideological redistribution of Marxist ideology that now concentrated on its political, and not economic, message. This revision was spearheaded by the French and Italian Sorelians – who supported the anti-liberal, anti-democratic and, indeed, anti-rationalist theories of Georges Sorel (1847–1922) – sought to adapt 'to [their] time Proudhon's ideas on the socialization of commerce and the State ... without touching private property'.[96] They combined this anti-materialist revision of Marxism, which married maximum political force with minimum economic interference by the state, with the concept of 'organic nationalism' – what Horkheimer called the 'national community' – and the belief that theory should be a product of action (and not vice versa). Onto this, they added the Marxist concept of revolution, and acceptability of violence in the name of the national community to forge an ideology that was, at once, both traditional and modern. Sternhell traces this Sorelian 'revolutionary syndicalism' through the phenomena of national Syndicalism, radical nationalism and futurism – noting the 'aesthetisation of politics' and primacy of the community over the individual that was increasingly inherent in all of these movements – finally, to Mussolini's nationalist-Socialist Fascism.[97] Lastly, the Fascist *Weltanschauung* was further complemented by the concept of myth as a motivating factor in a nation's history, a 'return to the basic values of a heroic society led by natural elites' – note the Spenglerian overtones – and, indeed, self-sacrifice in the name of the nation.[98] Or, as Benjamin succinctly concluded, 'the logical result of Fascism is the introduction of aesthetics into political life'.[99] Taken together, Sternhell's and Benjamin's conceptions of Fascism provide the best way to understand the phenomenon, certainly in its Italian incarnation, which is, ultimately, the form of Fascism that Ahimeir embraced.

Be that as it may, Ahimeir himself is never really clear on what he understands by Fascism, and he gives no indication of which facets of Fascist ideology he foresaw the Revisionists adopt, other than to elevate Jabotinsky's prestige to that of dictator. Undoubtedly, however – and certainly by April 1933 – he privileged Mussolini's 'pure' Fascism over Hitler's National Socialism. And he would also come to distance himself from Mussolini and the PNF once they introduced the Italian Racial Laws, in 1938.[100] Be that as it may, while Ahimeir undoubtedly recognised all of the 'mobilising passions' that Paxton identifies as underlying fascist action, so did, arguably, other ideological streams of Zionism. And such recognition only intensified with Hitler's rise to power, the subsequent war he waged and, of course, the most salient by-product of that war for world Jewry: the Holocaust. Ahimeir's articles from 1924 to 1928 demonstrate his already very solid rejection of Liberalism, class conflict and alien influences, and his belief in the detrimental effect that they had upon both the Zionist movement, in general, and the Yishuv and its leadership, in particular. Furthermore, Ahimeir was never a Marxist. This bears repeating. From his teenage years, when he made his first *Aliyah* to study at the Herzliya Gymnasium, to the period of his return to Bobruisk, where, when faced with the choice of becoming a Bolshevik and joining the Red Army – as had his favoured brother Meir – Ahimeir consistently eschewed Marxism and opted for Zionism. Thus, any comparison of Ahimeir's ideological development with that of Mussolini – a committed Marxist whose Fascism was predicated on his Marxist convictions, as per Sternhell's conclusions before – can be nothing more than superficial. In this very important respect, Ahimeir was not a true Fascist. Indeed, Ahimeir's own comment, that 'Syndicalism is not Marxism, in spite of the great resemblance', certainly lends credence to Sternhell's argument.[101] I would suggest that Ahimeir's own ideological trajectory saw him go from being a moderate Zionist-nationalist, to a 'revolutionary conservative' Zionist-nationalist, in other words, from moderate to extreme. And this was as much the result of historical development – or his perceived lack, thereof – within the Yishuv, as it was on any ideological change on Ahimeir's part. Sternhell notes the English critic and poet Thomas Ernest Hulme's (1883–1917) characterisation of the 'revolutionary conservative' – in his discussion related to Sorel and Hulme – as:

> [A] revolutionary who is also antidemocratic, an absolutist in ethics, rejecting all rationalism and relativism, who gives great importance to the mystical element in religion which he knows 'will never disappear', and who speaks contemptuously of modernism and *progress*, and uses a concept like *honour* with no sense of unreality.[102]

This is not to say that Ahimeir was a conscious Sorelian himself. Indeed, the French revolutionary Syndicalist was one of the few political figures from the period that Ahimeir appeared not to write about.[103] Nonetheless, if we examine Ahimeir's general disposition during the 1920s – as demonstrated innumerable times in his published articles – there is much that aligns him with Hulme's and Sorel's notion of the 'revolutionary conservative'.

All ideological posturing aside, Ahimeir most certainly identified with Mussolini the journalist, the editor of the Socialist papers *Avanti* and *Il Popolo d'Italia*, and he was undoubtedly inspired by the nonconformist 'man of action' who also founded *Utopia*.[104] Sternhell highlights the particular attractiveness of Fascism for many European intellectuals: it reflected their own nonconformism, while representing 'a new ideal of the beautiful and the admirable' that at the same time sought to orient the individual within the greater community.[105] Notably, in the 'Notebook of a Fascist' articles, Ahimeir makes very clear his own nonconformist spirit. He likens himself to an 'ancient pessimist [who] sometimes walks westward, sometimes eastward … [who] makes heard his Zionist ethic [without becoming interested] in the opinion of the crowd'.[106] Be that as it may, Ahimeir differed ideologically from Mussolini in one very important aspect. Mussolini saw Fascism in the same way that Lenin saw Marxist-Socialism: in a teleological context that allowed each to see his particular politico-ideological movement as, in historian Martin Malia's definition, 'a total project, aiming as it does at transcending present society completely and creating a whole new world and a new man'.[107] This was never Ahimeir's aim by embracing Fascism. For him, it served merely as a viable modus operandi that would best bring about the creation of a Jewish-Zionist nation state in Palestine. Ahimeir's Fascism was the means to an end, and was not intended to be the end itself. His article from 21 September 1928, quoted earlier, says as much: Socialism was an option to be considered once a Jewish state had been declared; until then, the Yishuv should operate as if under 'siege mentality'.[108]

Furthermore, in spite of all attempts to win over Jabotinsky and the non-Maximalist Revisionists to the Maximalist 'Fascist' programme, the party never adopted a Fascist platform, neither ideologically nor practically. And Jabotinsky – Ahimeir's unilateral claims that 'our *Duce*' had arrived, aside – spurned all efforts to create, in him, a leader, in the Fascist understanding of the word. As Shindler has shown, Ahimeir also privately pursued Jabotinsky's active leadership, asking him in a letter to 'Command us more … We have to obey your orders',[109] but Jabotinsky stuck to the position he held already in 1926, when he wrote: 'Duce … a translation of that most absurd of all English words – "leader" – buffaloes follow a leader. Civilized men have no "leaders".[110] That is not to say, however, that Jabotinsky did not play upon the Fascist sympathies of many of his younger adherents, when it suited his political agenda. Indeed, in an article that addressed Ahimeir's call for more decisive leadership, Jabotinsky noted that dictatorship could very well act as an ideological and practical stopgap at times, but could never function as a solid political modus operandi. Furthermore, as Daniel Heller recently highlighted, Jabotinsky had written to Mussolini himself, already in June 1922, and counselled him to best understand Zionist 'vitality' by adding 'only some tragedy, some tenacity – perhaps more experience' to the example of his own *fasci*.[111]

Yaacov Shavit posits that Jabotinsky understood Fascism as coming from an unstable organisation of the economy, which would result in a weakened middle class that would be obliged to turn to militarism in order to protect itself from an economically and organisationally stronger working class. Indeed, such was the case in the Yishuv, in his opinion.[112] However, unlike Fascism, mainstream Revisionism believed in the ability of compulsory arbitration by neutral parties to resolve labour disputes, and – in the case of the Yishuv – dilute the Histadrut monopoly by non-coercive means. In Shavit's analysis, this is its main point of divergence with Italian Fascism.[113] Be that as it may, Ahimeir undoubtedly believed that Zionist – and more specifically, Revisionist Zionist – ideology fulfilled the function of a civil religion:

> Up till now, Zionism had only the form of Social-Democratism. But during the last years, something has [changed] in Zionism: whether good or bad, but it [changed]. A Zionism with a backbone [now] goes [out] and crystallises; Zionism which is sure that the State will [be realised] in our generation. This Zionism will be fanatic, will have all the attributes of faith. This Zionism will take the place of moderate Zionism.[114]

And it is clear that Jabotinsky and Ahimeir had differing views on the utility of Betar. For the Revisionist leader, Betar was the party's youth group, and functioned much in the way that other Zionist youth groups did, in relation to their own parties. He emphasised military ceremony and precision in the name of *Hadar*, '[a] Hebrew word that ... comprehends some dozen different concepts: external beauty, pride, manners, loyalty'.[115] However, out of Jabotinsky's sight, the group could, at times, turn more obviously militaristic, and become rowdy, oppressive and violent. Ahimeir's reports of events following the Wailing Wall Incident, Jabotinsky's arrival in Palestine and the attack at the Left Poale Zion Club underscore this. Without a doubt, Ahimeir saw the group fulfil the same role as the *fasci* in Italy: a 'national guard' in which 'Hebrew culture permeated … from the Zionist public, from the Jewish youth'.[116]

Finally, it must be remembered that neither the General Revisionists nor the Maximalist Revisionists ever enjoyed a period of political rule in the Yishuv. Thus, we have no way of measuring how comprehensively either Jabotinsky's more liberal democratic or Ahimeir's and the Maximalists' more extreme revolutionary conservative ideologies might have played out, had they been realised in an applied political setting. To some degree, it is a moot point. Ahimeir's call for the Revisionists to adopt a Fascist platform was impossible to realise with no *Duce*. Jabotinsky did not want the job, and Ahimeir, by all accounts, was no leader, as will be discussed in further detail in Chapter 5.[117] This is not to say that Ahimeir did not achieve some degree of cult status, as will be discussed later, or that Jabotinsky did not – in many ways – fulfil the role of a charismatic leader. And while he was certainly happy to borrow from Fascist aesthetic for Betar, when it suited him, Jabotinsky was no Fascist; nor did he foresee a Revisionist embrace of Fascist ideology and practice. However, Ahimeir, as discussed earlier, was able to implement certain facets of Fascist ideology and practice into the youth of Betar, and the Maximalist Revisionists. If – in Walter Benjamin's assessment – Fascism was the result of introducing aesthetics into political life, then perhaps Jabotinsky, and most certainly Ahimeir were guilty of introducing Fascist aesthetics into Revisionist political life. That Benjamin saw war as the only possible outcome of such a diabolical combination is noteworthy indeed.[118]

The revolutionary[119]

National liberation movements are imbued with the idea of revolution. As Michael Walzer recently noted:

> Liberation is closer to revolutionary politics than to national aggrandizement. Like the liberationist militants, revolutionaries set themselves in opposition to established patterns of submission, accommodation, and (what Marxists call) 'false consciousness'. They aim at a radical transformation. Social revolution requires a struggle against the existing society; national liberation requires a struggle again, rather than an 'exultation' of, the existing nation.[120]

The common conception of Ahimeir is that he was a 'Fascist' who coined the provocative, but rather innocuous, term 'Revolutionary Zionism'. But is this a fair assessment? In point of fact, I would argue that we instead see Ahimeir first and foremost as a revolutionary – indeed a revolutionary conservative, as discussed earlier – who used Fascist aesthetic as the modus operandi for effecting his concept of Revolutionary Zionism. Such a revision in our perception of Ahimeir requires deeper engagement with two key questions. What was revolutionary about Ahimeir's 'Revolutionary Zionism', from an ideological point of view, and did he, in fact, catalyse a de facto revolution – in its modern, politico-scientific sense – in the Yishuv?

To this end, we should determine how best to analyse and classify the nature of the increasing incidences of anti-British and anti-Arab insurrection that occurred in the Yishuv from 1927 to 1948, from Ahimeir's first call for a revolution in Zionism to the end of the British Mandate and declaration of the State of Israel. Did they constitute a revolution or a revolt? Was this a protracted war of liberation or merely increasingly violent, armed resistance to the British Mandatory government and the Palestinian-Arab population?

The period in question began with the relatively moderate civil disobedience of Brit HaBiryonim, as will be discussed in Chapter 5, and reached a climax in the spring and summer of 1946 that was characterised by anti-British and anti-Arab violence by all three Yishuv paramilitary groups, Lehi, Irgun and Haganah. However, the latter group – which was the largest of the three and represented both the Yishuv leadership and its dominant political ideology – discontinued cooperation with its more extreme partners after they bombed the King David Hotel in Jerusalem on 22 July 1946, killing 91 people.[121] Nonetheless, the Haganah continued to act against the British in other ways, mainly through aiding Jewish illegal immigration to the Yishuv. Indeed, it was due to the unrelenting nature of both Zionist anti-British terrorism and illegal immigration that finally compelled Britain to appeal to the United Nations, in April 1947, to be released from the Mandate for Palestine. Thus, both the 'breakdown of sovereignty' and the chaotic element that historian Arno J. Mayer mandates as the 'essential precondition for the escalation of revolt into revolution' were present in the Yishuv.[122] And the events that occurred in the Yishuv certainly contained what Hannah Arendt terms the 'notion of irresistibility': the cumulative – eventually exponentially so – accrual of force that would render a revolt unstoppable 'beyond human power ... and hence a law unto itself', and that would transform it into a revolution.[123] Ahimeir, himself, absolutely recognised this fact when he wrote that the 'commencement of a revolution is like a small river and its end like [a] big ocean'.[124] Mayer further contends that extreme violence plays an integral role in revolution, since it 'entails both foreign and civil war'.[125] In line with his contention, we might recognise elements of both civil – directed against the Palestinian-Arab population – and foreign – directed against British Mandatory administration – violent action on the part of all of the Jewish paramilitary groups in the Yishuv, at some point between 1927 and 1948.

In spite of these rather compelling observations, we should remember that no transformation of class structure or a class-based revolt from below – necessary components of revolution, according to some social scientists – ever occurred, neither during the period under examination, nor after the founding of the State of Israel.[126] How could it? The Zionist project, both in Europe and the Yishuv, was absolutely rooted in Socialist ideals – to a fault, in Ahimeir's estimation, as has been discussed. As such it was inherently, in terms of class structure, downwardly mobile.[127] Thus the need for such a condition to be fulfilled as a vital component of revolution never existed in the first place in the case of Zionism, certainly not in Ahimeir's eyes.

Perhaps more important for our discussion is the fact that there was no ancien regime to overthrow – another key characteristic of revolution for historians and social scientists – only a colonial power that was mandated with the task of, inter alia, establishing a Jewish national home in Palestine.[128] While the traditional ancien regime in Palestine had been weakened – although by no means completely crumbled, since the hierarchical infrastructure that ranged from a Palestinian-Arab landowning elite of notables to peasant fellah remained intact – through the fall of the Ottoman Empire, Ahimeir did view the British Mandatory government – whom, as noted earlier, he called 'Perfidious Albion' and 'foreign occupiers' – as a regime to be overthrown. Furthermore, the British governed in the manner of an imperial power, not least in their bureaucratic and political inefficiency and ideology of 'divide and conquer', even if the latter policy was adapted somewhat to reflect its role as Mandatory Government. Although Britain was delegated with the task of creating a modern nation state for the Jews, it carried out the administration of its mandate using Imperialist methods. Not only was the form of administration and governance in Palestine determined by the Mandatory power, there was, outside of the various councils that acted as intermediaries – the *Va'ad Leumi*, for example – no political representation through suffrage, neither for the Jewish nor Arab citizens in Palestine. All aspects of the British Mandate leadership were decided in either Whitehall or in the office of the High Commissioner for Palestine.

Thus, for Ahimeir – from a political point of view – the British fulfilled the *function* of an ancien regime, if perhaps one that had been transposed from Europe to Palestine.

In addition, Ahimeir doubtless saw the Yishuv leadership – with its Labour-Left monopoly over all areas in the Yishuv – now fulfil the role similar to the traditional Jewish 'Old Regime' – the Kehillah – that the Zionists had sought to supplant in Europe. Indeed, for Ahimeir, the Yishuv leadership – which had become entrenched in partisan nepotism and bureaucratic inefficiency in only a few short years – represented nothing better than a 'Nouveau Ancien Regime in the *Altneuland*': a double slap in the face for a 'pure' Political Zionist like Ahimeir, and thus worthy of revolutionary supplantation. In his 1926 essay 'The Scroll of the Sicarii', it is clear that he sees what he calls the 'existing regime' as the focal point for the terror to be waged by the sicarius 'hero'.[129] Indeed, he uses the term no less than nineteen times, and although he is never specific in the essay, which remained unpublished until it was used as evidence at the Brit HaBiryonim trial in 1934, it is very likely that 'existing regime' refers to both the British and Yishuv leaderships, in toto. Thus, the condition that an old regime must be supplanted in a revolution was fulfilled to no small degree. Not only did the British administration leave Mandate Palestine on 14 May 1948 having not fulfilled the conditions of the Mandate, but did so, effectively, with its tail between its legs.

Furthermore – and notably – Mayer observes that 'although both revolution and revolt are turned against established elites and authorities, the former is driven by ideology and hope, whereas the latter is moved by traditional despair and disillusionment. Rebels, unlike revolutionaries, have a tendency to set upon local and tangible enemies who are readily vilified and turned into scapegoats'.[130] Without a doubt, Ahimeir's increasingly radical ideological development and actions were driven by a growing despair for, and disillusionment with, both the Yishuv and British leaderships. Not only do his 'Notebook of a Fascist' articles make this clear, but – as has been demonstrated in Chapter 2 – Ahimeir's 'despair and disillusionment' began already during his membership in HaPoel HaTzair. Nonetheless, he was still – ideologically – an unwavering, committed Zionist, and thus continued to be driven, at the same time 'by ideology and hope', in spite of his ever-increasing disillusionment with the Yishuv leadership and British administration.

If we want to find evidence of a revolution that would satisfy the conditions imposed by the social scientists, we should, more accurately, turn to the phenomenon of Zionism itself. As the Israeli social scientist Eyal Chowers notes:

> At its most basic level, Zionism aimed to restore to the Jews a political body they could claim as their own; national independence was seen as the way to guard the individual against physical threats and economic want, and the collective against the menace of assimilation and disintegration. ... But Zionism meant more than political independence in Palestine. It promised both material and spiritual transformation ... a modernized economy of and for the Jews ... and the revival of the Hebrew language. ... Some even hoped to form a new Jew: natural, assertive, self-reliant, productive, and so on.[131]

Thus Zionism as a social revolution needed to happen before Zionism as a political manifestation could occur, and therefore began much earlier, from the 1880s onwards, in Europe. The promise of the political manifestation of Zionism came only when Britain was granted the Mandate for Palestine, which had the implementation of the conditions of the Balfour Declaration as one of its principal tasks. But it slowly became clear to the Zionists – certainly by the time of the 1939 White Paper, which limited Jewish immigration to 75,000 people over the following five years, at which point it would cease, unless approved by the Arabs – that Britain was unable or unwilling to fulfil this fundamental mandatory requirement. Thus, anti-British political engagement on the part of the Zionists became necessary. And for Ahimeir this could occur only in the form of revolution.

So then, what characterised Ahimeir's own concept of revolution? As with his conception of Fascism, Ahimeir is likewise not overly forthcoming with regard to how he understands the concept. The clearest indication we get of any sort of ideology of revolution is in his article 'If Not for Myself, Who Will Be For Me', discussed in Chapter 2, where Ahimeir notes that revolution is the necessary consequence of a requisite 'imperialist moment' that had failed to deliver its 'utopian promise'. Nonetheless, in spite of his sparse ideological signposting, it is absolutely clear that Ahimeir understood revolution in its political, insurrectionary sense. The fact, therefore, that historians and social scientists have been unable to reach any scholarly consensus on how merely to define, let alone predict, revolution is something which Ahimeir – who again and again aggrandised men of 'action' over 'words' – would have noted with wry cynicism. Indeed, a straightforward dictionary definition of 'revolution' reads, quite simply, as 'a forcible overthrow of a government or social order, in favour of a new system',[132] and this is certainly how Ahimeir understood the term, fundamentally.

We should remember that Ahimeir, as a committed Revisionist, advocated a return to Herzlian Political Zionism: a 'revolution' in the most basic understanding of the word.[133] And that he foresaw the need for paramilitary action, if necessary, in order to achieve Zionism's political goal cannot be doubted. As he concluded:

> 'It is permissible to be nationalistic' – said Pinsker [and] Ahad Ha'am; 'It is permissible to pursue a Jewish state', said Herzl and Nordau. Jabotinsky and Trumpeldor came along and added: 'There is no state without a military'. Avshalom Feinberg and the brother and sisters from Zikhron Ya'akov came along and said: 'The Jewish State is such an important matter, that all means to achieve it are justified. No matter what [these] means [may be]. The enemy uses all means to fight'. And if we worry about [which] means we use – we will be conquered.[134]

By referring to Feinberg and other members of the Nili Group, Ahimeir makes it clear that his revolution must contain a militaristic underground component.[135] And, as will be discussed in Chapter 5, the fact that Ahimeir originally wanted Brit HaBiryonim to be named after the Nili Group's Sarah Aaronsohn leaves little doubt that he saw the Nili spy's willingness for self-sacrifice as a necessary character trait for a Zionist Revolutionary. All of these observations further buttress the contention that Ahimeir, himself, understood 'revolution' in a modern, political insurrectionary – if not socially scientific definitive – sense.

Indeed, already in his dissertation on Spengler, we see that Ahimeir viewed the Cromwellian Civil War as a political revolution; he uses that very term itself. This usage is noteworthy, as it was almost certainly not de rigueur in 1924, where the revolutionary definer would more likely have been the restoration of the English monarchy in 1660: a literal 'revolution' of the political status quo. In addition, it should not be forgotten that Ahimeir, again in his dissertation, considered Cromwell to be – in Spenglerian terms – 'morphologically contemporaneous' with Robespierre and Lenin, and therefore saw all three as political revolutionaries. And that blood must be shed in the name of revolution was an absolute necessity. Once again, Ahimeir's Notebook of a Fascist article from 9 November 1928 makes this fact absolutely clear, when he states that 'blood is the oil on the wheels of revolution'.[136]

Malia – ever the historian – suggested that 'each revolution learns from the experience of its predecessor and escalates that pattern each time to a more intense level of radicalism'.[137] It is a noteworthy comment. All of European and Yishuv Jewry – Zionist and otherwise – had been affected by the last great

European 'grand' revolution, the Russian Revolution of 1917: some, like Ahimeir, negatively; others, less so (cf. Ahdut HaAvodah's ultimate rejection of Marxism); and still others positively (cf. the Marxist-Zionist group HaShomer HaTzair). Had this not been the case – if we accept Malia's condition – it would, in fact, have been 'historically' impossible for Ahdut HaAvodah and the Haganah, in 1945, to join forces with the Irgun and Lehi in the Hebrew Resistance Movement, and thus eventually resort to violence against the British and Palestinian Arabs. Moreover, Malia's observation might also explain why Fascism – building as it did upon Marxism, whether positively as per Sternhell, or negatively as a revolt against Communism – was the most logical political ideology to catalyse what Ahimeir hoped would lead to a political revolution in Palestine. Not only was it more radical but it was – certainly in the eyes of its proponents – more ideologically evolved than Marxism.

Malia's claim is further buttressed, from a different ideological perspective, by Ahimeir's embrace of Oswald Spengler. Like his mentor, Ahimeir viewed Bolshevism as the epitome of 'Megalopolitan' *über*-civilization, a status quo which, in Spenglerian theory, signified that a societal Culture was in decline, and approaching the end of its life-cycle. Thus, in Ahimeir's eyes, Bolshevism could not serve as a viable modus operandi for a successful Zionist revolution in Palestine. This observation may also explain some of Ahimeir's ideological inconsistencies, for example, the fact that he could speak of the need for 'our own 1917' while, nonetheless, rejecting the ideological core of Bolshevism.[138] Furthermore – and rather notably, from an ideological perspective – it seems that Ahimeir the Spenglerian saw his Zionist Political Revolution as being 'morphologically contemporaneous' with the Jewish Revolt, from 66 to 70 CE. Both the Biryonim and Sicarii hail from this period, as will be discussed in more detail in Chapter 5. Ahimeir's appropriation of both terms for his modern-day purposes suggests – again, if we remember that Ahimeir was a Spenglerian – a very specific identification with both the nature and function of each group, that of revolutionaries who revolted against both the Roman regime and the Jewish moderates who were sympathetic to it. For Ahimeir the Spenglerian, the British Mandatory government was morphologically contemporaneous with the Roman regime in Judea, and the Labour-Left Yishuv leadership with the ancient Pharisees. Of course, the Jewish Revolt had ultimately failed; Ahimeir as both Spenglerian and historian expected his revolution to learn from the past, and succeed.

Without a doubt, Ahimeir and his cohorts espoused what Malia lists as a 'permanent feature of the revolutionary syndrome: ... a belief in a vast alien conspiracy against liberty'.[139] This was played out in several directions, all of which led to increasing radicalisation in the Yishuv: First, towards the Palestinian-Arab population and which became more radical with each successive round of Arab riot or revolt, from 1920 onwards. Second, towards Britain, which was seen – gradually, through various White Papers issued in the wake of each successive riot, and which further limited the parameters for the establishment of a Jewish state in Palestine – to be reneging on the promises made in the Balfour Declaration. Third, towards Europe in general, and – increasingly, from 1933 – Germany in particular, where antisemitism was institutionalised and, in Germany and the countries it occupied during the Second World War, eventually legalised.

Furthermore, it is illuminating to note several similarities between the political situation in pre-state Israel and revolutionary America (1776–87), which was in some ways anomalous to the English Revolution, and the modern European revolutions that followed. The American Revolution had started, Malia notes, 'as a reaction against royal state building and ended with a form of representative constitutional government'.[140] And in both America and the Yishuv, the sovereign was several thousand miles away, rendering each a 'territorial war of independence', although to be sure, the American Revolution was not a nationalist revolution but more a revolution of succession. Of course, Zionism, by contrast, was a nationalist movement that sought the creation of a modern nation state.[141] Malia further notes that 'within the [American] colonies themselves there were few entrenched hierarchical institutions to overthrow, thus obviating those serial upheavals within the rebellion that in England had radically transferred power from king to Parliament to army'.[142] Once again, this was the case in Mandate Palestine. There was no Parliament nor king to overthrow, only an administrative regime and army, that was – eventually – unwilling to continue to suffer the loss of human material of the magnitude that became the norm during the final years of the British Mandate. Furthermore, both populations perceived their indigenous populations as being 'savage', in need of taming. And in the Yishuv, as in America, the perception was – again to quote Malia – that the 'colonies … were on the edge of a thinly populated continent providing almost endless space for social mobility and sources of new wealth, [although] [t]o be sure, the continent was not "empty", as has often been assumed'.[143]

We should further note two final factors that, for Malia, set the American Revolution apart from its European counterparts. First, it constituted the 'creation of a democratic republic on an unprecedented continental scale, a feat moreover presented as the beginning of a New World, and a New Man, and a beacon for the rest of humanity'.[144] Certainly the Zionist project, in all of its various ideological forms, sought to do precisely this for world Jewry. Second, the new American republic 'had been born amidst an escalation of millenarian "fever" quite comparable to that driving earlier revolutionary episodes in Europe'.[145] Again, this was the case with the Zionist project, certainly by the time that the State of Israel was declared.

Finally, Malia notes that the aim of Socialism was to be a 'total project', a 'utopia'. And, he continues, 'for almost two centuries now we have talked as if capitalism and socialism were equally real historical formations between which society should choose'.[146] Indeed, it was the failure of both Socialism and capitalism to live up to the predictions that Marx made for each that led to the crisis of Marxism, discussed earlier. Furthermore, according to both Sternhell and Malia, it was the necessity to resolve this crisis that led – *at more or less the same time*, if we accept Sternhell's thesis – to the Socialist economic revisions of Marxism that became Lenin's Bolshevism, on the one hand, and Mussolini's Fascism, on the other.[147] Malia further notes that it was due to 'Communism's pretension to be the culmination of human progress, beyond which there is nothing but counterrevolution and the "restoration of capitalism"' that led to the phenomenon of 'revolution-as-regime'.[148] This observation might explain the holding pattern of the Labour-Left Yishuv leadership with regard to the formation of a Jewish state. As proponents of Socialism – to whatever degree – they were simply unable to begin a nationalist political revolution since they were stuck in an ideological paradox. Their 'permanent' revolution remained on the level of class struggle.[149] Thus, only a cynical and vehement opponent of Bolshevism and Socialism – such as Ahimeir was – could even entertain the thought of sparking a Zionist 'political', and indeed 'military', revolution. Fascist ideology espoused no less the concept of revolution, but did so rather, in the aid of national – and not international – Socialism.[150]

In reference to the Bolshevik Revolution, Malia concludes that 'All previous European revolutions, of course, had been fuelled by ideologies; but none had been guided by an ideology of history as a revolutionary process'.[151] However, Ahimeir, as a cultural historian, was practically obliged – if only unconsciously so – to be *guided by a history of ideology as a revolutionary process*. Quite simply put, he had revolution on the brain. His dissertation on Spengler – written in 1924 – already leaves no doubt about this. And again, Malia's contention that each revolution learns from its predecessor explains Ahimeir's embrace of Fascism: as the most current of the political 'isms' at the time, it could be his only choice *as a historian*, in a historical-teleological approach to revolution. And this approach was only buttressed by his earlier embrace of Spengler, as discussed earlier. Finally, it explains Ahimeir's own ideological trajectory, which can be summarised as follows: His first flirtation with Fascism, in his article in *HaToren* from 1923, which – in contrast to Shavit – I believe was more than ambivalent, but nonetheless did not yet result in any active engagement.[152] This was followed by a realisation, around the end of 1927, that revolution was necessary, as articulated in his Rosh HaShanah article in *HaPoel HaTzair*. However, he does not yet name – publicly, at least – any viable modus operandi for achieving this revolution. And finally, once the necessity for revolution was accepted, we see Ahimeir's embrace – both private and public – of Fascist aesthetic, as the viable – indeed, the *only possible* – modus operandi for achieving this revolution, as articulated in his 'Notebook of a Fascist' articles in *Doar HaYom* in September–November 1928.

Thus, Ahimeir's Fascism – to whatever degree he espoused it – was merely a function of his ideology of revolution. And we should remind ourselves of the historical context in which Ahimeir reached his conclusion. Our current tendency to view Marxism – and especially Leninist-Marxism – as a failed utopian social experiment, but Fascism as inherently sinister, is a product of the Second World War. We cannot apply such a viewpoint anachronistically to the population of the Yishuv in 1928, where familiarity with violent action and death – be it through pogroms in Russia, the Great European War, the October Revolution or, indeed, Arab attacks on the Yishuv – was part of the *Alltag*, and was experienced in every direction. The idea of revolution and 'revolution-as-regime' was rife in the Yishuv: the Marxist-Communist Party HaShomer HaTzair wanted to replicate the Bolshevik Revolution, alongside whatever violent action that might entail, in Palestine; Ahdut HaAvodah and HaPoel HaTzair called for a more moderate – without violence, to be sure – Socialist, but not Marxist, revolution; the Maximalist Revisionists – fuelled by Ahimeir's ideologies – called for a Zionist Political Revolution, one that could work only by embracing Fascism, or at the very least, Fascist aesthetics. Ahimeir pushed for Jabotinsky to become the *Duce* of the Revisionist Party. Indeed, why not himself? Because, by all accounts Ahimeir was shy, soft-spoken, neither a good public speaker nor suitable leader.[153] He was, however, a solid historical analyst who saw – by instinctively viewing revolution and revolutionary ideology as a teleological-historical process – that there could be no other way to spark a Zionist political revolution than through the embrace of Fascist aesthetic and ideology.

Nonetheless, all of his revolutionary posturing aside, Ahimeir led no actual revolution himself. To say, however, that he was a mere reactionary is also an unsatisfactory – and indeed, inaccurate – response. If not a revolution, what did he effect? Mayer provides a clue, when he notes that 'there can be no revolution without counterrevolution; both as phenomenon and process, they are inseparable ... Although counterrevolution is the other half of revolution, it tends not to be recognized and theorized as such'.[154] Counterrevolution is characterised by two major elements – reaction and Conservatism – although it is 'more doctrinal, principled, and impassioned' than either of these.[155] Counterrevolution is a product of the anti-Enlightenment; its 'prophets of despair' are pessimistic, decadent and rooted in a mythic past.[156] Mayer's definition of the counterrevolutionary appears to almost completely overlap that of the 'revolutionary conservative', and I propose that the two terms be used interchangeably.

Nonetheless, Walzer contradicts Mayer to a certain degree in his discussion of counterrevolution, and the distinction is worth noting. For him, the Conservatism and reaction in Mayer's depiction of counterrevolution are traditional-religious. Indeed, it is clear from his context that when Walzer speaks of 'Jewish zealotry in Israel' as an example of Zionist counterrevolution, he is speaking about modern-day ultra-orthodoxy:

> Their first allegiance is not to the nation-state but to something more like the traditional, pre-state community. After a time, when national liberation has receded in memory, these traditionalists stage a counterrevolution; thus the rise of Islamic radicalism in Algeria (and in Palestine), of Hindutva in India and of Jewish zealotry in Israel. The religious resurgence is a shock to the national liberation elites, who had grown complacent about the victory of newness.[157]

Walzer's counterrevolutionary Jewish zealots are truly Messianic, as opposed to those of Ahimeir and the Maximalists, for whom Messianism was secular, rhetorical and, indeed, far more sophisticated. I wonder, however, if the main difference between Mayer and Walzer is merely generational: Mayer is discussing the French and Russian Revolutions, while Walzer focuses on post–Second World War Israel, Algeria and India. Ideologically speaking, Ahimeir falls somewhere between the cracks. Perhaps, in the final analysis, it would be more accurate to call him a 'revolutionary counterrevolutionary', or possibly a counterrevolutionary whose counterrevolution took the form of a de facto revolution. Indeed, the fact that Mayer sees the culmination of European counterrevolution in the phenomenon of Fascism serves only to buttress this argument.[158]

Although he was no *Duce*, Ahimeir was certainly more than a mere ideologue. A counterrevolution needs counterrevolutionaries, and a counterrevolution predicated on Fascist aesthetics needs *fasci*. Ahimeir was instrumental in the creation of both, and on two very different realms. In the popular-public realm of the Revisionist Party, he was one of the leaders of the training school for Betar *madrikhim*. And in the more private-elite realm, he formed the first underground resistance group to the British, Brit HaBiryonim. These groups will be the foci of the next two chapters.

Betar leader, *madrikh l'madrikhim*, cultural historian

This chapter examines Ahimeir's involvement both as a *madrikh* (leader) with the Revisionist youth group Betar and as an instructor at the Betar Leadership Training School (BLTS). It begins by examining Ahimeir's ideological position vis à vis Betar, in order to indicate where it diverged from Jabotinsky's, and then, using unpublished contemporary training manuals from each group, undertakes a more detailed study of how members of Betar and the BLTS were trained. To be clear, although there was certainly much ideological overlap between the two groups, they organised – and acted – independently of each other, at first. While true that members of the BLTS were indeed also members of Betar, the converse was not necessarily true: the cadets at the BLTS were an elite group. Thus, throughout the chapter 'Betar', 'Betari' or 'Betar Youth' refers only to a member of the much larger youth group, Betar, while 'Cadet' or 'BLTS Cadet' refers to a member of the BLTS only. An examination of the two groups' training manuals gives us a unique insight into the nature of the ideological and practical training that both the Revisionist youth group members and their leaders received.

The last section of the chapter is devoted to a close reading of the first section of Ahimeir's final book *Yudaikah*, a work in which he provides a comprehensive presentation of his unique understanding of ancient Jewish cultural history. Although Ahimeir was responsible for instructing both the Betar Youth and BLTS Cadets in the Yishuv in Jewish history and culture, there is no material which bears his name in either of the training manuals studied earlier. *Yudaikah*, therefore, is unique in that it showcases Ahimeir the cultural historian, and is thus well worth a closer study.

Ideological differences

From the early 1930s onwards, Jabotinsky began to conceive of Betar as more than just another partisan Zionist youth group.[1] While he continued to see it as the vanguard of a Revisionist-Zionist youth that espoused the ideals of Political Zionism, he also came to recognise the necessity, in the Yishuv, for a more vigilantly active nationalist corollary to the Haganah. I suggest three overriding reasons for this change in tactic. First, Jabotinsky recognised – if perhaps only begrudgingly so – that the political climate in the wider world had changed in the years since he founded the group. The 'cult of the leader' that was a characteristic of both Communist and Fascist ideology had increasingly served to engage a post-war youth that lacked political motivation and direction. Second, the 1929 Palestine Riots – to be discussed in further detail later – reinforced Jabotinsky's belief in the necessity for a 'proper' Jewish army that was more proactively vigilant than the Haganah, which maintained a strict practice of *Havlagah* (restraint) as a strategic policy. He foresaw the Betar youth as a middle ground between these two ideological-tactical opposites. Third, Jabotinsky's change in approach was almost certainly also a reaction to the growing influence of the Maximalist arm of the Revisionist Party in Mandate Palestine.

Ahimeir had already in 1928 attributed the current stalemate on the part of the Zionist Organization – 'thirty years after the "Basel Programme", and ten years after the Balfour Declaration' – to a lack of national-political education.[2] Writing in the first edition of *Tel-Hai* – the journal of the Betar central command in Mandate Palestine – he differentiates between the need for a mere 'national' education for the youth of Betar and one that was more specifically 'political' in orientation, as taught by the leaders of its branches in Eretz Israel. Echoing the tenor of his 'Notebook of a Fascist' articles, Ahimeir reminds his reader that 'true redemption [in the form of a Jewish State] will not come until an iron bridge would be erected, over which the way of the Messiah would be prepared'.[3] His use of militaristic and Messianic imagery is apparent once again, but this time it is directed towards a Betar youth that, for Ahimeir, will provide this bridge in Eretz Israel. The difference in terminology – Ahimeir's 'Iron Bridge' (*gesher barzel*) versus Jabotinsky's 'Iron Wall' (*kir barzel*) – is seemingly deliberate. Jabotinsky's solution – military, to be sure, but defensively so – a wall through which the local population cannot break, is now supplanted by Ahimeir's Iron Bridge: a militarily proud, imposing structure over which the Messiah would pass. The ideological differences between the two men could perhaps not be better summarised. For Ahimeir, Jabotinsky's solution represented – if only cynically – nothing more than a relocation and replication of any one of Europe's many Jewish ghettos; Ahimeir's vision was of a physical and ideological final destination, cut off neither from its Arab neighbours – although it certainly passed over them – nor from a Galut which it, nonetheless, negated both geographically and spiritually.

As Shindler has pointed out, Ahimeir's concept of the utility of Betar differed somewhat in both ideology and practice from Jabotinsky's.[4] Certainly, both saw the group represent a 'national guard' – what Ahimeir called the group's '[one] clear objective' – that would aid in building the Jewish state by political, and not diplomatic, means. Furthermore, the group would set itself apart – and indeed, 'free itself' – from other Zionist youth groups through its unwillingness to compromise any part of its monistic, Political-Zionist ethos. The difference between the two leaders lay in the extremes to which each believed that one should go in this service. Echoing once again his 'Notebook of a Fascist' article from 4 November 1928, and using almost identical language – not surprising, as the two were written just five weeks apart – Ahimeir notes that a 'pure' political approach requires a necessary differentiation between 'morality of the individual' and 'morality of the collective'. Once again, 'What is forbidden [for] the individual, is allowed [for] the collective'.[5] And while Ahimeir was not the first Zionist ideologue to look to the Modern Hebrew poetical tradition – 'with Y.L.G. [Y.L. Gordon] at its head', he notes – for inspiration, the hero whom Ahimeir envisages is nonetheless very much literal, and not literary. For Ahimeir, the poetic-mythic Jewish hero is real in terms of both intention and deed, yet is nonetheless absolutely rooted in a Jewish primordial collective unconsciousness.

The fact that Ahimeir foresees an adoption of a Fascist ideological, and indeed tactical, approach in all of this – if not already clear in the main body of his article, as discussed earlier – is given little room for doubt if we look at the easily overlooked quote from Deuteronomy that he uses as its preamble:

> I am the LORD thy God, who brought thee out of the land of Egypt, out of the house of bondage. Thou shalt have no other gods before Me. Thou shalt not make unto thee a graven image, nor any manner of likeness, of anything that is in heaven above, or that is in the earth beneath, or that is in the water under the earth; thou shalt not bow down unto them, nor serve them; for I the LORD thy God am a jealous God, visiting the iniquity of the fathers upon the children unto the third and fourth generation of them that hate Me; and showing mercy unto the thousandth generation of them that love Me and keep My commandments.[6]

Ahimeir's use of such a fundamental biblical passage to underscore his call for Betar to adopt a Fascist modus operandi is perhaps not as curious as it may seem at first glance. The idea of a jealous God who – quite literally – dictates his laws to his masses, forbids the worship of all other 'false' idols, and who wreaks punitive damage upon his naysayers, embodies the *Urform* of the Fascist – or indeed totalitarian, in any sense – conception of the cult of the leader. And while this is perhaps an extreme secular application of the authoritarian God of traditional Jewish orthodoxy, it is nonetheless not illogical. Of course, Ahimeir's false idols are Socialism, Communism and the 'vegetarian' mainstream Zionism of the Yishuv, and although the jealousy – 'zealotry', perhaps – of a Jabotinsky foreseen by Ahimeir as the Zionist *Duce* is perhaps not as distinctive as that of a Mussolini, the comparison is, nonetheless, a strong one. Not only does Ahimeir further reinforce the quasi-Messianic overtones that formed part of his ideological world view for the youth of Betar but he also successfully links the political-Zionist aim to create a modern Jewish state in the whole of the ancestral homeland of the ancient Jewish nation, with the very foundation myth – indeed, the Western foundation myth par excellence – that sets out why the Jewish nation is unique from all others in the first place. The fact that Ahimeir is able to couple the Zionist present with the ancient Jewish past, and that he achieves this on an almost subliminal level, through the placement of the biblical quote as a mere prelude to the rest of the article, is masterful indeed.

Whatever he must have thought about the differences in their ideological outlooks, Jabotinsky nonetheless appointed Ahimeir to the editorial board of *Doar HaYom*, when he took over the paper's editorship on 7 December 1928. The appointment represented the curious relationship that the two men had with each other; sometimes mutually respectful, bordering at times on the reverential, but often curiously out of touch with each other, while both vied for ideological dominance within the Revisionist Party. Perhaps Jabotinsky's appointment of Ahimeir to the editorial board of *Doar HaYom* was as much an attempt to keep his younger colleague under control as it was a diplomatic effort to give voice to the various, often inconsistent, ideological streams within his party.

Indeed, Jabotinsky faced no small degree of ideological disparity within his own party. During the period under discussion, two main ideological streams within the Revisionist Party may be identified: the centrist stream, led by Meir Grossman, and the more radical – later, 'Maximalist' – stream, led by Ahimeir, Yevin and Greenberg.[7] Jabotinsky tried, with varying degrees of success, to oversee the two groups, which, it should be remembered, were also separated geographically: the first was based in London, and from April 1929 oversaw the world movement for Revisionist Zionism, while the second was based in the Yishuv. Thus the fact that such ideological incongruences should also find their way into the various incarnations of Betar is certainly not unsurprising. In Mandate Palestine, Betar developed a much more radical character, due on the one hand to the radical nature of Maximalist ideology, and on the other to the peculiar reality of the Yishv *Alltag*, which – through increasingly violent Arab resistance – directly informed such radicalness in both word and deed.

By October 1930, Ahimeir had further honed his ideological standpoint and presented it to the youth of Betar in an article in *Doar HaYom*. He addressed them directly:

> A true national movement knows not what pessimism is ... the path to Zion, to the Kingdom of Israel, is not strewn with roses. The people [literally 'The public', הציבור] that truly wants to be redeemed, needs to pay a great price for its redemption. ... The youth believes in his [own] private future, and therefore he is also able to believe in the future of a public ideal. ... You, the youth of Eretz Israel, are infected by two diseases. The first disease is the 'red sickness' [here he means 'communism', but Ahimeir makes a pun on 'measles', "מחלת ה"אדמת"], of which its most potent expression in 'Mops-ism'. The second disease is the disease of snobbery, of which the most dangerous expression is emigration abroad. ... Zionism is a goal unto itself. ... We are commanded to reject and fight every ideal except Zionism, no matter what it may be. ... For every ideal, there is only one [G]od, a jealous and vengeful [G]od who does tolerate other gods in his face.[8]

Now-familiar themes – the idea that service to the collective supersedes individual will; the necessity for self-sacrifice; the threats to Zionism posed by Socialism, Communism and assimilation; the monistic ideal of serving one overriding principal and indeed, leader; and the use of secular-Messianic imagery in aid of all of this – are, once again, given pointed expression. New, and noteworthy, is Ahimeir's use of imagery of 'disease' and 'infection' – a common Fascist metaphor – when presenting what he perceives to be the threats that currently faced the Zionism of his day.[9] And Ahimeir's article certainly rouses all of the 'mobilising passions' which Paxton believes 'underlie fascist action', as discussed in Chapter 3.

Without a doubt, Ahimeir – the 'well-known teacher' – knew well how to appeal to, and catalyse, a disengaged Zionist youth. He did this not only by instilling in it 'a sense of overwhelming crisis, beyond the reach of any traditional solutions', but also by underscoring the fundamental utility of the Betar youth in the resolution of said overwhelming crisis.[10] The fact that the youth could so easily be recruited for active resistance and even self-sacrifice is – once again – not as surprising as it may seem, at first glance. The 'sense of overwhelming crisis' which Ahimeir and his fellow Maximalists portrayed repeatedly to the Betari certainly made a significant impact on its intended audience. In addition – and perhaps equally as important – the concepts of (revolutionary-) violence and self-sacrifice in service of the nationalist – and indeed the 'internationalist' – myth were commonplace to many politico-ideological movements by the interwar period. The Maximalists glorified such acts, not least through their newspaper articles, literature and poetry. As historian Derek Penslar observes, 'Nationalist historical scholarship is by definition literary, for it invents a nation by constructing a coherent narrative in which the willingness to fight as and for the collective is a paramount indication of national identity'.[11]

Furthermore, for a Spenglerian like Ahimeir, the human impulse towards violence and bloodshed was not only the consequence of any particular 'sense of crisis' but , in fact, biologically predetermined. The contention that each human being possessed an inherent propensity for violence that had its roots in the primordial, lone warrior, was – perhaps not unsurprisingly – supported by the 'nationalist-historical' scholar, Spengler:

> The soul of these strong loners is warlike through and through, mistrustful, and jealous of its own power and booty. It knows the pathos not only of the 'I' but also of the 'mine'. It knows the intoxication of feeling when the knife pierces the hostile body, and the smell of blood and the sense of amazement strike together upon the exultant soul. Every real 'man', even in the cities of Late periods in the cultures, feels in himself the sleeping fires of this primitive soul from time to time.[12]

The psycho-sexual element – implicit in Spengler's description and thus, by interpolation, in any act that is rooted in such primordial warrior-ism – should not go unnoticed. And Adorno, once again, helps to bridge the philosophical, psychological, and ideological gap between Spengler's primeval warrior and the modern (F)ascist. Although he is discussing the operas of Richard Wagner, Adorno's observations may just as easily be applied to this discussion:

> We almost perceive some glimmering realization that the true nature of the hero lies in his self-knowledge. Self-praise and pomp – features of Wagner's

entire output and the emblems of Fascism – spring from the presentiment of the transient nature of bourgeois terrorism, of the death instinct implicit in the heroism that proclaims itself. The man who seeks immortality during his lifetime doubts that his achievements will survive him and so he celebrates his own obsequies with festive ceremonial. Behind Wagner's façade of liberty, death and destruction stand waiting in the wings; the historic ruins that come crashing down on the heads of the defeated Gods and the guilt-laden world of the Ring.[13]

The idea of the elite bourgeois terrorist would – in Zionism – find its consummate expression in the figure of Avraham Stern, and the underground paramilitary group that he founded, *Lohamei Herut Israel,* the 'Fighters for the Freedom of Israel', also known as Lehi or The Stern Gang. The ideological exemplar for Lehi was Ahimeir's semi-underground resistance group Brit HaBiryonim, which he founded in 1930, and which will be the focus of the next chapter. Ahimeir foresaw Betar and Brit HaBiryonim as two complementary groups. Betar was the larger group, sanctioned by the Revisionist Party; Brit HaBiryonim was its elite, semi-underground corollary, although it was neither organised nor recognised by the general Revisionists. Thus Ahimeir's engagement with the officially recognised Betar youth, and eventually also the BLTS cadets, occurred on an altogether different ideological and practical level than his engagement with Brit HaBiryonim.

For the youth of Betar, Ahimeir envisioned a group steeped in an understanding of Revisionist ideology, and a Jewish cultural and national historical past. To this ideological-historical education, Ahimeir mandated compulsory training in modern military discipline and exercise that went beyond Jabotinsky's concept of defensive militarism. The fact that his vision differed from Jabotinsky's became less and less of an issue by January 1930, after which Jabotinsky was barred by the British from returning to Mandate Palestine. Nonetheless, the lack of ideological uniformity in the party was apparent almost immediately upon Ahimeir's, Greenberg's and Yevin's joining the party, at the beginning of 1928. Such ideological disparity in the party could, at times, be exploited, certainly during the periods when Jabotinsky was absent. Indeed, *Beit HaSefer L'Madrikhei Betar* (The Betar Leadership Training School), founded by Yirmiahu Halpern and Moshe Rosenberg, was, in spite of its name, not originally sanctioned by Jabotinsky and the Revisionist Party. This occurred only after the school had been in operation for several months, upon Jabotinsky's return to Palestine, at which point the school was transformed into its own unit within Betar.

Yirmiahu Halpern was born in 1901 in Smolensk, and emigrated with his family to Palestine in 1913, where he was enrolled at the Herzliya Gymnasium. Thus, it is likely that he became acquainted with Ahimeir – who studied there from 1912 until the summer of 1914 – during this time. He came from a family with strong connections both to the idea of Jewish military engagement and to the figure of Jabotinsky himself. Halpern's father, Michael, had been one of the earliest advocates for a Jewish Legion, and Halpern had served as Jabotinsky's aide-de-camp during the 1920 Arab attacks in Jerusalem.[14] A certified naval captain from both the Italian Naval Academy (1917) and the London School for Captains and Engineers (1919), Halpern established a naval school in Civitavecchia, Italy, in 1931, which went on to become – in 1934, under Jabotinsky's directorship – the Betar Naval Academy.[15] The Academy represented the fulfilment of not only Jabotinsky's vision for a Jewish Marine that was trained in his beloved Italy, but no less the dream of the elder Halpern, who had proposed the idea of a resurrection of the ancient Hebrew navy 'already in the days of the *Biluim*'.[16] The school's co-founder, Moshe Rosenberg, had previously served as an officer in the Russian White Army, and went on to be commander of the Irgun in 1937–8.[17] From the autumn of 1931, at Jabotinsky's behest, and while the BLTS in Palestine was still operative, Halpern established a similar training school for Betar leaders.[18]

Madrikh l' Madrikhim

The *Beit Sefer L'Madrikhei Betar* began operation on 13 March 1929 and closed in January 1933.[19] Halpern maintained that the school was founded 'before the revolt in Betar', which – officially – revolved around the question of Betar's dependence on the Revisionist Party, but in reality was centred on the question of whether to give the group a more proactively defensive character.[20] Halpern was the chief commander, and he chose the remaining administrative leadership from within his circle of friends: Rosenberg was commander of weaponry, while Yosef Paamoni was administrator and commander of the Women's Unit, and Yehiel Kagan was bursar.[21] Instructors at the school included Abba Zelivnaski (Military Exercises), Arie Bayevsky (Tactic and Strategy), Abba Gilvitz (Ceremony and *Hadar*), Uziel Kaplan (Medicine and First Aid) and Abba Ahimeir (Ideology and Society).

During the course of its short history, the school graduated eighteen male and eleven female candidates. They hailed from far and wide: in addition to the Yishuv, they came from Odessa, the Caucasus, Poland, Galicia, Spain, Italy and America; there was even one graduate 'from Arabia'. Most of them were illegal labourers who came for training after a gruelling nine- or ten-hour workday, and lessons often continued until 1 or 2 am. Indeed, according to Halpern:

> There were occasions when students passed out from fatigue, [or] came to school ill with fever, with a high temperature. Only when a person couldn't stand upright anymore, were they freed from schoolwork. A lot of them didn't even have time to change [out of] their work uniform, and came punctually to lessons. This didn't give you any merit, it was seen as normal behaviour. Anyone who couldn't be a student of this leadership school without making the [necessary] sacrifices, couldn't remain enrolled.[22]

The school's motto – 'There is no order which cannot be obeyed, and we will carry it out' – underlined its ethos of producing strong military leadership for Betar. Indeed, the smallest misconduct, even tardiness, or a verbal dispute, was punished corporally, by 'metal to the knee'. Nonetheless, all such action was undertaken for the purpose of creating a strong personal and professional bond – 'a family of friends' – between the members of the training school. In Halpern's opinion, such a bond could be created only by instilling into the group a strong sense of discipline. Those who left the school prematurely were apparently shunned by their former colleagues.

The students shared a strong sense of camaraderie and common purpose. This had both positive and negative effects. Student of both sexes were instructed in *Hadar* – perhaps best described as 'dignified comportment' – and male students took on a protective role towards the younger, female students.[23] According to Halpern, however, it took time to instil in the older males a sense of respect and *Hadar* – indeed, *Gentlemeniut* – vis à vis their female colleagues. There was much discussion on how the two sexes should best relate to each other, not only because of the discrepancy in age but also because the female students did not want to 'owe any favours which could later be redeemed'. This is not to say that romantic relationships did not blossom, and Halpern reports instances of marriage between students. However, permission to marry had to be granted by Halpern who, as chief commander, apparently had the last word on every aspect of a student's life.

Both students and staff were part of the school's governing body, and thus bore equal responsibility in running the school. Those cadets guilty of misdemeanours – even if these occurred outside the auspices of the school –

were tried in a court made up of their peers. By all accounts, these 'comrade courts' were taken very seriously; every measure was taken to ensure that students projected the prestige and honour that went along with being a Betar *madrikh*-in-training.

Financial support for the school was by no means comprehensive, and it struggled with a hand-to-mouth existence throughout its short history. Nonetheless, the school's leaders and students showed no small degree of entrepreneurial spirit in organising fundraising activities, from staffing the cloakrooms at various social events, to putting on banquets, balls and parties. Materials for the school – everything from books and fencing foils to medicine, bandages, water bottles, and even paintings for the 'future corridors' of a permanent building – were bought with the proceeds, or donated, privately. Once Jabotinsky gave his official sanction to the school upon his return to Palestine in 1929, material goods became easier to acquire. In spite of this upswing in prestige and income, the school had no fixed location; lessons took places at students' homes, and on occasion, outdoors in the woods, often in the pouring rain.

Halpern's right hand man was Yosef Paamoni, who, in spite of an apparent short temper and anxious disposition, was put in charge of the school's female division. He was born Josef Glokman, on 20 July 1902, in St Petersburg. Imprisoned in Siberia for 'anti-national' – in other words, Zionist – activity during the 1917 Revolution, Paamoni was eventually allowed to emigrate to Mandatory Palestine in 1925, where he became actively involved in the newly formed Revisionist Party. He worked as a bacteriologist for the Pasteur Institute in Tel Aviv until 1927, when he was appointed director of the central laboratory of the Kupat Holim (health service) in the Histadrut. Notably, he was fired from this latter position in the wake of the Arlosoroff murder.[24]

Halpern considered Lieutenant Arie Bayevsky to be the best of the school's instructors, although he was, by all accounts, quite the character. The nephew of a former Admiral of the Russian Navy, Russko-Yaponskaya, Bayevsky was raised in the Russian Orthodox Church, and had considerable naval experience, before he ended up in Mandate Palestine 'by chance'. He would later become instrumental in assisting Halpern set up the Hebrew Naval Training Academy in Civitavecchia. According to Halpern, Bayevsky possessed an 'unbelievable encyclopaedic knowledge of both sea and land'. This 'wonderful person' was, however, also a 'scary alcoholic', and

we often had to postpone lectures because [he had drunk] one bottle too many.
In most cases, Bayevsky managed to read lectures properly and interestingly

... while still completely drunk. He read in Russian, and I translated to the Mother Tongue. At first, this shocked the school, but the [students] got used to it, accepted it, and got to like it.[25]

Towering in reputation over the rest of the instructors was the figure of Abba Ahimeir, who was already by this time well on his way to achieving the status of a cult figure within Revisionist ranks of the Yishuv, and was 'quite well-known' to the students of the Betar Leadership School. He had 'happily' accepted Halpern's invitation to instruct the future Betar leaders in Jewish history and culture. But, Halpern's seemingly innocuous reminiscences of his colleague and friend also reveal some rather telling information:

It was strange to see this bookworm in army fatigues, stretched out calmly in front of the leaders. By the way, this uniform changed him to the point of unrecognizability. This same bookworm later demonstrated how you should stand up for the truth. Because of his pointed actions, he sat [i.e., would end up sitting] in a Palestinian jail with Arab thieves on numerous occasions. Abba Ahimeir was one of those people who overstepped the boundary of logical battle, [and] showed his strength because of his nationalistic views. ... But in the school he always remained strictly within the given framework. And everything he taught was both necessary and interesting.[26]

Halpern's observations regarding Ahimeir's transformation, once he donned his army fatigues, not only are noteworthy but also, I would argue, go to the very crux of a study that attempts to define, explain and trace Ahimeir's ideology and ideological trajectory. The act of putting on his army fatigues was not only an aesthetic expression of Ahimeir's increasingly militaristic ideology but also, equally as important, it was an act that was apparently, for him, transformative. Ahimeir was no longer the shy intellectual 'bookworm', but rather the proud instructor – indeed 'commander' – of the BLTS cadets. And Ahimeir's was not an isolated case. Spengler's and Adorno's observations, noted earlier, that the sublimation and transformation of the primal, psycho-sexual instinct played a pivotal role in the behaviour of the 'bourgeois terrorist', are noteworthy. They attempt to philosophically explain what is empirically unprovable: that a 'repressed libido' – a heroic act, in and of itself[27] – is a contributing factor to 'bourgeois terrorist' action, to the 'heroism that proclaims itself'.[28] The fact that the need for the sublimation of the psycho-sexual desire into active engagement was present among the 'bourgeois terrorists' of the Maximalists, can be of no doubt. In a letter to Ahimeir from Brit HaBiryonim member Yosef

Hagalili that used as evidence in Ahimeir's trial, to be discussed in the next chapter, Hagalili writes:

> Yes Abba, I cannot live any longer without activity. ... I desire to live the life of the movement; I want to feel every day and every minute that [the] movement is alive ... otherwise I fear that I will become stuck in the boredom and lack of interest in life. ... Due to the great emptiness, questions of sexual life and other such like questions are taking place in my life and this is very very bad. Had I some kind of interest in my life there would be no room for such questions; at any rate not in such sharp form. Each one of the members in Jerusalem would surely sit down and write a letter similar to mine.[29]

Due to a move to Jerusalem, Ahimeir taught at the Betar Leadership School for only a short period of time. Nonetheless, his influence – both ideological and practical – persisted, and he continued to teach, and assisted in setting exams. And Halpern certainly remained proud of Ahimeir's attachment to the BLTS. Although Ahimeir perhaps did not have quite the same high regard for Halpern – he considered him to be ideologically inconsequent, and doubtless also recognised his rather self-inflated ego – the two remained on friendly terms for life.[30] Curiously, they died just over two months apart of each other: Ahimeir on 6 June and Halpern on 27 August 1962.

The BLTS was divided into three sections: nursing and housekeeping, which was exclusively female, and self-defence, which was split further into male and female groups. The nursing cadets often provided first aid at parties and other events that were held in Tel Aviv, and such endeavours contributed to the students' sense of accomplishment. Reflecting the school's ethos of 'active defence' – and once again, it should be stressed that this point of difference in ideology is what, for the moment, set the school apart from the official Betar position – the most important sections of the school were the male and female self-defence divisions. The students received comprehensive training that included instruction in military drill, tactics and strategy, basic weaponry, first aid, partisan warfare, espionage, map reading and topography, and fencing. They even received instruction in 'rock throwing'.

A close scrutiny of examination questions and exercises not only testifies to the great detail invested into all aspects of a cadet's military training and the great seriousness with which this training was all taken but also reveals how thoroughly the school placed emphasis on the fact that it was an institute for training future leaders and commanders who were destined to operate in Betar. Ideology never lurked too far below the surface. Thus, while examination cards for the first sergeant's course at the school tested the student's knowledge of both the theory and practice behind a particular military drill on the one hand, they also expected from the examinee the ability to explain the utility of the exercise from the perspective of both commander and student, on the other. Thus, for example, one of the exam cards is laid out as follows:

Card 1

Theory

1. What should the commander acquire?
2. How is the tuition of drill exercises for individuals different from drill exercises for leaders?

Explanation

1. Standing at ease (Placement of legs, heels, the toes, the arms, the body. What is permitted when standing at ease, and what is forbidden).
2. Creation of a tight unit (walking) – in single file, on the right [hand] side.
3. Build a column to the right.[31]

Other theoretical questions included: 'What are drill exercises created for?' 'What does the sergeant learn at the school?' 'How much time should the commander allow for the unit to understand that he commands the maximum discipline from it?' 'How is [this particular] command categorised [and] how is it given?' 'In which situation [state] does the commander find himself in the moment of [giving] a command?' 'What to do with those who lag behind?' and so on. Every aspect of command leadership was addressed, so that by the time a candidate reached his or her final test card, he or she would have demonstrated a solid ideological understanding, combined with the ability for the successful practical execution, of each exercise.

The highly worked-out night training exercises and espionage games on file, as well as copious letters, memos and dictates, all from Halpern and having to do with the Betar Leadership School, testify to the great care and attention to detail that he invested in the school's administration and creation of its curriculum.[32] They also reveal a rather strong, controlling personality, a man who took himself, perhaps – and without a doubt, his school – quite seriously. The acquisition of Ahimeir, as the school's instructor in Jewish history and culture, was doubtless a feather in his cap.

Halpern notes in his reminiscences that cultural education at the leadership school was divided into two parts: *Pegishot* (meetings) and *Hartzaot* (lectures).

Apparently, the lectures took on more the form of a seminar, where students spoke for 20–30 minutes on various topics set by the instructors, after which, 'Each student had the right to give his or her opinion – [but] not his or her reasoning – within a five-minute time limit. Five minutes taught them how to concentrate their thoughts.'[33]

Pegishot were more social gatherings – a typical meeting could include dancing and light-hearted entertainment, such as joke-telling – but although less formal they nonetheless counted as lessons. And the students could be called upon at any point to demonstrate with alacrity their newly learned proficiency with 'Jewish etiquette' and *Hadar*. Halpern gives an example of students being asked to propose a toast to, and 'declare their love' for, a particularly unpopular person, as an exercise in diplomacy and good etiquette.

A template for the organisation and running order of a successful *Pegishah*, along with suggested themes and so on, written in 1928 or 1929 by the instructor in 'Ceremony and *Hadar*', Abba Gilvitz, survives, and provides a fascinating glimpse into the ideology and practice behind one of the many varied facets of the training school:

Typical Running Order of a *Pegishah*

Cultural-Educational Section (1.15 [*sic*] hours)

A. Introduction
B. Lecture by one of the students on a predetermined subject (20–25 minutes)
C. Reason[ing] and expansion of the subject by [blank space, presumably for a person's name] [that] he will assist the lecturer during the order of the lecture … (10–15 minutes)
D. [word not clear, but probably has a meaning close to 'sharing'] of opinions on the subject of the lecture (20 minutes)
E. Assessment of the subject by the *Madrikhim* and the 'mature comrades' in the presence of the students of the BLTS, conclusion and issuing of the decisions [i.e., final verdicts] by vote.
F. Adjournment of the Cultural-Educational Section.

Educational Recreation Time

A. Introduction
B. Singing
C. Dinner (wine or non-alcoholic beverages)
D. Humorous lectures, solo songs, etc.
E. [unclear]

F. Adjournment

G. Anthem 'HaTikvah'[34]

In order to better stimulate a successful post-lecture discussion, students were informed of the lecture topic before the meeting. Furthermore, the evening's lecturer was given his or her topic by the particular *madrikh* responsible for a particular subject area. And regarding the second part of the meetings – Social Recreation Time – it was mandated that this began with choral singing of a 'fixed order' of songs, to which it was possible to add more.

Without a doubt, this second part of the meetings – the 'educational' or 'social' recreation periods – did not differ too much from similar events in other Zionist youth groups. Interest in choral singing reflected the Hebrew literary and cultural revival that permeated all levels of the Yishuv, and was certainly a feature of all of its youth group social gatherings, as was the singing of *HaTikvah*, the Zionist anthem, at their conclusion.[35] Where the meetings of the Betar Leadership School differed from those of other groups would have been on the concentration on comportment – once again, as understood in the concept of *Hadar* – that was so important to both Betar and the leadership school, and that was reflected in the choice of topics that the *madrikhim* chose for lectures and discussion (c.f. points D and G, in the following list):

A. Goals of our federation [הסתדרותנו: this could be read as either the leadership school or Betar; the meaning is unclear from the context]. The main thesis is the archetype of the 'New Jew' – citizen of Eretz Israel.

B. Expansion of our federation [again, it is unclear whether the reference is to Betar or the leadership school]

D. Behaviour of members of the federation. The internal concept inherent in external behaviour.

G. External image and its value.[36]

And we see evidence of Ahimeir's influence – if not his very hand – in a page that outlines some suggested 'Theses for the Lecture: The Individual and the Public, the Individual [Personality] and the Nation'.[37] The lecture posits the theory that the question of how to determine the essence of the state, and where to delineate its limits on the individual, is a fundamental question with which organised society has wrestled since the dawn of its existence. Who is subordinate to whom when there is clash of interests? In response, the author suggests two main streams of thought: First, that of the individual before the state, which views the state as a creation for the service of humankind. Second, the view that sees the state not as an artificial creation, but rather as a 'natural organism'; humans live societally and their 'essence and existence are embodied in societal and national life'.

The author contends that the usual tendency to separate the concept of the private individual who struggles against his world, his freedom, his very soul, from that of a public society that struggles against any individual who follows the natural tendencies of his heart, and strives to liberate himself from the yoke of the public, is fundamentally flawed. Indeed, he suggests that each individual possesses both a 'personal element' and a 'national element'; the two elements are complementary to each other, work in tandem and are inseparable. Just as there is no 'pure personality' that contains nothing of the national element, neither is there a 'pure nation[-ality]' that contains nothing of the personal element. The concept of family – 'the first link in the chain' that demands from its children to give themselves up for its sake – is found in other parts of society: social class, political party, church and so on. That the idea of such 'imagined' politico-social communities parallels the idea of a greater 'imagined' 'national' community is absolutely clear from the context of the lecture.[38] Furthermore, all of these 'physical' communal components influenced individual tendencies, choices and actions in many different 'conceptual' directions: 'ethics, laws, conventions, customs, manners, language, and literature'; inseparable elements from an individual's 'soul and essence'. Thus, only through a synthesis of the personal and national elements was the development of the individual, and development of the nation, possible. Such an ideological construct made it possible – indeed, necessary – for a person to dedicate himself to his nation, while continuing to maintain a sense of himself. Moreover, it allowed for self-sacrifice in every form, provided it was carried out in the name of the greater, national good.

While it is impossible to state categorically that the lecture was written by Ahimeir, certain elements in its composition lead to the fairly safe assumption that he was, in fact, its author, and that he most likely delivered it to students at the BLTS. First, we know that Ahimeir occupied himself with the idea of the individual versus society, and the question of whether something that was allowed one group should be allowed the other. Second, a curriculum for 'Ideology and Society' – the division for which Ahimeir was responsible, at the school – would almost undoubtedly broach the subject matter that the lecture addressed, certainly more likely so than any of the other curriculums offered. Third, the intellectual nature of the discussion, with its Spenglerian, Hegelian and Jungian overtones – even if pseudoscientific by today's standards – and the style in which it was written, suggest Ahimeir's authorship.[39] If indeed Ahimeir's work, the lecture testifies to the very particular ideological influence he had on the Betar leaders-in-training – certainly when it came to their understanding of the concept of the nation and its relation to the individual – and consequently on the 'general' Betar youth that they would go on to command.

Ideological overlap between Betar and the BLTS

Examination of the aforementioned document, while illuminating, nonetheless raises several further questions. In what other Jewish historico-cultural topics did the students receive instruction, and through which particular ideological filter were they presented? Did the choice of such topics, and the particular ideological bent in which they were presented correspond to the instruction given in similar subject areas to the 'general' Betar youth? Who influenced whom in this respect? Did the BLTS take its cue for the design of its Jewish historic-cultural and ideological courses from the general Betari, or vice versa? I suggest that we begin with the middle question first, and address the scope and nature of a Betari ideological and Jewish cultural education.

An examination of a Betar Youth-Eretz Israel training manual from 1927–28 gives a rather comprehensive overview of how the group educated its youth, and how it successfully differentiated itself ideologically from other Zionist youth groups.[40] Thus, the leaders of Betar youth group training sessions – to be clear, I refer here to Betar *Madrikhim*, and not to BLTS trainee cadets – were given points of discussion for their respective groups. These are listed in the training manual as 'Questions of the Stance in Betar', and cover topics as diverse as 'Legionary-ism and Betar', 'Compliance', '*Hadar* and Beauty', 'The Jewish State [literally, the 'Hebrew' State] and its Foundations', 'The Structure of Betar', 'The Tradition of Betar, and its Influence of the life of the Betari', 'The Historical Foundations of the Trumpeldor Union', 'Betar Public Opinion', 'Betar, Revisionist [Party], New Zionist Organisation', 'Why do the Jews have no right to exist in the Galut? Why was the Galut created?', 'How to Explain the Problem of Galut to Your Youth Group Students?' 'Evacuation of the Galut – Its Nature and Role', 'The False Messianic Movement – Its Essence and its Lesson', 'The Messianic Destiny in the Life of the Nations, and in Israel', 'What signifies the life of the ghetto Jewish people in the Diaspora?' 'Explain the concept of Zionism', 'Why do we need land? Can we not continue to exist in the Diaspora? If not, why?' '"First *Aliyah*"

– the essence and results', 'Land of Israel to the Jewish people in the Diaspora', 'The Rise in Illegal Immigration' and so on.

The final discussion point is noteworthy – appearing as it does in a document from 1928 – since it precedes 'official' Jewish illegal immigration to Mandate Palestine by ten years. Most likely a reaction to the 1922 Churchill White Paper, which was the first call for a reduction of Jewish immigration to Mandate Palestine, it demonstrates not only that Betar – and, by implication, the Revisionist Party – considered the possibility of, if not the necessity for, illegal immigration far earlier than other groups in the Yishuv but also that the group included the issue as a core ideological standpoint. Although there was certainly some overlap with other youth groups when it came to questions relating to the history of Zionism and Jewish life in the Galut, the sometimes defensive – if not somewhat antagonistic – tone in which the questions were posed ('Why do the Jews have no right to exist in the Galut?') reflects the uncompromising mind-set that certainly set Betar apart from other Yishuv Zionist youth groups.

Betar students in Mandate Palestine were also instructed in general knowledge, once per week.[41] It appears that courses on Jewish history and culture were offered at different levels of difficulty. The Betar handbook, to which I refer here, contains curriculum for the aforementioned course ('General Knowledge'), as well as a more advanced 'Program for Cultural Work – for Level 'C' [ג] of Betar in Eretz Israel'.[42] The first section of the latter course, while it focused primarily on history, current events and issues in European and Yishuv Jewish life, also – notably – studied other national liberation movements. Thus, the first themes that the course addressed surveyed the current state of affairs in recently 'emancipated' nations such as Italy, Greece, Serbia, Turkey, Czechoslovakia, Egypt, India and China. The choice of nations was certainly not accidental. At the time that the course curriculum was printed – 24 May 1928 – the governments of every one of the countries listed earlier contained national-liberationist political parties that enjoyed varying degrees of representation, from the uneasy political alliance between 'His Majesty's Government' and the Wafd Party in Egypt, to the overwhelmingly durable reign of the Fascist Party in Italy. That these nationalist movements were viewed in a positive light, and seen as role models for Betar's concept of Jewish nationalism cannot be doubted. Indeed, this claim is easily substantiated by an examination of the remainder of the topics that were covered in the first section of this course in general knowledge: the situation of the Jews before and after liberation, the role of Jews in liberation, ideologies of the Jews before and after liberation, the role of the youth movement in liberation and the influence of sport organisations on the liberation movement.[43]

Other subjects that contributed to the 'general knowledge' of the Betar youth included a thorough grounding in the knowledge of 'the land', a geographical study – similar to the German concept of *Landeskunde* – of Eretz Israel.[44] Thus, cadets studied not only history and political and physical geography but also topography – 'especially roads' and 'mountain[ous] border districts', local historical knowledge and 'how to exploit hiding places'. It is also interesting to note the emphasis that was placed on sport and the concept of the 'sporting movement', which was most likely a nod in the direction of European *Sportvereine.* Students learned the history of the sporting movement, its 'political and economic' worth and – most important – its value for the youth.

Betar youth were also educated in the theory of war, its historical importance and utility in the past, present and future, as well as its effect on international relations. That this was included in the syllabus of a 'general knowledge' course for a young Betari is noteworthy indeed, and demonstrates that the concept of – if not necessarily the necessity for – war was a key ideological tenet of Betar. Indeed, *Torat Milhamah* (The Teaching of War) preceded *Torat Tzionut* (The Teaching of Zionism), which was the final area of study in a Betar cadet's 'general knowledge' education. Not unsurprisingly – for a youth group that represented a political party that sought a revision back to 'pure' Herzlian Political Zionism – a young Betari was instructed in Zionist doctrines that emphasised Herzl's *Der Judenstaat* (The Jewish State), and divided the development of Zionist history into two parts: from the publication of Herzl's book until the Balfour Declaration, and from the beginning of the British Mandate, onwards. Indeed, the British Mandate government came under critical scrutiny; not only its 'value' but also its 'liabilities' were listed as points to be covered in the course. The leadership of the Yishuv was also scrutinised, and its physical and political makeup was discussed, as was the rather pointed question of 'how the Eretz Israeli government was fulfilling its obligations towards the Hebrew nation'.

The course outline is interesting, not only with regard to the content that it covered but also, equally, with regard to the order in which the subjects were taught. Notably, Betar cadets learned first about other national liberation movements; then about the 'general' situation of European Jewry, with the implied conundrum that it faced, both before and after emancipation. A student's attention was then focused on the 'land' itself. However, such an apparently innocuous focus on the 'geographical' also included a strong geopolitical element.[45] After that, more theoretical issues, such as youth, sport and war, were addressed, and only then did the student move on to the study of Zionist history, theory and practice. Consciously or unconsciously then, the course's design funnels downwards, both 'geographically' and 'theoretically', from the situation in the wider world to the situation in Zionism and the Yishuv. In other words, from 'World Current Events' (of a specific type, to be sure) to 'Jewish History' to 'Geography' (which addresses both physical and utilitarian issues regarding the land), 'Theory' (the ideological micro-trajectory 'Youth-Sport-War', as outlined in the course manual, is, in itself, not illogical) and finally, to 'Practice' (Zionism). The concept of 'land' stands – both literally and ideologically – in the centre of all of this.

The more advanced Betar 'Programme for Cultural Work' re-addressed and expanded upon many of the subjects covered in the 'general knowledge' course. It was split into three sections – historical, societal and political – and addressed issues in all of these subject areas in great detail, which apparently reflected the 'cultural' approach of the course. Not surprisingly, the study of the history of Israel began with the Patriarchs, and continued through the periods of the judges, kings, the Babylonian exile and Second Temple, down to the Talmudic period and the Middle Ages, after which the issues of 'emancipation and education' and 'assimilation and nationalism' were addressed, and finally, 'Zionism'. In spite – or perhaps because – of the Political-Zionist ideological stance of Betar, all forms – proto, political and practical – of Zionist ideology and history were taught, as were key contemporary issues that the Zionist movement was currently facing, such as the Churchill White Paper, and the period of Herbert Samuel's high-commissionership. And – important for the ideological education of a Betar youth – the course also taught the history of the Jewish Legion.[46]

Education in 'Knowledge of the Land' was expanded to include Hebrew and Arab economies, as well as a survey of the 'neighbours of Eretz Israel'. Furthermore – and rather pointedly – students were instructed in the 'history of settlement in America, Southern Africa, Australia and Greece', along with a survey of the 'political conditions in each location, relationships with local residents – the natives – and the 'question of cheap labour'. Such topics were then applied to the situation in the Yishuv, and addressed in that specific context; from the rise of the Biluim to the 'Third *Aliyah* and settlement based on the philanthropy of various Zionist organisations; the Fourth *Aliyah* and private initiative in industry and agriculture; [and] *aliyah* and settlement in the future'. Further discussion was given to the concept of the 'Pioneering' ethos, its degeneration in the Yishuv and the concept of the 'Betar Pioneer', which may be safely assumed was most likely an application of the ideology of the traditional Zionist *Halutz* to suit the specific ideological needs of the Revisionist youth group. That the Betar Pioneer was decidedly less agriculturally and more militarily oriented than his counterpart from HaPoel HaTzair may be deduced in consideration of the 'political' section of the course.[47] Here – in addition to the perhaps predictable education in Zionist and Yishuv institutions and political structures – topics such as the 'question of the colonising regime' and the 'question of security in the country' were also addressed. Finally, students were educated in the biographies of Joseph Trumpeldor and Ze'ev Jabotinsky.

What is perhaps most striking about the course outline is that – in terms of the division of Jewish historical periodisation, and the identification of salient political themes and security concerns – it might just as easily have come from a present-day course syllabus on Zionist history. Intellectual-historical terms such as the 'Third' and 'Fourth' *Aliyot* were used already in 1928 in the same way that we use them today. It should, however, be noted that, after approximately 1921, the term *Aliyah* had been appropriated by the Labour movement to refer only to the selective immigration of Zionist pioneers, and not to general immigration to the Land of Israel.[48] By 1928, such understanding of the term was de rigueur. Indeed, at the time of the course's inception, the 'Fourth *Aliyah*' was still an ongoing phenomenon.

I would suggest that the topics covered in the Betar courses, as outlined earlier, were almost certainly also addressed in the Betar Leadership Training School. The training manual is not only contemporary with the founding of the BLTS but also – in consideration of the fact that the very rationale for the school was to provide, inter alia, ideological training for Betar leaders – it was undoubtedly known, and referred to, by the members of the BLTS and certainly also Ahimeir, the school's instructor in 'Jewish History and Culture'. Nonetheless, at first glance there is little to suggest exactly how the themes discussed earlier were approached, neither in the context of the courses for Betari youth group members, nor that of the BLTS cadets, which – it goes without saying, but bears repetition – provided the training for leaders who would presumably eventually teach these self-same courses in Jewish history and culture to the Betari youth. The existing documentation provides only skeletal course outlines, not a comprehensive ideological picture. Presumably, the responsibility for all such course content was left to the individual instructor, provided he or she remained within the ideological parameters that delineated the particular Betari position. Sadly, there is no documentation in the archival material for the BLTS that is unequivocally the work of Ahimeir. We cannot know for certain how he approached his role as instructor in Jewish History and Culture at the BLTS, nor the actual content of his lectures. This unfortunate reality does not, however, prevent a certain degree of educated speculation, based on circumstantial evidence.

For example, the anonymous essay on the individual versus the collective, discussed earlier, further argues that the Hebrew Bible is 'not concerned at all with [the] singular ... but, rather, the collective'. Indeed, the author continues, the very concept of 'reward and punishment' in the *Tanakh* is directed towards the 'collective' and not the 'individual'. Putting aside the obvious similarities to Ahimeir's ideological outlook, which mandated the prioritisation of the collective over the individual, the essay holds a much more specific indication that its author is most likely Ahimeir. The essay contains a discussion that frames the biblical concept of 'reward and punishment' – in Hebrew, *sakhar v'onesh* – as a collective fate. In other words, the god of *sakhar v'onesh* rewarded and punished his collective people – and not a particular individual – appropriately. Thus, an individual bore great responsibility for his actions vis à vis his collective. This rather unique conceptual understanding of the term bears a striking similarity to the manner in which Ahimeir refers to the very same concept in his book *Yudaikah*, which was published over thirty years later, in 1960.[49] I would suggest that no other instructor at the BLTS had either the intellectual interest, or savvy, in engaging in such a sophisticated discussion, nor would he or she have occasion to do so within the context of a BLTS that saw Ahimeir as the sole instructor in Jewish history and culture. The similarity of the two discussions, which deal with both the priority of collective over individual interests and the concept of *sakhar v'onesh*, allows not only for the almost unequivocal identification of Ahimeir as the author of the BLTS lecture notes but also, furthermore and more important, for our use of *Yudaikah* – itself a collection of short essays that reflect the accumulation of Ahimeir's considerable knowledge of Jewish cultural history – as a springboard for a speculative discussion of how Ahimeir might have presented his lectures at the BLTS. At the very least, *Yudaikah* paints a comprehensive picture of Ahimeir's conception of ancient Jewish history and culture. But, assuming that Ahimeir is indeed the author of the BLTS lecture notes discussed earlier, I would further speculate that – since there is a striking degree of ideological and thematic similarity between the lecture and *Yudaikah*, which was published thirty years later – Ahimeir nonetheless retained a certain degree of ideological consistency throughout his life. Thus, a closer study of Ahimeir's conception of ancient Jewish history and culture as presented in *Yudaikah* should give us a fairly accurate indication of the content of Ahimeir's lectures in Jewish History and Culture at the BLTS in the late 1920s.

Ahimeir's cultural-historical conception of the Jewish nation

Published just two years before his death in 1962, *Yudaikah* offers a glimpse into the ideological thought of Ahimeir, the cultural historian. Nonetheless, it should be noted that for him (cultural-) history and (national-) politics were inextricably linked; indeed, he says as much, as will be discussed next. The book comprises eleven chapters, each of which contains several smaller sub-sections.[50] Not surprisingly, for a work written in the wake of the Second World War and the Holocaust, much of the book concentrates on these phenomena. Thus, I will limit my discussion of the book to its first three chapters – 'From Ur of the Chaldeans to the Present-Day', 'Ethics of the *Tanakh*' and 'What is Judaism?' – the contents of which are not informed by post–Second World War Europe, and hence may therefore be more safely projected backwards onto a speculative discussion of what Ahimeir's ideological content might have included during his tenure at the BLTS.

Already in the book's first sentence we see the similarity in ideological outlook and writing style with the essay on the individual and the nation, discussed earlier:

> The history of every nation [*leom*] is the history of the unbreakable physical bond between the nation and its land. There are no English outside of England. The English who emigrated from England became, with the passing of time, North Americans, Australians, Canadians, etc.[51]

Without its own land, then, a nation lost its particular national characteristics and became culturally bastardised, or transformed altogether. The almost pseudoscientific reasoning – a cultural-historical observation that presents such a polarised conclusion and is, itself, rather polarised and impossible to prove empirically – harks back to the essay discussed earlier. Indeed, we find ourselves back in the world of Ahimeir's doctoral dissertation on Spengler, where assimilation is a characteristic of Spenglerian 'Civilization', and thus, cultural annihilation. There is no middle ground. That Ahimeir saw things in terms of binary opposites is clear throughout *Yudaikah*, where such discussion could relate to historical figures (Moses and Aaron, Cain and Abel, and others), ideological concepts (individual and group, Zion and *Galut*, etc.), ethical-cultural constructs (reward and punishment, light and darkness) or geophysical constructs (Sinai and Negev, Dan and Beersheba, Zion and Galut, etc.).

It is interesting that he also divides the land of Israel into two binary opposing sections: the fertile, Mediterranean north, where the 'sea breeze permeates the air', and the desert south with its torrential winds and barren land. The town of Beersheba delineates the division between them. For Ahimeir, it was in the southern part, with the mountains and sunny blue skies of the Negev and Sinai deserts, where one truly felt not only the great expanse of the land but also its singular beauty. Here, in this land of contrasts, not only God but also Satan had spoken to his respective patriarchs and prophets. The desert thus inherently contained diametrically opposed – and competing – creative and destructive elements; it could therefore accommodate both God and Satan, Moses and Balaam, and so on. In line with his theory, Ahimeir divides the 'geopolitical history' of the Negev into four epochs, two creative and two destructive. The first period was the epoch of the patriarchs Jethro and Moses, where both the 'secret of iron was discovered' and the chronicler was 'invented'. Ahimeir believed that both of these two developments would have a far-reaching impact on a people that would eventually come to be divided between proponents of the pen and proponents of the sword. Most importantly, the Negev in its first period of flourishing was where the concept of the belief in one god was born, as was the weighty concept of 'reward and punishment', discussed earlier, which Ahimeir identifies as the 'secret of the relationships between man and his society'.[52] Finally, the Negev and Sinai were where the Jewish nation was born and in whom the 'Semitic spirit' of the desert – caring, subjective, ethical and, indeed, wandering – was embodied.

However, as stated, Ahimeir recognised in the desert also an ever-competing destructive element that constantly threatened the pastoral status quo. Hence the binary opposites represented by the figures of Yitzhak and Ishmael, Jacob and Esau, Moses ('The Prophet of Truth') and Balaam ('The False Prophet'). And he notes that the hunters of the desert – Nimrod, Amalek, Edom, and others – had rejected the shepherds who resided in the land that lay 'between Dan and Beersheba'. For Ahimeir, this eternal struggle, between hunter and shepherd, was epitomised in Jewish attitudes vis a vis the figures of Esau and Amalek; 'they became symbols … and the war between them and the nation became a war of life and death'.[53] The tribes of Israel went on to settle in the fertile north, the 'land of milk and honey', where the 'shepherd became farmer'. The Negev, by contrast, 'became a desert', abandoned, except by the 'hunters and thieves' who had caused the destruction of its pastoral element. Indeed, Ahimeir calls Herod – the cause of the destruction of the Second Temple – as 'a man of the Negev'.[54] And although the Jewish nation eventually became centred in the land 'between Dan and Beersheba', there was always a sector that would not forget its desert roots, and which continued to live the 'life of the Negev and Sinai', even in the north. Ahimeir identifies the Tribe of Levi as fulfilling this role during the First Temple period, and – notably – the Essenes, during the period of the Second Temple.

The Second Temple period also signalled for him the second blooming of the Negev, this time, however, not thanks to the children of Abraham, but rather to 'Jethro, Reuel, descendants of Midian' and the children of Nebaioth, the son of Ishmael. Unlike the Israelites – whose period in the Negev had created a written culture – the Nebaiothians had created a culture of edifice building, the 'perfect desert civilisation', but one that was however 'impossible to transport'. Thus, although 'Nimrod, Amalek, Ishmael, Edom destroyed the Negev', the Bnei Israel were nonetheless able to successfully flee from the desert with their holy scriptures, and transported them to the north. For Ahimeir, these were the two key factors that had preserved the survival of Jewish culture throughout its history: the Jewish ability to wander and adapt, and the creation of a self-defining culture that was written, and thus easily transportable from place to place. Finally, Ahimeir believed that this second 'blooming of the desert' was destroyed by the prophets of whom he calls 'Balaam the Second' – Mohammed – during the Arab-Moslem conquests in the seventh century. Unfortunately, however, this time 'Balaam had conquered Moses'.[55]

Ahimeir contends that the Jewish people stood at the crossroads of three great human civilisations throughout the course of history: first, the civilisation of the Ancient Orient; second, Mediterranean civilisation, to which the Northern Hebrews – 'Phoenicians' – joined first, and the Southern Hebrews – 'Canaanites and Hellenists' – joined only in the days of Alexander the Great; third, Western European civilisation, that 'began Muslim, in the south of Spain', but is essentially Christian. And here, for Ahimeir, is the crux of the matter:

> We are living now in the epoch of 'The Decline of the Christian West'. Could the Jewish People enjoy an independent existence without the Christian nations? At any rate, the Jewish People [now] close the circle of their historical circuit and return to their land.[56]

Thus, Ahimeir explains the return of the Jewish People to the Land of Israel in both quasi-Messianic – certainly from a Jewish perspective – and Spenglerian terms, that is to say both culturally religious and (pseudo-)empirically-meta-historically. Indeed, the nod to Spengler is deliberate.[57] The three cultural epochs, to which Ahimeir refers, correspond almost exactly to Spengler's Magian, Apollonian and Faustian Cultures. Thus, for Ahimeir, the decline of Western Christian, 'Faustian' Culture – and Magian and Apollonian Cultures, before that – in which the Jewish nation, 'standing at the crossroads', had participated but was nonetheless denied of any national-sovereign position, had created the conditions necessary for Jewish national rebirth and the re-emergence of the Jewish Nation in the land of its ancestors. The period of Galut represented the period of aimless wandering that, according to Spenglerian theory, each declining Culture was required to undergo before it qualified once again for cultural rebirth.

Ahimeir seems to suggest – although somewhat at odds with Spengler's own analysis of Jewish history – a Spenglerian reading of the Jewish historical trajectory that I would summarise as follows: A First Period of Jewish Culture, which contains – in Spenglerian terms – four stages in its cultural life: 'Pre-Cultural' (from Abraham to Moses), 'Youth' (The First Temple Period), 'Maturity' (The Second Temple Period) and 'Old Age' (from the relocation of the Jewish centre from Jerusalem to Yavne, and the period of the Jewish Wars). However, I would further posit that this final period remained incomplete, from a Spenglerian – and seemingly also an Ahimeirian – perspective. There were competing streams within Judaism during this time: the much more Jewish 'cultural' warrior-rebel Maccabees, who attempted – ultimately without success – to re-establish Jewish national sovereignty in Judea; and the more 'civilised' Pharisees, who went on to Yavne and the Diaspora.[58] The inability of the 'culturally-younger' Hasmoneans-Maccabees to restore Jewish national culture led to a dominance of the more culturally mature, 'civilised' Jewish communities – the Pharisees – in Yavne and Galut, where the Jewish people experienced a prolonged period of national decline and 'geographical longing'. Indeed, statements such as 'The spiritual history of our nation is the history of geographical longing' indicate not only the importance for both a physical homeland for its people but also the unescapable longing that occurs when the physical homeland is removed.[59]

However, Ahimeir believes that such 'geographical longing' did not only exist during the period of Galut but – notably – also in ancient Jewish civilisation, among the people of the fertile north who longed for the desert south; in other words, the population of the land 'between Dan and Beersheba' that had longed for the Sinai and Negev. From the beginning of Jewish history, 'Abel the shepherd, man of the desert, was righteous ... [w]hereas Cain, worker of the land, builder of cities, he was evil'.[60] The patriarchs and the tribes of Israel were righteous because they were nomads, but 'as soon as the tribes of Israel wandered into the desert, they longed for Egypt'.[61] For Ahimeir, this sense of longing – effectively, a sense of eternal dissatisfaction and internal contradiction – was a unique, integral characteristic of the Jewish nation. Thus, Moses leads the Jewish People to the land of Canaan, while Korach beckons them back to Egypt; the giving of the Torah at Sinai is countered by worship of the – 'Egyptian' – golden calf. And the prophet Jeremiah had considered the desert tribe of Yehuda 'more righteous', than the 'vintners' Noah and Ephraim. For Ahimeir it is noteworthy that the negative attitude to wine is found in Islam, the 'religion of the desert'; indeed, it fits perfectly into his ideology. And finally, Uz – home of Job the righteous – also bordered the desert.

Yudaikah, it should be remembered, was written after the foundation of the State of Israel. Hence, Ahimeir's pointed comment:

> Thanks to the longing for Zion, the Return to Zion was fulfilled. The State of Israel was established. Ostensibly: the end of longing, of spiritual wandering. And not. Yehuda Halevy said: 'My heart is in the East and I am at the edge [*sic*] of the West', that is to say, 'I'm situated in Spanish Castles and long for Zion'. But the nation that is located in Zion, in contrast to Halevy – sings: 'My heart is in the West and I am at the edge of the East.' We all enter into sharp criticism of the reality of our state. We all reject the reality that is in Zion.[62]

Ahimeir's observation is notable, and completely in line with his analysis of a Jewish history that is characterised by binary opposites that seem unable, or unwilling, to reconcile with each other.

He goes on to discuss, at great length, further binary opposites that were all bound up in Jewish history, in one form or another. He sees the Jewish spirit as having been equally influenced by two 'geophysical' influences: that of the sea versus the desert; north versus south; the Kingdom of Israel-Tribe of Ephraim versus Yehuda; the Mediterranean Sea versus the Dead Sea. And once again, pointedly, Ahimeir notes that the tribe of Benjamin – which was, after all, situated between Ephraim and Yehuda – was destroyed in the war between northern and southern Hebrew tribes. Indeed, for Ahimeir, such irreconcilable contrasts represented the second important ideological thread in the Torah: that of warring brothers.

He sees the 'patriarchs of the nation' as shepherds who came into constant conflict with their hunter-farmer brothers. The firstborn was evil, his younger brother, righteous but naïve. Thus: Cain is pitted against Abel; Ishmael against Isaac; Esau against Jacob; the older brother hailed from the north, the younger from the south. Ahimeir reminds his reader that it was, in fact, the pastoral Hebrews of the south who were the first to believe in one god, and who – with the Tribe of Yehuda 'at its head' – created the idea of superior morality and set out the conditions for good relations between an individual and his society that were the ideological cornerstones of Western civilisation.

Although interesting, and – at first glance – analytically accurate, Ahimeir's claim requires a certain amount of ideological expansion. We should remember that, although Ishmael did 'hail from the north', he was in fact, at the age of fourteen, banished to, and spent the remainder of his life in, the desert – that is to say, the 'south'. Ahimeir does not highlight this fact, probably because it would diminish the strength of his argument. However, he surely recognised the reality that Ishmael also possessed – if not by nature, then certainly by nurture – a certain degree of the spirit of the desert. His observation that the 'ground of the desert is good [*yafeh*] for the religious spirit … [n]ot only Judaism, but also Islam – by contrast – appeared in the desert' supports this interpolation.[63]

The figures of Esau and Jacob also require some contextual expansion. Esau – despite the fact that he is a hunter – nonetheless sells his birthright to his brother in order to acquire 'simple' food: 'bread, and pottage of lentils', in other words, a farmer's, and not a hunter's, fare.[64] This act is, at first glance, rather striking. In addition, Jacob, while perhaps a mild, 'simple' man, was arguably neither righteous, nor naïve. For it is Jacob who refuses to share any of his food until Esau promises to sell him his birthright. Furthermore, Jacob gains Isaac's blessing, becomes the favoured son – and thus also acquires his birthright – through deceit. In the analysis of the historian Israel Yuval, this action is justified because Isaac 'is blind and lives in the past'.[65] Interestingly, Yuval employs a similar typology to Ahimeir in this respect, when he concludes that the 'birthright passes from the man of the field to the man of the tent'.[66] Nonetheless, the 'man of the tent' – Jacob – flees Esau's fury at having been deceived, and goes into exile. It is only after his marriage, and siring of the twelve future leaders of the tribes of Israel, that Jacob returns. The 'chosen son' now heads the 'chosen family', and this time it is Esau who goes into exile.[67] Thus, as Yuval notes, rather pointedly: 'We have a denial of autochthony as the basis for any claims to the Land.'[68] In the story of Jacob and Esau, we see not only the 'superiority of the one who returns from exile over the native, since the foreign settler comes by dint of divine promise, not of original holding rights', but also the subjugation of the older brother by the younger brother.[69] It is striking that Ahimeir misses this very important connection to Zionist ideology, which recognised and privileged the rights of the Jews who were returning from exile, by 'dint of divine promise', over those of the indigenous Palestinian-Arab population.

Ahimeir might also have considered the parental relationships in each pair of brothers, named earlier. Adam and Eve hailed from the same 'land' and 'people' – in point of fact, the same person – but represent the *Urform* of each case. Again, Ahimeir almost certainly recognised this fact, as can be seen in his suggestion that the concept of the Garden of Eden represented the 'Mythological Period' in Israel's history.[70] Abraham and Sarah similarly hailed from the same land and people, but while Adam and Eve were the mythic 'father and mother' of humankind, Abraham and Sarah were the very real father and mother of the Hebrew nation. Abraham and Hagar, by contrast, hailed from both different lands and peoples. And finally, Isaac and Rebecca hail from different lands, but the same people. Thus the union between Isaac – the 'first farmer among the Patriarchs' and a 'man of the field' – and Rebecca – 'hidden in the tent' – thus symbolised the basic dichotomy – between 'culture' and 'civilisation' – within the Jewish nation that Ahimeir alludes to, earlier.[71] Indeed, as he remarks, cynically: Judaism 'destroys itself from within'. It is clear that from his discussion that the only 'true' successors to the father and mother of the Hebrew nation could – like Abraham and Sarah – only come from the same land, and the same people.

Moving forward in Jewish history, Ahimeir considers the House of David, which he divides into three epochs. The first two he designates, undramatically, to the periods of the First and Second Temples, in other words, to the 'historical' and 'post-historical' periods of the House of David, respectively. The third epoch, however, Ahimeir gives over to the whole period of Galut, or what he calls – notably – the period of 'Messianism'.[72] This period of Messianism had, in Ahimeir's eyes, been preceded by a significant degree, not only of political but also of cultural cooperation with 'foreign rule': the 'House of Zadok became a subject of Hellenism', he notes. This cooperation spawned the creation of the Hasmonean Dynasty, which rebelled against foreign rule, and:

> The Hasmonean priests put a royal crown on their heads. The House of David disappeared from the horizon of history, in fact, during the period of the Hasmoneans. And here also, the House of Hasmoneans was rejected from the House of Herod. The third period of the House of David begins with the concept of our nation. Perhaps the most important of all. Because this is the messianic period. The nation inherited disappointments from three of the dynasties of the Second Temple: The House of Zadok, the last Hasmoneans, and the House of Herod.[73]

Ahimeir believes that these disappointments awakened in the Jewish nation both a longing for the past, and – more importantly and as a result – a hope for the future that was embodied in Messianism. Hence, the fact that so many great historical figures had appeared during this period is no accident, in his eyes.

And Ahimeir singles out two figures – once again, binary opposites – who were representatives of this phenomenon: Hillel and Jesus. The former was the 'first and foremost of the biblical commentators', who had founded the 'Dynasty of Presidents'. And opposite the figure of Hillel – 'Jesus Christ'. Both were products of the end of the Second Temple Period – the 'period of disappointment' in Jewish history – and both preached messages of 'love and peace' that, in their different ways, would exert an influence over Western civilisation that continued to the present day. Nonetheless, as Ahimeir points out, it was the latter figure who was considered to be the Messiah for Europeans. For Jews, of course, the Messiah had not yet appeared, and all who had claimed the title, to that point, had been false messiahs. Nonetheless, he asks, 'would the concept of messiah have been connected to the House of David, if Zerubavel had been successful in controlling Yehuda … and would Christianity attribute the Messiah to the House of David if Zerubavel had been successful?'[74] It is an interesting question. Zerubavel, together with the High Priest Joshua, had led the first wave of Jews back to Jerusalem from Persian exile, and initiated the rebuilding of the Second Temple. In the Book of Haggai, Zerubavel is not only associated very strongly with the Davidic line but is also vested with Messianic expectation. Of course, Ahimeir's comment is pointed: all expectations – Messianic or otherwise – notwithstanding, Zerubavel had not successfully re-established the Davidic line. Indeed, he became nothing more than the governor of a vassal state: in other words, the servant of a foreign occupier.[75]

In reality, of course, as Ahimeir notes, rather dramatically: 'Moses dies and Jesus enters'.[76] Jewish Messianism, along with the Jewish nation, went into exile and both became subsumed by, and subordinated to, their Christian counterparts. Furthermore – and in Ahimeir's opinion, equally as tragic – Karaite Judaism had lost out to Rabbinic Judaism. Hillel and Jesus – 'heralds of peace and love' – were thus, for Ahimeir, both different products of the reactionary atmosphere that had characterised the Herodian period before the destruction of the Second Temple. After its destruction, their ideological crowns were passed to the figures of Rabbi Yohanan ben Zakkai and 'Saul-Paul'; the leading figures of Rabbinic Judaism and Western Christianity, respectively. In Ahimeir's eyes, each school – again, standing in binary opposition to the other – was a result of the 'Jewish Revolution', that had ended with the destruction of the temple. But for this defining event, neither Rabbinic Judaism nor Pauline Christianity could have developed as they had; indeed, they would not have needed to.

In Talmudic tradition, Rabban Yohanan ben Zakkai had been a student of Shammai and Hillel, and thus represented the last proponent of the Jewish scholarly tradition before the destruction of the temple and subsequent condition of Galut. He allegedly prophesied to Vespasian that the Roman soldier would become Emperor, for which Rabban Yohanan received – when prophesy became reality – royal permission to settle in Yavneh. Rabban Yohanan was a pacifist, who preached negotiation with the Romans during the siege of Jerusalem. To this end – again, according to Talmudic tradition – he feigned death and had himself smuggled out of the besieged city in a coffin to a waiting Vespasian, who was still an army captain at this time. The school he established at Yavneh represented the Pharisaic tradition that came to dominate post–Second Temple Judaism: the rabbinic tradition that focused on oral and written tradition – Talmud and Torah – and strict adherence to Halakhah, or Jewish Law. And notably, Rabban Yohanan's sister had a son named Abba Sikra, whose importance to this study will be discussed in Chapter 5.

Ahimeir pits Rabbinic Judaism – 'Written Prophecy', or the 'Prophecy of Halakhah' – against the 'Prophecy of Action' that had preceded it, and whose ideological trajectory Ahimeir traces from Moses through Samuel, and Elijah: the 'Prophets of Rage'.[77] Indeed, Ahimeir notes, in regard to these latter two figures, posterity had recorded much more detail surrounding their actions, and much less regarding what they actually said. And in a further nod to Spengler, he sees in Samuel the father of Christian activism, the spiritual father of Calvin and Calvinism, Knox, and Cromwell. Of course, Ahimeir's implication is that Judaism, by contrast, had receded into inaction behind the ghetto wall and the Yeshiva; it had become ossified through Talmudic pseudo-argument. As previously noted, we know that Ahimeir admired Cromwell for his revolutionary spirit; hence, it is relatively clear on which side of the fence Ahimeir sits in this discussion.

I would therefore suggest – again from both a Spenglerian and Ahimeirian-Spenglerian perspective – that the result of Judaism's recession behind the ghetto walls was that of a Jewish Culture that was forced to undergo Spenglerian pseudomorphosis; much less, however, with its host culture in Galut, although this certainly occurred, but – more importantly – with itself. The Jewish-Desert-South-Warrior-Maccabean Culture went into decline, and was thus obliged to undergo the period of 'aimless wandering' that characterised a Spenglerian Culture that was at its end. At the same time, Jewish-Fertile-North-Rabbinic-Pharisaic Culture – which had begun much later – had reached the final stage in its Spenglerian life-cycle: Civilisation. Thus the two remaining 'competing'

Jewish Cultures were locked in a Spenglerian pseudomorphical deadlock with each other, one that was characterised, at one and the same time, by aimless wandering and *über*-civilization. Moreover, we know from Ahimeir's dissertation that he believed that such a pseudomorphical existence would signal the Culture's death knell. In this case, 'cultural', heroic, active, *Tanakh*ic Judaism was being bastardised by 'civilised', rabbinic, passive, Talmudic Judaism.

The period of Galut also witnessed the flourishing and subsequent decline of Magian, Apollonian and Faustian Cultures. These phenomena, ironically, thus also led to the second life of a renewed – indeed, modern – Jewish Culture that was once again nationally sovereign, and back in its ancestral land: what Ahimeir apparently saw – although, to be sure, it is only implied – as the Second Period of Jewish Culture. To put it more simply: The First Period of Jewish Culture (Ancient) – *Galut* [Exile] (Dormant: the Spenglerian period of Aimless Wandering) – The Second Period of Jewish Culture (Modern). Although Ahimeir does not say as much, I would contend that he understood the development of Jewish history in such a manner. The use of Spenglerian theory – in the background, to be sure – in all of this, in a book written almost forty years after Ahimeir's doctoral dissertation, is noteworthy indeed. It suggests a much more watertight ideological basis – if perhaps a flawed one, by today's standards – for Ahimeir's own reading of Jewish history than is perhaps commonly recognised.

Judaism had rejected the prophets of rage, its hunters and fighters. Esau, Elijah, Samuel, the Hasmoneans, even Moses had been rejected for the pacifism of Aaron, Hillel and Yohanan ben Zakkai. Once again, living culture had been rejected for stagnant civilisation. For Ahimeir, this rejection even represented one of the main reasons for the current crisis in Jewish tradition. Indeed, he says as much:

> The crisis of 'tradition' is not an accidental crisis. This is a crisis associated with the elimination of the eastern European Galut. The nation, which in the last generations passed from Europe to America, from the town to metropolis, did not transfer with it the 'Yavneh' Judaism, but rather revived the 'Alexandrian' Judaism [Hellenism]. We don't know if Alexandrian Judaism will last as long as Yavneh Judaism, but we know [nonetheless] that the 'Third Temple' will not built in the spirit of Yavneh.[78]

Neither could Ahimeir envisage the long-term success of any transplantation of Lubavitch or Volozhin Hasidism – 'Yavneh Judaism' – to New York, 'nor to Tel Aviv'.[79] For him, Jerusalem must absolutely once again replace Yavneh:

'The Talmud not only united the nation. It also divided ... No book arouses such a negative attitude as [does] the Talmud'.[80] Hence, for him, on the 'eve of destruction of the European Galut', and the beginning of the third period of Jewish independence, it was secular and not religious leaders such as 'Pinsker, Herzl, Nordau, Jabotinsky, etc.' who had 'arisen' as leaders, and the rabbis had played almost no role in either Jewish political or spiritual revival.[81]

In a more metaphorically expansive passage, Ahimeir seeks to illustrate his point by likening 'every human society, every nation' to an 'old ship' that requires three necessary components if it is to function successfully: an anchor, sails and a rudder. Every society goes through necessary periods of 'mooring' that are characterised by strong conservative elements. Indeed, the 'Ship Israel' had become 'anchored' during the period of exile, and thus unable to move forward. And its conservative elements had certainly been strong during this time. However, even during the adverse conditions of Galut, Ahimeir notes that the Jews had never forgotten their 'national pledge'.[82] During the past three generations, the ship had indeed 'lost its anchor' and was being driven anew by the wind in its sails, but for Ahimeir, the current 'steersman' was of doubtful expertise and ability. Although referring to the political leadership in the State of Israel when *Yudaikah* was published, in 1960 – in other words, a Mapai coalition government that was headed by David Ben-Gurion – Ahimeir's comment could just as easily be transposed backwards, to a Mapai-dominated Yishuv leadership led by David Ben-Gurion, in 1930. For him, throughout this whole period, the 'Ship Israel' continued to lack a suitable anchor.

Ahimeir returns again and again to discussions of binary opposites, and more specifically to the theme of warring brothers:

> The story of Cain and Abel contains all of the complete philosophy of the brutal history of humankind: brother rises up against brother. Not the serpent, not the stranger, but rather, the brother. At the beginning of the history of Rome, Israel's great antagonist, brother rose up against brother, as well: Romulus slew Remus. And they weren't just brothers, but rather, twins. Also Esau and Jacob were twins.[83]

It should also be remembered that Esau, upon giving up his birthright – and in spite of all apparent dishonesty on Jacob's part, in its procurement – now not only became the 'bad' Jew who stood opposite the 'good' Jew, Jacob. He also became – once again, in Israel Yuval's analysis – the 'brother-nation Edom [who] was the rival of the kingdoms of Judea and Israel, and therefore he imposed the resentments of the present on the embryonic, dim, mythic past'.[84] Thus – from a

Jewish perspective – Esau-Edom would also eventually 'become' Rome. But, of course, Esau-Edom-Rome would eventually also become Christian. Therefore, for Christians, we have precisely the opposite reading: Esau, who had sold his birthright to his younger brother Jacob, not only once again represented the 'bad' Jew but now also the omnipresent Jew who lived in the midst of a 'New Israel', a dominant Christian society headed by Jacob-Jesus, and where the elder was obliged to 'serve the younger'.[85]

Indeed, for Ahimeir – summing up, in another curious metaphor – the 'concept of Judaism' had continually 'descended' throughout its own body over the course of the past 3,000 years. It had begun in the 'head', with Moses, and moved to the 'heart', with Jesus. More recently, it had moved even lower, due the influence of the two 'False Messiahs': first to the 'stomach', with Marx, and finally to the 'groin', with Freud.[86] That Ahimeir doesn't put Jesus in the same category as Marx and Freud is probably best explained through his apparent continual embrace of Spenglerian theory. We know from his doctoral dissertation that – in a reading as Spenglerian as it is Christian – Ahimeir considered Jesus to be morphologically contemporaneous with Moses. Furthermore, Ahimeir is once again adamant that history is made by 'heroes' who act, and not by sedentary, obsolete figures who had become anachronistic. Thus, Moses and Jesus – both men of action who, in Ahimeir's estimation, shared a parallel function in their respective cultures – enjoy a higher status than Marx and Freud – men of words – who had only served to bring Judaism down to ever-lower levels of debasement.

We cannot be certain as to what degree Ahimeir's conception of Jewish cultural history changed between the period that he taught at the BLTS and the final years of his life, when he wrote *Yudaikah*. Nonetheless, we may be certain that – however much else of his concept of Jewish cultural and historical development, as outlined in *Yudaikah*, was already worked out in the late 1920s – Ahimeir certainly conveyed one very key ideological element to his students at the Betar Leadership Training School: that history is created and progressed by active heroism. And his words cannot have fallen on deaf ears: it would be students from the BLTS who espoused the very ethos of heroic action, and who played a key role in demonstrations at the Western Wall in Jerusalem, in August 1929.

Tisha B'Av 1929

Jewish-Arab tensions had been steadily increasing ever since the incident at the Western Wall on Yom Kippur, in September 1928. The following summer, on 15

August 1929, on the fast-day of Tisha B'Av (The Ninth of Av) – traditionally, the saddest day on the Hebrew calendar, in which the destruction of both Temples, among other calamities in Jewish history, are said to have occurred and are mourned – the 'Zionist Revolutionary Youth' in the Yishuv organised a march to, and demonstration in front of, the Wall.[87] The Jewish demonstration sparked not only an Arab counter-demonstration the next day but also an ever-increasing wave of violence over the following two weeks that, at final count, resulted in 133 Jewish and 120 Arab deaths.[88] According to Revisionist biographers, the march was organised by recent graduates of the Betar Leadership Training School, although Halpern's own testimony is equivocal.[89] On one hand, he states that the school merely 'provided the security' for the march; on the other, he claims that he was 'blamed as the leader of this demonstration'. Either way, the sense of proud nationalism that the participants in the march felt is clear from his testimony:

> The danger was great. For the first time in a millennium, there was a handful of brave men who walked with their heads held high through the Damascus Gate, through the narrow Arab streets of the Old City. ... The demonstration was allowed on the condition that the flag wouldn't appear. However, the flag did [appear], but initially [it] was rolled up and was unfurled only at the Western Wall. For the first time since the destruction of the Temple, the Jewish flag flew at the Western Wall, and for the first time, the gloomy stones heard hymns of hope rather than wailing.[90]

Jewish prayer had taken place at the Western Wall regularly since the seventeenth century, and pilgrimage to the Western Wall on Tisha B'Av was an annual event that had intensified with Zionist settlement in Palestine. Indeed, in 1929, in spite of the fact that, in Halpern's opinion, 'everything passed quietly', events took a decidedly more nationalistic turn.[91] That afternoon, an assembly at Beit Haam in Tel Aviv 'adopted a resolution protesting against the infringement of Jewish rights at the Wall and demanding "the dismissal of the anti-Zionist officials" as well as "the sending of a Parliamentary Commission from London to Palestine to investigate the position on the spot."'[92] The resolutions were given to the acting chief secretary by representatives of the demonstrants, who had marched down Jaffa Road towards the Old City. Contemporary accounts list 2,000 participants; however, more recent scholarship claims that there were, in fact, only 300.[93] Whatever the real number, Halpern and Ahimeir were certainly both present.

Halpern's testimony supports all accounts of a quiet demonstration. Perhaps not unsurprisingly, however, he makes the claim that peace had prevailed due to the exceptional training and control that he and the members of the BLTS exercised over the crowd. As he later recollected:

> The crowd – having seen in what order [and] in grave silence the male and female students of the school marched, and how they followed orders which I gave them, not verbally, but simply with some pre-determined sign – decided that we were the main demonstrators, and so followed us without asking questions. At one point there was some provocation in the crowd, and some lowly shouting started. I stopped the demonstration and announced that if the shouting wouldn't stop, we would go no further, and on top of this, I would kick out everyone who would dare not listen to my orders. After all [that], someone shouted and within a minute flew head over heels out of the row. The general who eventually ended up being part of the commission defending Jews became the leader of a strong police guard made up of cavalry and infantry of Englishmen, Jews, and Arabs. The general noticed that we had a lot more influence over the crowd than his force.[94]

Although Halpern's recollections of the event are perhaps overblown, it is clear that the Betar Leadership Training School not only filled a practical and ideological void in the Yishuv but also – in spite of the school's relatively short life-span and modest means – it exerted both a practical and ideological influence there for years to come. According to Halpern, all of the members of the BLTS met at the end of the events of August 1929, to discuss the Haganah's policy of *Havlagah*. He noted with pride that the BLTS had received compliments from the Haganah representative Avraham Ikar – who had been a fellow student of Ahimeir and Halpern at the Herzliya Gymnasium – who nonetheless mocked the group's exaggerated discipline and behaviour, and suggested that the school disband and join the Haganah.

Regardless of whether or not the BLTS had actually organised the demonstration, the march took place absolutely outside the auspices of Betar, a fact which Jabotinsky – ever the politician – came to regret. Behind all of this – practically and, indeed, ideologically – stood the dual figures of Ahimeir and Halpern.

It is one of the main purposes of this book to reweight Ahimeir's position, without prejudice, in the trajectory of Revisionist-Zionist history. In so doing, it is absolutely incumbent upon us to also recognise Yirmiahu Halpern's considerable achievements with regard to the Betar Leadership Training School. Be that as it may, the school's accomplishments were, ultimately, not enough for Ahimeir. For him, neither the Jewish nation nor the Jewish youth were yet 'trained for the[ir] considerable role in the establishment of the kingdom of

Israel'. As he would eventually conclude in an open letter to the youth of Betar – written, ironically, from a cell in the Jerusalem Central Prison – the 'maximalist Israeli ideal was being attempted by minimalist means'.[95] To combat this lack of progress, Ahimeir foresaw the creation of an underground group that was much more elite, and more ideologically driven, than the cadets of the BLTS. The tradition of Rabban Yohanan ben Zakkai and the spirit of the Pharisees and the dominance of Yavneh over Jerusalem that had dominated Jewish culture and practice throughout the period of Galut now required an altogether different strategical approach, one that was both traditional and modern. The fighting spirit of the ancient Jewish fourth sect, the mythical Zealots – and, indeed, their Sicarii elite – would be liberated from their pseudomorphical deadlock with Pharisaic tradition, and resurrected in the form of the modern Brit HaBiryonim. The group would come to represent, at once, Ahimeir's proudest achievement, and the source of his greatest defeat.

Political activist

This final chapter examines the two phenomena that marked, on the one hand, the pinnacle of Ahimeir's ideological development, and, on the other, the nadir of his political activity: his creation of the underground, anti-British resistance group Brit HaBiryonim, and his implication in the murder of Chaim Arlosoroff and the trials that followed in its wake. The ever-widening division between Jabotinsky and the Maximalists that grew from 1930 onwards has been well-documented, and Colin Shindler, in particular, has comprehensively chronicled Ahimeir's involvement in Brit HaBiryonim, and the Arlosoroff and Brit HaBiryonim trials. I do not intend to revisit these discussions here, nor to recount, once again, their histories. Neither will I attempt to solve the Arlosoroff murder: to my profound sadness, the examination of hundreds of documents pertaining to the murder did not lead me to the proverbial smoking gun. As stated throughout, this study seeks not only to examine and understand Ahimeir's ideological development per se but also to place it within the wider ideological frameworks of both Revisionist Zionism and the broader organisation of the Yishuv. With this aim in mind, it should be noted that the documents discussed in this chapter provide a unique insight into the ideological and practical worlds of Maximalist Revisionism. Not only do they augment but they very often challenge our previous understanding of the ideological realm in which the group acted.

The first section of the chapter will present a comprehensive ideological overview of Brit HaBiryonim by using evidence gathered for the Arlosoroff murder and Brit HaBiryonim trials, as well as two further publications: a pamphlet that Ahimeir authored in the 1950s and a booklet published in 1982, in which various essays and reminiscences by members of the group – including Ahimeir – appeared.[1] In addition, I will trace the nature and trajectory of Chaim Arlosoroff's ideological outlook, with the intention of assessing to what degree his very specific idea of 'Jewish People's Socialism' overlapped with some of the Maximalists' – and especially Ahimeir's – own ideological position. Indeed,

I would contend that – at times – the degree of similarity in both men's thinking is overshadowed only by the magnitude of the tragedy that would come to befall them.

The turning point II

The Western Wall riots in 1929 had served only to buttress Ahimeir's, Greenberg's and Yevin's convictions that the only possible course of action for dealing with both the increasing active resistance to Jewish settlement by Palestine's indigenous Arab population and the inaction of the British Mandatory government, Yishuv leadership and – not least – Jabotinsky himself could be a militant, revolutionary approach that was predicated on Fascist ideology and engagement. In the wake of the riots, the trio and their radical agenda enjoyed a surge in popularity within the Revisionist Party in the Yishuv. Years later, Ahimeir identified – and over-romanticised – Jabotinsky's two major shortcomings:

> He wasn't a politician, but rather, a prophet. And he wasn't an architect. Herzl was an architect. What was built, remained: A Congress, A Bank, a Zionist Organisation. Jabotinsky was Don Quixote, in the positive understanding of the word.[2]

In point of fact, Jabotinsky had been in Europe when the riots occurred, and returned only briefly to Palestine, in December 1929. The Maximalists seized the day, and took advantage of Jabotinsky's increasingly precarious situation vis à vis both the Yishuv Revisionists and the British. On 22 November 1930, they put themselves in control of the Revisionist Party in the Yishuv.[3] In January 1930, Jabotinsky – who had gone off again to London to testify before the Shaw Commission and South Africa to fulfil various speaking engagements – was notified by the British that they had barred his return to Palestine. It was a stroke of luck for the Maximalists. Jabotinsky would never return to Palestine, and his continued absence certainly made it easier for the Maximalists to hold on to their power over the Revisionist Party in the Yishuv. Indeed, by the time of the Revisionist Conference in Katowice, in March 1933, the party had split in three directions: Meir Grossman's faction, which argued for the party to remain within the Zionist Organisation; Jabotinsky, who recommended the party's secession from the ZO; and the Maximalists, who – like Jabotinsky – wanted the party to leave the ZO, but also, and in contrast to Jabotinsky, wanted the party to adopt a Fascist platform.[4]

In the months following the 1929 riots, Ahimeir penned three short essays – 'The Desert and the Garden of Eden', 'Shall We Miss the Hour of Opportunity?' and 'From Tel-Hai to Beer Tuvia' – which summarised not only his frustration and anger with the events themselves but also provided some tactical suggestions for the future.[5] And while none of these suggestions should have come as a surprise to anyone who had been au courant with Ahimeir's ideological positions to that point, he nonetheless now delivered them with a greater sense of vitriolic – one might say Messianic – urgency.[6] He places culpability for the recent bloodshed equally on the shoulders of the British and Arabs, and addresses them directly, while the 'blood of the murdered and wounded had not yet been erased from the steps of Jaffa Street':

> You erred, Gentlemen and Effendi; you erred, Governors. Your attempt to overthrow the 160,000 Children of Europe in the country was unsuccessful and will not succeed. It is impossible to turn the nation of Herzl and Einstein into spiritual slaves. And [our] neighbours will also know: We will not go from here, only our enemies – they [are the ones] that will go from here.[7]

Ahimeir blames the British, and more specifically, the current British Labour government under Ramsay MacDonald, for appearing to have lost not only its 'talent for ruling nations' but – more importantly – its will to rule, at all. Referring pointedly to the Egyptian Revolution of 1919, and the Great Iraqi Revolution of 1920, Ahimeir remarks that perhaps the Zionist movement should 'also be ready in the near future, for the evacuation of Eretz Israel by the armies of Britain'.[8] Indeed, he notes that the Zionist movement now stood before 'difficult trials, the likes of which it had not seen since [the discussion of the] Uganda [Plan]', and it should, therefore, 'be ready for anything'.[9] And balancing the fallout of recent events, Ahimeir counsels: 'There is no room for despair. There is room for gnashing of teeth and clenching of fists. No path of national revival is strewn with roses'.[10]

Ahimeir's vision for a Zionist youth that would serve as the vanguard in bringing about swift retaliation to both the British and Arabs for the recent events and for forging a path towards a Jewish national home in Palestine is not new, it merely assumes a greater sense of impetuosity. Where he departs from his usual rhetoric, however, is in his curious appeal – perhaps borne out of despair, in view of the recent violence – that the Jews could 'better instil in themselves pride and courage' by adopting and internalising the attitude of the anti-Semites', and also themselves begin to see that the question of the 'Nation of Israel' was one of the greatest issues that currently faced humanity. 'If nothing else', he adds,

'Maybe we can derive this simple conclusion at this moment of such world [im-] balance?'[11]

To be sure, Ahimeir and his fellow Maximalists had, at times, a rather curious attitude to the most notorious of the 'anti-Semites', the Nazi government, certainly during its first four months in power. While not staunchly pro-Nazi, the Maximalists did support the party's anti-Communist stance, its revolutionary nature and – as with Mussolini's Fascists – ability to look back to a rich, brilliant and, indeed, heroic, historical past.[12] They also – mistakenly – believed, at first that they could successfully separate the Nazi's 'antisemitic shell' from its 'anti-Marxist content'.[13] Furthermore, and using rather tenuous ideological reasoning, they believed that the rise of Nazism would jog Germany's assimilated Jewish population into re-embracing its Jewish identity and stimulate further emigration to Palestine.[14]

Nonetheless, in spite of overwhelming support for the Maximalist agenda from the Betar camp, the three Maximalist leaders slowly came to realise that the Betar youth, alone, were not capable of implementing some of the more sophisticated acts of civil disobedience that their radical agenda mandated. Years later, Ahimeir wrote that he and many other Revisionists had eventually concluded that

> even Jabotinsky would find it difficult to convince those responsible for the British colonisation policy that what benefitted us also benefitted them, and vice versa. Thus, one began to draw a comparison between Irish and Polish liberation [movements]. And each person asked himself ... 'How were they liberated? How did the communists come to power? Was it not [in fact] by means of revolution?' And the conclusion was clear: 'The world is a world of bandits', and 'You find yourself among wolves, and you take the trouble to learn to bay like them' ... and Jabotinsky sang that 'Silence is Filth'. ... Thus was born Brit HaBiryonim.[15]

Interestingly, Ahimeir notes that they were not the first Zionist revolutionary group to exist. As discussed in Chapter 3, he looked to Avshalom Feinberg, Sarah Aaronsohn and other members of the Nili group for inspiration, and he highlights the fact that the group's ideologies were not yet widely known when Brit HaBiryonim were formed.[16] Equally interesting – and often overlooked – is that he also cites the Russian-Turkish Zionist Marco Baruch (1872–99), a member of *Hovevei Tzion* (Lovers of Zion), who had, in his day, proposed the creation of a Jewish army to engage in armed struggle against the Ottomans in Palestine, as inspiration for the group.[17] Furthermore, Baruch's ideological successors were – in Ahimeir's estimation – the Zionist agricultural pioneer

Yehoshua Barzilai (Eisenstadt), and Michael Halpern, the father of the Betar Leadership Training School founder, Yirmiahu Halpern. Alongside the 'forgotten' elder Halpern, Ahimeir further lists the figure of A. D. Gordon – remembered 'now' (that is to say, at the time of writing, in 1962) only because the mention of his name continued to 'ignite fiery discussion in the country's classrooms'.[18] Ahimeir provides no explanation for this curious comment, but presumably he is referring to Gordon's anti-Marxist stance, which, in 1962, may have been a ground of contention for young Israeli students. The comment is noteworthy, as it further demonstrates that he remained – on some level – inspired by Gordon's concept of the Zionist Pioneer throughout his life. We should assume, however, that Ahimeir – certainly by 1962 – is referring more to the nationalistic content bound up in Gordon's ideology than to any actual 'pioneering' ethos. Or perhaps, by the 1960s, Ahimeir was seeking to somehow reconcile the myriad ideological streams that had influenced him throughout his life, and present them as some of sort of comprehensive ideology. In any case, we may be sure that Brit HaBiryonim did not spring up out of nowhere, but had solid ideological models.

The events of August 1929 had set a new precedent, and had further underscored, for Ahimeir, the necessity for more direct action, carried out by an elite few. Indeed, it is at this chronological juncture that we see Ahimeir's concept of the 'individual hero' really begin to take shape, and gain its own momentum. As he observed:

> This year, ten years after Tel-Hai, was discovered in the Yishuv the tradition of the Galut in its most typical form, in the catastrophes of Hebron and Safed [pogroms of 1929], compared to the signs of the correct political path that were budding in other parts of the land. The youth know that more days such as [those of] Tel-Hai were expected, and it was up to us to memorise the words of Trumpeldor – 'It does not matter!' Tel-Hai is the workshop of the state. The youth take care not to return to the days of Hebron and Zefat, otherwise how would we carry our shame? We do not need saints, but rather heroes. Not Hebron, but rather Tel-Hai.[19]

In spite of the anti-Arab rhetoric implied in his statement before, Ahimeir and Brit HaBiryonim concentrated their efforts on other groups which they believed posed a greater threat to the status quo in the Yishuv, and to the establishment of a Jewish nation state in Palestine. First, were the Socialists. Ahimeir – as evidenced in previous chapters – and his colleagues in Brit HaBiryonim absolutely rejected Socialism, which they considered to be a 'catastrophe for

Judaism', one of the main 'diseases' that had rotted it out. It was the Socialist leanings of the Yishuv leadership that had created a division within the Yishuv itself, and it was thus no better – in the eyes of Brit HaBiryonim – than the British Mandatory government.[20] Furthermore, Ahimeir notes, the 'fact that the Gentile world saw the Jews as the standard bearers of communism, and the Left in general', had justified – in their eyes – antisemitic engagement, not only by 'traditional' anti-Semites but – more importantly – now also by the 'neutral masses'.[21] Second, the group declared that a war on Socialism was equal to a war on antisemitism. They believed that the two issues were inextricably linked to one another, and therefore needed to be fought as a single phenomenon.[22] Third, Brit HaBiryonim rejected the ideology of defensive resistance. The 1929 riots had exposed the weakness in the general Yishuv policy of *Havlagah*. To that point, all Yishuv groups, including Betar, had practised the policy of 'defensive restraint' vis à vis Arab anti-Zionist action. But the events of 1929 had exposed the Jews of the Yishuv to the fact that they were, in historian Anita Shapira's words, 'living in the shadow of a volcano'.[23] Furthermore, as she notes:

> The theory of the volcano was diametrically opposed to the defensive ethos. Indeed, even at the time of Tel-Hai, the idea of sacrifice had been integrated into the complex and had become a part of that ethos. However, there was a natural limit on the level of tension and intensity of confrontation that the defensive ethos was able to absorb while still remaining intact. It should be recalled that this ethos rested on a fundamental supposition, namely, that realization of the Zionist project would not require the use of force.[24]

The 1929 riots had set a precedent whereby the willingness to actively defend the community now became 'an identity symbol of the new Jewish Yishuv'.[25] After August 1929 – according to Ahimeir – Betar split into two factions. The first – 'The Nationalist Defense' (*HaHaganah HaLeumi*) was militaristic in nature, ideology and organisational structure. It incorporated the majority of Betar members, and maintained a military command structure, with Jabotinsky as chief commander. The second – 'Brit HaBiryonim' – was revolutionary, in a political, insurrectionary sense. It differed from the first group in size, ideology and intention. Notably, Ahimeir observed that Brit HaBiryonim – in contrast to Betar – 'did not see the Arabs as the great enemy for the nation'.[26]

Brit HaBiryonim had no overall organisational structure, 'only soldiers and commanders'. Nonetheless, Ahimeir stood at both the group's ideological and tactical heads.[27] Furthermore, the group was an elite unit. As Ahimeir noted, the 'point was not quantity, but rather, quality'.[28] Brit HaBiryonim identified four 'fronts' for direct action: 1. The British Mandate, 2. Socialist Zionism, and Socialism in the Yishuv, in general, 3. Russian Communism, 4. German National Socialism.[29] The group prided itself in being not only the first anti-Socialist group in the Yishuv but also being first group whose members would happily go to prison for their actions.

Excursus: Female influences on the Maximalists

Brit HaBiryonim was unique – certainly among other such Fascist, or Fascist-inspired groups – in that it looked not only to the 'nationalist youth' but also to women, for inspiration for, and execution of, its ideological platforms.[30] The group embraced an ideology which recognised, and moreover celebrated, the act of female heroism, a phenomenon that certainly had its roots in the individual ideologies of the Maximalist leaders themselves. The personal lives of Ahimeir, Greenberg and Yevin during the early 1930s were themselves influenced and affected at times by some very complicated relationships with female figures that were close to them. Indeed, the personal and ideological spheres seem to have collided within Ahimeir and Greenberg in particular. By all accounts – and in spite of their cocky self-confidence when seated behind a keyboard – both men cut apparently shy, reserved and retiring figures, in person. Perhaps the love and influence of the women in their lives spurred Greenberg and Ahimeir on to rise above their seemingly docile exterior natures.

The theme of strong women as both role models for, utilitarian members of, and indeed, active heroines within, an underground organisation was first broached by Ahimeir in his essay 'The Scroll of the Sicarii'. Ahimeir dedicated the work to the memories of Charlotte Corday – the Girondin sympathiser who, in 1793, had stabbed Jacobin leader Jean Paul Marat to death in his bath – and Dora Kaplan, who had shot Lenin in 1918.[31] Both women were subsequently executed for their crimes. And, once again: Ahimeir heroised Sarah Aaronsohn, who had committed suicide rather than betray any information that she had gathered as a spy in the Nili group. Moreover – and rather notably – in Ahimeir's eyes, women and youth shared a particular utility:

> Youth and women especially get caught up in sicariness. They bond easily with the malady of the sicarii. A man over the age of 40 is rarely infected by such a malady. The youth and the woman – they who understand less of politics – in reality it is they who are the real Sicarii: the youth lives in a world of ideals, and

the woman is as strengthened by hate as by love. The youth and the woman tend more towards ideals, towards extremes. Their attitude to walking on the 'tried and true path of gold' is negative. They also tend not to take moderate measures.[32]

Ahimeir's comments are noteworthy. They highlight the fact that an ideology of strong feminine influence could characterise the ideology of Brit HaBiryonim and inspire its actions, to a significant degree. And here there is a marked overlap with Ahimeir's own personal situation, a fact that is often overlooked. Ahimeir was, throughout his life, almost continually supported and encouraged by a close female companion. His years in Vienna are the one notable exception. We should not forget that Ahimeir had first travelled to Ottoman-Palestine, to attend the Herzliya Gymnasium, in 1912, under the chaperoneship of his older sister Bluma, who remained an ardent Socialist and *kibbutznik* throughout her entire life. And she was there upon Ahimeir's return to Mandate Palestine, in 1924. By 1930, Ahimeir had married his first wife, Hasia, who was born Hasia Gerchikov in 1900. Very little biographical information about Hasia exists, but we know that she also hailed from Bobruisk, where she had given up her medical studies to come to Palestine to be with Ahimeir.[33] Their daughter, Ze'eva – ostensibly, the first female to be named after Jabotinsky – was born on 10 November. Within two weeks of the birth, Hasia – who apparently became mentally ill during the process of childbirth – was deemed unsuitable to care for the baby, and confined to a sanatorium.[34] It has been suggested that she suffered from severe post-natal depression, although the condition would not have been recognised as such, at that time.[35] She died in 1938, and is buried on the Mount of Olives, in Jerusalem.

Presumably in order to protect the baby from a mentally ill mother, and a father who was in and out of prison as a result of his political activities, Bluma took over Ze'eva's guardianship. Ze'eva thus grew up believing that Bluma was her mother and Ahimeir her uncle. She learned the truth only at the age of fourteen, when she accidentally discovered a letter from Ahimeir that was in Bluma's possession.[36] It is tragically ironic that Ahimeir's first wife was – in no small way – thus 'sacrificed' in the service of some greater good. Perhaps Ahimeir's familial situation and recognition of Hasia's passive heroism influenced his own embrace of tragic heroines as role models for the Sicarii and Biryonim. Indeed, it has been further suggested that Ahimeir's love for Hasia was unrequited and that she overplayed her mental state in order to 'liberate' Ahimeir from the marriage. Furthermore, Ahimeir wanted Ze'eva's daughter – born in 1960 – to be named after Hasia. Both of these facts – if true – buttress not only the argument for a heroic element in Hasia's character but also its inspiration for Ahimeir.[37]

Ahimeir's second wife, Sonia – born Sonia Estherhan in 1908, in Minsk – was a no less heroic figure, if only stoically so. A distant cousin, whose family, like Ahimeir's, were timber merchants, Sonia first met Ahimeir when she was fifteen years old. Like Ahimeir, Sonia also studied at the University of Vienna, and the University of Brussels, and she was also a committed Zionist from a young age.[38] The two corresponded over the years, and when Ahimeir came to lecture in Poland in September 1932, they met again, and a closer relationship developed.[39] Sonia moved to Palestine in 1934 so that she could be closer to the now-imprisoned Ahimeir. She often visited him there, where the two spoke with each other 'through the fence', and Sonia acquired books and writing paper for him.[40] They married upon Ahimeir's release, in 1935, and had two children: the prominent journalist Yaakov Ahimeir (b. 1938), and journalist and former politician, Yosef Ahimeir (b. 1943), who is currently the Director of the Jabotinsky Institute in Tel Aviv. Sonia's devotion to Ahimeir was unwavering.

More complicated, by far, were the relationships between Ahimeir's fellow Maximalist, Uri Zvi Greenberg and two formidable women who figured prominently in his life during the era of Brit HaBiryonim: his own mother and Miriam Yevin. During the Brit HaBiryonim trial, two lengthy letters that Greenberg had written to Yevin's wife were produced as evidence. Miriam Yevin had apparently acted as the go-between for the two men while Greenberg was in Lviv, in February 1932. They reveal a Greenberg who was melancholy and restless, somewhat self-obsessed and – notably – apparently also romantically attracted to Yevin's wife. Moreover, the frank nature with which Greenberg expresses himself towards her suggests no small degree of complicity on the part of Miriam Yevin:

> Towards the morning of yesterday I dreamt that you went down to a well, for some reason or another, and when you came up again there was an old man with a beard and moustache, I think 'who helped you' come up from the well, but he seized this opportunity for passing his chin over your neck and also touched your face. ... I, of course, became furious at this, but during this whole day I had a longing to be with you, say, in Italy, in a place to ourselves and that you should be utterly dishevelled and sweat[y]. Very strange ... and it is because I am always frank with you that I also now divulge to you my secret and my erotic dream.[41]

In spite of Greenberg's feelings, he finds himself nonetheless unable to return, at present, to Palestine, and cites two somewhat delusional reasons for this fact:

A – My miserable mother, whom I influence by my presence and prolong her days.

B – The necessity to arouse a tumult and to rouse the conscience in the Diaspora and the possibility of establishing a non-British and non-Sanballatian front behind the Palestinian apparatus, etc.[42]

In any case, Greenberg ends the letter by attempting to justify their relationship with an almost pagan-like superstition:

> Goodbye Miriam. Do not be sad. You must feel that 'in effect' there has not been, for the time being, any catastrophe which, however, will probably befall us. And perhaps this is the Zionist catastrophe or possibly the personal catastrophe: that somebody beloved and dear will die … I am glad you are alive, that my mother is still alive and that I live and feel that I have something about which to feel pain and tremble. It always pains and I tremble. My mother understands and listens to me as far as such a mother can listen and understand'.
>   Goodbye and I kiss you "a lot"
>   Yours, Uri.[43]

It is not clear whether Yevin himself knew the true depth of Miriam and Greenberg's friendship. The passages quoted before were probably not read aloud in court; they do not appear in the selections from the letter that were marked for reading out at the trial. Nonetheless, the letters are interesting to note here. Not only do they reveal a side of Greenberg that is not consistent with the image of him that comes across in print, that of a strong-willed, provocatively ultra-nationalist Hebrew poet and Maximalist Revisionist leader. Rather, the Greenberg who is portrayed in these letters comes across as an equivocal, melancholy, and indeed neurotic, individual.

Likewise, a recording of a lecture given by Ahimeir at the Jabotinsky Institute, where he shares his reminiscences at a conference marking the thirtieth anniversary of the Betar Leadership Training School, reveals a surprisingly shy, painfully introverted figure.[44] The Ahimeir that is revealed in recording – a man who speaks Hebrew with a strong Russian accent, stammers, leaves sentences incomplete and repeats others unnecessarily – stands directly at odds with our image of Ahimeir the provocative and somewhat cynical cultural historian and literary figure, who wrote in a rather elevated, uncompromising Hebrew.

It would appear possible then, that both Greenberg and Ahimeir sought out, and required, the constant support of strong women. Such support – for whatever reason – enabled them to overcome their natural social awkwardnesses and thereby project a more confident public persona.

Brit HaBiryonim

A connection to the ancient Biryonim had already been established in Revisionist circles through writings by historian Josef Klausner and poetry by Yaakov Cahan and Uri Zvi Greenberg.[45] It had served as inspiration for the youth of Betar and doubtlessly influenced the Maximalists' decision in naming the new group. Interestingly, Ahimeir – perhaps not unsurprisingly, in line with his reminiscences earlier – actually wanted the group to be named after Sarah Aaronsohn, whom he called the 'Joan of Arc of Israel'.[46]

As noted earlier, Ahimeir foresaw Brit HaBiryonim as a small, elite unit that would lead the movement for Revolutionary Zionism in the Yishuv. Certainly, his original plan for an organisational 'meeting of responsible persons, not more than 12 from all over the country' suggests this desire.[47] But the group was, in reality, apparently larger than this. By 1953, Ahimeir could comfortably name former members of Brit HaBiryonim, and he lists well over one hundred member names – sometimes whole families – who were organised in six major centres: Tel Aviv, Jerusalem, Hebron, Samaria, Haifa and the Jezreel Valley-Galilee.[48] According to him, the Jerusalem Brigade was the most dedicated, and Ahimeir participated in every one of its activities. Stalwarts of the Jerusalem Brigade – Chaim Diviri, Yaacov Orenstein, and Josef Gurevitz, are notable examples – were also occasionally joined by students and 'other sympathisers'.[49] Thus, Brit HaBiryonim was – if Ahimeir's reminiscences are accurate – a much larger group than he perhaps originally intended it to be. Nonetheless, and notably, there is almost no overlap in personnel between members of Brit HaBiryonim and the BLTS. Besides Ahimeir, apparently only Moshe Segal and Chaim Eliayhu participated in both groups.[50]

Brit HaBiryonim identified with their namesakes from the Second Temple period. They took their name from a band of Zealots – the Biryonim – who were said to have gone out to actively resist the Romans, and who subsequently set fire to all stores of wheat and barley remaining in besieged Jerusalem.[51] The Jastrow dictionary – to which the defence referred during the Brit HaBiryonim trial – lists *biryon* as 'palace guard',[52] but has a second entry for *biryona*,[53] which he translates as 'rebel', 'outlaw', or 'highwayman'. The Eliezer Ben Yehuda dictionary – to which the British referred, during the same trial – lists both 'praetorian guard' and 'terrorist' for *biryon*.[54] The Evan Shoshan Dictionary lists a similar meaning for *biryon*: a 'terrorist' or 'aggressive person, who rules by force', but it has no separate listing for *biryona*.[55] The etymology of Biryonim is unclear. It has been suggested that *biryoni* is derived from the Hebrew root for 'empty',[56] since the *Biryonim* were 'empty men with a propensity to violence'.[57]

The temptation simply to understand *biryoni* in its Modern Hebrew translation – that of 'thug' or 'hooligan' – does not take into consideration the nuances which exist in a more historical understanding of the word: that of a defender of the capital city – the *bira* – in other words, Jerusalem[58]. The *Biryonim* could thus also be understood to be civic guardsmen, indeed *neteuri karta* in a most literal sense.[59] The *Sans-culottes* of the French Revolution and Bolsheviks were understood to have had their ideological roots in the *Biryonim*, a fact with which Ahimeir and Yevin were familiar.[60] Nevertheless, Ahimeir – the ideological agent provocateur of the group – could not have been unaware of the word's double-edged meaning. And any lingering doubt about the word's potential for wide-ranging and politically charged interpretation is quickly eradicated when one considers the variety of ways in which both *biryoni(m)* and Brit HaBiryonim appear in translation: from 'thugs',[61] 'terrorists',[62] 'Praetorian Guard',[63] 'ruffians',[64] and 'palace guards',[65] to 'Covenant of Thugs',[66] 'League of the Sicarii',[67] 'Brotherhood of Hoodlums',[68] 'The Union of Zionist Rebels',[69] 'Covenant of Brigands'[70] or 'Alliance of Warriors'.[71] Usually, an author's particular translation also betrays his or her own political agenda or affiliation.

In spite of all rhetoric to the contrary, Brit HaBiryonim limited its activities to non-violent acts of civil disobedience; bloodshed and terror would come later, with the Irgun and Lehi. Its first organised act was a demonstration on 9 October 1930 outside the Tel Aviv hotel where the visiting British under-secretary, Dr Drummond Shiels, was staying. The group protested against the Second British Census on 18 November 1931, and the appointment in 1932 of Norman Bentwich to professor of international relations at the Hebrew University of Jerusalem.[72] It was the sympathies of the latter to the bi-nationalist *Brit Shalom* (Covenant of Peace) movement – which called for peaceful coexistence between Jews and Arabs in Palestine – that prompted the interruption of Bentwich's inaugural lecture by members of Brit HaBiryonim. In the context of their ideology, Bentwich was akin to the Rabbis who, during the siege of Jerusalem, wanted to go out and make peace with the Roman Emperor Vespasian: now, as then, the *Biryonim* were required to ensure that this would not transpire.[73]

At the conclusion of the 1930 Yom Kippur services at the Western Wall, it was a member of Brit HaBiryonim – Moshe Segal – who blew the traditional shofar blasts, in defiance of a British ruling designed to placate the Arabs, and 'against the wishes of the Mufti, of (Lord) Plummer II, of Chaim II (Arlosoroff), of the Bund in *Eretz Israel*, of the *Va'ad Leumi* (Jewish Agency) and of others'.[74] Brit HaBiryonim was also the first group to undertake acts of civil disobedience against the Nazi regime, although not until it became clear to the Maximalists – after the anti-Jewish economic boycott that came into effect on 1 April 1933 – that the Nazi government intended to follow through on its antisemitic rhetoric.[75] In May 1933, members of Brit HaBiryonim set fire to the door of the German Consulate in Jerusalem and removed the swastika flag from its consular offices in Jerusalem and Jaffa.[76] Although the Maximalists had at first spoken favourably about Hitler's election, seeing it as a victory against Communism and Socialism, as discussed earlier, they quickly disassociated themselves once it was clear to them that Nazi antisemitism was an integral ideological element.

Members of Brit HaBiryonim themselves often met with violent reaction from the British authorities; Ahimeir was beaten and arrested at the Shiels, Bentwich and British Census protests, and served prison time in Acre, Jerusalem and Jaffa. Indeed, it was revealed at the Arlosoroff trial that Ahimeir had been arrested for 'insulting the police', three days after Arlosoroff's murder. Two days later, he was sentenced to one month's imprisonment. Ahimeir used this incident in his defence to show that he had no fear of imprisonment, not even while the Arlosoroff murder investigation was ongoing.[77]

Another member of Brit HaBiryonim, Yehoshua Lichter, founded the newspaper *Hazit HaAm* (The People's Front), in 1931. Ahimeir and Yevin were editors, and Greenberg a regular contributor. The paper was published weekly until its demise, in 1934, and reflected the radical, at times pro-Fascist, attitudes of its writers. Although not the official organ of Brit HaBiryonim, the fact that all of its contributors were associated with the semi-underground group made the paper an ideological and intellectual place of assembly for like-minded individuals in the Yishuv.

Incriminating evidence

Unlike Betar and even the Betar Leadership Training School, about both of whom copious contemporary records abound, there is a lack of contemporary documentation surrounding Brit HaBiryonim and its activities. Even less material exists that originated from within the group itself. Owing to the illegal nature of the organisation, its members regularly destroyed any incriminating evidence as a matter of course.[78] Nonetheless, enough contemporary evidence and ex post facto testimony exists to allow us to paint a comprehensive ideological picture of the group. Most of the documentation that has survived was seized during police raids in conjunction with the Arlosoroff murder, and used subsequently as evidence in both the Arlosoroff and Brit HaBiryonim trials.[79] Aside from letters, personal testimonies and trial transcripts, two main documents stand out: a copy of the group's periodical, *HaBiryon*, and Ahimeir's notebooks and diaries, which included the sketches for two essays, 'The ABC of Revolutionary Zionism', and 'The Scroll of the Sicarii'.[80]

The extant copy of *HaBiryon* is a six-page mimeograph in the style of a newsletter. It was mainly typewritten, with a few larger headlines added in handwriting. The newsletter contains no identifying information other than the words 'Brit HaBiryonim' above the main title '*HaBiryon*'. The copy used in the trials is labelled 'No. 5', and the newsletter was apparently published monthly, boasting that it 'does not need the authority of the Hebron Government'. The title page also bore the motto of Brit HaBiryonim: 'With Fire and Blood Judea Will Rise'. Due to two statements within the body of text, we can be almost certain that the newsletter was written and published after November 1931 and before June 1932. Not only does the paper compel its reader to remember the heroism of Sara Aaronsohn, the 'hero whom England threw into the sea', and the '137 victims of August [1929]', but also the heroism of 'Stahl and Zohar'. Saliah Zohar and Johanan Stahl were a young couple who had disappeared while backpacking, in June 1931. Their bodies were discovered months later, on 13 November, in the grisliest of conditions. Stahl had been stabbed and buried face down while still alive, and Zohar had been raped repeatedly before being stabbed to death.[81] Although five Bedouin Arabs were arrested in connection with the murders, eventually only two were finally charged. One received a fifteen-year sentence, the other was released, possibly because he was a minor.[82] Although the paper may have appeared before the trial of Zohar and Stahl's murderers, the comments made in *HaBiryon* about the couple's heroism, almost certainly would not have been made before the discovery of their bodies, in November 1931.

An excerpt from the bulletin – presumably Ahimeir's contribution – appears in the collection of articles that Ahimeir's son, Josef, included in the book *Brit HaBiryonim*.[83] Here, he lists the publication date as 17 April 1932; however, he also lists the issue as 'No. 1'. This could be an oversight, although it might also indicate that only one issue of the newsletter was ever printed and distributed.

Certainly, the content of the copy labelled 'No. 5' gives the impression – in spite of its numbering – of being the first bulletin that the new group produced.

Furthermore, in the English translation of *HaBiryon* that was used during the Brit HaBiryonim trial, there is an extra page – apparently, the final page – that is missing from the copy of the Hebrew original. It includes a 'Chronicle', which lists the group's activities up to that point. It notes that the 'Organisation of Revolutionary Zionists in Palestine' had come into being 'a few months ago', and had protested successfully against the British Census, in July 1930, and the 'activity of a number of youths within the walls of the University'; a reference to the disruption of the Bentwich lecture, which occurred on 10 February 1932.[84] In addition, there is a pronouncement that states that – 'commencing in June' – *HaBiryon* would appear monthly. Doubtless, this refers to June 1932, since the bulletin makes no mention of the Nazi victory in January 1933, or of any of the group's efforts to protest against it – which by 28 May 1933, had included the removal of the Nazi flag from the German consulate in Jerusalem – activities which the group would certainly have proudly documented in its bulletin. All of these facts, together, point to Yosef Ahimeir's accurate dating of the article to 17 April 1932.

The paper is less a manifesto – although certainly also that – than a rallying cry, a call to arms for a Hebrew youth whom its authors admonish to:

> Be ashamed at the desolation which betook you after the laconic reply of the Government of Palestine. You, Hebrew youth, who, when seeking your personal luck, courageously faced all obstacles in entering the United States, Argentina, Chile, Australia, and all parts of the world, are you, Hebrew youth, unable to overcome the obstacles in entering your own country, in order to stand at the front in the war for the esteemed idea of the resurrection of the Kingdom of Israel? ... Not by efforts of supplication to the Mandatory Government and the fat officials of the [Jewish] Agency will salvation come; but only thanks to the flame which flares in your heart due to your diligence and arrogance of spirit. You diligent and prideful Hebrew, there are many ways ahead of you to immigrate; choose one of them; immigrate and succeed.[85]

The newsletter is replete with Messianic rhetoric, now so extreme that it can no longer be called merely 'quasi' Messianic. Certainly, the language used in *HaBiryon* is much more politically charged than even in Ahimeir's 'Notebook of a Fascist' articles, and more accurately fits the definition of what Shavit terms 'national Messianism'.[86] *Malkhut Israel*, the 'Kingdom of Israel' – Greenberg's term, full of ecstatic, eschatological, national fervour – is used throughout the publication, which in any case, is saturated with biblical imagery and syntax:

An Eye for an eye, a tooth for a tooth.

Inscribed in the heart with characters of blood are the names of the pioneers who fell as prey to wild animals. A day will come and we shall repay these savages seven-fold; they who are afraid to meet in open war and who attack from behind. But you, cowards, who hide yourselves under cover of the darkness of night in order to cut off the lives of trees which cannot defend themselves or flee from the sword of the murderer, the outcast of humanity, you and all those assisting you, be careful; the property of the Jew will not be unclaimed. We shall revenge upon you sevenfold; for each tree of our groves, seven of yours will we take.

And to you, Hebrew Youth, we say: At these moments of hatred, throw away modern doctrines and remember those of the ancient legislator – 'An eye for an eye, a tooth for a tooth' – and you shall then be safe in your life, honour, property, and land.[87]

The paper's authors – the varying writing styles point to more than one pen – refer to the Yishuv leadership as the 'Hebron Government', and accuse it of relinquishing its 'obligations to Zionism and the Jewish nation'. They call the British, variously, the 'Pogrom Government' and 'Esau', whose 'hairy hand' had closed the doors of immigration and 'wrenched' from the Jews 'our sacred right to the Land of Zion' by limiting Jewish land purchase and settling Arabs 'in the most flourishing strips of the county in order to frustrate the aspiration of the Jewish Nation for liberation, and to turn us here, in our native land, into loathsome and downcast slaves – in a worse position than Czarist Russia'.[88]

The paper's first section – signed 'Brit HaBiryonim Revolutionary Zionists' – concludes with the slogans:

Shame to the Pogromist Hebron Government.
Shame to its agents, its servants in the Jewish Agency.
Long live the war for the liberation of the People.
Long live the Kingdom of Israel.[89]

Throughout the newsletter, the Hebrew youth is co-opted to fulfil its 'historical function', to serve as 'pioneers at the front of the war for deliverance'. Any lingering doubt as to what form such a war might take is eradicated by the explanation that the authors were calling for 'an actual war against the enemy Government and the administration which is the agent of the former'. What is striking about *HaBiryon* is that it appears not to be intended only as a newsletter for members of Brit HaBiryonim, but rather as a missive from Brit HaBiryonim to the 'Hebrew Youth'. It is as uncompromising in its implication of the Yishuv and British leaderships as it is in its directives to the 'Hebrew Youth' to join the Zionist Revolution:

And to show you the only way to save your nation – the way of the Zionist Revolution, the way of terrorism and disobedience – we are organising this new stage in Zion without the authority of the Hebron Government and without the legality which binds and closes the mouth from telling the full truth.[90]

It is clear from the context of the newsletter that Brit HaBiryonim and the Organisation of Revolutionary Zionists were not only one and the same, but that they saw themselves in the role of an elite command vis à vis the 'Hebrew Youth'. Indeed – its authors continued – recent attacks 'by Arabs on Jewish land, which came as a direct result of the policy of the bloody Government', would require 'special reaction' for which the order would come – rather ominously – 'in due course'.[91]

This single, extant copy of *HaBiryon* is unique in that it gives us an unredacted glimpse into the ideological and practical world of Brit HaBiryonim. The material contained in the bulletin was intended only for the eyes of other members of the group and a presumably sympathetic 'Hebrew Youth', and was thus neither edited for a less compassionate audience, like a newspaper article, nor distorted by the passage of time, like a personal reminiscence. The irony, of course, is that had Ahimeir and other members of the group not been arrested, there would be probably no extant documentation at all that was contemporary with the existence of Brit HaBiryonim.

The same holds true for 'The ABC of Revolutionary Zionism', which exists in an English translation that was used as trial evidence.[92] Like 'The Scroll of the Sicarii', as we shall see, the essay – in point of fact, less an essay than an outline for a projected essay on Ahimeir's concept of 'Revolutionary Zionism' – was unpublished, and was found in one of Ahimeir's seized notebooks. It is, nonetheless, important as a document, since it not only makes the connection between members of Brit HaBiryonim as the prime executors of 'Revolutionary Zionism' but also provides some form of practical-ideological instruction for its members. In the spirit of 'whoever is not with us is against us', Ahimeir mandates that

a member of 'Brit HaBiryonim' has no private life. To be more correct, the aims of Brit HaBiryonim are more important than his private life. A member of Brit HaBiryonim is definitely at the disposal of the Brit.

The ideal personality of Brit HaBiryonim is Sara Aaronsohn.[93]

Once again, Ahimeir demands the primacy of the group and total suppression of individual desire in its service. Once again, Sara Aaronsohn is named as a role model. And to be sure, years later, Ahimeir listed the key difference between Brit HaBiryonim and the Irgun and Lehi in the fact that Brit

HaBiryonim 'did not see public action as its mission'.[94] Like the ancient Sicarii and the Nili Group, they withdrew from action at the first opportune moment. Indeed, the first-century Jewish-Roman chronicler, Flavius Josephus – who was contemporary with the Sicarii – described the nature of one of the group's successfully executed crimes:

> When [the victims] fell, the murderers joined in the cries of indignation and, through their plausible behaviour, were never discovered. … The panic created was more alarming than the calamity itself, everyone, as on a battlefield, hourly expecting death. Men kept watch at a distance on enemies and would not trust even their friends when they approached.[95]

Ahimeir's claim – made almost twenty years after the group's demise – that Brit HaBiryonim shied away from public action, may seem contradictory at first. Ahimeir, and other members of Brit HaBiryonim very publicly demonstrated, were very publicly arrested, and very publicly went to prison as a result of their actions. However, the group's members always acted as if individually. The existence of Brit HaBiryonim was kept secret, no one acted in the name of the group during a protest. The impression – once again, like the Sicarii or Nili's – was one of individual, if also perhaps coincidentally like-minded, engagement and protest. The moment that the existence of the group was discovered – during the Arlosoroff murder investigation – Brit HaBiryonim dissolved. Nonetheless, the fact that Brit HaBiryonim served as the direct ideological precursor to the more public and militant Irgun and Lehi was confirmed years later by Ahimeir.[96] His comment is perhaps somewhat self-serving, but demonstrates, nonetheless, that he himself recognised the ideological similarity between the three groups. And although Brit HaBiryonim acted less frequently, and less radically, than either of its two successors, the ideological link that it provided – through the concept of Revolutionary Zionism – was integral to the character of both groups.

In the few short pages that make up Ahimeir's notes on 'The ABC of Revolutionary Zionism', we gain an insight into practically all of the issues that informed his ideological world: the role of Jewish history in reproving the nations; the importance of Messianism; the need for a new type of Zionism; assimilation as 'conversion en masse'; the equation of 'liberalism, socialism and assimilation, Christianity and Islam and conversion'; the difference between Western 'liberal' antisemitism and 'socialist' antisemitism in Russia, etc.

Also noteworthy, is Ahimeir's treatment of two further topics: racial theory and Messianism. Regarding the former, he notes that – in contrast to racial theorists, who concentrate only on the physiological development of race – race, in a 'spiritual' sense, had evolved in a cultural-historical manner. Thus:

> The Romans looked upon the Germans in their times as Barbarians, as we look upon the negroes. ... Tacitus would surely have been doubtful had he [been told that] out of this race there will once spring Dürer, Kant, Goethe. *A fortiori*, we can say the same thing of the Negro race, which is so much hated by the Americans.[97]

Ahimeir's statement reinforces the fact that he continually viewed the world's historical development in cultural-historical – indeed, Spenglerian – terms. And here we find the ideological link to Ahimeir's embrace and advocacy of Messianism, an otherwise seemingly illogical phenomenon for a man educated to the degree that Ahimeir was, and it is worth quoting him at length:

> Is [here] the place to explain that Zionism in its 'un-modern' form, known under the name of Messiani[sm], has existed from the first moment of the destruction of Jerusalem, or more correct, from the first moment danger lurked for [the] political existence of our Nation? ... Modern Messianism, or Zionism, has been in existence for fifty years. ... Until less than fifty years ago, there were communal ideas which tried to solve the question of our nation. Liberal assimilation tried, whose failure is sufficiently conspicuous in the light of the happenings in Hitler's Germany, without mentioning the Dreyfus question in France. It tried to solve the question of the revolutionary-socialist Jews; if [we see it] in the light of the catastrophe of Russian Jewry, [then] the picture of failure is sufficiently clear. And orthodox Jewry, surely, is no solution. Because to return to the shtetl, heder, yeshiva, we cannot, even [if] we wanted to. ... So [only] the Zionist truth remains. But can Zionism solve the question of the Jews (Nordau) or even the question of Jewry (Ahad Ha'am) within fifty years? In the light of the happenings in the Diaspora – we must be truthful and say: Zionism is not capable. [At least not the] Zionism which [existed] up till now. There is a Zionism which is capable. That is Revolutionary Zionism.[98]

Thus, for Ahimeir the Spenglerian, modern Zionism was not merely similar to, but absolutely morphologically contemporaneous with, ancient, biblical Messianism. This reasoning explains how he could so easily use quasi-Messianic or national-Messianic rhetoric, without any sense of traditional religious Messianic expectation. It further buttresses my contention, in Chapter 4, that Ahimeir split Jewish history into two separate Spenglerian Cultures: one ancient, the other modern, while the period of Galut represented the dormant period of 'aimless wandering' that Spengler foresaw as the necessary precursor to cultural reawakening. Indeed, in this respect, Ahimeir's employment of secular Messianism appears to be much more ideologically watertight than Greenberg's, which I would argue is rooted more in the realm of poetic pathos and metaphor than in the systematic realm – flawed as it may be – of Spenglerian meta-history.

The Scroll of the Sicarii

In 1926, a failed attempt on Mussolini's life prompted Ahimeir to write *Megillat HaSikarkin* (The Scroll of the Sicarii). In the essay, he compared the relationships between acts of the ancient Sicarii and modern-day political assassination.[99] The historical Sicarii were understood to be the extremists among the Zealots,[100] active at the time of the destruction of the Second Temple, and so-named for the daggers – *sicae* – concealed beneath their clothing, with which they would stab Jewish moderates sympathetic to the Roman regime.[101] They saw the Roman rule as illegitimate and sought to liberate the Jewish People from it through 'deliberately planned strategy'.[102] In spite of this fact, it would appear that the Sicarii focused their attention on Jewish notables and ruling groups. Josephus gives 'not the slightest indication that the Sicarii ever attacked a Roman official or a Roman military object'.[103] Historian Martin Goodman notes that Josephus believed the Sicarii to be 'deceivers and imposters'.[104] Notably, Richard Hornsley suggests that the sicari phenomenon was a result of the 'alienation of the intellectuals' within Jewish society during the Roman occupation of Jerusalem, and that its leadership and a significant number of members were drawn from the Jewish intelligentsia; a pointed coincidence when considering Ahimeir and his colleagues in this respect.[105] It has also been posited that the Biryonim – who had been 'organized at a stage when the situation in Jerusalem had not yet been totally hopeless' – preceded the Sicarii, who were an 'extreme offshoot' of the former that added a 'Messianic-social' streak to the 'national-political' struggle of the Zealots.[106] Israeli historian Josef Klausner – who was a member of the Revisionists, and edited the *Hebrew Encyclopaedia*, alongside Ahimeir – believed them to be 'activist Essenes', communistically inclined, aiming at an egalitarian society and the abolition of poverty'.[107] It was indicated during their trial that the various members of Brit HaBiryonim, including Ahimeir, understood the two different factions in this way.

In point of fact, Ahimeir would often publish articles under the name Abba Sikra – literally, 'Father of the Sicarii' – who, according to the Babylonian Talmud, was not only the leader of the Biryonim but also the nephew of Yohanan ben Zakkai, the founder of the Pharisaic tradition in Judaism. Furthermore, it is recounted that the Rabbis had asked the Biryonim for permission to leave the city to attempt to make peace with the Romans. However:

> They would not let them, but on the contrary said Let us go out and fight them. The Rabbis said: You will not succeed. They then rose up and burnt the stores of wheat and barley so that a famine ensued. … Abba Sikra the head of the biryoni in Jerusalem was the son of the sister of Rabban Yohanan b. Zakkai. The [latter] sent to him saying, Come to visit me privately. When he came he said to him, How long are you going to carry on in this way and kill all the people with starvation? He replied: What can I do? If I say a word to them, they will kill me.[108]

Historian Josef Nedava believed that this exchange pointed to 'basic political schisms within the leadership of the revolt'.[109] As noted earlier and elsewhere, there was, by 1930, an ever-widening split between the various factions of the Revisionist Party. Indeed, in one of Greenberg's letters to Miriam Yevin, he states that not only was Jabotinsky not a great leader, he was, in fact, 'dangerous'.[110] And in a letter to his wife, written on 29 October 1931, Yevin noted that

> everyone knows that J. has become a 'rag' and has become Grossman's lackey. … The trouble is that one cannot carry on an open campaign against J. because of his popularity amongst the Youth, which serves as an attraction.[111]

According to Nedava, Abba Sikra bridged the gap between the *biryoni* and the Sicarii, and was seen as a moderate rather than a 'mere, irresponsible "brigand."'[112] Certainly the Talmudic passage quoted before would seem to support Nedava's reading.[113] Indeed, Ahimeir was much more equivocal than his colleagues with regard to Jabotinsky's leadership abilities. In a letter written shortly after Yevin's, on 1 November 1932, and – according to the trial notes – 'probably [in] Ahimeir's handwriting', he maintained that 'We remain the Revisionist Zionist Organisation because of J. Besides the fact that he is popular, we have not lost our confidence in him yet'.[114]

Be that as it may, Ahimeir certainly saw in the figure of Abba Sikra someone who would not sanction those from within the Jewish community itself who were ready to compromise at any cost with the ruling power. And his identification with the Sicarii leader went beyond the pages of *Hazit HaAm*: as leader and commander of Brit HaBiryonim, Ahimeir became the morphological contemporary of Abba Sikra, and not only in his own eyes. A letter from Brit HaBiryonim member Shlomo Varde confirms that Ahimeir was widely recognised as the leader of this group of modern-day Sicarii. Furthermore, it also demonstrates the degree to which, by 1933, Ahimeir had himself, become a charismatic, cult leader in his own right:

> My beloved lord and admired Dr. Abba Ahimeir,
>
> I am unable to tell you of the feelings of happiness that filled my heart. ... Can I express in words what my hearts feels? Your few letters were as a balsam to my heart. If the number of your admirers is big, then I, the poor, am one of them who understands you and shares your sorrow ... the sorrow of all the Sikarikin and zealots. ... In Bialystok itself, the Betarim expect you and see in you the image of the Head of the Sikarikin and Biryonim, which serves them as a symbol and miracle. ... I am expecting to hear from you as the Jew expects the deliverer. Sprinkle me with the marrow and juice of your pen and my heart will delight.[115]

The fact that a man who was apparently as shy and reserved as Ahimeir could assume such a position of leadership and reverence is striking. Perhaps his adoption and portrayal – 'putting on the uniform' – of the figure of Abba Sikra served, for him, as a way to overcome his natural introversion.

In 'The Scroll of the Sicarii', Ahimeir uses the imagery of the Sicarii as a vehicle for the presentation of a hero who – as an 'anonymous' individual acting alone – 'makes' history through deeds and not words, and who is ready to sacrifice and, indeed, be sacrificed, in the name of the greater good. He notes that this precedent was, in fact, set in the *Tanakh* – which, Ahimeir notes, 'in general is fond of the sicarii' – in figures such as Ehud, Yonatan and the sons of Benjamin. Not surprisingly, Ahimeir believed that the Marxist 'negates the hero's value in history' because 'he is jealous of individual heroism', unlike in ancient Greek society, where 'every killer of a tyrant is considered a native hero'. In spite of this observation, Ahimeir wrote that sicari-ness appeared, nonetheless, as a last resort, only 'when there is the feeling that liberal-parliamentary means are not enough' to bring down the existing regime. Sicari killing could thus only be justified because it served a public objective. As such, killing was rendered permissible because it constituted a form of (national) self-defence.[116] Even so, far from glorifying the sicari deed, Ahimeir describes *sicari*-ness as a 'sickness which is contagious and dangerous'; a necessary evil perhaps, but a bad sign for the society held in its sway, nonetheless.

As we have seen in the previous chapter, Ahimeir's conception of the hero-as-doer remained an important theme for him: in *Yudaikah* he wrote that the idea of the hero-as-maker-of-history embodied the 'historical philosophy of the *Tanakh*' and, as such, had preceded the philosophies of Carlisle and Nietzsche by thousands of years.[117] Indeed, he sees the Hebrew Bible as being much more interested in individual – and not 'mass' – heroism. Furthermore, in terms of bloodshed, the 'Book of Books' – 'bleeding with blood' – was superseded only, in Ahimeir's estimation, by the works of Homer and Shakespeare.[118]

We should remember that 'The Scroll of the Sicarii' was written in 1926, while Ahimeir was still a member of HaPoel HaTzair. It was handwritten into one of his notebooks. He apparently never sought its publication, and doubts remain as to whether he would ever have done so.[119] Ahimeir almost certainly would have found an opportunity had publication been his intention: by this time he was already a well-established journalist in the Yishuv, and, as we have seen, did not shy away from journalistic provocation. He began to write his column From the 'Notebook of a Fascist' just two years after penning 'The Scroll of the Sicarii', and had begun to write about Italian Fascism and its possible suitability as a political model, already from 1923.[120] Be that as it may, 'The Scroll of the Sicarii' sat unpublished – and in all likelihood unread – for seven years among Ahimeir's many writings, in the room that he shared with Avraham Stavsky.

In no small sense is it remarkable that an essay that most likely never saw the light of day could, seven year later, come to play so central a role in serving to determine the further course of its author's life. The judge who sentenced Ahimeir concluded that 'a society does not depend upon its name but upon its propaganda and its aims', yet how effective is propaganda which does not propagate? Although produced as one of the central pieces of evidence in the trial of Brit HaBiryonim, no proof – indeed, not even an indication – exists that 'The Scroll of the Sicarii' was ever used as some sort of manifesto for the group. The article was not published, neither in the public nor underground press.[121] While we will never know his true intentions for the essay, it is important to remember that Ahimeir had no qualms about courting controversy in print. This was the man who, in 1933, had implored the masses 'to learn from the success of Nazism'.[122]

Regarding the essay's content, it is true that there are passages that condone political killing, but it is equally clear that Ahimeir saw this not only as a last resort but also as indicative of a diseased society. Furthermore, the concepts discussed in the essay do not stray too far from the Talmudic discussion of the *din rodef*, or law of the pursuer.[123] Ahimeir, while an avowed enemy of Rabbinic Judaism, had nonetheless received a certain degree of Talmudic education. And we should also not forget his early article on Savinkov, where he first broaches the question of 'killing by acceptable means'.[124] Indeed, Ahimeir sketched 'The Scroll of the Sicarii' only one year after he wrote the essay on Savinkov. Thus, he had precedents. It is perhaps not unthinkable that all of this helped him to justify the acceptability of the type of political assassination described in 'The Scroll of the Sicarii'. In a later essay, also found in one his notebooks and used as evidence in the Brit HaBiryonim trial, Ahimeir underscores – albeit in the context of a discussion on Socialism – his belief that 'Only the one who is able to die for his ideas is able also to kill'.[125] Be that as it may, Ahimeir's justification is hardly the 'glorification of political murder' that the sentencing judge concluded in the Brit HaBiryonim trial. Moreover, a critical reading of 'The Scroll of the Sicarii' shows Ahimeir's own position on the matter to be more equivocal than it is generally understood to be, and the text itself is not without thematic inconsistencies. The question remains as to why he would write a treatise expounding a belief in the societal benefits of the individual terror act, when such an act had just recently very nearly taken the life of his great ideological hero, Mussolini, and that this event had, in fact, been the catalyst for the whole exercise. It is very likely that 'The Scroll of the Sicarii' represents nothing more than an unpolished essay – dealing with contentious themes, to be sure – that had the simple misfortune to be discovered among Ahimeir's personal effects when his room was raided.

All ideological bravado aside, Ahimeir did in fact practise what he preached. He was arrested and went to prison on several occasions before the Arlosoroff and Brit HaBiryonim trials, for participating in acts of civil disobedience that were connected to Brit HaBiryonim activities. And Ahimeir made what must have been a profoundly horrible personal sacrifice – that of his own identity – when he sent his infant daughter to be raised by his sister, as her own. At the end of the manuscript of 'The ABC of Revolutionary Zionism', he adds the following, poignant note to Ze'eva, who was an infant at the time:

> These lines you will understand after many, many years. The good aunt will hide the picture for the moment and guard it. The first letter you will receive will be from your father, who has created among the Jewish youth in Palestine a Zionist revolutionary movement. Your good aunt and uncle do not understand. In Degania B a reception was given to the High Commissioner, the representative of the wicked rule which robbed 5000 dunums of Jewish land in Wadi Hawareth. (Crossed out)
>
> My heart breaks of longing for you without an end. But, never mind, it is grand to live. (Crossed out).[126]

The Jewish *Volks* Socialist

On 16 June 1933, the prominent Mapai leader and spokesman Chaim Arlosoroff was shot and killed while walking with his wife along the beach in Tel Aviv. He had just returned two days earlier from Nazi Germany where he had negotiated an agreement that would oversee the emigration of German Jews to Palestine. The Nazi government had been unwilling to let its Jewish émigrés leave with their possessions, and the new agreement sought to resolve this by permitting the transfer of Jewish capital from Germany to Palestine by immigrants or investors in the form of goods. This, of course, assisted the Germans through increased production and export of goods which, technically, were bought by Jews at the other end. This, in turn, staved off any anti-German boycott in Palestine, for the time being, and gave the economy in the Yishuv a much-needed injection.[127] It was dubbed 'The *Haavara* Agreement', or 'The Transfer Agreement', and was highly controversial.

Ahimeir was just over a year older than Arlosoroff, who was born on 23 February 1899 in Romny, Ukraine. Arlosoroff's father, Shaul, was – like Ahimeir's – a successful timber merchant, and the family – again, like Ahimeir's – enjoyed a comfortable existence that combined some degree of Jewish tradition with an overall Russian cultural identification. Both boys studied Hebrew, privately, from a young age. Albeit for completely different reasons, both families moved when each boy was set to begin school. In the Arlosoroffs' case, the move was to East Prussia, in the wake of the 1905 pogroms. The family moved once again, in 1912, to Konigsberg, where the young Arlosoroff entered Gymnasium, the same year that the young Gaissinovitch entered the Herzliya Gymnasium in Tel Aviv.[128]

In spite of their Russian citizenship, the Arlosoroffs remained in Germany during the First World War, where they relocated to Berlin. Nonetheless, Shaul Arlosoroff returned to Russia to conduct business during the war, and died from cholera in St Petersburg in June 1918 – less than a year before Meir Gaissinovitch was killed in battle – without having been reunited with his family. As in Ahimeir's case, the death of a close family member had a profound impact upon the young Arlosoroff.

In spite of both his family's overall identification as Russian, and his own still slightly Russian-accented, spoken German, Arlosoroff embraced German culture, wholeheartedly. He even sought placement in the German army during the war, although his application was rejected because of his Russian citizenship. Perhaps Arlosoroff's newfound identification as a German was really due to his gratitude for his family having been given asylum there, as Shlomo Avineri suggests. Or perhaps it was due to some deeper psychological coping mechanism on Arlosoroff's part: the need of a foreigner to fit in to his new host society. In Arlosoroff's case, however – and to no small degree – one might say that the flesh was willing, but the spirit was weak. In spite of his undoubted love of German culture, Arlosoroff's love was the fascination of an outsider looking inwards. Indeed, his 'Oriental' ancestry rendered any such love as nothing more than superficial, the 'product of an inner rift due to rootlessness…and unknown to the racial German'.[129] Notably, the teenage Arlosoroff wrote poetry that, by any definition, could be considered Jewish-nationalist in orientation. Not unlike that of the Maximalists, Arlosoroff's poetry looked to the ancient Maccabees and the Bar Kochba revolt for inspiration.[130] The *Zerrissenheit* that the young Arlosoroff experienced regarding his inability to reconcile his conflicting German, Jewish – and presumably also, although to a lesser degree, Russian – identities was a dilemma in which the young Gaissinovitch appears never to have found himself, and marks a notable psychological-developmental divergence between the two men.[131]

Be that as it may, Arlosoroff – like Ahimeir – fell under the ideological spell of A.D. Gordon and his idea of the Zionist 'pioneer' who sought 'redemption' through the 'upbuilding of Eretz Israel on the foundations of self-labour and national ownership of land', etc.[132] Like Ahimeir, Arlosoroff also completed doctoral studies – in his case in economics, at the University of Berlin – advocated the programme *HeHalutz*, joined HaPoel HaTzair, and contributed to the party's publications. Indeed, he became editor of HaPoel HaTzair's German-edition journal *Die Arbeit*. Furthermore, both men emigrated to British Mandate Palestine in 1924, where each intensified his activities – both journalistic and political – within the party. Thus, a cursory comparison of Ahimeir's and Arlosoroff's biographies to this point demonstrates an often uncanny degree of similarity, certainly more than we might expect, given each man's eventual fate. Such similarities were, at times, also mirrored in the two men's ideological outlooks.

Arguably Arlosoroff's best-known work, *Der Jüdische Volkssozializmus* – written in 1920, before he had ever visited Palestine – provides a salient case in point. The typical English translation of the essay's title – 'Jewish People's Socialism' – lacks the multilayered sophistication of meaning that the German word *Volk* conveys. As George Mosse elucidated:

> *Volk* signified the union of a group of people with a transcendental 'essence' [that] might be called 'nature' or 'cosmos' or 'mythos', but in each instance it was fused to man's innermost nature, and represented the source of his creativity, his depth of feeling, his individuality, and his unity with other members of the Volk.[133]

Mosse further stipulated that in the German understanding of *Volk*, the 'human' – indeed 'national' – soul was inextricably bound to its 'natural surroundings'.[134]

Indeed, it is clear through the context of Arlosoroff's essay that he understood *Volk* in this way.[135] Thus – in Mosse's example of a typical application of *Völkisch* theory – the Jews were as spiritually 'dry' and 'barren' as was the desert landscape from which they came forth.[136] We should also remember that Ahimeir – who, in *Yudaikah*, used the Hebrew equivalents of *Volk: Am* and *Umma* – also considered a people's natural habitat to be one of the elemental determinants of 'national' character. Not surprisingly, however, Ahimeir – and we might safely also assume Arlosoroff – saw the desert as a positive influence, where the 'Semitic spirit' – 'caring, subjective, ethical, and wandering' – had been imbued into the nascent Jewish nation.[137]

Arlosoroff argues the case for a *Jewish Volks Socialism* that is 'born from the needs and soul of the Jewish *Volk* alone'; a movement that would

> engage the Jewish Volk as a constructive and equally entitled member in the association of socialist nations, in which it nonetheless remains authentic[ally] and proud[ly] national. A movement that does not want to base its socialism on the egoistic interests of one class, but rather on the renewal of production and revival of labour; [a movement] whose means are neither class rule nor class sedition, but rather the establishment of the basic convictions of the community [*Gemeinschaftsgesinnung*] and positive economic make-up [*Aufbau*]. A movement that will conquer Palestine with the will of idealism, lead the Diaspora towards a national and social future, renew and promote Hebrew culture in the consciousness of the historical integrity of its *Volk* [*im Bewusstsein der geschichtlichen Einheit des Volkes*].[138]

Like Ahimeir, Arlosoroff rejected orthodox Marxism, and bemoaned the over-emphasis that had developed, towards the end of the nineteenth century and in the first decade of the twentieth, on its class-based, anti-capitalist, economic message that had resulted in a break with – indeed, negation of – a nation's sense of evolutionary-historical, cultural-national, self-identification.[139] Such negation was doubly dangerous for the Jews. First, the fate of the cultural-national self-identity of Europe's Jewish population was on an already slippery slope due to the bastardisation of assimilation.[140] Second, there was almost no Jewish working class, neither an agrarian peasantry, nor industrial proletariat. But neither were there many Jewish industrial magnates. In contrast to the situation with Jewish industrial entrepreneurs in America, for example, Arlosoroff saw the majority of Europe's Jewish masses as acting in some sort of undertaking where they would fulfil the role of both proprietor and worker, at the same time. And while the Jewish bourgeois perhaps did, to a certain degree, possess a certain means of production, the success of a particular venture depended on no small measure of manual labour by the business's proprietor, himself.[141] And no matter where a business was based, all profits from Jewish, capitalist, entrepreneurship served only to benefit the economic life of whatever country the particular business happened to operate in.[142] There was no 'Jewish' economy, no 'Jewish' class struggle. Of course, Arlosoroff saw his concept of *Jewish Volks Socialism* as the only way out of this conundrum.[143]

Arlosoroff believed that a basic ideological schism existed between a European Jewish majority in Russia that was dominated by the Poale Zionists and Bundists, and HaPoel HaTzair in Palestine. The latter group had just begun to cooperate with Ahdut HaAvodah at around the time that Arlosoroff wrote his treatise, and their joining of forces led to the establishment of some of the most iconic Labour Zionist institutions: the Histadrut, *Va'ad Leumi* and Bank HaPoalim, etc. Eventually, in 1930 – through the efforts of Arlosoroff and David Ben-Gurion – the two groups would merge into the political party, Mapai. Perhaps somewhat surprisingly – given Arlosoroff's own Russian-Jewish pedigree – he foresaw the German *Landesverband* (national association) of HaPoel HaTzair as specially situated; an elite group with 'a special role to fulfil' that would act as the necessary unifying agent between the two ideologically disparate – and by his implication, less ideologically evolved – groups.[144] Indeed, in spite of Arlosoroff's utopian vision for a nationalist Socialism for all of the Jewish Volk, a close reading of *Jewish Volks Socialism* – especially in its original German form – often betrays an exceedingly smug, Western Euro-centricity.[145]

Ahimeir, all of his illiberal posturing aside, espoused a traditional liberal approach when it came to economics. He believed that the state should stay out of socio-economic enterprise, but should retain control of 'political and legal superstructures', and steer the national economy by providing incentives and setting tariffs.[146] Nonetheless, Ahimeir was a historian, and not an economist. He was neither au fait with – nor most likely very interested in – highly worked out economic theories. With Arlosoroff, an outstanding economist, we have an altogether different story. His economic recommendations for the Yishuv play a central role in his concept of *Jewish Volks Socialism*, and – it goes almost without saying – they were based on very strong Socialist foundations. Arlosoroff lists six ideological principles that he believed to be fundamental to the success of his concept of *Jewish Volks Socialism*:

1. Public ownership of land.
2. The creation of a national fund for investment [and] the nationalization of production.

3. The placing under national control of transit commerce arising from Palestine's geographical position.
4. The launching of a world-wide Jewish loan for Palestine.
5. Extensive encouragement of co-operative societies in Palestine.
6. The introduction of wide-ranging social legislation regulating working hour, guaranteeing collective bargaining, freedom of association for trade unions, as well as fixing a maximum price on land in private hands.[147]

A comparison of Arlosoroff's six principles with the demands of *Gush HaAvodah HaRevizionisti*, discussed in Chapter 3, is striking in the degree of ideological overlap that exists between the two, and it is rendered all the more striking when we remember that Ahimeir, Greenberg and Yevin – all three of whom had literally just resigned from HaPoel HaTzair – appeared as representatives of the *Gush*. Rather than two diametrically opposed ideological streams, we are presented almost with two versions of a similar ideology. The main difference is the question of ownership of land, but to a certain degree this is a moot point. At the time of the first *Gush HaAvodah HaRevizionisti* conference, all of the members of the group lived and worked on kibbutzim or moshavim. And Arlosoroff's treatise was written in 1920, eight years before Ahimeir and company split from HaPoel HaTzair, and one year before Arlosoroff had even visited Palestine, let alone emigrated there. Indeed, by 1925, Avineri notes that Arlosoroff 'appeared to suggest for the first time that a laissez-faire policy, and a middle-class immigration could prove to be successful and that the Yishuv could develop along capitalist lines, and did not have to follow the pioneering and socialist-oriented directions taken by the Second and Third *Aliyah*'.[148]

Furthermore, by 1932 – in the wake of ever-increasing Arab resistance, and British vacillation vis à vis its position on the Zionist project – Arlosoroff laid out the only four possible options that he saw as being currently viable for the Zionist movement: to continue on, with 'passive' hope, as was the way of Galut; to abandon the Zionist project, altogether; to partition Palestine; or to establish a revolutionary Jewish dictatorship, 'aimed against both the British and the Arabs'.[149] Remarkably, at the time of writing, Arlosoroff saw the last option as the only possible solution. And with amazing ideological similarity to Ahimeir, Arlosoroff concluded that

Zionism cannot, in the given circumstances, be turned into reality without a transitional period of the organised revolutionary rule of the Jewish minority, that there is no way for a Jewish majority ... without a period of a nationalist

minority government which would usurp the state machinery, the administration
and the military power in order to forestall the danger of our being swamped by
numbers and endangered by a rising.[150]

Avineri contends that had Arlosoroff lived to see the immigration boom of
1933–7, he would have no longer seen the option of revolutionary dictatorship
as the only possible course of action for the Zionists. But while the population
of the Yishuv had indeed doubled during this period, and the idea of partition
had indeed been broached – although by no means adopted as official policy –
in the Peel Commission Report published on 7 July 1937, Arab resistance and
violence had nonetheless also increased exponentially. Thus, we have no way of
knowing if Arlosoroff would so easily have discarded his claim that a period of
Jewish revolutionary dictatorship was the only viable option for the Zionists,
and Avineri's comment seems more to betray his own political agenda.

Once again, the impression we get from a comparison between Arlosoroff
and Ahimeir is not one of polar opposites, but rather one of two men whose
ideologies developed – at times – in an uncannily parallel manner. There is a
similarity here to the relationship between Weizmann and Jabotinsky; one that,
in the public sphere, could be uncompromisingly contentious, but upon closer
study of each man's ideological position, one that reveals more common ground
than is generally recognised. Arlosoroff the Socialist economist was convinced
that theory would determine action; Ahimeir the historian believed the opposite
to be true. What is often overlooked in the whole Arlosoroff-Ahimeir debate is
that the conclusions both men reached were as much intellectual as they were
political or practical. And on a purely intellectual level, the two men had few
other peers in the Yishuv, during this period. Where they really differed was
in tactic, not so much in strategy. Indeed, the attitude of each man towards
the newly elected Nazi government serves as a tragically ironic example of this
difference.

In the spring of 1933, the Revisionists had proscribed all political and economic
relations with Germany, and, following the lead of members of Brit HaBiryonim,
had instigated a boycott of German goods. Although the Maximalists could not,
at first, see past the Nazi victory as representative of anything more than a victory
of Fascism over Communism, once it became clear to them that the 'Hitlerists'
would not renounce their antisemitism, Ahimeir and Brit HaBiryonim were the
first in the Yishuv to take action against the Germans.[151] Arlosoroff's visit and
subsequent negotiations with the Nazi leadership was thus viewed as betrayal
by the Revisionists, who now began to attack him openly in their press organs.
They branded him a traitor, who 'offers not only to lift the ban but to guarantee a

market for German exports', and concluded that 'by this action, Mapai is stabbing our people in the back'.[152] Furthermore, on the day of Arlosoroff's assassination, *Hazit HaAm* had published an article describing Arlosoroff as willing to 'deal away the most sacred Jewish assets and values' for money and wealth.[153]

Trials

Thus it is perhaps not surprising that in the wake of Arlosoroff's murder an accusatory finger was pointed in the direction of the Revisionists. Five weeks after the murder, Ahimeir was among fifteen members of Betar, the Revisionist Party and Brit HaBiryonim arrested in connection with it. At that time the police seized the Revisionist archives and Ahimeir's writings, including the notebook discussed earlier. Ahimeir was formally charged by the British Mandatory police with plotting the murder, while two Betari – Avraham Stavsky, Ahimeir's roommate and Zvi Rosenblatt – were charged with carrying it out. This brought the increasingly hostile relationship between the Revisionists and the Labour Zionists to a head, with the Revisionists accusing Mapai and the Left of waging a 'witch hunt' and 'blood libel'[154] against them.[155] Copies of some of the documents seized, including 'The Scroll of the Sicarii' were transferred to Prague in August 1933, where the 18th Zionist Congress was to take place. Berl Katznelson called for a commission of inquiry to be appointed which would scrutinise the documents. This, in spite of claims by several Zionist council members that such a commission might influence the judges, as well as public opinion, to the detriment of the accused during their subsequent trial.[156] Their claims notwithstanding, a majority of 92 to 67 voted in favour of setting up the council of inquiry. Through the establishment of the council, it was hoped to bring the results of the investigation to the Zionist General Council so that it could take steps to 'put an end to such trends should they be found to exist and to root out all elements guilty or responsible for such trends from within the Zionist movement'.[157]

On 16 May 1934 Ahimeir was acquitted of the charges relating to the Arlosoroff murder, but Rosenblatt and Stavsky stood trial. They were eventually acquitted due to lack of corroborating evidence, although, in Stavsky's case, only on appeal. Jabotinsky, for his part, spoke out in support of all men charged, in an effort to maintain a show of solidarity in a trial that was as much about its perception as part of a world struggle between right and left, as it was about the actual murder of Arlosoroff. [158]

Although acquitted, Ahimeir remained in jail and began a hunger strike, which he continued for four days and ended only at the prompting of the Chief Rabbi, Avraham Yitzhak HaCohen Kook. On 12 July 1934 he was further charged, alongside other members of Brit HaBiryonim Yehoshua Yevin, Yehoshua Lichter, Chaim Diviri, Moshe Svorai and Yacob Orenstein, with 'conspiring to effect acts in furtherance of a seditious intention, advocating and encouraging unlawful acts, being a member of an unlawful and seditious association, and being in possession of seditious literature'.[159] The major piece of 'damning' evidence used against Ahimeir was 'The Scroll of the Sicarii'.[160]

During the trial, much emphasis was given to the question of semantics. Although the defendants agreed that the word *sikarikim* meant 'terrorist', there was less of a consensus on the translation of *biryon* or *Biryonim*.[161] This suggests that Ahimeir and his group may well have understood the Sicarii to have been 'extreme offshoots' of the *biryonim*, as discussed earlier. While the prosecution maintained that *biryon* was synonymous with 'terrorist', the defence claimed that they understood the word in its old Hebrew meaning of 'Praetorian Guard'.[162] Both sides produced dictionaries – the Eliezer Ben Yehuda Dictionary on the part of the prosecution, and the Jastrow Dictionary of the Talmud on that of the defence – to support their claims. The judge, in his ruling, questioned whether this differentiation was 'of very much importance, because the object of nature of a society does not depend upon its name but upon its propaganda and its aims'. He finally concluded that 'in certain circumstances "*Biryonim*" can be translated as "terrorists"'. Similarly, with regard to the word 'revolutionary'; while accepting the word's potential for a many-faceted interpretation, the judge nonetheless ruled that when 'used in documents which include references to murder, revolvers, knives, the shedding of blood, blowing up of trains etc., the word acquires a much more sinister meaning'.

Ahimeir defended 'The Scroll of the Sicarii' by claiming that it was a historical essay, written out of a keen interest in terrorism and its history, and with the desire to write a history of the Russian Revolution in the future.[163] He attributed no serious meaning to the work, but confirmed that its writing had been catalysed by an attack on Mussolini's life several years earlier. Nonetheless, regarding 'The Scroll of the Sicarii', the judge ruled that

> there is no doubt that it can be given a meaning which is more seditious than any other document in the whole of this case. … It is in effect a glorification of political murder. Killing from a Sicarii point of view and for political reasons is permitted.

Ahimeir, as leader of Brit HaBiryonim, was deemed 'head and shoulders above anyone else in ability, intelligence and education', and sentenced to twenty-one months' imprisonment with hard labour. The judge had spotted a clear difference between the Revisionists and Brit HaBiryonim, finding that 'a dangerous conspiracy had been unearthed'. Jabotinsky appeared to use this fact for political gain, and effectively let the group's members hang themselves with their own rope. Certainly his support of Ahimeir throughout the trial was nothing like what he gave to Avraham Stavsky. Ahimeir and Diviri appealed, and were eventually found guilty only of 'being members of an unlawful association', and 'being in possession of documents containing seditious intentions'. Notably, they were found not-guilty of 'conspiracy to do acts in furtherance of a seditious intention', and Ahimeir's sentence was thus reduced to eighteen months.[164]

Years later, Ahimeir provided reasons for the ultimate failure of Brit HaBiryonim. The self-destructive element in the group's nature – its unwillingness to act publicly as one organisation, as described earlier – was, by its very definition, a significant reason for the group's failure. The group was neither an underground nor a public group, but rather a 'semi-underground' organisation, whose emphasis was on propaganda that sought to re-educate and re-engage a pacifist youth into one that was ready for revolutionary war. Ahimeir saw the courtroom as the best forum for waging this propaganda war, but – once again, by definition – the moment that such a war could be waged would at the same time spell the automatic destruction of the group. More importantly, Ahimeir lists the group's inability to successfully adopt Fascism as a modus operandi as one of the key causes that prevented the group's success. He suggests that this was due to the fact that – by the 1930s – Fascism had been unable to disassociate itself from antisemitism. When we consider that he wrote these lines in 1953, Ahimeir's claim seems rather striking. Nonetheless, it is unclear whether Ahimeir's comments reflect his position in 1953, or whether they merely reflect his analysis of the failure of Brit HaBiryonim in the 1930s. Finally – unlike the Irgun and Lehi, who fought their wars 'on only one front', and thus with more success – Brit HaBiryonim had fought a war on four fronts, as listed earlier, and had not differentiated between the British Mandatory and Yishuv leaderships.

The negative press generated by their initial support for the Nazis coupled with the fallout of the two trials against them signalled the end of the Brit HaBiryonim, and, in point of fact, also the Maximalists. It is generally believed that upon Ahimeir's release from prison, he devoted his time to intellectual pursuits – publishing articles, and serving on the editorial board of the Hebrew Encyclopaedia, to which he was a significant contributor – and that he eschewed any organised political activity. That is not to say that Ahimeir did not remain active within the Revisionist Party – he famously clashed with Jabotinsky at the fourth national convention of Betar in 1936 in Poland – but his activities were confined to the realm of party politics, not direct political action.[165] However, a memorandum dated 15 or 25 September 1937, which deals with the murder investigation of a young Irgun member, Zvi Frankel, and marked simply, 'From Police', claims that

> after the Arlosoroff trial, Ahimeir proceeded abroad, and handed over the organisation of the group to Haim Diviri. The group was then named HaNoar HaMari [*sic*] … . After Ahimeir had left Palestine, rumours were spread by the Party that he had given up politics. This, however, was not true as when in Poland he immediately organised the *Kvutzat Berionim* [*sic*], which is an extremist organisation and formed the opposition to the Zionist Organisation and the Revisionist Party there. Actually, they were closely connected with the Palestine Extremist Party, which was being run by Diviri. They were executing terrorist acts during the last month of the disturbance of 1936. At the beginning they directed their attacks against Arabs in retaliation for the murders of Jews, but since the suggestion of partition they decided to commence acts of terrorism against Jews, in order to intimidate them against the support of partition.[166]

There is no mention of either *HaNoar HaMari* [*sic*] (The Youth of Resistance)[167] or the *Kvutzat Biryonim* (Biryonim Group) in the body of scholarship on Ahimeir, nor indeed – apparently – anywhere else. In 1936, he had gone to Poland on a lecture tour on behalf of the Revisionists in Warsaw. It is interesting that Ahimeir apparently did attempt to organise, once again, a group that espoused an 'extremist' platform in deed, and presumably also ideology. Nonetheless, the lack of any further documentation surrounding *Kvutzat Biryonim* points to the group's failure – if indeed, it existed at all – to attain any real position of importance within the Zionist resistance movement. Although outside of the scope of this book, this one small clue that points towards the existence of *Kvutzat Biryonim* and *Noar HaMeri* begs for further research in this direction.

No matter what did or did not happen in Poland after his release from prison, in Palestine itself Ahimeir never really recovered politically or personally from the events of 1933 and 1934. Although acquitted before even going to trial, the notoriety he gained during the Arlosoroff murder inquiry would hang like an albatross around his neck for the rest of his life. While proud of his involvement and achievements with Brit HaBiryonim, Ahimeir steadfastly maintained his innocence with regard to the Arlosoroff murder throughout his whole life, both publicly, and – more pointedly – privately. Many years later, in a letter to his daughter Ze'eva, he outlined the events which led to the accusation.[168] As a member of HaPoel HaTzair, Ahimeir had fought:

> Together with Arlosoroff against the adoption of the socialist program and against a merger with Ahdut HaAvodah. Arlosoroff surrendered and joined Mapai, and I didn't. Since then I hadn't seen him. ... I was informed about the Arlosoroff murder 12 hours after his murder. Neither I, nor Stavsky, nor Rosenblatt, nor any person from Jabotinsky's movement had any relevance to this crime. But Mapai, who thus found themselves in a difficult situation, exploited the murder and in the light of the propaganda the Palestine Foundation Fund potentially conducted a blood libel.[169]

Ahimeir believed that there was a plot against him because of his activity in Brit HaBiryonim. Stavsky was accused because he shared a room with Ahimeir, and Rosenblatt came into the picture because he was still a youth and presumably naïve, and a third person was needed in order to correspond with Mrs Arlosoroff's eyewitness account. Privately, Ahimeir believed that Arlosoroff had been murdered by the British secret police. 'The question', he continued, 'is whether some of the Mapai leadership weren't also involved (Berl Katznelson, Dov Hoz, Eliyahu Golomb, and others)'.

It had been Berl Katznelson who was instrumental in establishing the commission of inquiry in Prague and throughout the whole affair had maintained a dogged anti-violence stance which would eventually serve to isolate him from his own party. Nonetheless, behind closed doors he was nagged by a sense of culpability from all sides involved: 'A great deal of emotional preparation was required of these people before they arrived at this state. And who can tell whether or not one of us did not expedite this process?'[170]

Indeed, it would appear that, privately, Katznelson came to doubt Ahimeir's guilt but did not voice this openly since the presumed guilt of all three men charged was a 'tenet of faith for the leaders of the Histadrut and Mapai', and thus unchallengeable.[171] Ahimeir, perhaps more than anyone, understood how difficult it was to dispel the rumours of his guilt in the matter. At the end of his letter to his daughter he repeats once again, emphatically:

> I swear on all that is holy to me, I swear on the memory of my parents who were murdered at the hands of the Germans, I swear on the lives of my children – that neither I, nor Stavsky, nor Rosenblatt, and neither any person from the membership of Jabotinsky's movement had a hand in the murder of Arlosoroff. ... My soul has been extremely wounded. I traversed a path of life which was very difficult. But I was sincere. In a sense I succeeded. Not in everything. I could not save a few souls which were dear to me.

The controversy around the Arlosoroff murder and subsequent trial of members of Brit HaBiryonim were defining moments in Ahimeir's life. Misconceptions and inaccuracies continue to persist, not only regarding the circumstances surrounding Ahimeir's involvement in the murder and command of the resistance group but also surrounding the writing of 'The Scroll of the Sicarii'. Indeed, some sections of Israeli society remain polarised to this day.[172] Nonetheless, Brit HaBiryonim set an important precedent with its ideologies of anti-British resistance, pointed political action, willingness to go to prison and for self-sacrifice, and – not least – in acting as the vanguard for the concept of a militaristic, Revolutionary Zionism that Ahimeir so strongly advocated that the Yishuv adopt as praxis.

Conclusion: The bourgeois revolutionary

As of 1855 and the death of Nicholas I the modern Russian political tradition was scarcely fifty years old, yet in that relatively short space of time it had undergone a remarkably swift process of radicalization. ... In the thirty years of repression under Nicholas the idea of revolt became the ideal of revolution, and the goal was no longer a change in the political regime or legal status of the citizenry but a total social and moral renovation of the nation. Indeed, this 'socialist' goal had assumed the form of the most extreme and uncompromising theory of revolutionary liberation – anarchism. Throughout this whole process of radicalization, however, there is one remarkable element of continuity: with each shift leftward the impetus came predominantly from men of the same social group – the gentry.[1]

So observed Martin Malia at the conclusion of his biography of Alexander Herzen, in a chapter entitled 'The Gentry Revolutionary'. Some of the parallels with this study are striking. By 1933, with the murder of Arlosoroff, the 'modern Jewish political tradition' – Zionism – was also scarcely fifty years old, and in its somewhat younger, Herzlian-Political ideological form, had also, in a relatively short space of time, undergone a remarkably swift process of radicalisation.[2] In the thirty years since Herzl's death, the gradual 'repression' of Political Zionist ideology – by Practical Zionist settlement that was willing to compromise its terms – led to a situation where Jabotinsky's 'idea of revolt', as embodied in the foundation of Revisionist Zionism, became Ahimeir's 'ideal of revolution'. Of course, in this case – in a movement that was nationalistically political – a 'change in the political regime or legal status of the citizenry' absolutely superseded any 'social and moral renovation of the nation.' Indeed, this 'nationalist-political' goal had assumed the form of the most extreme and uncompromising theory of revolutionary *nationalist* 'liberation': Fascism. And again, as was the case with the modern Russian political tradition, the modern Zionist political tradition was likewise characterised by 'one remarkable element of continuity': with each shift to the right, the impetus also came predominantly from men of the same social group – in this case, the bourgeois intelligentsia.

From Herzl through Nordau, to Jabotinsky and Ahimeir, the gradual radicalisation of Political Zionism was not only led by the bourgeois intelligentsia but, furthermore, one that had – in character and orientation – shifted gradually from Western to Eastern Europe, from 'more bourgeois' to 'more *intelligent*', as it were. Indeed, the very concepts of intelligentsia and the *intelligent* are, themselves, Russian in origin.[3] Moreover, for an Eastern European Jew of Jabotinsky's and Ahimeir's generations, the intelligentsia – whose first members had, in fact, come from the gentry – *had become* the gentry of the bourgeoisie, albeit one that was 'landed' with *Bildung*, and was thus a group to which one could realistically aspire to, and attain membership in. The fact that both Jabotinsky and Ahimeir were cosmopolitan products of both realms – Eastern European by birth and upbringing, Western European by education – only buttresses this argument. In this – very important – respect, both men had followed in the long ideological-historical trajectory that had its origins in the Westernisation programme of Peter the Great, one that saw a selected few – at this point still members of the gentry – go to Western Europe for a 'higher' education, before returning to Russia to assume some sort of civic leadership role.[4] Not only did Ahimeir recognise, and place a high value upon, Peter the Great as a moderniser – specifically through his Westernisation programme, as discussed in his dissertation on Spengler – but Ahimeir himself represented, at once, the pinnacle and terminus of its ideological, and historical, development. In contrast to Ahimeir, Jabotinsky had, in 1901, after his studies in Rome, returned to Russia. And he did, in fact, as both a prominent journalist and eventually also Zionist politician, assume a leadership role, albeit one within a 'smaller' Russian – in this case, Jewish – community. Of course, there was no question of Ahimeir returning to Russia at the end of his education, a fact due not only to his ardent Zionism, but – equally as important – to the reality that, in post-revolutionary Russia, the anti-Western character of the new, Communist, intelligentsia had now rendered the classic Western-educated Russian *intelligent* undesirable.

Nonetheless, Ahimeir – as both a Russian and a Zionist – certainly upheld the ideals of the traditional Russian intelligentsia, one that was, in the words of the distinguished intellectual historian, Isaiah Berlin:

> Founded, broadly speaking, on the idea of a permanent rational opposition to a status quo which was regarded as in constant danger of becoming ossified, a block to human thought and human progress. This is the historic role of the intelligentsia as seen by itself, then and now.[5]

This elitist – we might even say Messianic – attitude informed Ahimeir's role, not only as a member of a 'traditional' Russian intelligentsia but – more important – as a 'modern' Political Zionist who stood in permanent opposition to a Jewish national movement that was – through its lack of forward motion – 'in constant danger of becoming ossified'. Indeed, in this latter – more pronounced – role, Ahimeir embodied Berlin's quintessential 'real' member of the intelligentsia, whom he characterised as the 'political pamphleteers, the civic-minded poets, the forerunners of the Russian Revolution – mainly journalists and political thinkers who quite consciously used literature, sometimes very poor examples of it, as vehicles for social protest.'[6] The only difference, in Ahimeir's case, was that he no longer looked to Russia, but to Zion, for his revolution. In the Yishuv, Ahimeir, now no longer a member – neither geographically, nationalistically, nor ideologically – of a bourgeois Russian intelligentsia, and catalysed in no small way by what he saw as a 'truly repressive regime,' became instead, the leading figure of a new Zionist nationalist *intelligentsia militans.*[7]

Perhaps the simple recognition that Jabotinsky was living in London during the period of the October Revolution, while Ahimeir experienced it first-hand in Bobruisk, may provide a further telling explanation for both this 'geographically' eastward shift as a key element in the radicalisation of the ideology of Political Zionism, and the fact that it was Ahimeir, and not – indeed, *could not* be – Jabotinsky, who was able to effect it. The year 1917 had, for Jabotinsky – with the formation of the Zion Mule Corps – sowed the seeds for Jewish military organisation. For Ahimeir – who experienced the Bolshevik Revolution first-hand – it sowed the seeds for Jewish revolutionary organisation. One gesture recognised and advocated the utility of European Jewry in the service of modern European politics; the other decried the uselessness of Europe in the service of modern European Jewish politics. Thus, by 1933, Jabotinsky's Zionist Bourgeois Gentleman had been transformed into Ahimeir's Zionist Bourgeois Revolutionary, his 'Iron Wall' (*kir barzel*) into Ahimeir's 'Iron Bridge' (*gesher barzel*), if still yet only in ideology.[8]

Jabotinsky and Ahimeir could both trace their ideological positions back to the Nietzschean concept of *Macht* (power), as understood (or perhaps misunderstood, in the estimation of Israeli philosopher, Jacob Golomb) and expanded upon by Max Nordau.[9] Nietzsche distinguished between 'positive, authentic' and 'negative, inauthentic' power; the former was symptomatic of a strong, confident personality, the latter, of a weak, insecure – what Nordau termed 'degenerative' – personality. Hence Nordau's concept of *Muskeljudentum* (Muscular Jewry), in which the negative, degenerative manifestation of power that he believed prevailed among Europe's Jews by the end of the nineteenth century, would be transformed into its positive, authentic form. Nonetheless – as Golomb notes – Jabotinsky, in his personality and ideology, embodied elements of both positive- and negative-degenerative manifestations of power; he was, equally, a child of fin de siècle liberal decadence, and a more tempered liberal politics.[10] Ahimeir – through his radicalisation of Jabotinskian politics, and a concept of *Macht* that saw him solidly embrace Fascist ideology and aesthetic – shifted yet further towards what he believed to be Nietzsche's concept of a positive manifestation of power. The paradox, of course, is that – if we accept Nietzsche and Nordau – this fetishisation of power, certainly in a 'Fascist' sense, represented, in reality, a far greater insecurity and degeneration than it purported to negate, and was thus, ultimately, a shift further towards a Nietzschean negative manifestation of power.

The difference between Jabotinsky's and Ahimeir's 'degeneration' is that of a bourgeois-indulgent versus a bourgeois-existential decadence. Much in the way that Spenglerian philosophy was a more desperately existential manifestation – and therefore a necessary consequence – of a more indulgently bourgeois Nietzschean philosophy, so was Ahimeir's embrace of 'degenerative' power a more desperately existential manifestation – and therefore a necessary consequence – of Jabotinsky's more indulgently bourgeois mixture of Nietzschean 'positive' and 'negative' concepts of *Macht*. More simply put, Jabotinsky – and indeed, Herzl and Nordau before him – was decadently liberal, while Ahimeir – and Stern and Begin after him – was decadently illiberal. Indeed, the fact that it is often so difficult to unequivocally explain Jabotinsky's political positions can almost always be attributed to his liberal leanings. We have no such difficulty with Ahimeir. In this respect, Jabotinsky was still more a child of a Western European-, and Ahimeir of an Eastern European bourgeois intelligentsia. This argument is buttressed by Herzen's contention that the 'bourgeoisie does not have a great past and has no future. It was good only for a moment, as a negation, as a transition'.[11]

We should assume that Herzen was speaking of a Russian bourgeois intelligentsia, and to a certain degree Ahimeir must also have understood his own Russian bourgeois-*intelligent* roots in such a manner, if perhaps only subconsciously so. Indeed, Ahimeir fits Malia's definition of the Russian *intelligent* – 'any able, sensitive, and ambitious individual, from a more or less privileged group, who lives under an inflexible and "closed" old regime which does not offer adequate scope for his energies, and who consequently goes over to integral, as well as highly ideological, opposition to that regime' – to a tee.[12] In Ahimeir's case, the 'inflexible' and 'closed old regime' was less the British Mandatory government than it was the Zionist leadership of the Yishuv. Such an analysis would explain Ahimeir's permanent sense of what might be called 'desperate transience', which – be it as rootless Jew, stateless Zionist or anachronistic Russian bourgeois intellectual, and which in the final analysis is more than just a historian's worry, although it is also that – led to his frustrated cynicism and eventual emergence as a 'bourgeois terrorist', the spiritual leader and ideologue of the new Zionist *intelligentsia militans*.[13]

Nonetheless, we should see Ahimeir's 'bourgeois terrorism' in a positive light. This may appear to be a difficult admission; however, I offer no apology in my attempt at an accurate analysis of Ahimeir's historical position. In his study, Malia distinguishes between the 'positive anarchism' of Herzen and the 'negative anarchism' of Bakunin that was characterised by an emphasis on

> disorganisation, destruction, and negation. ... Herzen, on the other hand, only rarely ... chose to revel in the drama of destruction. ... Nor does one have the feeling with Herzen, as one does with Bakunin, that destruction was an end in itself.[14]

Similarly, in our case, we should distinguish between the 'positive Fascism' of Ahimeir and the 'negative Fascism' of, say, Avraham Stern who – in the final analysis – was much more nihilistic in his ideology, approach and, ultimately, fate.[15] Once again, Ahimeir's Fascism and his advocacy for bourgeois terrorism were the means to one end only: the long overdue (re-)establishment of a Jewish national home in all of the historical biblical Land of Israel. And Ahimeir's desire for this end – and therefore, also the means that he advocated to achieve it – was imbued with a sense of existential desperation that explains the illiberally decadent, radical incarnation of those means.

On 1 February 1944, Menachem Begin – who that previous December had taken over the commandership of the Irgun – proclaimed a revolt against the British Mandatory government in Palestine. With his proclamation, the long trajectory of Revolutionary Zionist ideology that Ahimeir had first broached in November 1927, in his article for *HaAretz*, 'If I Am Not For Myself, Who Will Be For Me?' now matured into practical application. Both the Irgun and Lehi had already carried out various attacks, mainly against Arabs and British policemen, over the past six years, attacks that had only increased in the wake of the British government's 1939 White Paper. The latter highly contentious document, issued with the aim to end three years of Arab Revolt in the Yishuv, limited Jewish immigration to Palestine to 75,000 people over the next five years. After that, no more Jews would be allowed into Palestine without Arab agreement. In a rare moment of unity, all of the various political factions in the Yishuv condemned the Paper outright. Why should the Jews – they believed – in their most desperate hour, be forced to abandon both the hope and possibility of coming to Palestine, merely to appease an Arab population that had rebelled against the very British Mandatory government with whom the Yishuv, in its eyes and for the most part, sought to cooperate? Did the increasing occurrences of institutionalised antisemitism on the continent, above all in Hitler's Germany, not underscore the bleak predictions for the fate of European Jewry that began in earnest with Herzl, and continued with Jabotinsky and later his younger Maximalist adherents, all of whom embraced an ideology of Political and indeed, military, Zionism? Desperate times now called for desperate measures.

Be that as it may, with the outbreak of the Second World War, the Yishuv – including its paramilitary groups, the Haganah and Irgun, but not Lehi – agreed, if only begrudgingly, to support the British and the Allied powers in their campaign against Hitler and the Axis powers. By 1944, however – in the wake of Britain's steadfast refusal, both to allow the establishment of a dedicated Jewish army to fight the Germans and to relax the immigration quotas of the White Paper, in spite of Hitler's now clear intention to destroy European Jewry – the Irgun under Begin now took matters into its own hands. Its lengthy declaration of Revolt, which it postered throughout the Yishuv on 1 February, addressed not the British administration, but the 'Hebrew Nation in Zion', directly:

> Jews!
> Our fighting youth will not be deterred by victims, blood and suffering. They will not surrender, will not rest until they restore our past glory, until they ensure our people of a homeland, freedom, honour, bread, justice and law. And if you help them, then your own eyes will soon behold the return to Zion and the rebirth of Israel. May God be with us and aid us![16]

In its imagery and tone – biblical, Messianic, proud, unapologetic and unforgiving – the proclamation evoked the Brit HaBiryonim pamphlet, *HaBiryon*, from April 1932:

> At these moments of hatred, throw away modern doctrines and remember those of the ancient legislator – 'An eye for an eye, a tooth for a tooth' – and you shall then be safe in your life, honour, property, and land.[17]

The Revolution that Ahimeir had foreseen seventeen years earlier now began in earnest, although he himself would not play a leading role in its execution.

As noted in Chapter 5, Ahimeir himself considered Lehi and the Irgun to be the ideological successors of Brit HaBiryonim. The groups' most well-known leaders – Avraham Stern and Menachem Begin, respectively – were themselves certainly influenced[18] by both Ahimeir the ideologue and person, although these relationships could, at times, be strained. Begin, for his part, completely whitewashes Ahimeir out of his two biographical accounts.[19] And although the two men remained friends until Ahimeir's death, Begin kept him at bay, politically. He is reported to have told Ahimeir that, should he ever come to power, Begin would appoint him as the 121st member of his Knesset.[20] For Begin, the politician, it was doubtless seen as bad public relations to be associated with a man who had once represented such a controversial figure as Ahimeir, Begin's own controversial past notwithstanding. Nonetheless, Begin aligned himself spiritually with Ahimeir and Brit HaBiryonim already in 1933, when he joined the Betar Head Command in Warsaw.[21] As Shindler notes, 'Clearly Begin had a psychological need to remember and reshape the past'.[22] Nonetheless, it is clear that he was influenced by Ahimeir's ideology.[23] Indeed, the cynic would certainly see Begin's call, at the Third World Convention of Betar in 1938, to usher in a new period of 'Military Zionism' – and, more pointedly, Ben-Gurion's, call for 'Fighting Zionism' only two months later – as nothing more than an opportunistic repackaging of Ahimeir's concept of 'Revolutionary Zionism' from ten years earlier.[24]

The historian Eric Hobsbawm cites the relevance of the 'date when the first adult generation of "children of the revolution" emerge on the public scene, those whose education and careers belong entirely to the new era'.[25] The original 'children' of Ahimeir's revolution came of age with the eventual election of Begin as prime minister of Israel, in 1977. Yet, by the time of Begin's speech in 1938, Ahimeir's political revolution had been gaining ground for almost a decade.

Avraham Stern, one of the Brit HaBiryonim 'sympathisers' listed by Ahimeir (see Chapter 5), likewise fell under his influential spell, although perhaps more that of Ahimeir the 'man of action' than Ahimeir the ideologue. Stern, like Ahimeir, was also ideologically informed by Savinkov, and similarly rejected Marxism while he remained nonetheless impressed by the Left's 'technique of taking power'.[26] And like his older mentor, Stern strongly advocated individual heroism and self-sacrifice. Nonetheless, the two men differed ideologically in three different respects. First, Stern did not share Ahimeir's negative impression of diaspora Jewry, and believed that in spite of their long history of persecution, Europe's Jews, even during the Middle Ages, had remained strong as a people through their unwavering faith and ethic-national self-identification.[27] Second, as Heller notes, Stern was less influenced by the 'axioms' of Jabotinsky and Ahimeir as he was by their 'operative conclusions'.[28] Thus, while he respected the Ahimeir who called for revolutionary war, he rejected the Ahimeir who led Brit HaBiryonim in 'mere' acts of civil disobedience. Third, Ahimeir and Stern were completely at odds over Stern's attempt to ally with Nazi Germany and Fascist Italy in 1941. Ahimeir, in spite of all his earlier bravado to the contrary, was absolutely convinced that Germany and its allies represented for the Jews, by 1941, a much great enemy than Britain.[29]

Be that as it may, those looking for perfect ideological consistency in Ahimeir will be disappointed. This fact is perhaps not surprising, and we need only take a cursory glance at Jabotinsky's or Ben-Gurion's – or indeed a myriad of public figures' – respective oeuvres to realise that Ahimeir is certainly not alone, in this respect. Ahimeir once described himself as an 'ancient pessimist' who sometimes walked 'westward, sometimes eastward', taking no notice of the 'opinion of the crowd', being interested only in sharing his own, sometimes idiosyncratic, 'Zionist morality'.[30] Thus, for example, he could accept Lenin as a revolutionary but not Leninism as a doctrine, and – for a time, at least – the anti-Marxist kernel of Nazism while rejecting its antisemitic 'shell'. And in spite of the fact that he distanced himself from even Italian Fascism, once its racial laws were introduced in 1938, Ahimeir could, in 1953, blame part of the failure of Brit HaBiryonim on the fact that they had been unsuccessful in adopting a Fascist modus operandi. It is an astonishing claim, to say the least, but one which nonetheless points to the fact that Ahimeir drew a clear – if flawed – distinction between Italian Fascism and Nazism. Likewise, he could use Spenglerian theory to explain away any sort of universal aspect to Judaism, but could just as easily ignore the universalist message in Jerimiah's prophesy.[31] And not least, he could be at once a revolutionary and a counterrevolutionary. Indeed, in the final analysis, we might say that Ahimeir's counterrevolution took the form of a de facto political insurrectionary revolution, one which opposed not only the very 'real' British Mandatory government but also the more conceptual 'social revolution' that was embodied in the Zionist project.

As discussed in the previous chapter, Ahimeir and Arlosoroff were products of a similar Zionist ideological strain that had its roots in the moderately labour-oriented pioneering ethos of HaPoel HaTzair. Arlosoroff – perhaps because of his background in economics – took a more tempered, 'nationalist-socialist' stance, while Ahimeir – perhaps because of his background in history – took a more radical, overtly 'nationalist-nationalist' and eventually 'Pro-Fascist-nationalist' position. Arlosoroff saw Socialism similar to the way in which

Ahimeir saw Fascism: as a modus operandi for effecting his nationalist vision, the creation of a Jewish nation state in Palestine. Thus, both men were not on different sides of the same coin, but rather on the same – Bourgeois–Intellectual – side of the same Zionist coin: Arlosoroff more in the 'Western–Bourgeois', 'Nationalist–Socialist' middle, Ahimeir on the 'Eastern–*Intelligent*', 'Nationalist–Nationalist' edge; Jabotinsky and the more moderate Revisionists occupied the space in between the two. In this formulation, the true opposite side of the coin would then see the more traditionally Labour Ahdut HaAvodah – led by David Ben-Gurion – at the 'Western–Bourgeois', 'Socialist–Nationalist' centre, and HaShomer HaTzair at the 'Eastern–*Intelligent*', 'Marxist–Socialist' edge. Indeed, Arlosoroff and Ahimeir were both products of the – Western and Eastern, respectively – European bourgeoisie, and thus not wholly dissimilar in outlook to the bourgeois elements of the World Zionist Organisation, which, as Derek Penslar has noted, were decidedly anti-Labour in the 1920s.[32] Ahimeir's letter to his daughter Ze'eva, quoted in the previous chapter, makes it clear that both men had originally fought 'against the adoption of the socialist program and against a merger with Ahdut HaAvodah'.[33] Nonetheless, Arlosoroff eventually 'surrendered' when the two centrist groups – Ahdut HaAvodah and HaPoel HaTzair – merged into Mapai, in 1930.[34] Ahimeir, of course, did not.

Notably – and again, perhaps owing to each man's bourgeois-intellectual upbringing – both Arlosoroff and Ahimeir had more or less formulated their particular ideological positions already by the end of their doctoral studies. Arlosoroff may have re-evaluated parts of his economic theories in *Der Jüdische Volkssozializmus* after living in the Yishuv for several years, but not his nationalist-Socialist position. Indeed, his student essay – and the ideological position which it outlines – remains the work that is most readily associated with Arlosoroff.

Likewise, Ahimeir. Practically every one of his future ideological cornerstones – the power of youth; the preference for men of action over word; the concept of active heroism; the importance of drawing on a rich historical past; the acceptance of violence, indeed the readiness for self-sacrifice in the service of the national cause; the rejection of Marxism, Bolshevism, Socialism and Liberalism; and not least, a preoccupation with revolution and the Messianic element that was implicit in all of this – is addressed already in his dissertation on Spengler. This fact is as surprising in its revelation as it is frustrating in the recognition, inherent therein, that the lack of scholarly engagement with Ahimeir's student work has allowed this key observation in his ideological development to be overlooked, until now. And the further fact that Ahimeir was, as has been demonstrated, enamoured already by 1923 with Mussolini and Fascism in a less than superficial way leads to the conclusion that Ahimeir's complete ideological path was set already at the time of his emigration to Palestine in 1924, a conclusion as unexpected as it is critical to our understanding of his ideological development. Ahimeir would return time and again to these various ideological markers, and would certainly develop and refine his position on all of them, but rarely would he introduce any serious new themes into his ideological admixture, during the period under discussion. His practical path, however, would require almost ten years to catch up. One needs only to consider Ahimeir's gradual embrace of Fascism – first in theory, then in practice, as outlined in Chapter 3 – to support this contention.

Thus, in no small way, all roads lead to Spengler. For whatever reason – and like many of his contemporaries – Ahimeir became enamoured with *The Decline of the West* and Spenglerian theory. In spite of the exceptions that he takes with Spengler's conceptions of Russian and Jewish history, Ahimeir remained – be it through an intellectual justification that equated Zionism with ancient Messianism, or a pitting of various 'morphological contemporaries' against each other in his final book, *Yudaikah* – ideologically, intellectually and methodologically loyal to Spengler on some level, throughout his life. Spengler provided an intellectual fascination and methodological framework that enabled Ahimeir's continued ideological growth. We need only to consider Spengler's own later work, *Man and Technics*, published in 1931 and quoted in Chapter 4 – with its critique of a modernity that refused to recognise the primeval instinct of the 'individual warrior' that was inherent in every man – to see that the continued similarity in ideological development between Ahimeir and Spengler was borne out, not least by reading Spengler himself, in his conclusions.[35] The fact that Spenglerian ideology was so easily misappropriated by 'fascism's most extreme and calamitous incarnation', Hitler's National Socialists – the Austrian political satirist Karl Krauss (1874–1936) pointedly referred to them as *Die Untergangster des Abendlandes* – points to just how thick an ideological quagmire Spengler had wandered into.[36] Likewise, Ahimeir. His initial inability to see past his love for Fascist ideology, which culminated in his appeal to 'learn from the success of Nazism', underscores the danger of such blind faith.[37]

If the years 1924–34 saw Ahimeir's practical path catch up with his ideological path, the ten years previous – 1914–24 – saw events unfold that would steer Ahimeir's ideological path, *imprimis*. First, his time at the Herzliya Gymnasium strengthened Ahimeir's love for the land, and further reinforced his already strong Zionist leanings. Similarly – and second – the outbreak of war that prevented his immediate return to Palestine instilled in Ahimeir an even deeper longing and nostalgia for the land to which he could not return. Third, the Bolshevik Revolution simultaneously reinforced both his Zionist and anti-Marxist leanings, as did the death of his brother that was a result of that revolution. It nonetheless also planted in Ahimeir the idea of the utility of revolution, and perhaps even the question of the permissibility of killing. And both events numbed Ahimeir to an existential *Alltag* of violence, bloodshed and death. Finally, his stint at university and his introduction to Spengler gave Ahimeir both the intellectual clout that he needed to become a 'member of the bourgeois intelligentsia', and the methodological tools to develop further, as such. In short: Zion nourished his soul; war, revolution and his brother's death informed his body, heart and psyche; and Spengler his brain. The rest – as it were – are details.

There are two broad, underlying theses in this study. One has to do with the proverbial throwing of the baby out with the bathwater, or perhaps better put: the danger of taking an all-too-easy, dismissively au courant, methodological approach. The fact that Spengler is now considered rather outmoded has, in the past, perhaps prevented a deeper engagement with both Spenglerian theory, and its profound and lasting influence on Ahimeir. I have demonstrated the danger that such a methodological shortcut may pose. Furthermore, Ahimeir's own claim – made stronger by his journalistic bravado in the Notebook of a Fascist articles, and indeed, beyond – that he was a 'bona fide' Fascist has perhaps led to a scholarly complacency that has, until now, taken Ahimeir's claim at face value. Thus, Ahimeir's true importance as a revolutionary figure has been overshadowed by a superficially raised arm towards the unquestioned acceptance of Ahimeir as a 'mere' Fascist. This study has provided a more sophisticated analysis of his embrace of both phenomena. Finally, Zionist historiography has – until now, and with few exceptions – been dismissive of the historical role that Ahimeir, himself, played. This study, with its focus on ideology, has not only confirmed that Ahimeir was a key figure in the development of the ideology of Revisionist Zionism and its legacy but also demonstrated how and why that is the case.

The second underlying thesis is tied to the first, and concerns the writing of 'difficult' history. Even today, more than fifty years after his death, Ahimeir's name and legacy are still able to provoke polarised reactions and heated debate. Nonetheless, I have approached this study with neither a preconceived outcome, nor political agenda. The only agenda of which I have allowed myself the luxury is that of painting as accurate a historical picture as possible, with the means at my disposal. Of course, there are limitations. As the American author Thornton Wilder (1897–1975) once observed:

> There is only one history. It began with the creation of man and will come to an end when the last human consciousness is extinguished. All other beginnings and endings are arbitrary conventions – makeshifts parading as self-sufficient entireties, diffusing petty comfort or petty despair. The cumbrous shears of the historian cut out a few figures and a brief passage of time from that enormous tapestry. Above and below the laceration, to the right and left of it, the severed threads protest against the injustice, against the imposture.[38]

Be that as it may, I hope that any petty comfort that was diffused in this study has not been all-too supplanted by petty despair, and indeed, vice versa. Responsibility for any injustice, or imposture, is completely my own.

There is a third underlying thesis in this study, although I am hesitant to name it as such, if only because of my incapacity for doing any more than hinting at its presence. But its presence is all-pervading. As noted in Chapter 4, the inability to introduce – empirically – the psychological element into this study represents at once the major weakness in, and also very likely also the key to, a completely comprehensive understanding of Ahimeir's ideological and practical development. Thus, at the end of a study that has offered a more ideologically focused, intellectual biography of Abba Ahimeir during the years when he was most politically active, I likewise admit my frustration at being unable to more successfully delineate the human aspect that most certainly also informed Ahimeir's ideology and practice, during that time. But it is there, whether in Ahimeir's longing for Zion, or heartbreak at the death of his brother, or indeed loss of his first wife and temporary 'loss' of his daughter. Ahimeir was not a journalist and political activist who happened to have a few close relationships, but rather a brother, husband and father, who also happened to be a notorious journalist and political activist. The fact that Ahimeir's love for Zion was perhaps as strong as his love for those close to him does not, nonetheless, mitigate the latter observation. And the fact that the consequences of his political activism, in the service of Zionism, would come to overshadow his reputation, historical legacy and reception should not mitigate the observation that Abba Ahimeir occupied an integral ideological position in the history of the Zionist Right.

Appendix A

Espionage game

Devised by Yirmiahu Halpern, 1928[1]

1. Division into two groups, A and B.
2. For each camp, fix a Commander and two Deputies.
3. The Commanders choose a Referee.
4. The Referee divides [up] all the players in the exercise, except for the Commanders and deputies; notes are signed.
5. 'Spy' is written on some of the notes.
6. He who is issued a note [with] 'Spy', is considered a Spy for the opposing camp. That is to say, if a person from Camp A is issued with a 'Spy' note, he must deliver [information] about all that is done in this camp to the Commander of Camp B.
7. The notes are opened at home or in a place out of sight.
8. The next day, [and after] division of the notes, the game as explained below becomes valid.
9. The Commanders set the Command Headquarters and inform the Deputies of this. The Commanders set an assembly point, day, and time, of the camp and inform the people in their [respective] camp[s] of this.
10. The Spies try to immediately inform the opposing camp about the assembly point, and time, the Commanders try to find the Spies, and to thwart the delivery of correct [information]. So, for example, they could fix an assembly in one place and immediately in the same place, or at another time, [they could] concentrate on changing the assembly point to a new assembly point [by pulling] out two by two. These pairs watch over one another, and the Spy will [find it] difficult to get away in order to inform of the change of location; also on the chance that one of the people will see the suspect, he is to immediately inform the Camp Commander about this and he [the Commander] marks him as a Spy.
11. The notifications of the assembly point and also reports of Spies and their notifications should be put down in writing. These reports and the copy of

all notifications will be kept at the Command Headquarters. Aside from this, a flag specially made for this game will be kept at the Command Headquarters. The Command Headquarters can be replaced at the Commander's discretion.

12. The two camps try to discover the assembly point and time of gathering, location of the Command Headquarters, and the whereabouts of the documents. Aside from this, people of the two camps try to pull off each other's caps. Those whose caps have fallen, are not allowed to pull off the caps of others. The caps will be kept for 24 hours at the Camp Command and after that are returned to the Commander of the opposing camp. In the event of such an 'assassination' [of those from whom their caps are pulled off], [they] try to defend their colleagues and not allow them to be approached, however it is forbidden to use tactics of battle or beating.

13. Both the flag and all the documents must be brought to the assembly, however it is forbidden to bring [them] to the place any earlier than two hours before the assembly. The Deputies are forbidden to be Flag Bearers.

14. The two camps, after they have learned the assembly point, try to close all the paths and entrances to the assembly and to capture the flag. The flag will be captured only with the successful pulling off of the caps of the Flag Bearer, and the Guard (a body of two people). After the caps of the Flag Bearer and the Guard have fallen, it is required to place the flag on the opponent's side, and to let them move [get] away to a distance of half an hour from the place.

15. A special group is sent to the assembly point. Their role is to disturb and to prevent entrance to the assembly point. If the cap from the Commander is pulled off – the assembly is cancelled. Also, in the event that the flag is captured, it is necessary to cancel the assembly. (The flag must be returned within 24 hours.)

16. The two camps try to inform on the location of Command Headquarters and steal its items, especially the file of documents.

17. A person captured as a Spy is brought before the Commander who investigates him and if necessary, hands him to neutral Arbiter, who is decided at the beginning.

18. The Arbiter, after hearing the testimonies for and against the accused and the defence, rules a verdict of innocent or guilty.

19. [If] a verdict is incorrect (that is to say, in the event that [the accused] wasn't really a Spy). 4 points are given to the opposing side.

20. After notice of the verdict, the Referee, who knows who the Spies are, informs whether or not the Arbiter was correct.

21. An Arbiter who rules incorrectly twice is dismissed, and another is chosen in his place.

22. The Spy gives all of his written notices. In the event that he is caught at the time of writing the notice, or if a notice is in his handwriting, he is considered 'Invalid'. The 'Invalid [player]' transfers automatically to the service of espionage of the camp in which he finds himself. [Notice] about this betrayal is kept secret and keeps up [his] appearance as a spy towards his previous Commander, thereby giving the opposing camp the opportunity to inform on all that is done in their previous camp, and especially to put false notices about the actions in their camp.

23. In the event that a Spy is caught, and deemed 'Invalid', he leaves the game.

Note: The Spies, immediately after being informed of their necessary roles, are required to present themselves by written notice. That is to say, to transfer their slip on which is written 'Spy' and their name, to their Commander.

1. Pulling off a cap is [good for] 2 points
2. Pulling off a cap from a Flag Bearer – 6 points
3. For each of the Guards – 3 points
4. From the Guard and Flag Bearer at one go – 18 points (that is to say, capturing the flag)
5. Theft of the file of documents from the Command – 16 points
6. Theft of each 5kgs of items from the Command room – 2 points
7. Cancellation of Assembly – 18 points
8. Assembly that takes place, with the attendance of the Commander, flag and all documents – and exactly on time set for the assembly – 16 points.
9. Capture of a Spy – 8 points
10. Discovery of an 'Invalid' – 12 points
11. Notice of an incorrect verdict – 4 points

The winner is [the camp] [that] gains 50 points more than the opposing camp. It is also possible to set a number of known points, and whoever reaches this number first, wins.

Defensive Training Department of Betar Rule

קה"ש

Y. H

Halpern

Notes

Introduction

1 E. Salaman, 'A Talk With Einstein', *The Listener*, vol. 54 (1955), pp. 370–1.

2 Colin Shindler, *The Triumph of Military Zionism: Nationalism and the Origins of the Israeli Right* (London: I.B. Tauris, 2010), p. 10.

3 See, for example, Gideon Shimoni, *The Zionist Ideology* (Hanover and London: Brandeis University Press, 1995), pp. 85–6. 'Political Zionism' stood in contrast to 'Practical Zionism', which privileged settlement over diplomacy.

4 See Anonymous, 'Ma Rotzim HaMaximalistim?' (What Do the Maximalists Want?), *Hazit HaAm*, 7 April 1933.

5 See, for example, Colin Shindler, *The Rise of the Israeli Right: From Odessa to Hebron* (Cambridge: Cambridge University Press, 2015), p. 100, which lists the Maximalists' main demands to the Revisionists at the Fifth World Revisionist Conference in Vienna, in 1932: '1. To raise the prestige of the leader to that of dictator. 2. To propose that Maximalist Zionist institutions be a tool for national liberation. 3. To transfer the political department to one of the centres of the Jewish masses. 4. To organise Diaspora youth to fight antisemitism.'

6 See Raymond Williams, *Keywords* (London: Fontana Press, 1988), pp. 153–7 for a more comprehensive discussion on the etymology and understanding of 'ideology'.

7 Ibid.

8 Shimoni, *The Zionist Ideology*, p. 3.

9 Williams, *Keywords*, pp. 31–3.

10 Merriam-Webster's Online Dictionary, http://www.merriam-webster.com/dictionary/aesthetics, accessed 3 April 2018.

11 The converse is also true, but is not so applicable to the aims of this study.

12 See, for example, see Shlomo Avineri, 'The Political Thought of Vladimir Jabotinsky', and Israel Eldad's rebuttal, 'Jabotinsky Distorted', both in *The Jerusalem Quarterly*, no. 16 (Summer 1980).

Chapter 1

1 Abba Gaissinovitch, *Bemerkungen zu Spenglers Auffassung Russlands*, Abba Ahimeir Archive 'Beit Aba', Ramat Gan.

2 See George L. Mosse, 'Lecture 25', in *European Cultural History 1880–1920* (30 November 1979), 'Minds@UW Madison', University of Wisconsin-Madison, https://minds.wisconsin.edu/handle/1793/35030, accessed 3 April 2018.

3 'Dr. Abba Ahimeir: Luah Ta'arikim b'Hayav', in *Abba Ahimeir v'HaTsionut HaMahapkhanit* (Tel Aviv: Jabotinsky Institute, 2012), p. 140.

4 Uriel Abulof's adaptation of Milan Kundera's eponymous concept. The definition, presented earlier, is an amalgamation of their two formulations. See Uriel Abulof, '"Small Peoples": The Existential Uncertainty of Ethnonational Communities', *International Studies Quarterly*, vol. 53 (2009), pp. 227–8.

5 In a diary entry from 26 April 1926, he notes that it was perhaps only to the British Mandatory police that he was still known as Gaissinovich. Presumably, this fact was due to Ahimeir's growing reputation as a journalist, and not yet his notoriety as a political activist. See Abba Ahimeir, *Atlantidah, O-HaOlam She Shakah: Sippurim v'Zikhronot* (Tel Aviv: Or Am, 1996), p. 11.

6 See Abba Ahimeir, *Moto shel Yosef Katznelson* (Tel Aviv: Shamgar Press, 1974), pp. 63–74, for Ahimeir's reminiscences of this period.

7 See Carl E. Schorske, *Fin-de-siècle Vienna: Politics and Culture* (New York: Vintage Books, 1981), pp. 120–33, and Brigitte Hamann, *Hitlers Wien* (Munich: Piper, 2012), pp. 337–64.

8 David Rechter, *The Jews of Vienna and the First World War* (Oxford and Portland: The Littman Library of Jewish Civilisation, 2008), p. 48 and Hamann, *Hitlers Wien*, p. 487.

9 See Phil.Nat. 1921/22-SS 1924, Archiv der Universität Wien.

10 See Rechter, *The Jews of Vienna*, pp. 46–57.

11 According to Ahimeir, their first meeting had occurred when he spotted Stricker sitting at his *Stammtisch* (usual seat) in Stricker's favourite Viennese Coffeehouse. See Abba Ahimeir, 'Robert Stricker', Corrected proof copy for *Herut*, 22 August 1949, Abba Ahimeir Archive, 'Beit Aba', Ramat Gan.

12 See Ibid., and PH RA 5935/Gaissinowitsch, Archiv der Universität Wien.

13 For more on the historiographical trends of 'German-Austrian' Viennese historians during the interwar period, see Gernot Heiss, *Willfährige Wissenschaft. Die Universität Wien 1938–1945* (Vienna: Verlag für Gesellschaftskritik, 1989), pp. 39–76.

14 See Peter Thaler, *The Ambivalence of Identity: The Austrian Experience of Nation Building in a Modern Society* (West Lafayette: Purdue University Press, 2001), p. 153, fn. 91.

15 In the case of Uebersberger, the same one – *Albia* – that Theodor Herzl joined in 1880, although he later resigned in protest of the group's increasingly antisemitic nature.

16 *Vorschriften für das Abfassen von Dissertationen an der Philosophischen Fakultät* (Specifications for the Compostion of Dissertations in the Faculty of Philosophy),

Universität Wien, Reformgesetzen (Reform Laws), 1872, Archiv der Universität Wien.

17 Oswald Spengler, *The Decline of the West Volume 1: Form and Actuality* (New York: Alfred A. Knopf, 2003), p. 3.

18 I use 'Culture' as opposed to 'culture', throughout, in order to denote the use of the word in a specifically Spenglerian sense, that is, as 'Babylonian' or 'Western.' Rather confusingly, the evolutionary lifespan of each Spenglerian Culture also sees it transform from a 'culture' into a 'civilisation', as outlined in more detail, earlier.

19 Spengler, *Decline of the West: 1*, p. 106.

20 Oswald Spengler, *The Decline of the West Volume 2: Perspectives of World History* (New York: Alfred A. Knopf, 1976), p. 48.

21 Ibid., p. 37.

22 Ibid., p. 32.

23 Spengler, *Decline of the West: 1*, p. 100. For a more detailed explanation of Spengler's concept of Morphology, see Ibid., pp. 93–113, and Harry Infield, *Israel in the Decline of the West* (New York: Bloch, 1940), pp. 9–19.

24 Spengler, *Decline of the West: 1*, Table 1, following p. 428.

25 Infield, *Israel in the Decline of the West*, p. 29, and Spengler, *The Decline of the West: 2*, p. 196: 'Tolstoi's Christianity was a misunderstanding. He spoke of Christ and he meant Marx. But to Dostoyevski's Christianity the next thousand years will belong.'

26 George L. Mosse, *The Culture of Western Europe: The Nineteenth and Twentieth Centuries* (London: John Murray, 1963), pp. 306–7.

27 For a detailed discussion on Spengler's conception of Judaism, see: Infield, *Israel in the Decline of the West*, pp. 43–62.

28 A juxtaposition of the two cultures, but not a Spenglerian cultural pseudomorphosis, to be clear.

29 Infield notes (p. 55) that Spengler offers no explanation for how the Jews became *fellaheen*, nor for the fact that they do not experience a 'Second Religiousness.' The obvious candidate for this phase would, of course, be Zionism, since it is congruent (albeit cynically so) with Spengler's theory. The omission is all the more noteworthy since he does mention Zionism – fleetingly – in a more general discussion on the first Jewish Dispersion (Spengler, *Decline of the West: 2*, p. 210).

30 Ibid., p. 317.

31 Spengler remarks: 'That of Russia is another problem', without elaborating what that problem might be. Ibid., p. 323.

32 Ibid.

33 Gaissinovitch, *Bemerkungen*, p. 4. All translations from Gaissinovitch's dissertation are mine.

34 Ibid., p. 11.

35 See Ibid., pp. 12–28.

36 Ibid., p. 12 and Spengler, *Decline of the West: 2*, pp. 204–5.

37 Yaacov Shavit, *Jabotinsky and the Revisionist Movement 1925–1948* (London: Frank Cass, 1988), p. 132. Ahimeir's particularistic conception of ancient Jewish culture and history will be discussed in detail in Chapter 4.

38 Shavit's focus on Ahimeir takes place within the greater context of how the idea of land and its ownership was a key metaphorical link between two ideological movements, as Canaanism emerged from Hebraism. See Yaacov Shavit, *The New Hebrew Nation: A Study in Israeli Heresy and Fantasy* (London: Routledge, 1987).

39 Ibid., p. 16.

40 Ibid. He goes on to show how Ahimeir's conception of Zionism as a 'secular, territorial phenomenon', in combination with his 'alegal approach' was an influence on Yonatan Ratosh's Canaanite movement. Interestingly, Shavit cites two of the main characteristics of Hebraism as 'an unmediated, intimate link with the landscape of the country and a feeling of ownership and political, meta-historical *Adnot* [*sic*] that is, 'sovereign lordship' over it' (Ibid., p. 14). Although outside of his discussion of Ahimeir, it is interesting to note the Spenglerian overtones inherent in such an ideology. It is thus not surprising that such seemingly disparate ideological movements could nonetheless still find much common ideological stimulus.

41 Gaissinovitch, *Bemerkungen*, pp. 14–15.

42 Eduard Meyer's books include, *Geschichte des Altertums* ('History of Antiquity') (1884–1902), *Die Entstehung des Judentums* ('The Genesis of Judaism') (1886), and *Israeliten und Ihre Nachbarstömme* ('Israel and Her Neighbouring Tribes') (1906).

43 Shavit describes Gaissinovitch-Ahimeir's world as one of 'dialectic contrasts within a whole'. He notes Ahimeir's rejection of the traditional Judeo-Christian 'morphological and meta-historical division between Judaism and Hellenism' and his conviction that the task of modern nationalism was to buttress the '"Hellenistic element" – in other words the earthly, territorial and political dimensions – that had been weakened during the long years of Jewish exile'. However, from the discussion earlier, it is clear that Gaissinovitch considered Hellenism to be a sign of Spenglerian 'civilization'. Thus between Shavit's conclusions that Ahimeir saw a task of Zionism to be redemption of the Jewish people from the decadence of civilisation (in *The New Hebrew Nation*, as discussed earlier), and that modern nationalism should reinforce the 'Hellenistic element', we are confronted with a contradiction. Shavit does succeed in highlighting how Ahimeir could paint 'in the blackest and most extremist terms' those who questioned or rejected the need for politico-territorial organisation – specifically that of the Jewish people – and who were thereby committed to their destruction: Titus, Rabbi Yohanan ben Zakkai, the apostle Paul and Marx. He demonstrates clearly Gaissinovitch's conception of the

'Talmudic-Yavnist' tradition as being equal to Spengler's concept of civilization';
and its antithesis – the 'Tanakhic-Jerusalemite' tradition – being equal to
Spengler's concept of 'culture'. Ahimeir thus favoured those who fought in the
three great Jewish revolts against the Romans, fighters for national – and not
religious – freedom. In addition, Shavit discusses a segment of Ahimeir's ideology
that is often overlooked: his rejection of there being any universal aspect bound up
within Judaism. Thus, 'Moses was a prophet and lawgiver for his people only and
not a prophet and lawgiver for the nations.' Gaissinovitch's embrace of Spenglerian
theory buttresses such a contention, which is completely congruent with his
assertion that Moses was a 'morphological contemporary' of Zarathustra, Paul,
Mohammed and Confucius, discussed earlier. His Spenglerian reading could only
allow him to view each figure as a mere religious leader and lawgiver to his own
respective people. See Shavit, *Jabotinsky and the Revisionist Movement*, pp. 132–3.

44 Italics mine. The embrace of 'Monism' – the idea of serving one overriding belief
or principle – was a central tenet of Revisionist Zionist ideology. Gaissinovitch,
Bemerkungen, p. 28.

45 Ibid., pp. 29–33.

46 Spengler, *Decline of the West: 2*, p. 194. See 'St. Petersburg, or the Russian City', in
Gaissinovitch, *Bemerkungen*, pp. 36–41.

47 Eran Kaplan, *The Jewish Radical Right: Revisionist Zionism and its Ideological Legacy*
(London and Madison: University of Wisconsin Press, 2005), p. 18.

48 Ibid. Lenin also believed that Russia was a 'terribly backward country.' See, inter
alia, Vladimir I. Lenin, 'Critical Remarks on the National Question', quoted in
Lenin on Literature and Art (Rockville: Wildside Press, 2008), p. 75.

49 Gaissinovitch, *Bermerkungen*, pp. 42–66.

50 According to Gaissinovitch, Eduard Bernstein acted similarly as a revisionist of the
Socialists.

51 Spengler, *Decline of the West: 2*, p. 194.

52 See Chapter Three.

53 Gaissinovitch, *Bemerkungen*, pp. 15–16.

54 The Essenes were an extreme Jewish sect, during the Second Temple period, whom
some scholars believe were the authors of the Dead Sea Scroll found at Qumran.
The Sicarii were Jewish terrorists, also during the Second Temple period, who
concealed knives under their robes, which they used to murder other Jews who
were sympathetic to their Roman occupiers.

55 Or indeed Zionism, in Ahimeir's case.

56 Spengler, *Decline of the West: 1*, p. xiv.

57 Ibid., p. 70.

58 Ibid., p. 79.

59 However, his assertion that Ahimeir saw as a strength of the Russian Revolution its
'ability to draw on Russian roots, on the Russian anarchism of Tolstoy rather than

on the Western decadence of Dostoyevsky' is not supported by the earlier discussion. Kaplan, *The Jewish Radical Right*, p. 18.

60 'To Whom the Last Word in Europe', in Gaissinovitch, *Bemerkungen*, pp. 85–7.

61 'Beurteilung der Dissertation des Cand. Phil. Aba Gaissinowitsch' (13 June 1924), PH RA 5935/Gaissinowitsch, Archiv der Universität Wien.

62 Ibid. (10 June 1924).

63 Ibid.

64 Shavit, *Jabotinsky and the Revisionist Movement*, p. 131.

65 Cf. Kaplan, *The Jewish Radical Right*, p. 18, where he takes a different position.

66 Interestingly, in Ahimeir's first article for *HaToren*, on the figure of Moses Hess ('HaRishon' (The First), August 1922) he traces a Russian-Jewish national consciousness and its subsequent literary expression back to the emergence of *Kabbalah* and *Hassidism*. For him, these had effected two logical paths of development: the national-individualist path of the *haskalah* and Zionism, and the universalist path, embodied in the demand for individual autonomy and social reform. Frankfurt and Hamburg had evolved into important Jewish religious centres *(kehillot kedushot)*, yet no Jewish national spirit had yet been awakened there. In Ahimeir's opinion, the religious reforms that had taken place in Germany had failed in awakening any sort of original, public Jewish-cultural engagement there. However, he stops short at classifying the German Reform movement as an assimilationist undertaking; the reformers were simply a by-product of their generation. The 'nationalist' value of the Reform movement was, in Ahimeir's eyes, equal to than that of the *haskalah;* indeed, he calls the German Reform movement the '*haskalah*' of German Jewry, much in the same way that the *haskalah* was the 'reform' of Russian Jewry. Nonetheless, the *haskalah* had led to a Jewish national awakening in Russia; German Reform would, in Ahimeir's opinion, be followed by nothing.

67 Shavit, *Jabotinsky and the Revisionist Movement*, pp. 135–6.

68 Kaplan, *The Jewish Radical Right*, p. 40.

69 What Mosse would have called the 'New Barbarian.'

70 Abba Ahimeir, *Yudaikah* (Tel Aviv: Ankor, 1960), pp. 40–1.

71 See Alan J. Mintz, 'A Sanctuary in the Wilderness: The Beginnings of the Hebrew Movement in America in *HaToren*', *Prooftexts*, vol. 10, no. 3, Tenth Anniversary Volume, Part 3 (September 1990), pp. 389–412, for a full discussion of the genesis and publication life of this seminal American Hebrew publication.

72 Ibid., p. 392.

73 Indeed, as Mintz notes, 'Hebrew is the only component of the Zionist dream whose realization not only remains uncompromised but surpassed the expectations placed upon it' (Ibid., pp. 390–1).

74 Ibid., p. 394.

75 *HaToren*, June 1913, quoted in Ibid., p. 398.

76 Ibid., p. 399.

77 Ibid.

78 Abba Ahimeir, 'Rayonot Bodedim al HaFashizm', *HaToren*, August 1923, pp. 150–5.

79 Ibid., p. 150.

80 Ibid., pp. 150–1.

81 In his earlier articles in *HaToren*, Ahimeir also highlights the 'military' nature of Hess's and Bialik's writing. Nonetheless, he apparently ignores the fact that the only Jewish Fascists were assimilationists, probably because, by definition, they privileged Italian- over Jewish- nationalist self-identification. Stanislao G. Pugliese suggests that Italy's Jews were supportive of the PNF due to their 'socio-economic status ... as members of the bourgeoisie, not as Jews'. Whatever the reason, the fact remains that Italy's Jewish community as a whole was highly assimilated. The rate of intermarriage was fifty per cent by the time that Italian Racial laws came into effect, in 1938. See Shindler, *The Rise of the Israeli Right*, p. 82, and Stanislao G. Pugliese, 'Resisting Fascism: The Politics and Literature of Italian Jews, 1922–45', in Michael Berkowitz, Susan L. Tananbaum and Sam W. Bloom (eds), *Forging Modern Jewish Identities: Public Faces and Private Struggles* (London and Portland: Valentine Mitchell, 2003), pp. 270–2.

82 Ahimeir, *HaToren*, August 1923, p. 152.

83 The *Bund* and *Yevsektsiya* were the Jewish sections in the Soviet Communist Party from 1918–22. The *Kultur Lige* (Culture League) was a Jewish association linked to the Jewish Labour Bund, active mainly in Russia in the interwar years, and dedicated to the promotion of Yiddish culture.

84 Although in reality, perhaps, they had merely placed less emphasis on a 'brilliant Jewish past' by looking forward to a universal-socialist future.

85 Ahimeir, *HaToren*, August 1923, p. 152.

86 Ibid., p. 153.

87 Ibid., p. 154.

88 In this article he uses both 'גבורים היסטוריים' and 'גבורים, יוצרי ההיסטוריה'.

89 Spengler, *Declilne of the West: 1*, p. 149.

90 Oswald Spengler, *Der Untergang des Abendlandes* (Berlin: Albatros, 2014), p. 194.

91 Shavit is the notable exception, although he states that Ahimeir's attitude towards the burgeoning political movement was, in 1923, still 'ambivalent,' a conclusion with which I disagree. Although Ahimeir's political views were evolving during this period, his article on Fascism betrays a certain measure of attraction to the movement, if only subconsciously so. See Shavit, *Jabotinsky and the Revisionist Movement*, p. 363.

92 See Yaacov Orenstein's testimony in Brit HaBiryonim trial evidence, Exhibit Y.L. 27, 1\6\14ב, Jabotinsky Institute Archive. Notably, the same piece of evidence also contains a postscript – signed merely 'Rachel' – which states: 'Joseph Hagalili says that he has already found him, Orenstein also says so. They undoubtedly refer to Abba.'

Chapter 2

1 *Aliyah* (singular) and *aliyot* (plural) denote the various waves of Zionist immigration to Palestine. The Second *Aliyah* occurred from approximately 1903 to 1914, the Third *Aliyah*, from 1919 to 1924. Nonetheless, the serialised Aliyot, as we understand them today, were constructs that privileged the ideological Zionist 'Pioneer' *Oleh* over the 'immigrant' who had come to Palestine in the hope of a better existential future. See Hizky Shoham, 'From "Great History" to "Small History": The Genesis of the Zionist Periodization', *Israel Studies*, vol. 18, no. 1 (Spring 2013), pp. 31–55. As Shoham notes: 'The 1920s were years in which mythologization was enhanced in the Yishuv. The myths of the Second and Third Aliyot were part of a series of local myths that were created in the Yishuv after the War, along with the *Tel–Hai* myth, Tel-Aviv's foundation myth, and more' (p. 48). Jabotinsky imbued the myth of the Pioneer with a further dimension, deeming her/him as 'somebody prepared to carry out any task required of him by the national movement'. See Anita Shapira, *Land and Power: The Zionist Resort to Force: 1881–1948* (Oxford: Oxford University Press, 1992), p. 161.

2 Gideon Shimoni's term, see Shimoni, *The Zionist Ideology*, p. 207.

3 See Anita Shapira, *Israel: A History* (London: Weidenfeld and Nicholson, 2014), pp. 42–2 for a more thorough discussion on the ethos of the Second *Aliyah*.

4 From *HaPoel HaTzair*, vol. 1 (1919–20), quoted in Shimoni, *The Zionist Ideology*, p. 207.

5 The question of Fascism and how Ahimeir understood it in the late 1920s will be discussed in the following chapter.

6 Josef Nedeva in Josef Nedeva (ed.), *Abba Ahimeir: HaIsh she Hitah et HaZerem* (Tel Aviv: Association for the Dissemination of National Consciousness, 1987), p. 8.

7 Ahimeir wrote regularly to Katznelson, during his stint in Vienna. The letters are preserved at the Beit Aba Archive.

8 See Shindler, *The Rise of the Israeli Right*, p. 69.

9 Ze'ev Sternhell, *The Founding Myths of Israel* (Princeton: Princeton University Press, 1998), p. 179.

10 See discussion, below.

11 Joseph Trumpeldor (1880–1920) had, with Ze'ev Jabotinsky, formed the Zion Mule Corps, a group of Jewish volunteers who formed the 38th to 42nd Battalions of the Royal Fusiliers of the British Army during the First World War. He established *HeHalutz* in 1918, in order to prepare Jewish youth for emigration to Palestine. In spite of having lost an arm fighting in the Russo-Japanese War, he continued to be an active soldier throughout his life, and was mortally wounded in the Battle of *Tel–Hai* (1 March 1920), while defending the Jewish settlement from Arab attack. His apparent final words, 'It is good to die for our country', helped bestow upon

him national hero status, and Trumpeldor was considered – and exploited as – a mythical cult figure by both the Left and Right in the Yishuv.

12 Abba Ahimeir, 'M. Gershonzon', *HaPoel HaTzair*, 8 April 1925.

13 Ibid.

14 Abba Ahimeir, 'HaDon Quixote shel HaMahapekhah HaRussit' ('The Don Quixote of the Russian Revolution'), *HaPoel HaTzair*, 5 June 1925. As historian Peter Kenez has noted: 'After the November Revolution [Savinkov] showed a statesmanlike understanding of the need for cooperation between all the enemies of Bolshevism, and that he was willing to make personal and ideological sacrifices for this cause'. Ahimeir would make it clear in his articles penned for the tenth anniversary of the 1917 Revolutions (see below) that Lenin's strength lay in his ability to adapt ideology in the service of pragmatism. See Peter Kenez, *Civil War in South Russia, 1918: The First Year of the Volunteer Army* (Los Angeles and Berkeley: University of California Press, 1971), p. 82, and Alexander Rabinovitch, *The Bolsheviks Come to Power: The Revolution of 1917 in Petrograd* (Chicago: Haymarket Books, 2004), pp. 98–100.

15 Ahimeir, 'The Don Quixote of the Russian Revolution'.

16 Abba Ahimeir, 'San Simonizmus' ('Saint Simonianism'), *HaPoel HaTzair*, 10 July 1925.

17 The idea that Marxist Socialism contained a 'religious' dimension (in its fervency) was a subject to which Ahimeir would return, see below.

18 Ibid.

19 Abba Ahimeir, 'Shtei Torot al HaMin' ('Two Sexual Theories'), *HaPoel HaTzair*, 18 September 1925.

20 Otto Weininger, *Sex and Character* (London: William Heinemann, 1906), p. 33.

21 See D. H. Robinson, 'A Narrative of the General Strike, 1926', *The Economic Journal*, vol. 36, no. 143 (September 1926), pp. 375–93.

22 D. F. Calhoun, *The United Front: The TUC and the Russians, 1923–1928* (Cambridge: Cambridge University Press, 1976), p. 234. See pp. 233–53 for a discussion of the strike and attempts by the Soviets to assist the miners financially.

23 Ibid., p. 233.

24 Ibid., p. 236.

25 *British Worker*, 8 May 1926, p. 2.

26 Calhoun, *The United Front*, p. 250.

27 Abba Ahimeir, 'Hirhurei Proletari al HaShvitah HaAnglit', *HaPoel HaTzair*, vol. 29, 1926.

28 Ibid.

29 "סטרייק-ברכריות".

30 Ecclesiastes 11.1.

31 Ahimeir, *HaPoel HaTzair*, vol. 29, 1926.

32 Ibid.

33 Ibid.

34 Ibid.

35 Calhoun, *The United Front*, p. 250. Bernard Pares was a British historian who concentrated on Russia, and was a contemporary of the period in question.

36 'Shvitat Hakorim B'Anglia: HaLaylah HaAharon lefi Hakhrazat HaShvitah', *Davar*, 3 May 1926.

37 'Government's Ultimatum to Trade Unions', *The Palestine Bulletin*, 3 May 1926.

38 Abba Ahimeir and M.S. (Moshe Shertok), *Davar*, 26 June 1926.

39 Ahimeir, *Davar*, 26 June 1926.

40 Ibid.

41 Shertok, *Davar*, 26 June 1926.

42 'The Churchill White Paper', reprinted in Walter Laqueur and Barry Rubin, *The Israel-Arab Reader* (New York: Penguin, 2001), pp. 25–9.

43 Abba Ahimeir, 'Mahutah shel HaLeumiut etzel Ahad Ha'am' (The Essence of Ahad Ha'am's Nationalism), *HaPoel HaTzair*, vol. 39–40, 1926.

44 Ibid.

45 The concept of *Volk*, and its application to nationalism, will be discussed in Chapter Five.

46 Abba Ahimeir, 'Gorelam shel HaTurkim HaTzairim' (The Fate of the Young Turks), *Davar*, 15 September 1926. The Young Turks movement (approximately 1902–18) was a revolutionary movement comprised of bourgeois liberals and military cadets who, in 1908, overthrew Ottoman Sultan Abdul Hamid II, and introduced Turkey's first multiparty system of democracy in the Ottoman Empire. The Young Turk Empire – which had fought on the side of Germany during the First World War – collapsed at the war's end. Kemalism was Mustafa Kemal Atatürk's eponymous politico-ideological movement that was based on six unwavering 'fundamental tenets': Republicanism, Secularism, Populism, Nationalism, Reformism and Statism. The movement successfully established the first Republic of Turkey in 1923, with Atatürk as its first president.

47 Ahimeir did mention the Sicarii in his dissertation on Spengler, but only fleetingly, and the dissertation was not published.

48 Abba Ahimeir, 'Le'an P'niah shel HaDemokratiah Muadot?' (Where is Democracy Headed?), *HaPoel HaTzair*, vol. 42, 1926.

49 In Ahimeir's eyes, Spain, Greece and China were characterised by a 'General Puritanism'. Bonapartism had sought to consolidate French Revolutionary ideals while reinstating direct, imperial rule, perhaps not surprisingly, under Napoleon Bonaparte, himself. See Steven Englund, *Napoleon: A Political Life* (Cambridge: Harvard University Press, 2004), pp. 458–9.

50 Ahimeir, *HaPoel HaTzair*, vol. 42, 1926.

51 Ibid.

52 Kant believed that all democracy is despotism (on perpetual peace) as it represents tyranny of the majority. My thanks go to Derek Penslar for this observation.

53 Ibid.

54 Abba Ahimeir, 'Gorelam shel Idealim Hevruti'im' (The Fate of Societal Ideals), *HaPoel HaTzair*, Year 20, no. 1–2.

55 Ibid.

56 Ibid.

57 Ibid.

58 In issues Year 20, Numbers 6 and 9.

59 Abba Ahimeir, 'HaMaskanot MeShvitat HaKorim' (The Wretchedness of the Striking Miners), *HaPoel HaTzair*, Year 20, no. 5 (1926).

60 Abba Ahimeir, 'Sotzializmus uFashizmus' (Socialism and Fascism), *HaPoel HaTzair*, Year 20, no. 6 (1926).

61 The similarity to Ahimeir/Gaissinovitch's conclusion in his dissertation on Spengler – that elements of both 'Culture' and 'Civilization' (in this case, Fascism and Bolshevism, respectively) could coexist in a particular ethnic culture – is noteworthy here.

62 Abba Ahimeir, 'Yihusei Miflagot B'Anglia' (Allocation of Political Parties in England), *HaPoel HaTzair*, Year 20, no. 19 (1927).

63 Ibid.

64 Abba Ahimeir, 'Mediniut Gosseset' (Dying Policy), *HaPoel HaTzair*, Year 20, no. 20–1 (1927).

65 Ibid.

66 Abba Ahimeir, 'Trotzkizmus' (Trotzkyism), *HaAretz*, 12 June 1925.

67 Abba Ahimeir, 'Eser Shanim L'Revolutzia HaFebruarit' (Ten Years [Since] The February Revolution), *HaPoel HaTzair*, no. 23, 'HaHaga HaOktoberit' (The October Terror), 07 November 1927, *HaAretz*, 'HaYotzer HaShalom HaBriskai' (The Creator of the Treaty of Brest-Litovsk'), 23 November 1927, *HaAretz*.

68 Ahimeir, *HaPoel HaTzair*, no. 23.

69 See Also Shindler, *The Rise of the Israeli Right*, p. 81.

70 Ahimeir, *HaPoel HaTzair*, no. 23.

71 Ibid.

72 Ibid.

73 Ahimeir, *HaAretz*, 7 November 1917.

74 Ahimeir, *HaAretz*, 23 November 1917.

75 Ahimeir, *HaAretz*, 12 June 1925.

76 Ahimeir, *HaAretz*, 7 November 1917.

77 See Shindler, *The Triumph of Military Zionism*, p. 156.

78   Abba Ahimeir, 'Italiah keNeged Versailles' (Italy vs. Versailles), *HaAretz*, 24 May 1927.

79   See Abba Ahimeir, 'HaSikhsukh HaAnglo-Russi' (The Anglo-Russian Conflict), *HaAretz*, 8 June 1927, and 'HaPolitikah HaShamranit shel Angliah' (The Conservative Politics of England), *HaAretz*, 19 June 1927.

80   Abba Ahimeir, 'HaOlam b'Rosh HaShanah 5688' ('The World at Rosh HaShanah 5688'), *HaAretz*, 26 September 1927.

81   Abba Ahimeir, 'Catalonia', *HaAretz*, 4 November 1927.

82   *Pronunciamiento* was a declaration of intent to effect a coup d'état that was a trademark of Spanish, Portuguese, and Latin American politics in the previous century.

83   By 1928, there were approximately 2,500 Jewish members in the Partito Natzionale Fascista (out of a total Jewish population in Italy of approximately 45,000), a figure which had tripled by 1933. As Michael E. Ledeen notes: 'Three of the "Fascist martyrs" were Jewish, as were ... two of the most important *"sansepolcristi"*, the Fascists of the first hour. As time passed, Jewish participation in the Fascist state continued to be quite active, from the highest rungs of the Army and Navy to the Ministry of Finance.' See Michael A. Ledeen, 'The Evolution of Italian Fascist Antisemitism', *Jewish Social Studies*, vol. 37, no. 1 (Winter 1975), p. 4.

84   Abba Ahimeir, 'Yad Israel v'Kol Yaacov' (Hand of Israel and Voice of Jacob), *HaAretz*, 24 November 1917.

85   He uses the term 'Salon Socialists'.

86   Ibid.

87   Ibid.

88   Abba Ahimeir, 'Im Ein Ani Li – Mi Li?' (f I Am Not For Myself, Who Will Be For Me?'), *HaAretz*, 15 November 1927. The quote is from Hillel, the Elder, Pirkei Avot 1:14.

89   Ibid.

90   Abba Ahimeir, 'Problimot HaTalush v'Hahalutz' (Problems of the Unrealistic and of the Pioneer), *HaAretz*, 08 December 1927.

91   'Haver Kaslo', 'Kismon', *Davar* (undated).

92   Abba Ahimeir, 'Tirol HaDromit' (South Tirol), *HaAretz*, 13 December 1927.

93   In Jewish Law an *Agunah* is a woman 'anchored' to her marriage through the unwillingness (or inability) or her husband to issue a *get* (bill of divorce).

Chapter 3

1   Shavit states that Ahimeir had not yet become a member of Jabotinsky's party when he penned his 'From the Notebook of a Fascist' articles in *Doar HaYom* at

the end of 1928. However, Yosef Ahimeir and Shmuel Schatzky refute this, and claim that around the time of the Revisionist conference on 10 February 1928, the trio joined the Revisionist Party, having 'just retired from the party HaPoel HaTzair', as does Shindler in *The Rise of the Israeli Right*. The claim for Ahimeir's joining the Revisionist Party at the beginning of 1928 is further upheld by the recent publication of *Abba Ahimeir and Revolutionary Zionism*, in 2012 (perhaps not unsurprisingly, since it was edited by Yosef Ahimeir). See Shindler, *The Rise of the Israeli Right*, p. 71, and Yosef Ahimeir and Shmuel Shatzki, *Hineinu Sikrikim* (*We were all* Sicarii) (Tel Aviv: Shamgar, 1978), p. 236.

2 Ibid. Although Shindler, *The Triumph of Military Zionism*, p. 156 writes that the trio were (variously), 'originally members of Ahdut HaAvodah and Hapoel HaTzair', Yosef Ahimeir and Shatzky claim that all three were members of HaPoel HaTzair.

3 See Y. Ophir, *Sefer HaAvodah HaLeumi* (*The Book of National(ist) Labour*) (Tel Aviv: The Executive Committee of the National Worker's Union, 1959), pp. 50–64, and Yaacov N. Goldstein, 'Labour and Likud: Roots of their Ideological-Political Struggle for Hegemony over Zionism', *Israel Affairs*, vol. 8, Issues 1–2 (2001), pp. 79–90, for further discussions of the Bloc for Revisionist Labour.

4 See Ophir, *Sefer HaAvodah*, p. 50.

5 Ibid.

6 Ibid., p. 52.

7 The most important decisions registered at the end of the conference were as follows:

  A. In consideration of the abnormal situation of the Histadrut … and in consideration that this situation causes its administrative and moral failure of the institutions of the Histadrut, the conference therefore finds correct to declare the recognition of a revision in the Hebrew Worker's Movement in the country. This revision should especially call for:
    1. Reorganisation of the Histadrut on purely professional foundations
    2. Cementing the Histadrut into democratic foundations and a wide autonomy of professional guilds
    3. Disconnect of cooperative institutions from the Histadrut and elimination of parallel institutions [in] departments of the Zionist executive.

  B. The conference recognises the national coalition as supreme regulator in building the Hebrew State and as the foundation of this, demands:
    1. Immediate organisation of neutral [labour] exchanges in town and country
    2. Compulsory arbitration as a tool for resolution of social conflicts in town and country

E. In consideration of the decisions of the second conference of the Revisionist Party in Eretz Israel regarding mandatory Hebrew Labour in the Hebrew economy. The conference turns to the central committee of the Revisionist Party with the suggestion to visit [or possibly, 'to criticise', it is not clear from the context] the network of branches, and to remove from the Histadrut [those branches] reluctant to establish the decisions [if there are any].

F. The conference deems correct the suggestion of the Revisionist fraction in the national committee to declare public and economic sanctions on destroyers of the national and state foundations of the Yishuv.

G. The conference turns to the central committee of the Revisionist Party to begin a public operation in the Diaspora to favour Hebrew work in the Hebrew economy.

H. The demoralisation in the institutions of the union of workers that penetrated into all of its individual activities, the poisoned atmosphere surrounding the household and financial institutions and the disorder in the financial accounting of the institutions above, lacking neutral criticism – all this enables the compromising of [i.e. this compromises] the Histadrut and its officials.

I. Politicians and bureaucrat members of the union of workers, who are deemed to be at fault, need to be suspended from their public figures [roles] until the end of the inquiry and the trial. See Ibid., pp. 52–3.

8   Abba Ahimeir, 'Mond v'Strauss o HaProblemah shel HaKapitalim' (Mond and Strauss, or the Problem of Capital), *HaAretz*, 8 February 1928.

9   Ibid.

10 Ibid. See the Conclusion for further discussion on the concept of the Russian *intelligent*.

11 Mussolini, quoted in George L. Mosse, 'Toward a General Theory of Fascism', in *The Fascist Revolution* (New York: Howard Fertig, 1999), p. 42.

12 Abba Ahimeir, 'Me"Krim" Le"Emor"' (From Crimea to "Emor"), *HaAretz*, 15 February 1928. Emor is the weekly Torah portion which outlines the purity rules for *Cohanim* and lists all Holy Days. It is perhaps not out of place in consideration of Ahimeir's discussion of the current 'impurities' that existed within the Jewish community, in this case the Territorialists, for whom Crimea had represented one option for a Jewish national home.

13 Literally זהו התוכן עמנו

14 Ahimeir, 'Me "Krim" L"Emor"'.

15 Abba Ahimeir, 'Eyropah HaMitorreret' (Europe Awakened), *HaAretz*, 12 September 1928.

16 For a more complete discussion of *Doar HaYom* see the entry for the newspaper on the National Library of Israel website, http://web.nli.org.il/sites/JPress/English/Pages/DoarHayom.aspx, last accessed 19 April 2018.

17   See Hillel Halkin, *Jabotinsky: A Life* (New Haven and London: Yale University Press, 2014), pp. 163–7, for a concise discussion of Jabotinsky's editorship of *Doar HaYom*.

18   Abba Ahimeir, 'Opozitziah shel Kollelim' (Opposition of [the] Included), *Doar HaYom*, 10 August 1928. It is noteworthy that Ahimeir refers to himself as a 'Political Zionist', and not (yet) a 'Revisionist.' Perhaps he wanted to underscore the ideological trajectory that had led to the formation of the Revisionist party.

19   Ophir, *Sefer HaAvodah*, pp. 57–8.

20   Ibid.

21   Ibid.

22   'Doar HaYom BeDrakho Kadima' ('*Doar HaYom* on its Way Forward'), *Doar HaYom*, 21 September 1928.

23   This is not to say that Ahimeir and the Yishuv nationalists never referred to themselves as rightist, which they did.

24   Ibid.

25   Abba Ahimeir, 'BeInyan HaVizah l'Jabotinsky' (In the Matter of Jabotinsky's Visa), *Doar HaYom*, 21 September 1928.

26   I use 'Fascist' and not 'fascist' throughout, to denote Ahimeir's particular affinity to Mussolini Fascism, which, as is clear already from his articles in *HaPoel HaTzair*, he saw as the ideological and practical vanguard of the new European political movement.

27   He uses 'vegetarianism' pejoratively to describe weakness of the Socialist ideals of the Yishuv leadership and the Labour Zionist Left, and their willingness to compromise on Zionist territorial ambitions.

28   Shavit reaches the same conclusion, see Shavit, *Jabotinsky and the Revisionist Movement*, p. 364.

29   Lit. יפיתניקים.

30   Ahimeir, *Doar HaYom*, 21 September 1928.

31   See Jewish Telegraphic Agency dispatch, 11 September 1928, *Palestine Government Reluctant to Admit Vladimir Jabotinsky*, http://www.jta.org/1928/09/11/archive/palestine-government-reluctant-to-admit-vladimir-jabotinsky, accessed 25 April 2018.

32   See *The Palestine Bulletin*, 21 September 1928, p. 3 and *Jewish Telegraphic Agency* dispatch, 18 September 1928, 'Palestine Asks Guarantee Against Jabotinsky's Political Activities', http://www.jta.org/1928/09/18/archive/palestine-asks-guarantee-against-jabotinskys-political-activities, accessed 24 April 2018.

33   See Joseph Schechtman, *The Life and Times of Vladimir Jabotinksy: Fighter and Prophet* (Silver Springs: Eschel Press, 1986), p. 87.

34   See *Jewish Telegraphic Agency* dispatch, 25 September 1928, 'Jabotinsky Says London Not Responsible for His Visa Troubles', http://www.jta.org/1928/09/25/archive/jabotinsky-says-london-not-reponsible-for-his-visa-troubles, accessed 25 April 2018.

35 Ahimeir, *Doar HaYom*, 21 September 1928.

36 Ibid.

37 Ibid.

38 Lit. 'Siege Mode', Ibid.

39 Josephus, *Jewish Wars*, Book II, Chapter 14.

40 Abba Ahimeir, *Doar HaYom*, 8 October 1928.

41 See Ahimeir's comment re the Hindus, below.

42 See *The Palestine Bulletin*, 25–28 September 1928.

43 *Davar*, 25 September 1928.

44 *Doar HaYom*, 25 September 1928.

45 M.B., '*Davar HaYom*', *Davar*, 25 September 1928.

46 *Doar HaYom*, 27 September 1928.

47 *The Palestine Bulletin*, 1 October 1928.

48 Abba Ahimeir, *Doar HaYom*, 8 October 1928.

49 *Kahal* means 'public', or 'street', but in this context he is most likely referring to
    the diaspora community as a whole, or possibly pejoratively, to the executive organ
    of the *kehilah*/Gemeinde).

50 Abba Ahimeir, 'B'Kesher Im Bo'o shel Ha"Duce" shelanu' (Pertaining to the
    Coming of our 'Duce'), Doar HaYom, 10 October 1928.

51 Ibid., here Ahimeir quotes the Mishneh Torah, Book of Love, Law of Blessings,
    Chapter 71.

52 See Yaacov Shavit, 'Realism and Messianism in Zionism in the Yishuv', in Jonathan
    Frankel (ed.), *Studies in Contemporary Jewry, An Annual, VII: Jews and Messianism
    in the Modern Era: Metaphor and Meaning* (Oxford, 1991), pp. 100–27 for a
    discussion of the distinction between Messianic ideology and Messianic metaphors
    and rhetoric, etc.

53 Shimoni, *The Zionist Ideology*, p. 406, fn. 19. See also Ibid., p. 434, fn. 37.

54 See *The Palestine Bulletin*, 8 October 1928.

55 *Doar HaYom*, 12 October 1928.

56 Abba Ahimeir, *Doar HaYom*, 19 November 1928.

57 Ibid.

58 See Ze'ev Jabotinsky, *On the Iron Wall*, in Eran Kaplan and Derek Penslar (eds),
    The Origins of Israel, 1882–1948: A Documentary History (Madison: University of
    Wisconsin Press, 2011), pp. 257–63.

59 See Shindler, *The Triumph of Military Zionism*, pp. 49–52, etc., for a discussion
    about the group's foundation.

60 I am indebted to Abigail Green and David Rechter for pointing out the martial
    character inherent to both examples, above.

61 See, for example, 'Betar ke'Tefisat Olam' (Betar as World-View) in Abba Ahimeir,
    HaTzionut HaMahapekhanit (Revolutionary Zionism) (Tel Aviv: Simhon, 1966),
    p. 21.

62 Abba Ahimeir, *Doar HaYom*, 28 October 1928.

63 Abba Ahimeir, *Doar HaYom*, 4 November 1928.

64 Abba Ahimeir, *Doar HaYom*, 9 November 1928.

65 Notably, Ahimeir – and indeed his colleagues Beilinson and Gluckson, judging from the context of his article – viewed the events which had led to the Declaration of Czechoslovak Independence, on 18 October 1918 as a 'revolution', if perhaps only a 'bloodless' one, as Beilinson and Gluckson believed.

66 See Kaplan, *The Jewish Radical Right*, pp. 31–2 for a discussion of fascist ideology as a result of 'evolutionary Monism.' However, he does not make the necessary distinction between Jabotinsky's and Ahimeir's understanding of Monism.

67 Abba Ahimeir, *Doar HaYom*, 19 November 1928.

68 Agostino Lanzillo, *La Disfatta del Socialismo*, quoted in Zeev Sternhell, *The Birth of Fascist Ideology* (Princeton: Princeton University Press, 1994), p. 180.

69 Abba Ahimeir, *Doar HaYom*, 19 November 1928.

70 Abba Ahimeir, *Doar HaYom*, 23 October 1928.

71 Ophir, *Sefer HaAvodah*, p. 53.

72 Ibid.

73 Ahimeir, *Doar HaYom*, 23 October 1928.

74 Shindler, *The Triumph of Military Zionism*, p. 155. In Shindler, *The Rise of the Israeli Right*, he is less categorical, and asks 'So were Ahimeir, Greenberg and Yevin – these intellectuals of the Left – true Revisionists?' (p.79).

75 See Shindler, *The Rise of the Israeli Right*, pp. 97–104.

76 See Joseph Heller, *The Stern Gang: Ideology, Politics and Terror, 1940–1949* (London: Frank Cass, 1995), p. 19.

77 See Robert O. Paxton, *The Anatomy of Fascism* (London: Penguin, 2004), pp. 218–20.

78 Walter Benjamin, 'The Work of Art in the Age of Mechanical Reproduction', in *Illuminations* (London: Fontana Press, 1999), p. 234.

79 According to Martin Malia, Bismarck 'had learned from the example of Napoleon III that universal suffrage could be turned to conservative uses'. See Martin Malia, *History's Locomotives: Revolutions and the Making of the Modern World* (New Haven and London: Yale University Press, 2006), p. 237. As had Benjamin Disraeli, cf. 'The Representation of the People Act, 1867'.

80 Benjamin wrote *The Work of Art in the Age of Mechanical Reproduction* in 1936 in Paris, which he had reached by way of Nice, Svendborg and Sanremo; Adorno and Horkheimer wrote *Dialectic of the Enlightenment* in 1944 in California; and Horkheimer wrote *The Eclipse of Reason* in 1947, likewise in California.

81 Max Horkheimer, *The Eclipse of Reason* (London and New York: Continuum, 2004), p. 5.

82 Ibid., p. 6.

83 Ibid., p. 9.

84 Ibid., p. 13.

85 Theodor Adorno and Max Horkheimer, *Dialektik der Aufklärung* (Frankfurt am Main: Fischer, 1993), p. 23 (my translations). This particular quote is taken somewhat out of context, but I believe, nonetheless, that it serves the overall tenor of the discussion.

86 Ibid.

87 Horkheimer, *The Eclipse of Reason*, pp. 14 and 83.

88 Adorno and Horkheimer, *Dialektik der Aufklärung*, p. 22.

89 Ibid., p. 19.

90 Horkheimer, *The Eclipse of Reason*, p. 86, see also Benjamin, *The Work of Art*, p. 234.

91 Adorno and Horkheimer, *Dialektik der Aufklärung*, p. 23.

92 Jacob Talmon, *The Origins of Totalitarian Democracy* (London: Sphere Books, 1970), pp. 249ff.

93 Ibid.

94 Ibid.

95 Ibid.

96 Édouard Berth, *Politique et Socialisme*, quoted in Sternhell, *The Birth of Fascist Ideology*, p. 101. For a summary of Sternhell's conclusions, see Ibid., pp. 233–58. See also Kaplan, *The Jewish Radical Right*, pp. 56–7.

97 'Aesthetisation of politics' is Walter Benjamin's term, quoted in Sternhell, *The Birth of Fascist Ideology*, p. 235.

98 See Ibid., p. 251.

99 Benjamin, *Illuminations*, p. 234.

100 Both the concluding discussion on Ahimeir's Fascism and the discussion on Revolution are based on my chapter, 'Revolutionary Fascist or Fascist Revolutionary: Abba Ahimeir and the Success of Revolutionary Zionism' (Peter Bergamin) in Jacob Frank and Sebastian Kunze (eds), *Jewish Radicalisms: Historical Perspectives on a Phenomenon of Global Modernity. European Jewish Studies*, vol. 39 (forthcoming). It is used here by the kind permission of the publishing house Walter DeGruyter.

101 Abba Ahimeir, 'Two Nations', unpublished article used as evidence in the Brit HaBiryonim trial. Exhibit Y.T. 12, 1\6\14ב, Jabotinsky Institute Archive.

102 Hulme, quoted in Sternhell, *The Birth of Fascist Ideology*, p. 241.

103 Although not conclusive evidence, it is interesting to note that no works by Sorel appear in Ahimeir's personal library, which has been preserved in situ in his house in Ramat Gan, since his death in 1962. Similarly, Walter Laqueur considered Jabotinsky to be 'a Sorelian who may have never read Sorel.' See Walter Laqueur, *The History of Zionism* (London: Tauris Parke, 2003), p. 360.

104 See Sternhell, *The Birth of Fascist Ideology*, pp. 195, 204, 214, 254.

105 Ze'ev Sternhell, 'Fascism: Reflections of the Fate of Ideas in Twentieth Century History', *Journal of Political Ideologies*, vol. 5, no. 2 (2000), p. 150.

106 Ahimeir, *Doar HaYom*, 4 November 1928.

107 Malia, *History's Locomotives*, p. 226. Although Malia is speaking only of Socialism, I suggest that his definition applies also the aims of Mussolini's Fascist project.

108 Ahimeir, *Doar HaYom*, 21 September 1928.

109 Shindler, *The Triumph of Military Zionism*, p. 162.

110 Jabotinsky, quoted in Ibid., p. 125.

111 Jabotinsky to Mussolini, 21 July 1922, quoted in Daniel Kupfert Heller, *Jabotinsky's Children: Polish Jews and the Rise of Right-Wing Zionism* (Princeton and Oxford: Princeton University Press, 2017), pp. 79ff. and 121.

112 Shavit, *Jabotinsky and the Revisionist Movement*, p. 357.

113 Ibid., p. 362.

114 Ahimeir, 'Two Nations'.

115 Jabotinsky, quoted in Shimoni, *The Zionist Ideology*, p. 245.

116 Ahimeir, 'Betar ke'Tefisat Olam', p. 24.

117 See Shavit, *Jabotinsky and the Revisionist Movement*, p. 87. Both Yosef and Yaacov Ahimeir have confirmed in interviews with the author that their father was not a 'natural' leader, but rather a shy, soft-spoken figure who was much more at home in the worlds of scholarship and journalism.

118 See Benjamin, *Illuminations*, p. 234.

119 Much of the following discussion has appeared (in a slightly altered form) in Bergamin, 'Revolutionary Fascist or Fascist Revolutionary'. Again, I am grateful to the publishing house Walter DeGruyter for their kind permission to use it.

120 Michael Walzer, *The Paradox of Liberation: Secular Revolutions and Religious Counterrevolutions* (New Haven and London: Yale University Press, 2015), p. 5.

121 Steven Wagner, 'The Zionist Movement in Search of Grand Strategy', *Journal of Military and Strategic Studies*, vol. 16, Issue 1 (2015), p. 86.

122 Arno J. Mayer, *The Furies: Violence and Terror in the French and Russian Revolutions* (Princeton and Oxford: Princeton University Press, 2002), p. 35.

123 Arendt, *On Revolution*, pp. 37–8.

124 Abba Ahimeir, undated letter. Exhibit Y.T. 9, Brit HaBiryonim Trial, 1\6\14ב, Jabotinsky Institute Archive.

125 Mayer, *The Furies*, p. 5.

126 Theda Skocpol's classic definition of 'social revolution' reads: 'a basic, rapid transformation of a society's state and class structure, accompanied and in part carried out through class-based revolts from below'. See Theda Skocpol, *States and Social Revolutions: A Comparative Analysis of France, Russia and China* (Cambridge: Cambridge University Press, 1979), p. 287. Notably, this definition

was challenged almost immediately upon publication by the unfolding events of the Iranian Revolution, in 1979.

127 See Shimoni, *The Zionist Ideology*, p. 195.

128 Eric Hobsbawm defines 'revolutionary eras' as a 'series of events, generally associated with 'revolt' and capable of transferring power from an 'old regime' to a "new regime."' However, he notes that such a transformation does not necessarily always occur. See Eric J. Hobsbawm, 'Revolution', in Roy Porter and Mikulas Teich (eds), *Revolution in History* (Cambridge: Cambridge University Press, 1986), pp. 5–46.

   Martin Malia likewise sees, in what he calls a 'European grand revolution', a 'generalized revolt against an Old Regime'. For Malia, however, this can occur only once in a nation's history, since it also represents the 'founding event for the nation's future "modernity."' See Malia, *History's Locomotives*, p. 3. Malia, in variance to Hobsbawm, implies a necessary transfer of power as a measure of a revolution's success. Despite this apparent contradiction, I believe that both observations are noteworthy.

129 [המשטר הקיים.] Abba Ahimeir, 'Megillat HaSikrikin', in *Brit HaBiryonim* (Tel Aviv: Shamgar Press, 1972), pp. 217–33. The historical sicarii were understood to be the extremists among the Zealots, active at the time of the destruction of the Second Jewish Temple, and named for the daggers – *sicae* – concealed beneath their clothing.

130 Mayer, *The Furies*, p. 30.

131 Eyal Chowers, *The Political Philosophy of Zionism: Trading Jewish Words for a Hebraic Land* (Cambridge: Cambridge University Press, 2012), p. 7. See also Benjamin Harshav, *Language in Time of Revolution* (Berkeley, Los Angeles and London: University of California Press, 1993).

132 Henry W. Fowler and Francis G. Fowler, eds, *The Concise Oxford Dictionary of Current English* (Oxford: Clarendon Press, 1995), p. 1180.

133 See the discussion on Ahimeir's first 'Notebook of a Fascist' article, above.

134 Abba Ahimeir, 'HaShalav HaShilshi' (The Third Phase), in Ahimeir, *Revolutionary Zionism*, p. 13.

135 The Nili Group, based in Zikhron Yaakov, had been a Jewish espionage ring working on behalf of the British, and Aaronsohn had committed suicide rather than disclose information while enduring torture at the hands of the Ottoman Turks. See Shapira, *Land and Power*, p. 69.

136 Ahimeir, *Doar HaYom*, 9 November 1928.

137 Malia, *History's Locomotives*, p. 5.

138 Shindler, *The Triumph of Military Zionism*, p. 156.

139 Malia, *History's Locomotives*, p. 149.

140 Ibid., p. 163.

141 I am indebted to Derek Penslar for pointing out this distinction. See e.g. Dror Wahrman, 'The English Problem of Identity in the American Revolution', *The American Historical Review*, vol. 106, no. 4 (October 2001), pp. 1236–62.

142 Malia, *History's Locomotives*, p. 162.

143 Ibid., p. 164.

144 Ibid., p. 162.

145 Ibid.

146 Ibid., p. 226.

147 See Ibid., pp. 249–52 for a discussion of Lenin's economic revision of Marxism.

148 Ibid., p. 256.

149 Although to be clear, Ahimeir does not use the term 'permanent revolution', himself.

150 Although the nationalist-socialist nature of Fascism rendered the Marxist need for 'permanent revolution' obsolete.

151 Malia, *History's Locomotives*, p. 256.

152 See Shavit, *Jabotinsky and the Revisionist Movement*, p. 363.

153 See Ibid., p. 87.

154 Mayer, *The Furies*, p. 45.

155 Ibid., p. 52.

156 Ibid., pp. 61–2.

157 Walzer, *The Paradox of Liberation*, pp. 55–6.

158 Ibid., p. 67.

Chapter 4

1 See Shindler, *The Rise of the Israeli Right*, pp. 149–54 for a discussion on Jabotinsky's concept for Betar youth in the early 1930s.

2 Abba Ahimeir, 'HaTzorekh B'Hinukh Medini' (The Need For Political Education), 1928, reprinted in Yosef Kister (ed.), *Ahimeir u'Betar* (Tel Aviv: A. Oren, 1982), pp. 47–8.

3 Ibid., p. 47.

4 See Shindler, *The Rise of the Israeli Right*, pp. 93–104.

5 Abba Ahimeir, 'Betar k'Tefisat Olam' (Betar as Worldview), *Masu'ot*, 10 December 1928, reprinted in Kister, *Ahimeir u'Betar*, pp. 49–51.

6 Deuteronomy 20:2–5.

7 See, *inter alios*, Shindler, *The Triumph of Military Zionism*, pp. 148–62, and Schechtman, *The Life and Times of Vladimir Jabotinsky*, vol. 1, pp. 139–83.

8 Abba Ahimeir, 'Davar el HaNoar HaTzioni' (A Word to the Zionist Youth), *Doar HaYom*, 21 October 1930.

9   Mussolini called Religion a 'disease of the psyche', and Hitler made the eradication of the 'Jewish disease' a cornerstone of Nazi ideology.

10 See Robert Paxton's 'nine mobilising passions, which underlie fascist action', Chapter Three.

11 Derek Penslar, *Jews and the Military: A History* (Princeton and Oxford: Princeton University Press, 2013), p. 5.

12 Oswald Spengler, *Man and Technics: A Contribution to a Philosophy of Life* (United Kingdom: Arktos, 2015), p. 45.

13 Theodor Adorno, *In Search of Wagner* (London: Verso, 2005), p. 4.

14 Laqueur, *The History of Zionism*, p. 343.

15 Although there seems to be discrepancy on this point. Shindler (*The Triumph of Military Zionism*) states merely that naval training for Betar cadets was provided in Civitavecchia from 1934. However, a Bulletin from the Recanti Institute for Maritime Studies (University of Haifa) states that Halpern established a naval training school there in 1931, and was appointed 'Director of the Naval Department in Betar', in 1932. This suggests that the training school in Civitavecchia preceded its affiliation with Betar, as was in fact the case with the Betar Leadership Training School, in Jerusalem. See *Report of the Leon Recanti Institute for Maritime Studies, University of Haifa*, Report No. 31 (2005), p. 5.

16 Yirmiahu Halpern, *Tehiat HaYamaut HaIvrit* (Revival of the Hebrew Marine) (Tel Aviv: Hadar, 1982), p. 40. The *Biluim* were the first agricultural pioneers to set out for Eretz Israel, in 1882.

17 Shindler, *The Rise of the Israeli Right*, pp. 86, 181–2.

18 See Heller, *Jabotinsky's Children*, pp. 181ff.

19 I am grateful to Yossi Ahimeir for clarifying these dates, although they contradict other recent scholarship. See Shindler, *The Rise of the Israeli Right*, p. 87.

20 See Halpern's testimony, in Hebrew and Russian, on file at the Archives of the Jabotinsky Institute, Tel Aviv, 2\3\77פ and 19\3\77פ. Although File 19\3\77פ is labelled 'Betar Leadership School in Lithuania', it is clear that Halpern's reminiscences refer to the school in Mandate Palestine. I am indebted to Lova Chechik for translation of the documents from Russian.

21 According to Halpern's testimony, he was the school's director only for the first 'year and a half' of its operation.

22 Ibid.

23 There is some parallel here with the interaction between children raised on Kibbutzes. See, i.e., Yosef Criden, *The Kibbutz Experience* (New York: Schocken, 1987), p. 117.

24 See entry for 'Josef Paamoni', in *Entziklopaedia l'Halutzei HaYishuv U'Bonav* (Encyclopaedia of the Pioneers of the Yishuv and Its Foundations) (Tel Aviv, 1947), p. 601.

25 See Halpern's testimony.

26 Halpern testimony.

27 I am indebted to Will Ferris, Oxford, for pointing out this connection, although he did not specify whether he arrived at his conclusion by way of reason, or personal experience.

28 See also the introduction to Kaplan, *The Jewish Radical Right*, p. 1, where he documents a Betar recruitment mission in Europe, that saw its leaders ride in 'on motorcycles and dressed in leather jackets'. See also George Mosse's fascinating study, *Nationalism and Sexuality* (New York: Howard Fertig, 1985). And Derek Penslar, albeit in a much different, if not completely-unrelated context (that of Theodor Herzl's views on the Palestinian Arabs, as recorded in his diaries) wonders, 'How much of what was scribbled in the diary was an outpouring of the id or the libido, released verbally only to be sublimated into constructive political action?' (Derek Penslar, 'Herzl and the Palestinian Arabs: Myth and Counter-Myth', *The Journal of Israeli History*, vol. 24, no. 1 (2005), p. 73).

29 Letter from Josef Hagalili to Ahimeir, sometime between 1930 and 1933, Exhibit B.G. 18, Brit HaBiryonim trial evidence, in 1\6\14ב, Jabotinsky Institute Archives.

30 Shindler quotes Ahimeir as saying that Halpern's 'head is full of porridge from an ideological point of view'. See Shindler, *The Triumph of Military Zionism*, p. 153.

31 Jabotinsky Institute, File P 77-2/3.

32 See, for example, the rules for an espionage game that Halpern devised for the leadership school, Appendix A.

33 Halpern's testimony.

34 Jabotinsky Institute, File B 8a-9.

35 For example, Ruth Rosowsky – who joined HaShomer HaTzair in 1946 in Tel Aviv – confirmed in a telephone interview (7 October 2015) that the programme, above, was typical of any Zionist youth group meeting. Moreover, she stated that 'Every meeting of every Zionist youth group began with choral singing, and ended with the singing of *HaTikvah*, although we [i.e. HaShomer HaTzair] would then also sing *The International*'.

36 Jabotinsky Institute, File B 8a-9.

37 Ibid.

38 For more on the idea of 'Imagined Communities', see Benedict Anderson, *Imagined Communities: Reflections on the Origin and Spread of Nationalism* (London: Verso, 1991).

39 Certainly the idea of an individual who inherits various societal instincts from his ancestors, is reminiscent of the Jungian concept of the 'collective unconsciousness', which sees man inherit what Jung terms 'primordial images' or 'archetypes' from his ancestors. And knowledge of his previous discussions on Freud and Weininger shows that Ahimeir was, to some degree, familiar with certain psychological concepts. And, of course, as always, we should note the similarity with Spenglerian theory.

40 See Betar Training Manual (1927), Jabotinsky Institute, File B 8a-8.

41 See Ibid.

42 Ibid.

43 Ibid. Although I have translated שחרור in its most literal sense - 'liberation' – I would suggest that, certainly for the first three topics listed, it might also be understood as 'emancipation', i.e., as referring backwards to the concept of 'Jewish Emancipation' and not forwards to 'Jewish [national sovereign] Liberation'. The fact that שחרור is used throughout, makes it difficult to ascertain exactly the author's meaning.

44 ידיעת הארץ.

45 It would seem, from the context of the course outline, that 'land' means 'Eretz Israel', although I am hesitant to state this conclusively.

46 'Tochnit HaAvodah HaTarbutit: L'Daregah Gimel shel Betar B'E.I'. (The Programme for Cultural Work [for] Level C, of Betar in Eretz Israel'), Jabotinsky Institute, B 8a-8.

47 See Footnote 1 in Chapter Two, which notes Jabotinsky's ideological addition to the concept of the 'Zionist Pioneer'.

48 See Shoham, 'From "Great History" to "Small History"'. As Shoham notes: 'After 1921, when it was clear that the mass immigration plan stayed on paper, the narrative of the great history disappeared in favour of the narrative of the small history' (p. 45).

49 Ahimeir refers to the concept no less than three times in the first three chapters, alone.

50 See Ahimeir, *Yudaikah*.

51 Ibid., p. 12.

52 Ibid., p. 14.

53 Ibid., pp. 14–15.

54 Ibid., p. 15.

55 Ibid.

56 Ibid., p. 16.

57 And is clearer in the original Hebrew, where Ahimeir writes, ''שקיעת המערב "הנוצרי"''.

58 In this context, I would categorise the remaining two Jewish ideological streams at that time, as follows: the Sadducees as Hellenistic-assimilationists, and the Essenes as proto-Christians; both, therefore superfluous to a discussion of the 'Jewish' cultural position.

59 Ahimeir, *Yudaikah*, p. 20.

60 Ibid.

61 Ibid.

62 Ibid., p. 21. Ahimeir misquotes Halevy, slightly: ''לבי במזרח ואני בקצה מערב'', instead of ''ליבי במזרח ואנוכי בסוף מערב''.

63 Ibid., p. 24.

64 Genesis 25:34. See also Israel Yuval, *Two Nations in Your Womb* (Berkeley, Los Angeles and London: University of California Press, 2006), p. 7.

65 See Ibid., pp. 1–30, for a detailed discussion of the Jacob and Esau story, and its application to Jewish and Christian typological history.

66 Ibid., p. 7.

67 Ibid., p. 8.

68 Ibid., p. 9.

69 Ibid.

70 Ahimeir, *Yudaikah*, p. 26.

71 And which Shavit also highlights. See Shavit, *The New Hebrew Nation*, p. 15. The phrases in quotations are reproduced as in Yuval, *Two Nations in Your Womb*, p. 6.

72 Ahimeir, *Yudaikah*, p. 59.

73 Ibid., p. 60.

74 Ibid., p. 61.

75 See John Kessler, 'Haggai, Zerubbabel, and the Political Status of Yehud: The Signet Ring in Haggai 2:23', in Michael Floyd and Robert D. Haak (eds), *Prophets, Prophecy, and Prophetic Texts in Second Temple Judaism* (New York and London: T&T Clark, 2006), pp. 102–19, for a more detailed discussion on the significance of the Zerubbabel story.

76 Ahimeir, *Yudaikah*, p. 31.

77 Ibid., p. 47. Note, once again, Ahimeir's use of binary opposites.

78 I.e., Hellenism. See Ibid., p. 73.

79 Ibid.

80 Ibid., pp. 63 and 92.

81 Ibid., p. 79.

82 Ibid., p. 65.

83 Ibid., p. 46.

84 Yuval, *Two Nations in Your Womb*, p. 4.

85 Genesis 25:23. See, once again, Yuval's fascinating discussion of the Jacob-Esau story in Yuval, *Two Nations in Your Womb*, pp. 3–20.

86 Ahimeir, *Yudaikah*, p. 50.

87 See Shindler, *The Rise of the Israeli Right*, pp. 87–9, and Shindler, *The Triumph of Military Zionism*, p. 153, for further discussions of the demonstration.

88 For a comprehensive discussion of the events of August 1929, see Hillel Cohen, תרפ"ט ('1929') (Jerusalem: Keter, 2013), (Hebrew).

89 19\3\77פ Jabotinsky Institute Archive.

90 Ibid.

91 *The Palestine Bulletin*, 16 August 1929.

92 Ibid.

93 See Ibid., and Shindler, *The Rise of the Israeli Right*, p. 88.

94 19\3\77ɔ Jabotinsky Institute.

95 Abba Ahimeir, 'Mikhtav el HaNoar HaBetari' (Letter to the Betar Youth), *Hazit HaAm*, 29 March 1932.

Chapter 5

1 Abba Ahimeir, *Brit HaBiryonim*, Pamphlet published by the Jabotinsky Institute, Tel Aviv, August 1953, and Moshe Menor (ed.), *Brit HaBiryonim* (Jerusalem: WZO, 1982). Neither of these pamphlets should be confused with the collection of Ahimeir's writings that appeared as *Brit HaBiryonim* (Tel Aviv: Shamgar, 1972).

2 Abba Ahimeir, 'Ma Haitah Brit HaBiryonim?' (What Was Brit HaBiryonim?), lecture delivered in April 1962, reprinted in Menor, *Brit HaBiryonim*, pp. 10–17.

3 Joseph Heller, 'The Failure of Fascism in Jewish Palestine 1925–1948', in Stein U. Larsen (ed.), *Fascism Outside Europe* (New York: Columbia University Press, 2002), p. 376.

4 For a detailed discussion of the party split, and the Katowice Conference, see Shindler, *The Rise of the Israeli Right*, pp. 115–19.

5 Abba Ahimeir, 'HaMidbar v'Gan HaEden' (The Desert and the Garden of Eden), September 1929, 'Hanahmitz et Sha'at HaKusher?' (Shall We Miss the Hour of Opportunity?), September 1929, 'M'Tel Aviv ad Beer Tuvia' (From Tel Aviv to Beer Tuvia), March 1930, all reprinted in Menor, *Brit HaBiryonim*, pp. 37–42.

6 Although it is not clear if the essays were published at the time. The reprint in Menor lists only when they were written (see footnote, above).

7 Abba Ahimeir, reprinted in Menor, *Brit HaBiryonim*, p. 37.

8 Ibid., p. 38.

9 Ibid., p. 39.

10 Ibid., p. 38.

11 Ibid., p. 40.

12 See Shindler, *The Rise of the Israeli Right*, p. 106.

13 See Heller, *The Stern Gang*, p. 21.

14 Shindler, *The Rise of the Israeli Right*, p. 107.

15 Ahimeir, *Brit HaBiryonim* (1953), p. 4.

16 See also Shindler, *The Triumph of Military Zionism*, pp. 161, 167, and Shindler, *The Rise of the Israeli Right*, pp. 121–2.

17 See Paula Daccaratt, '1890s Zionism Reconsidered: Marco Baruch', *Jewish History*, vol. 19, no. 3/4 (2005), pp. 315–45, for a comprehensive discussion of this somewhat forgotten early Zionist figure.

18 Abba Ahimeir, in Menor, *Brit HaBiryonim*, pp. 14.

19 Abba Ahimeir, 'From Tel-Hai to Beer Tuvia', in Menor, *Brit HaBiryonim,* p. 42.

20 Ahimeir, *Brit HaBiryonim* (1953), p. 4.

21 Ibid., pp. 4–5.

22 Ibid., p. 4.

23 See Shapira, *Land and Power,* p. 175.

24 Ibid. See also Ehud Luz, *Wrestling With An Angel: Power, Morality, and Jewish Identity* (New Haven and London: Yale University Press, 2003), pp. 198–220, for a discussion on the debate over *Havlagah* in the Yishuv.

25 Ibid., p. 177.

26 Ahimeir, *Brit HaBiryonim* (1953), p. 5.

27 Ibid., p. 11.

28 Ibid., pp. 4–5.

29 Ibid., p. 5.

30 Robert Paxton notes the exclusivity of 'male chiefs' in fascist action, see Chapter Three.

31 Ahimeir, 'Megillat HaSikrikin', p. 217. Interestingly, Jabotinsky had written a poem about Corday in 1902, 'Charlota HaUmlalah'..

32 Ibid., p. 219.

33 Biographical information for Hasia Ahimeir was taken from https://www.geni.com/people/Hasia-Ahimeir/6000000015925786149, accessed on 9 May 2018, and an interview with Ada Zavidov (Hasia's and Ahimeir's granddaughter), 29 March 2016.

34 The issue of Hasia Ahimeir succumbing to mental illness during childbirth is also noted in the sworn witness testimony of Rebecca Chasan – Ahimeir's and Stavsky's landlady in Tel Aviv – during the Arlosoroff trial. See Exhibit RH94, in 4\8ח, Jabotinsky Institute Archive, Tel Aviv.

35 The information – speculative and otherwise – concerning Hasia was gathered in an interview with Ada Zavidov, 29 March 2016.

36 Interview with Ada Zavidov.

37 'Hasia' became Ada Zavidov's second name.

38 See Uri Dromi, 'Always At His Side', *HaAretz,* 2 February 2006, http://www.haaretz.com/print-edition/features/always-at-his-side-1.178973, accessed 9 May 2018; and a film interview with Sonia Ahimeir by Yehuda Kaveh, https://youtu.be/upgexWxqJ-I, accessed 9 May 2018.

39 See 'Dr. Abba Ahimeir: Luah Ta'arikim b'Hayav', p. 145.

40 See Kaveh's interview with Sonia, above.

41 Exhibit JK 31, produced in the trial for Brit HaBiryonim members, Jabotinsky Institute Archive, 1\6\14ב. The letter appears in the trial records – like most of the evidence – in an uneven English translation. Unless otherwise stated, I quote all court transcripts as they appear, that is, almost always in English and often in a translation that can, at times, be broken, or stylistically rough. Original documents

are almost completely absent from the trial transcripts, a fact that becomes less important if we remember that for many – indeed, most – of the people called upon during the course of both the Arlosoroff and Brit HaBiryonim trials, Hebrew was not their mother tongue. Greenberg's letter, quoted above, was written originally in Yiddish. The Arlosoroffs spoke German with one another, Stavsky testified in Yiddish, Ahimeir in Hebrew; the judges spoke English, and relied heavily on translations, both verbal and written.

42 Ibid. The reference to the Samaritan leader Sanballat, who scorned the Jewish governor Nehemiah's intentions of building the walls of Jerusalem, is almost certainly a reference to the British Mandatory government.

43 Ibid.

44 See Jabotinsky Institute Archive: 1\134 קל, 2\134 קל and 316 סל.

45 Shavit, *Jabotinsky and the Revisionist Movement*, p. 88, and Kaplan, *The Jewish Radical Right*, p xiii.

46 See Heller, *The Stern Gang*, p. 22.

47 Letter to Josef Katznelson, Exhibit Y.T. 2, in Brit HaBiryonim trial evidence, in 1\14-6ב, Jabotinsky Institute Archives. Undated, but almost certainly written before the first Brit HaBiryonim activity, the demonstration against Drummond Shiels, in October 1930.

48 Ahimeir, *Brit HaBiryonim*, p. 12.

49 Two notable 'sympathisers' whom he lists are Avraham Stern and Ben-Zion Netanyahu (father of the current Israeli prime minister, Benyamin Netanyahu).

50 See Ahimeir, *Brit HaBiryonim*, pp. 11–12 and 19\3\77פ, Jabotinsky Institute Archive.

51 See B. Gittin 56a.

52 ביריון, see Marcus Jastrow, *A Dictionary of the Targumim, The Talmud Babli and Yerushalmi, and the Midrashic Literature* (London: Luzac, 1903).

53 ביריונא, in Ibid. In spite of the discrepancy in spelling, he claims it is the latter group which is referred to in B Talmud Gittin 56a as discussed next.

54 Eliezer Ben Yehuda, *MilonHaLashon HaIvrit HaYeshanah yeHaHadashah* (Dictionary of Ancient and Modern Hebrew) (Jerusalem: Hotsat HaAm, 1948–1959). My thanks go to Martin Goodman and Cesar Merchan-Hamann at the Centre for Hebrew and Jewish Studies, Oxford, for providing some much-appreciated advice with regard to the various meanings of *biryon, biryona and sicarrii*.

55 See *Milon Evan Shushan* (Jerusalem: Magnes Press, 2007).

56 בור.

57 See B. Gittin 56a, note 27 in the Schottenstein edition, Artscroll Publications, Brooklyn, 2005.

58 Yosef Ahimeir, interview 8 June 2010.

59 I am indebted to Derek Penslar for pointing out this connection to me.

60 See, for example, Ahimeir, 'Davar el HaNoar HaTzioni' and Shindler, *The Triumph of Military Zionism*, p. 159.

61 Gail Lichtman, 'Abba Ahimeir', *The Jerusalem Post Magazine*, 31 May 2002, p. 16, etc.

62 The definition put forth by the prosecution when Ahimeir and other members of the Brit HaBiryonim stood trial, charged under the 'Seditious Offences Ordinance No. 41 of 1929' ((PRO) London, CO733/266/1).

63 The definition put forth by the defence during the same trial.

64 Rashi, in B.Gittin 56a, in its English translation in the Babylonian Talmud, Schottenstein edition (Brooklyn: Artscroll, 2005).

65 The same passage in B.Gittin 56a, in its English translation in the Babylonian Talmud, Isidore Epstein (ed.) (London: Sonico, 1978), p. 256.

66 Ehud Sprinzak, *The Ascendance of Israel's Radical Right* (Oxford: Oxford University Press, 1991), p. 315 and others.

67 Heller, *The Stern Gang*, p. 15, etc.

68 Kaplan, *The Jewish Radical Right*, p. 181.

69 Yosef Ahimeir (ed.), 'Dr. Aba [*sic*] Ahimeir: The Man Who Turned the Tide', http://beitaba.com/index.php?dir=site&page=content&cs=19, accessed 9 May 2018.

70 Shimoni, *The Zionist Ideology*, p. 250.

71 Anita Shapira, *Berl: The Biography of a Socialist Zionist* (Cambridge: Cambridge University Press, 1984), p. 195.

72 There was a general call from the Revisionists to boycott the census. They feared that the data collected would be used by the British to establish a Legislative Council in Palestine that would have proportional representation that reflected its population demographic, that is, with an Arab majority. See, e.g., *JTA Bulletin*, 23 September 1931.

73 B. Gittin 56a.

74 Abba Ahimeir, 'HaTekia HaGadola' (The Great Shofar Blast), *Hazit HaAm*, 11 November 1932, reprinted in Ahimeir, *Revolutionary Zionism*, pp. 64–8.

75 See Shindler, *The Rise of the Israeli Right*, p. 108.

76 Shimoni, *The Zionist Ideology*, p. 434, fn. 43.

77 See page 2, 8.19ח, Jabotinsky Institute Archives.

78 See Ahimeir and Shatzki, *Hineinu Sikrikim*, p. 8.

79 See investigation and trial evidence held at the Jabotinsky Institute: 19\8ח, 5\8ח, 4\8ח, 3\8ח, 2\1\8ח, 3\1\1\8ח, 2\1\1\8ח, 1\1\1\8ח.

80 See 1\6\14ב for *HaBiryon* and *The ABC of Revolutionary Zionism*. See 3\1\1\8ח for 'The Scroll of the Sicarii', Jabotinsky Institute Archives. An original Hebrew copy of *HaBiryon* is held at the Beit Aba Archive, in Ramat Gan.

81 *The Palestine Bulletin*, 15 November 1931.

82 *Jewish Telegraphic Agency*, 10 May 1932.

83 Ahimeir, *Brit HaBiryonim* (1972), pp. 217–23.

84 Brit HaBiryonim members feared that the Census was being carried out with the intention of creating a 'representative legislative assembly with an Arab majority'. See Shindler, *The Rise of the Israeli Right*, p. 91.

85 See Exhibit B.S. 38 in Brit HaBiryonim trial evidence, in 1\14-6ב, Jabotinsky Institute Archives.

86 See Shavit, *Jabotinsky and the Revisionist Movement.* He defines 'national Messianism' as the 'redemption of a national body, rather than with individual Messianism, which concerns individual redemption' (p. 139).

87 Exhibit B.S. 38.

88 Ibid.

89 Ibid.

90 Ibid.

91 Ibid.

92 See Exhibit Y.T. 10, Brit HaBiryonim trial evidence, in 1\14-6ב, Jabotinsky Institute Archives.

93 Ibid.

94 Ahimeir, *Brit HaBiryonim* (1953), p. 10.

95 Josephus, in Martin Goodman, *Rome and Jerusalem* (London: Penguin, 2006), p. 407. It is interesting to note that the term survives in Spanish, as *sicario*, or 'hitman'. My thanks go to Cesar Merchan-Hamann for this insight.

96 Ahimeir, *Brit HaBiryonim* (1953), p. 10.

97 Ibid.

98 Ibid.

99 Three years later, in the wake of the 1929 Arab Riots, Greenberg would also begin to use sicari imagery in various poems. (Note the difference between Sicarii (noun) and sicari (adjective.)

100 Although Solomon Zeitlin understood them to be 'two distinct, mutually hostile groups'. See Solomon Zeitlin, 'Zealots and Sicarii', *Journal of Biblical Literature*, vol. 81, no. 4 (December 1962), pp. 395–8.

101 See Goodman, *Rome and Jerusalem*, p. 407, Shimoni, *The Zionist Ideology*, p. 434, fn. 39, Shavit, *Jabotinsky and the Revisionist Movement*, p. 388, fn. 58, etc.

102 Richard A. Horsley, 'The Sicarii: Ancient Jewish Terrorists', *The Journal of Religion*, vol. 59, no. 4 (October 1979), p. 444.

103 Ibid., p. 445.

104 Goodman, *Rome and Jerusalem*, p. 407.

105 See Horsley, 'The Sicarii', p. 448.

106 Josef Nedava, 'Who Were the Biryoni', *The Jewish Quarterly Review*, New Series, vol. 63, no. 4 (April 1973), p. 321.

107 Ibid., pp. 318–9.

108 B.Gittin 56a.

109   Nedava, 'Who Were the Biryoni', p. 319.

110   Exhibit J.K. 31, Brit HaBiryonim trial evidence, in 1\14-6ב, Jabotinsky Institute Archives.

111   Exhibit J.K. 33, Brit HaBiryonim trial evidence, in 1\14-6ב, Jabotinsky Institute Archives.

112   Nedava, 'Who Were the Biryoni', p. 318.

113   The comments of Klausner and Nedava are relevant from both a historical and political perspective. Klausner was a professor and chief editor of the *Hebrew Encyclopedia*, and had established the 'Pro-Wailing Wall Committee' in 1929. Nedava was a historian who went on to become professor of Political Science at the Universities of Bar Ilan and Haifa, and Dropsie College. He wrote the Forward to Ahimeir's *Brit HaBiryonim* and *HaMishpat*, and edited the book about him, *HaIsh she Hitah et HaZerem (The Man Who Turned the Tide)*. Both men were engaged Revisionists.

114   Exhibit J.K. 32, Brit HaBiryonim trial evidence, in 1\14-6ב, Jabotinsky Institute Archives.

115   Exhibit Y.T. 13, Brit HaBiryonim trial evidence, in 1\6\14ב, Jabotinsky Institute Archives. The letter is dated 'Bialystok, 22 Shevat 5693' (18 February 1933).

116   For commentaries on the permissibility of killing in Jewish Law see B. Talmud, Sanhedrin 74a-b.

117   Ahimeir, *Yudaikah*, p. 39.

118   Ibid., pp. 40–1.

119   See Josef Nedava's Forward to Abba Ahimeir, *HaMishpat* (The Trial) (Tel Aviv: Ramah, 1968), p. ט"ו.

120   Ahimeir, 'Some Ideas on Fascism', and 'If I am not for myself who will be?'

121   The original manuscript has disappeared. It was most likely destroyed by the British, along with other trial evidence. When Yosef Ahimeir published *The Scroll of the Sicarii* as an appendix to the edition of Ahimeir's collected writings *Brit HaBiryonim* (1972), he reconstructed the essay from excerpts that appeared in various Yishuv newspapers at the time of the trial. My examination of the printed copy (in Hebrew and English) used as trial evidence reveals the order of the essay to be somewhat different than in the 1972 book, is thus probably more accurate. This fact, however, does not substantially change our reception of the essay's content.

122   See Heller, *The Stern Gang*, pp. 20–1.

123   Of course we cannot know for certain if Ahimeir was familiar with this, nor if it carried any weight for him had he been. For commentary surrounding the application of the principle of the *din rodef* to contemporary society, see 'War and Non-Jews', in J. David Bleich, *Contemporary Halakhic Problems, Volume II* (New York: Ktav, 1983), pp. 159–66.

124   Abba Ahimeir, *HaPoel HaTzair*, 5 June 1925.

125 Exhibit Y.T. 12, Brit HaBiryonim trial evidence, in 1\14-6ב, Jabotinsky Institute Archives.

126 Exhibit Y.T. 10, Brit HaBiryonim trial evidence, in 1\14-6ב, Jabotinsky Institute Archives.

127 See Yf'aat Weiss, 'Haavara Agreement', Yad Vashem Chronology of the Holocaust, https://www.yadvashem.org/odot_pdf/Microsoft%20Word%20-%20 3231.pdf, accessed 9 May 2018.

128 Arlosoroff's biographical information for this comparison comes from Shlomo Avineri, *Arlosoroff* (London: Peter Halban, 1989), pp. 5–10.

129 Arlosoroff quoted in Avineri, *Arlosoroff*, p. 7.

130 Ibid.

131 Avineri uses '*Zerissenheit*' (inner turmoil) in the original German, which suggests that it is the term that Arlosoroff used, himself, to describe his situation.

132 See Chapter Two.

133 George L. Mosse, *The Crisis of German Ideology: Intellectual Origins of the Third Reich* (New York: Schocken, 1981), p. 4.

134 Ibid.

135 Avineri suggests that Arlosoroff's use of the 'German romantic anti-industrialist ideas associated with the *Volk* [that] would be, in one of its manifestations, contaminated by its association with Nazism, should not detract from our understanding of the authentic social criticism expressed by it and its emancipatory potential as one of the many intellectual modes of protest against alienation in modern, industrialized society'; a statement as apologetic as it is, apparently, unapologetic. See Avineri, *Arlosoroff*, pp. 15–16.

136 Ibid.

137 See my discussion on *Yudaikah* in Chapter Four.

138 Chaim Arlosoroff, *Der Jüdische Volkssozializmus* (Berlin: HaPoel HaTzair, 1920), pp. 70–1. All tranlations are mine.

139 Ibid., pp. 9–16.

140 Ibid., p. 12.

141 Ibid., pp. 19–21.

142 Ibid., p. 22.

143 Ibid., p. 28.

144 Ibid.

145 See Sternhell, *The Founding Myths of Israel*, pp. 3–46, for a thorough discussion of the nature of Arlosoroff's 'nationalist socialism'. See also Derek Penslar's critique of Sternhell, 'Ben Gurion's Willing Executioners', *Dissent* (Winter 1999), which paints Sternhell as an (Isaiah) Berlin-ian 'hedgehog' whose every argument is a product of his singular belief that 'fascism originated as a mutation of Marxist social democracy into an ethnocentric "nationalist socialism."'

146 Kaplan, *The Jewish Radical Right*, p. 59. See also pp. 51–74, for Kaplan's detailed discussion of Revisionist economics.

147 Avineri, *Arlosoroff*, pp. 31–2.

148 Ibid., p. 3.

149 Ibid., pp. 93–4.

150 Arlosoroff, letter to Chaim Weizmann, 30 June 1932, quoted in Ibid., p. 95.

151 See Kaplan, *The Jewish Radical Right*, pp. 12 and 182, fn. 22, Heller, *The Stern Gang*, pp. 21–2, and Shindler, *The Triumph of Military Zionism*, pp. 174–5, etc.

152 *Hazit HaAm*, 9 June 1933, quoted in Kaplan, *The Jewish Radical Right*, p. 12.

153 'Brit Stalin-Ben Gurion-Hitler', *Hazit HaAm*, 16 June 1933, in Kaplan, *The Jewish Radical Right*, p. 183, fn. 23.

154 Nedava, Forward to *HaMishpat*, p. ט"ו.

155 See Yosef Ahimeir (ed.), 'Beit Aba: Abba Ahimeir Archive, Ramat Gan', http://www.beitaba.com/content.php?id=19, accessed 9 May 2018 and *Encyclopedia Judaica*, vol. 2, pp. 471–2.

156 Nedava, Forward to *HaMishpat*, pp. ט"ו–ט"ז.

157 Ibid., see also Shapira, *Berl*, pp. 194–5.

158 See Heller, *The Stern Gang*, p. 22.

159 National Archives (PRO) London, CO733/266/1.

160 Nedava, Forward to *HaMishpat*, p. ט"ו.

161 *Sikarikim* is the Greek form of Sicarii.

162 This, and subsequent citations from the trial, taken from National Archives (PRO) London, CO733/266/1.

163 In point of fact, Ahimeir did write a history of the Russian Revolution. The manuscript – in excess of 300 pages – is held at the Beit Aba Archive.

164 7\14כ, Jabotinsky Institute Archive.

165 See Heller, *The Stern Gang*, pp. 30–1. Ahimeir (and Greenberg, and Yevin) also lent ideological and moral support to Menahem Begin in Poland in 1935 and beyond, see Shindler, *The Rise of the Israeli Right*, pp. 160–71.

166 Memorandum, 'From Police', 15 or 25 September 1937, Beit Aba Archive. For more information on the circumstances surrounding Frankel's murder, see John Boyer-Bell, *Terror Out of Zion* (London and New Brunswick: Transaction Publishers, 2009), p. 37.

167 The Hebrew transliteration is almost certainly incorrect. *Mari* means 'bitterness' – a not unlikely pairing – but *meri* means 'resistance' or 'insubordination'; a much better fit. Either way, both words are nouns, rendering the *Ha* before *Noar* incorrect.

168 Letter to Ze'eva Ahimeir-Zavidov, 6 February 1952, Beit Aba Archive.

169 Ibid. The sentence underlined is reproduced as in the original letter.

170 Mapai Central Committee minutes, 31 January 1934, quoted in Shapira, *Berl*, p. 196.

171 Ibid., p. 197.

172 A recent article in the Israeli daily *Yediot Ahronot* mistakenly refers to 'The Scroll of the Sicarii' as having been written *in the wake of* the Arlosoroff murder. The comments which followed when Yosef Ahimeir corrected the error give a good indication of how polarising the affair remains within Israeli society. See Aviel Mignazi, 'Telegramti, ein teshuva mimekh, katav Eshkol l'Ishto', *Ynet News*, http://www.ynet.co.il/articles/0,7340,L-4027803,00.html, accessed 9 May 2018.

Conclusion: The Bourgeois Revolutionary

1 Martin Malia, *Alexander Herzen and the Birth of Russian Socialism: 1815–1855* (Cambridge: Harvard University Press, 1961), p. 416.

2 I use 'political' versus 'Political' to differentiate between Zionism as an expression of modern Jewish 'political' organisation, and the tradition of Herzlian 'Political Zionism' as a specific ideological strain of Zionism.

3 See Isaiah Berlin, 'The Role of the Intelligentsia', in *The Power of Ideas* (London: Chatto and Windus, 2000), pp. 103–10.

4 See Inna Kochetkova, *The Myth of the Russian Intelligentsia: Old Intellectuals in the New Russia* (London: Routledge, 2009), p. 19.

5 Berlin, *The Power of Ideas*, p. 107.

6 Ibid., p. 106.

7 Berlin defines the *intelligentsia militans* as being generated – historically and 'essentially' – by 'truly oppressive regimes.' See Ibid., p. 108.

8 Or indeed, the 'Bourgeois Terrorist'; Adorno's term, see Chapter Four.

9 See Jacob Golomb, *Nietzsche and Zion* (Ithaca and London: Cornell University Press, 2004), pp. 46–64 for a detailed discussion of Nordau's application of Nietzsche.

10 Ibid., p. 59. See Michael Stanislawski, *Zionism and the Fin de Siècle: Cosmopolitanism and Nationalism from Nordau to Jabotinsky* (Berkeley, Los Angeles and London: University of California Press, 2001) for a comprehensive discussion on Herzl, Nordau, and Jabotinsky *vis à vis* the *fin de siècle*. 'Decadence' here, and as follows, might best be understood as 'being characterised by some degree of licentious self-indulgence.'

11 Herzen, quoted in Malia, *Alexander Herzen*, p. 358.

12 Ibid., p. 5.

13 'Bourgeois terrorist' is Adorno's term, see Chapters Four and Five.

14 Malia, *Alexander Herzen*, p. 417.

15 Avraham Stern, on the run from British authorities, was eventually tracked down to a flat in Tel Aviv, and shot dead by police, on 12 February 1942.

16   Text of the Irgun Declaration of Revolt, 1 February 1944, https://www.
jewishvirtuallibrary.org/revolt-is-proclaimed-by-the-irgun, accessed 22 November
2018.

17   Exhibit B.S. 38 in Brit HaBiryonim trial evidence, in 1\14-6ב, Jabotinsky Institute
Archives.

18   Ibid.

19   Menachem Begin, *The Revolt* (New York: Dell, 1977), and *White Nights* (London:
Futura, 1978).

20   This anecdote was related by Yossi Ahimeir. The Knesset, Israel's national
legislature, has only 120 members. Begin finally did become prime minister of
Israel in 1977, fifteen years after Ahimeir's death.

21   Heller, *Jabotinsky's Children*, p. 219, and Shindler, *Rise of the Israeli Right*, p. 126.

22   Shindler, *The Triumph of Military Zionism*, p. 18.

23   Ibid.

24   Ibid., pp. 7–8, 17 and 205–12. Begin's 'Military Zionism' was to supplant the two
earlier periods in Zionist history, 'Practical Zionism' and 'Political Zionism'. See
Heller, *The Stern Gang*, p. 41.

25   Hobsbawm, 'Revolution', p. 32.

26   Heller, *The Stern Gang*, p. 103. Although after Stern's death, Lehi would gradually
reject his anti-socialist stance, and, by 1944, advocate 'National Bolshevism.'

27   Ibid., p. 25.

28   Ibid., p. 75.

29   Ibid., p. 86.

30   See *Doar HaYom*, 4 November 1928.

31   Jerimiah 31:31-4.

32   Derek Penslar, 'Ben Gurion's Willing Executioners.' This is not to say that
Ben-Gurion was not a product of a similar eastern European bourgeoisie, but he
was not a bourgeois intellectual in the same way that were Ahimeir, and Arlosoroff.
As a student of law, Ben-Gurion lent his energies to what Berlin calls the 'ordinary
pursuits' (i.e. of the intelligentsia). Berlin, *The Power of Ideas*, p. 108.

33   Letter to Ze'eva Ahimeir-Zavidov, 6 February 1952, Beit Aba Archive.

34   An observation that is neither new, nor original, to be sure.

35   This is not to say, of course, that Spengler knew of Ahimeir.

36   Karl Krauss, *Die Dritte Walpurgisnacht* (Munich: Fischer, 1967), p. 82.

37   See Heller, *The Stern Gang*, pp. 20–1.

38   Thornton Wilder, *The Eighth Day* (New York: The Library of America, 2011), p. 339.

Appendix A

1   19\3\77ב Jabotinsky Institute Archive.

Bibliography

Primary sources

Interviews with Yaacov Ahimeir, Yosef Ahimeir, Ada Zavidov

Adorno, Theodor W., *Aesthetic Theory* (London: Continuum Press, 2004).

Adorno, Theodor W., *In Search of Wagner* (Norfolk: Verso Press, 1985).

Adorno, Theodor W. and Horkheimer, Max, *Dialektik der Aufklärung: Philisophische Fragmente* (Frankfurt am Main: Fischer Verlag, 1993 (German)).

Ahimeir, Abba, *Atlantidah, O-HaOlam She Shakah: Sipporim v'Zichronot* (Tel Aviv: Or Am, 1996 (Hebrew)).

Ahimeir, Abba, *Bemerkungen zu Spenglers Auffassung Russlands* (Unpublished, Abba Ahimeir Archive 'Beit Aba', Ramat Gan (German)).

Ahimeir, Abba, *Brit HaBiryonim* (Tel Aviv: Shamgar, 1972 (Hebrew)).

Ahimeir, Abba, *HaMishpat* (Tel Aviv: Ramah, 1968 (Hebrew)).

Ahimeir, Abba, *HaTziyonut HaMahapekhanit* (Tel Aviv: Simhon, 1966 (Hebrew)).

Ahimeir, Abba, *Im Kriat HaGever* (Tel Aviv: Rav Guterman 1957 (Hebrew)).

Ahimeir, Abba, *Moto shel Yosef Katznelson* (Tel Aviv: Shamgar, 1974 (Hebrew)).

Ahimeir, Abba, *Reportage shel Bahor 'Yeshiva'* (Tel Aviv: Hidkel, 1984 (Hebrew)).

Ahimeir, Abba, *Yudaikah* (Tel Aviv: Ankor, 1960 (Hebrew)).

Arlosoroff, Chaim, *Der Jüdische Volkssozialismus* (Berlin: Verlag HaPoel Hazair, 1919 (German)).

Arlosoroff, Chaim, *Yoman Yerushalayim* (Israel: Worker's Party Press, 1949 (Hebrew)).

Begin, Menachem, *The Revolt* (New York: Dell, 1977).

Begin, Menachem, *White Nights* (London: Futura Publications, 1978).

Ben Yehuda, Eliezer, *MilonHaLashon HaIvrit HaYeshanah yeHaHadashah* (Dictionary of Ancient and Modern Hebrew) (Jerusalem: Hotsat HaAm, 1948–1959).

Benjamin, Walter, *Illuminations* (London: Fontana Press, 1992).

Horkheimer, Max, *The Eclipse of Reason* (London and New York: Continuum Press, 2004).

Jastrow, Marcus, *A Dictionary of the Targumim, The Talmud Babli and Yerushalmi, and the Midrashic Literature* (London: Luzac and Co., 1903).

Krauss, Karl, *Die Dritte Walpurgisnacht* (Munich: Kösel, 1967).

Lenin, Vladimir I., *Lenin on Literature and Art* (Maryland: Wildside Press, 2008).

Orenstein, Yaakov, *B'clevim* (Tel Aviv: Elisha Press, 1973 (Hebrew)).

Shushan, Evan, *Milon Evan Shushan* (Jerusalem: Magnes, 2007 (Hebrew)).

Tidhar, David (ed.), *Entziklopedia l'Halutzei HaYishuv U'Bonav* (Tel Aviv: David Tidhar, 1947 (Hebrew)).

Journals and newspapers

Betar
Betar Monthly
The British Worker
Davar
Doar HaYom
HaAretz
HaMashkif
HaPoel HaTzair
HaToren
Hazit HaAm
Herut
The Jerusalem Post
Jewish Telegraphic Agency
Kuntres
Madrikh Betar
The Palestine Bulletin
The Revisionist
The Revisionist Bulletin
Yediot Ahahronot

Archives

Abba Ahimeir Archive, 'Beit Aba', Ramat Gan
Beit Ariela, Tel Aviv
Jabotinsky Institute, Tel Aviv
Lavon Institute, Tel Aviv
University of Vienna
National Archives, Kew

Secondary sources

Aberbach, David, *Jewish Cultural Nationalism: Origins and Influences* (London: Routledge, 2007).
Abulof, Uriel, '"Small Peoples": The Existential Uncertainty of Ethnonational Communities', *International Studies Quarterly*, vol. 53 (2009), pp. 227–48.
Ackerl, Isabella, *Geschichte Österreichs in Daten* (Wiesbaden: Marix Verlag, 2013 (German)).

Ahimeir, Yosef (ed.), *Abba Ahimeir v'HaTsiunut HaMahapekhanit* (Tel Aviv: Hadkel, 2012 (Hebrew)).

Ahimeri, Yosef and Shatzki, Shmuel (eds), *Hineinu Sikrikim* (Tel Aviv: Shamgar, 1978 (Hebrew)).

Anderson, Benedict, *Imagined Communities: Reflections on the Origin and Spread of Nationalism* (London: Verso, 1991).

Arendt, Hannah, *On Revolution* (London: Penguin Books, 2006).

Avineri, Shlomo, *Arlosoroff* (London: Peter Halban Publishers, 1989).

Avineri, Shlomo, 'The Political Thought of Vladimir Jabotinsky', *The Jerusalem Quarterly*, no. 16, Summer (1980), pp. 3–26.

Baldwin, P. M., 'Liberalism, Nationalism, and Degeneration: The Case of Max Nordau', *Central European History*, vol. 13, no. 2 (June 1980), pp. 99–120.

Ben-Israel, Hevda, 'Zionism and European Nationalisms: Comparative Aspects', *Israel Studies*, vol. 8, no. 1 (2003), pp. 91–104.

Berkowitz, Michael, Tananbaum, Susan L. and Bloom, Sam W. (eds), *Forging Modern Jewish Identities: Public Faces and Private Struggles* (London and Portland: Valentine Mitchell, 2003).

Berlin, Isaiah, *The Power of Ideas* (London: Chatto and Windus, 2000).

Ben-Hur, Rafaella Bilski, *Every Individual a King: The Social and Political Thought of Ze'ev Vladimir Jabotinsky* (Washington DC: B'nai B'rith Books, 1993).

Bleich, J. David, *Contemporary Halakhic Problems, Volume II* (New York: Ktav, 1983).

Boyer-Bell, John, *Terror Out of Zion: The Fight for Israeli Independence* (New Brunswick and London: Transaction Publishers, 2009).

Burleigh, Michael, *Sacred Causes: Religion and Politics from the European Dictators to Al Qaeda* (London: Harper Perennial, 2007).

Calhoun, Daniel F., *The United Front: The TUC and the Russians 1923–1928* (Cambridge: Cambridge University Press, 1976).

Cohen, Hillel, תרפ"ט ('1929') (Jerusalem: Keter Books, 2013 (Hebrew)).

Crenshaw Hutchinson, Martha, 'The Concept of Revolutionary Terrorism', *The Journal of Conflict Resolution*, vol. 16, no. 3 (September 1972), pp. 383–96.

Criden, Yosef, *The Kibbutz Experience* (New York: Schocken Books, 1987).

Daccaratt, Paula, '1890s Zionism Reconsidered: Marco Baruch', *Jewish History*, vol. 19, no 3/4 (2005), pp. 315–45.

Don-Yehiya, Eliezer, 'Hanukkah and the Myth of the Maccabees in Ideology and Society', in Deshen, Shlomo A., Charles S. Liebman and Moshe Shokeid (eds), *Israeli Judaism: The Sociology of Religion in Israel* (London: Transaction Publishers, 1995), pp. 303–22.

Don-Yehiya, Eliezer and Liebman, Charles S., *Civil Religion in Israel: Traditional Judaism and Political Culture in the Jewish State* (Berkeley, Los Angeles, London: University of California Press, 1983).

Don-Yehiya, Eliezer and Liebman, Charles S., 'Zionist Ultranationalism and Its Attitude toward Religion', *Journal of Church and State*, vol. 23, no. 2 (1981), pp. 259–27.

Englund, Steven, *Napoleon: A Political Life* (Cambridge, MA and London: Harvard University Press, 2004).

Evron, Boas, *Jewish State or Israeli Nation?* (Bloomington: Indiana University Press, 1995).

Feiner, Shmuel, *Haskalah and History: The Emergence of a Modern Jewish Historical Consciousness* (Oxford: The Littman Library of Jewish Civilization, 2004).

Floyd, Michael and Haak, Robert D. (eds), *Prophets, Prophecy, and Prophetic Texts in Second Temple Judaism* (London and New York: T&T Clark, 2006).

Frankel, Jonathan (ed.), *Jews and Messianism in the Modern Era: Metaphor and Meaning, Studies in Contemporary Jewry VII* (Oxford: Oxford University Press, 1991).

Frye, Northrop, '"The Decline of the West" by Oswald Spengler', *Daedalus*, vol. 103 (1974), pp. 1–13.

Garau, Salvatore, 'Anticipating Norwegian Fascism: The Radicalization of Urban Right-Wing Nationalism in Inter-war Norway', *European History Quarterly*, vol. 43, no. 4 (October 2013), pp. 681–706.

Garau, Salvatore, 'The Internationalisation of Italian Fascism in the Face of German National Socialism, and its Impact on the British Union of Fascists', *Politics, Religion and Ideology*, vol. 15, no. 1 (2014), pp. 1–19.

Gentile, Emilio, 'Fascism as Political Religion', *Journal of Contemporary History*, vol. 25, no. 2/3 (May–June 1990), pp. 229–51.

Goldberg, Jonah, *Liberal Fascism: The Secret History of the Left from Mussolini to the Politics of Meaning* (London: Penguin, 2009).

Goldstein, Yaacov N., 'Labour and Likud: Roots of their Ideological-Political Struggle for Hegemony over Zionism, 1925–35', *Israel Affairs*, vol. 8, no. 1 (Autumn/Winter 2001), pp. 79–90.

Golomb, Jacob, *Nietzsche and Zion* (Ithaca: Cornell University Press, 2004).

Griffin, Roger, *Fascism* (Oxford: Oxford University Press, 1995).

Halkin, Hillel, *Jabotinsky: A Life* (New Haven and London: Yale University Press, 2014).

Halpern, Yirmiahu, *Tehiat HaYamaut HaIvrit* (Revival of the Hebrew Marine) (Tel Aviv: Hadar, 1982 (Hebrew)).

Hamann, Brigitte, *Hitlers Wien: Lehrjahre eines Diktators* (Munich: Piper, 2012 (German)).

Heiss, Gernot, *Willfährige Wissenschaft: Die Universität Wien 1938–1945* (Vienna: Verlag für Gesellschaftskritik, 1989).

Heller, Daniel Kupfert, *Jabotinsky's Children: Polish Jews and the Rise of Right-Wing Zionism* (Princeton and Oxford: Princeton University Press, 2017).

Heller, Joseph, 'Jabotinsky's Use of National Myths in Political Struggles', *Studies in Contemporary History: An Annual*, vol. XII (1996), pp. 189–91.

Heller, Joseph, *The Stern Gang: Ideology, Politics and Terror, 1940–1949* (London: Frank Cass, 1995).

Heller, Joseph, 'The Zionist Right and National Liberation: From Jabotinsky to Avraham Stern', *Israel Affairs*, vol. 1 (1995), pp. 85–193.

Hobsbawm, Eric J., 'Revolution', in Roy Porter and Mikulas Teich (eds), *Revolution in History* (Cambridge: Cambridge University Press, 1994), pp. 5–46.

Infeld, Harry, *Israel in the Decline of the West* (New York: Bloch, 1940).

Kaplan, Eran, *The Jewish Radical Right: Revisionist Zionism and its Ideological Legacy* (Madison: University of Wisconsin Press, 2005).

Kenez, Peter, *Civil War in South Russia, 1918: The First Year of the Volunteer Army* (Los Angeles and Berkeley: University of California Press, 1971).

Kochetkova, Inna, *The Myth of the Russian Intelligentsia* (London: Routledge, 2009).

Laqueur, Walter, *The History of Zionism* (London: Tauris Parke, 2003).

Laqueur, Walter and Rubin, Barry, *The Israel-Arab Reader* (New York: Penguin, 2001).

Larsen, Stein U. (ed.), *Fascism Outside Europe: The European Impulse Against Domestic Conditions in the Diffusion of Global Fascism* (New York: Columbia University Press, 2002).

Laybourn, Keith, *The General Strike of 1926* (Manchester: University of Manchester Press, 1993).

Ledeen, Michael A., 'The Evolution of Italian Fascist Antisemitism', *Jewish Social Studies*, vol. 37, no. 1 (Winter 1975), pp. 3–17.

Luz, Ehud, *Wrestling with an Angel: Power, Morality, and Jewish Identity* (New Haven and London: Yale University Press, 2003).

Maier, Charles S., *Recasting Bourgeois Europe: Stabilization in France, Germany, and Italy in the Decade After World War I* (Princeton: Princeton University Press, 1988).

Malia, Martin, *Alexander Herzen and the Birth of Russian Socialism: 1812–1855* (Cambridge, MA: Harvard University Press, 1961).

Malia, Martin, *History's Locomotives: Revolutions and the Making of the Modern World* (New Haven and London: Yale University Press, 2006).

Marchand, Suzanne, 'German Orientalism and the Decline of the West', *Proceedings of the American Philosophical Society*, vol. 145 (2001), pp. 465–73.

Mayer, Arno J., *The Furies: Violence and Terror in the French and Russian Revolutions* (Princeton: Princeton University Press, 2000).

Mazza, Roberto, *Jerusalem: From the Ottomans to the British* (London: I.B. Tauris, 2014).

Mintz, Alan J., 'A Sanctuary in the Wilderness: The Beginnings of the Hebrew Movement in America in *HaToren*', *Prooftexts*, vol. 10, no. 3, Tenth Anniversary Volume, Part 3 (September 1990), pp. 389–412.

Mosse, George L., *Confronting the Nation: Jewish and Western Nationalism* (Hanover: Brandeis University Press, 1993).

Mosse, George L., *The Crisis of German Ideology: Intellectual Origins of the Third Reich* (New York: Schocken Books, 1981).

Mosse, George L., 'Fascism and the French Revolution', *Journal of Contemporary History*, vol. 24, no. 1 (January 1989), pp. 5–26.

Mosse, George L., 'Fascist Aesthetics and Society: Some Considerations', *Journal of Contemporary History*, vol. 31, no. 2, Special Issue: The Aesthetics of Fascism (April 1996), pp. 245–52.

Mosse, George L., *The Fascist Revolution: Toward a General Theory of Fascism* (New York: Howard Fertig, 1999).

Mosse, George L., *Nationalism and Sexuality: Respectability and Abnormal Sexuality in Modern Europe* (New York: H. Fertig, 1985).

Mosse, George L. and Laqueur, W. (eds), 'International Fascism: 1920–1945', *Journal of Contemporary History*, vol. 1 (1966).

Mosse, George L., 'Who Were the Biryoni', *The Jewish Quarterly Review*, New Series, vol. 63, no. 4 (April 1973), pp. 317–22.

Nedeva, Josef, *Abba Ahimier, HaIsh She Hitah et HaZerem* (Tel Aviv: Carmel, 1987 (Hebrew)).

Ophir, Y., *Sefer HaAvodah HaLeumi (The Book of National Labour)* (Tel Aviv: The Committee of the National Worker of the Histadrut, 1959 (Hebrew)).

Overy, Richard, *The Morbid Age: Britain between the Wars* (London: Allen Lane, 2009).

Paxton, Robert O., *The Anatomy of Fascism* (London: Penguin, 2004).

Paxton, Robert O., 'The Five Stages of Fascism', *The Journal of Modern History*, vol. 70, no. 1 (March 1998), pp. 1–23.

Peleg, Ilan, 'The Zionist Right and Constructivist Realism: Ideological Persistence and Tactical Readjustment', *Israel Studies*, vol. 10, no. 3 (Fall 2005), pp. 127–53.

Penslar, Derek J., 'Ben Gurion's Willing Executioners', *Dissent* (Winter 1999).

Penslar, Derek J., 'Herzl and the Palestinian Arabs: Myth and Counter-Myth', *The Journal of Israeli History*, vol. 24, no. 1 (March 2005), pp. 65–77.

Penslar, Derek J., *Jews and the Military: A History* (Princeton and Oxford: Princeton University Press, 2013).

Penslar, Derek J., *Zionism and Technocracy* (Bloomington and Indianapolis: Indiana University Press, 1991).

Penslar, Derek J. and Kaplan, Eran, *The Origins of Israel, 1882–1948: A Documentary History* (Madison: University of Wisconsin Press, 2011).

Porter, Brian, *When Nationalism Began to Hate: Imagining Modern Politics in Nineteenth Century Poland* (Oxford: Oxford University Press, 2000).

Rabinovitch, Alexander, *The Bolsheviks Come to Power: The Revolution of 1917 in Petrograd* (Chicago: Haymarket Books, 2004).

Ravitzky, Aviezer, *Messianism, Zionism, and Jewish Religious Radicalism* (Chicago and London: University of Chicago Press, 1996).

Rechter, David, *The Jews of Vienna and the First World War* (Oxford: The Littman Library of Jewish Civilisation, 2008).

Robinson, H. D., 'A Narrative of the General Strike, 1926', *The Economic Journal*, vol. 36, no. 143 (September, 1926), pp. 375–93.

Salaman, E., 'A Talk With Einstein', *The Listener*, vol. 54 (1955), pp. 370–1.

Schechtman, Joseph B., *The Life and Times of Vladimir Jabotinsky, Volume 1: Rebel and Statesman* (Silver Springs: Eschel Press, 1986).

Schechtman, Joseph B., *The Life and Times of Vladimir Jabotinsky Volume 2: Fighter and Prophet* (Silver Springs: Eschel Press, 1986).

Schechtman, Joseph B. and Benari, Yehuda, *History of the Revisionist Movement: Volume One 1925–1930* (Tel Aviv: Hadar, 1970).

Schorske, Carl E., *Fin-de-siècle Vienna: Politics and Culture* (New York: Vintage Books, 1981).

Shapira, Anita, 'The Debate in Mapai on the Use of Violence, 1932–1935', *Zionism*, vol. 2, no. 1 (spring 1981), pp. 99–124.

Shapira, Anita, *Berl: The Biography of a Socialist Zionist* (Cambridge: Cambridge University Press, 2009).

Shapira, Anita, *Israel: A History* (London: Weidenfeld and Nicholson, 2012).

Shapira, Anita, *Land and Power: The Zionist Resort to Force* (Oxford: Oxford University Press, 1992).

Shavit, Yaacov, *Jabotinsky and the Revisionist Movement 1925–1948* (London: Frank Cass, 1988).

Shavit, Yaacov, *The New Hebrew Nation: A Study in Israeli Heresy and Fantasy* (London: Frank Cass, 1987).

Shavit, Yaacov, 'Politics and Messianism: The Zionist Revisionist Movement and Polish Political Culture', *Journal of Israeli History*, vol. 6, no. 2 (1985), pp. 229–46.

Shavit, Yaacov, 'Realism and Messianism in Zionism in the Yishuv', in Jonathan Frankel (ed.), *Studies in Contemporary Jewry, an Annual, VII: Jews and Messianism in the Modern Era: Metaphor and Meaning* (Oxford: Oxford University Press, 1991), pp. 100–27.

Shimoni, Gideon, 'Postcolonial Theory and the History of Zionism', *Israel Affairs*, vol. 13, no. 4 (October 2007), pp. 859–71.

Shimoni, Gideon, *The Zionist Ideology* (Hanover: Brandeis University Press, 1995).

Shindler, Colin, *The Land Beyond Promise: Israel, Likud and the Zionist Dream* (London: I.B. Tauris, 2002).

Shindler, Colin, *The Rise of the Israeli Right: From Odessa to Hebron* (Cambridge: Cambridge University Press, 2015).

Shindler, Colin, *The Triumph of Military Zionism: Nationalism and the Origins of the Israeli Right* (London: I.B. Tauris, 2006).

Shoham, Hizky, 'From "Great History" to "Small History": The Genesis of the Zionist Periodization', *Israel Studies*, vol. 18, no. 1 (Spring 2013), pp. 31–55.

Skocpol, Theda, 'Cultural Idioms and Political Ideologies in the Revolutiony Reconstruction of State Power: A Rejoinder to Sewell', *The Journal of Modern History*, vol. 57, no. 1 (March 1985), pp. 86–96.

Skocpol, Theda, *States and Social Revolutions: A Comparative Analysis of France, Russia, and China* (Cambridge: Cambridge University Press, 1979).

Sofer, Sasson, *Begin: An Anatomy of a Leadership* (Oxford: Basil Blackwell Ltd, 1988).

Spengler, Oswald, *The Decline of the West: Form and Actuality: Volume 1* (New York: Knopf, 2003).

Spengler, Oswald, *The Decline of the West: Perspectives of World History: Volume 2* (New York: Knopf, 1976).

Spengler, Oswald, *Der Untergang des Abendlandes* (Berlin: Albatros, 2014 (German)).

Spengler, Oswald, *Man and Technics: A Contribution to a Philosophy of Life* (United Kingdom: Aktos, 2015).

Sprinzak, Ehud, *The Ascendance of Israel's Radical Right* (Oxford: Oxford University Press, 1991).

Sprinzak, Ehud, 'The Emergence of the Israeli Radical Right', *Comparative Politics*, vol. 21, no. 2 (January 1989), pp. 171–92.

Stanislawski, Michael, *Zionism and the Fin de siècle: Cosmopolitanism and Nationalism from Nordau to Jabotinsky* (Berkeley, Los Angeles, London: University of California Press, 2001).

Sternhell, Ze'ev, 'The Anti-materialist Revision of Marxism as an Aspect of the Rise of Fascist Ideology', *Journal of Contemporary History*, vol. 22, no. 3 (July 1987), pp. 379–400.

Sternhell, Ze'ev, *The Birth of Fascist Ideology* (Princeton: Princeton University Press, 1994).

Sternhell, Ze'ev, 'Fascism: Reflections on the Fate of Ideas in Twentieth Century History', *Journal of Political Ideologies*, vol. 5, no. 2 (2000), pp. 139–62.

Sternhell, Ze'ev, *The Founding Myths of Israel* (Princeton: Princeton University Press, 1998).

Sternhell, Ze'ev, *The Intellectual Revolt Against Liberal Democracy* (Jerusalem: Israel Academy of Sciences and Humanities, 1996).

Tagore, Rabindranth, *Nationalism* (London: Penguin, 2010).

Talmon, J. L., *The Origins of Totalitarian Democracy* (London: Sphere Books, 1970).

Thaler, Peter, *The Ambivalence of Identity: The Austrian Experience of Nation Building in a Modern Society* (West Lafayette: Purdue University Press, 2001).

Tocqueville, Alexis de, *The Ancien Regime and the French Revolution* (Cambridge: Cambridge University Press, 2011).

Tzahor, Ze'ev, 'The Struggle Between the Revisionist Party and the Labor Movement: 1929–1933', *Modern Judaism*, vol. 8, no. 1 (February 1988), pp. 15–25.

Wagner, Steven, 'The Zionist Movement in Search of Grand Strategy', *Journal of Military and Strategic Studies*, vol. 16, no. 1 (2015), pp. 61–89.

Wahrman, Dror, 'The English Problem of Identity in the American Revolution', *The American Historical Review*, vol. 106, no. 4 (October 2001), pp. 1236–62.

Walzer, Michael, *Just and Unjust Wars: A Moral Argument with Historical Illustration* (New York: Basic Books, 2000).

Walzer, Michael, *The Paradox of Liberation: Secular Revolutions and Religious Counterrevolutions* (New Haven and London: Yale University Press, 2015).

Weininger, Otto, *Sex and Character* (London: William Heinemann, 1906).

Yoder, Dale, 'Definitions of Revolution', *American Journal of Sociology*, vol. 32, no. 3 (November 1926), pp. 433–41.

Yuval, Israel J., *Two Nations in Your Womb: Perceptions of Jews and Christians in Late Antiquity and the Middle Ages* (Berkeley, Los Angeles, London: University of California Press, 2006).

Index

www.ingramcontent.com/pod-product-compliance
Lightning Source LLC
Chambersburg PA
CBHW050412280326
41932CB00013BA/1831